W9-CYZ-489

DOMUS UNIVERSITATIS 1650

VERÖFFENTLICHUNGEN
DES INSTITUTS FÜR EUROPÄISCHE GESCHICHTE MAINZ
BAND 98
ABTEILUNG FÜR ABENDLÄNDISCHE RELIGIONSGESCHICHTE
HERAUSGEGEBEN VON PETER MEINHOLD

THE LATE CITY REFORMATION IN GERMANY

THE CASE OF COLMAR 1522—1628

BY
KASPAR VON GREYERZ

FRANZ STEINER VERLAG GMBH · WIESBADEN
1980

THE LATE CITY REFORMATION IN GERMANY

THE CASE OF COLMAR 1522—1628

BY

KASPAR VON GREYERZ

FRANZ STEINER VERLAG GMBH · WIESBADEN
1980

CIP-Kurztitelaufnahme der Deutschen Bibliothek

Greyerz, Kaspar von:
The late city reformation in Germany: the case of Colmar, 1522–1628 / by Kaspar von Greyerz. – Wiesbaden: Steiner, 1980.
(Veröffentlichungen des Instituts für Europäische Geschichte Mainz; Bd. 98: Abt. für Abendländ. Religionsgeschichte)
ISBN 3-515-02997-4

 Satz und Druck: Rheinhessische Druckwerkstätte Alzey.

Printed in Germany

To Deborah

TABLE OF CONTENTS

Preface IX

Sigla XII

Introduction 1

I. Sixteenth Century Colmar 12
A. The geographical location: its significance 12
B. The social structure and political constitution of the city community 16
C. Colmar as a member of the Alsatian *Decapolis* 22
D. Colmar's ecclesiastical institutions 25
E. The intellectual life 34

II. From the social and religious unrest of the 1520's to the introduction of the Reformation in the neighboring principality of Horbourg-Riquewihr in 1535 37
A. Community and church at the beginning of the 1520's 37
B. The city government and the church in the early 1520's 41
C. The urban unrest of 1524/25 44
D. The conditions and causes of the unrest 56
E. Colmar's ecclesiastical, religious and social policy following May, 1525 64
F. The Reformation movement in Colmar, 1525–1535 69

III. From 1535 to the Peace of Augsburg, 1555 71
A. The introduction of the Reformation into the neighboring territory of Horbourg-Riquewihr 71
B. The ecclesiastical politics of the city government 74
C. Hieronymus Boner and Matthias Güntzer: their influence on city politics 84
D. The Reformation movement, 1535–1555 90

IV. From the Peace of Augsburg, 1555, to the introduction of the Reformation in 1575 94
A. The impact of the Augsburg treaty on urban church politics in Alsace and in Colmar 94

B. The influence of the Reformation in Haguenau on the religious climate in Colmar: 1565–1574 95
C. Gradual shifts in the official church policy, 1555–1575 99
D. The joint mission of Haguenau and Colmar deputees to the imperial court in Vienna (November, 1574–January, 1575) 108
E. The Reformation movement, 1555–1575 111

V. The Protestant community and church from 1575 to 1628 124
A. The ministerial recruitment and doctrinal development of the Protestant church: The transition from Lutheranism to Calvinism . . 124
B. The communal institutionalization of the Reformation 154

VI. The late city Reformation in Germany 163
A. The characteristic aspects of the Colmar Reformation 163
B. The Reformation in Essen, Dortmund, Aachen, Aalen and Haguenau 169
C. Patterns of the late city Reformation in Germany 196

Bibliography 206
A. Manuscript Sources 206
B. Printed Sources 207
C. Literature 208

PREFACE

One tends to think of the late urban Reformation in the 16th century as a "late bloomer", a less exciting version of a well-known earlier phenomenon. The halcyon days of the Reformation had indeed long passed when events in Colmar marked the climax of an unspectacular revival of the urban Reformation in German cities. Yet, the investigation of this revival is more than a mere exercise in historical thoroughness. The example of the Colmar Reformation and some of its "late bloomer friends" confronts us with the puzzling situation of Reformations essentially sneaking in "from above", that is, without significant participation by the common man. This book argues that the study of the late city Reformation in Germany forces us to abandon preconceived assumptions of similitude and reconsider typological categories of "early" and "late".

A book largely concerned with Alsatian history and written in English by a Swiss historian requires some explanation as to its origin. The intensive exposure to personal and scholarly cross-cultural influences that has accompanied my work of the last six years has played an important part in shaping the present study. My interest in the manifold aspects and problems of urban Reformation history was first awakened in 1974 by Professor Lewis W. Spitz during my days as a graduate student at Stanford University. A subsequent stay in Mainz enabled me to pursue my research and writing in the congenial atmosphere of the Institut für Europäische Geschichte and in close cooperation with the team of Section Z 2 of the Sonderforschungsbereich Spätmittelalter und Reformation at Tübingen University. In November 1978, the original version of this investigation was presented to Stanford University as a doctoral dissertation. I have since had the opportunity to review the original manuscript, revise parts thereof and include references to, and the discussion of, additional source material.[1] My genuine hope is that this investigation will serve equally the European and the trans-Atlantic readership and community of historians. As a result, all quotations from German or Latin originals appearing in the text have been translated into English. In the footnotes, however, I have in most cases rendered the original version and spelling of quotations. When referring to the names of Alsatian cities and villages, I have generally adhered to the French spelling currently in use (*Sélestat* rather than *Schlettstadt*, *Rouffach* rather than *Ruffach*), but have retained most of the original German spelling in dealing with the names of 16th century Alsatians (*Egenolph von Rappoltstein* rather than *Egenolph of Ribeaupierre*).

In the course of the present undertaking, I have incurred more debts than I could possibly account for here. Above all I am indebted to Professor Lewis W. Spitz, whose

[1] In particular, I have expanded the quotations from archival sources in the footnotes, with the exception of sources contained in a forthcoming *compendium* on Alsatian Reformation history edited by Professor Jean Lebeau of Strasbourg University. The latter sources are identified in the proper places below.

wisdom, proverbial humour and contagious enthusiasm for Reformation history have had a profound effect on my current outlook. His encouragement and friendship have guided me through the various stages of preparing this study. I owe my deep appreciation to Professor Ernst Walder of the University of Bern for stimulating my initial interest in 16th century studies more than ten years ago and for establishing exacting research guidelines at the earliest stage in my development. While pursuing this investigation, I have received important material support for a period of more than three years form the Institut für Europäische Geschichte, Abteilung Religionsgeschichte, in Mainz. My gratitude goes to the now deceased expert in Reformation history, Professor Joseph Lortz, for having arranged my stay in Mainz, and to his successor, Professor Peter Meinhold, who generously continued to sponsor this study and offered me its publication in the Institut series. I would also like to express special thanks to Dr. Silvia Gräfin Brockdorff who has guided this book through printing.

This study owes more than I am able to express here to the encouragement and the fruitful suggestions received during repeated discussions of my work from the members of Section Z 2 of the Sonderforschungsbereich Spätmittelalter und Reformation at Tübingen University. I am especially grateful to this great group of scholars for the entire day they dedicated to the discussion of the original version of this manuscript in December 1978. My deep appreciation goes in particular to the leader of Section Z 2, Dr. Hans-Christoph Rublack, and to his assistants Drs. Ingrid Bátori, Dieter Demandt and Erdmann Weyrauch. The latter two colleagues have both furnished me with the manuscripts of forthcoming articles covering aspects of Colmar's late medieval and Reformation history.

In addition to these Tübingen fellow historians, my friends and colleagues Mark Friedrich of the University of Rochester and Professor Frank Roberts of Calvin College, Grand Rapids, have granted this study the benefit of their helpful scrutiny. I am greatly indebted to them, as well as to Rolf Decot of the Institute in Mainz, who took the time to secure for me copies of the *Colmariana* kept at the Haus-, Hof- und Staatsarchiv in Vienna. For further assistance, constructive criticism and encouragement I would also like to extend my thanks to Professors Marc Lienhard, Bernard Vogler, Dr. Jean Rott, and to their Strasbourg colleagues, to Professor Hans Rudolf Guggisberg of Basel University, to Professor Heiko A. Oberman of Tübingen University, and to my friends and colleagues at the Institut für Europäische Geschichte in Mainz.

My research has been eased considerably by various archive and library staffs. I am very much indebted to all of them. Special thanks are due to the patient library staff of the Institut für Europäische Geschichte, and to Gabriel Braeuner and his assistant Francis Lichtlé of the Archives Municipales at Colmar for the gracious reception, help and friendship I have received from them. My thanks also go to M. C. Wilsdorf, director of the Archives Départementales du Haut-Rhin at Colmar, and to the staff of the Archives Municipales at Strasbourg, to its director M. F.-J. Fuchs, and his assistants MM. G. Foessel and E. Ponsing. Finally my appreciation must go to Susan Hensel and Roland Siegrist for their technical assistance.

The greatest debt of all I owe to my wife Deborah who has patiently encouraged and helped me throughout all phases of my work and without whose assistance this study would not have found the present form. She has spent more time working on this manuscript than anyone else excepting myself. It is to her that I dedicate this book. I must acknowledge regretfully, however, that the actual formulation and therefore the responsibility for any shortcomings in what appears below rests with myself alone.

Frankfurt am Main, September 1979 *Kaspar von Greyerz*

SIGLA

AAEB	Archives de l'Ancien Evêché de Bâle, Porrentruy (Switzerland)
ADB	Allgemeine Deutsche Biographie
ADBR	Archives Départementales du Bas-Rhin, Strasbourg
ADHR	Archives Départementales du Haut-Rhin, Colmar
AMD	Archives Municipales de Colmar
AMS/AST	Archives Municipales de Strasbourg/Archives du Chapitre de Saint Thomas
Annales ESC	Annales: Economies-Sociétés-Civilisations
Annuaire de Colmar	Annuaire de la Société d'Histoire et d'Archéologie de Colmar
Arch. EA	Archives de l'Eglise d'Alsace (Same periodical as Arch. EKG).
Arch. EKG	Archiv für Elsässische Kirchengeschichte (Same periodical as Arch. EA)
ARH	Archive for Reformation History – Archiv für Reformationsgeschichte.
AS/EA	Amtliche Sammlung der älteren eidgenössischen Abschiede
Auctarium Parisiensis	Auctarium Chartulari Universitatis Parisiensis, Tomus VI, ed. by Astricus L. Gabriel and Gray C. Boyce
BHP	Bulletin philologique et historique
BHPF	Bulletin de la Société de l'histoire du Protestantisme français
BMC	Bibliothèque Municipale de Colmar
BNUS	Bibliothèque Nationale et Universitaire de Strasbourg
Dortmunder Beiträge	Beiträge zur Geschichte Dortmunds und der Grafschaft Mark
Essener Beiträge	Beiträge zur Geschichte von Stadt und Stift Essen
Esslinger Studien	Esslinger Studien: Jahrbuch für Geschichte der oberdeutschen Reichsstädte
HBL	Historisch-biographisches Lexikon der Schweiz
H.H.St. A	Haus-, Hof-, und Staatsarchiv, Vienna
HZ	Historische Zeitschrift

Jb.GSL	Jahrbuch für Geschichte, Sprache und Literatur Elsass-Lothringens
Kirchners Elsässische Chronik	"Kirchners Elsässische Chronik": BMC, Fonds Chauffour, I.Ch.1.
Matr. Basel	Die Matrikel der Universität Basel, ed. by Hans Georg Wackernagel
Matr. Freiburg i.Br.	Die Matrikel der Universität Freiburg im Breisgau von 1460–1656, ed. by Hermann Mayer
Matr. Heidelberg	Die Matrikel der Universität Heidelberg, ed. by Gustav Toepke
Matr. Köln	Die Matrikel der Universität Köln, ed. by Hermann Keussen
Matr. Wien	Die Matrikel der Universität Wien, ed. by Willy Szaivert and Franz Gall
MKR	Monatshefte für Evangelische Kirchengeschichte des Rheinlandes
NDB	Neue Deutsche Biographie
Publ. Arch. Colmar	Publications des Archives de Colmar
QFRG	Quellen und Forschungen zur Reformationsgeschichte
RCA	Revue Catholique d'Alsace
RdA	Revue d'Alsace
REThK	Realencyklopädie für protestantische Theologie und Kirche
Rh.Vb.	Rheinische Vierteljahresblätter
RST	Reformationsgeschichtliche Studien und Texte
SMRT	Studies in Medieval and Reformation Thought
STA	Staatsarchiv
SVRG	Schriften des Vereins für Reformationsgeschichte
Th.B.	"Thesaurus Baumianus epistolarum reformatorum alsaticorum": BNUS
Theol. Arbeiten	Theologische Arbeiten aus dem Rheinischen wissenschaftlichen Prediger-Verein
TLA	Tirolisches Landesarchiv, Innsbruck
UB Basel, Hs.	Universitätsbibliothek Basel, Handschriften-Abteilung
VKBW	Veröffentlichungen der Kommission für geschichtliche Landeskunde in Baden-Württemberg
VSWG	Vierteljahrschrift für Sozial- und Wirtschaftsgeschichte
VVKB	Veröffentlichungen des Vereins für Kirchengeschichte in der evangelischen Kirche Badens

ZBRG	Zürcher Beiträge zur Reformationsgeschichte
ZB Zürich	Zentralbibliothek Zürich
Zedler's Universal Lexicon	Großes Universal Lexicon aller Wissenschaften und Künste . . ., ed. by Johann Heinrich Zedler
ZGORh	Zeitschrift für die Geschichte des Oberrheins
ZKG	Zeitschrift für Kirchengeschichte
Zs. Aachen	Zeitschrift des Aachener Geschichtsvereins
ZSKG	Zeitschrift für schweizerische Kirchengeschichte
ZSavRG, Kan. Abt.	Zeitschrift der Savigny-Stiftung für Rechtsgeschichte, Kanonistische Abteilung
ZWLG	Zeitschrift für württembergische Landesgeschichte

INTRODUCTION

Historiography to date has largely neglected the spread of the urban Reformation in Germany beyond the years of the Protestant cities' defeat in the Smalkaldic War of 1546–47. The present study attempts to show that the city Reformation in Germany was not uniquely a phenomenon of the first two or three decades of the Reformation era, as most recent research implies.[1] By overlooking cases of the further spread of the Reformation in German cities after 1555 one is led to assume that studies of these late and unusual products of a waning epoch would confirm patterns observed in the earlier city Reformations, and therefore be anti-climactic examples of already established paradigms. I will argue in this book that they were not.

Essentially a "magistrate's Reformation" introduced by the ruling oligarchy, the late city Reformation was devoid of the various forms of popular social and religious unrest so prominent in the early city Reformation. Although it remains an open issue as to whether the early city Reformation can actually be considered a revolution[2], there can be no doubt that the late city Reformation was not revolutionary at all. It was, however, more than a simple reflection of the fairly languid situation of German Protestantism in an era of increasing confessionalism that stifled the original dynamism of the Reformation movement.

To be sure, urban Protestantism did not remain "the solid substructure of the Reformation" after 1555, as has recently been claimed, but this late movement was far more widespread than is now generally assumed.[3] In fact, it is no exaggeration to speak of a "second wave" of the urban Reformation in the period 1555 to 1581. The majority of these local movements did not reach their destination and fell prey to the consolidating Counterreformation. Nevertheless, the urban Reformation movement was still capable

[1] Such a concentration on the first years of the Reformation era is warranted only in the study of the city Reformation in German-speaking Switzerland because the stalemate reached through the battle of Kappel in 1531 effectively forestalled the further spread of the Reformation in the free cities of the Confederacy.

[2] This has been argued in the case of the Reformation in Geneva and implied in most other cases of urban Reformation by *Robert M. Kingdon*, "Was the Reformation a Revolution? The case of Geneva", Studies in Church History, XII (1975), 203–222.

[3] This is clearly evidenced by the two studies cited below, n. 7. The quotation is from *A. G. Dickens*, The German Nation and Martin Luther (London 1974), pp. 182, 196, and 219. Compare with *Bernd Moeller*, "Imperial cities and the Reformation", in idem, Imperial Cities and the Reformation: Three Essays, trans. and ed. by H.C. Erik Midelfort and Mark U. Edwards, Jr. (Philadelphia 1972), p. 114: "After 1550 the spiritual center of Germany shifted rapidly away from southern Germany to the princely courts of northern and central Germany." For the early disintegration of urban solidarity, cf. the recent studies by *Sigrid Jahns*, Frankfurt, Reformation und Schmalkaldischer Bund: Die Reformations-, Reichs- und Bündnispolitik der Reichsstadt Frankfurt am Main 1525–1536, Studien zur Frankfurter Geschichte Book IX, Frankfurt a. M. 1976; and by *Martin Brecht*, cited below, n. 20.

of mustering enough strength to reach victory in the six free and imperial cities of Colmar, Haguenau, Aalen, Essen[4], Dortmund and Aachen.

Since the publication of Bernd Moeller's study *Reichsstadt und Reformation* in 1962[5], research on the German city Reformation has experienced a revival. A number of thorough local monographs on the Reformations in various German cities have since been published. Moeller's argumentation has found both praise and criticism in several more recent comprehensive accounts of the early spread of the Reformation in and through the German cities. Yet, this entire recent revival in urban Reformation history has generally concentrated on the first half of the 16th century and has failed to stimulate badly needed research on the continued spread of the German Reformation beyond 1555. Gerhard Ritter's admonition – that the historians' interest in this period, 1555–1618, has subsided considerably of late and finds itself close to extinction – has inspired little concern on the part of urban Reformation historians.[6]

To date, there are only two accounts that transcend the confines of local history and draw attention specifically to the phenomenon of the late Reformation movement in German cities.[7] Among the late city Reformations discussed in this study, only the Reformation in Aachen (largely due to the significant repercussions it had on imperial politics in the 1580's and 1590's) has received widespread interest. Although the Reformations in Essen and Dortmund have found considerable attention on the level of local historiography[8], the reception and discussion of this research in more general accounts of the German Reformation still remains a *desideratum*. What follows responds to this need by combining a local case study on the Reformation in Colmar with a comparative analysis of the late Reformations in Essen, Dortmund, Aachen, Aalen and Haguenau.

From the beginning of my research, I have found striking differences between specific aspects of the Colmar Reformation and the general patterns of the early city Reformation. I came to conclude that the Reformation in Colmar was part of a relatively widespread second wave of the urban Reformation movement within Alsace and other cities of the Holy Roman Empire during the decades following the drafting of the Peace of Augsburg in 1555.[9] Hence, my decision to combine this local study with a more general comparative analysis of the late Reformation in other German imperial cities.[10]

[4] For the particular constitutional status of Essen, cf. below, p. 172.

[5] *Bernd Moeller*, Reichsstadt und Reformation, SVRG, No. 180, Gütersloh 1962. For an English translation of Moeller's essay, cf. above, n. 3.

[6] *Gerhard Ritter*, Die Neugestaltung Europas im 16. Jahrhundert: Die kirchlichen und staatlichen Wandlungen im Zeitalter der Reformation und der Glaubenskämpfe (Berlin 1950), p. 367.

[7] *Gerhard Pfeiffer*, "Der Augsburger Religionsfriede und die Reichsstädte," Zeitschrift des historischen Vereins für Schwaben, LXI (1955), 213–321; and *Hans-Christoph Rublack*, Gescheiterte Reformation: Frühreformatorische und Protestantische Bewegungen in süd- und westdeutschen geistlichen Residenzen, Spätmittelalter und Frühe Neuzeit: Tübinger Beiträge zur Geschichtsforschung, Vol. IV, Stuttgart 1978. For an earlier essay by Rublack covering part of the same topic, cf. idem, „Reformatorische Bewegung in Würzburg und Bamberg", in Stadt und Kirche im 16. Jahrhundert, ed. by Bernd Moeller, SVRG, No. 190 (Gütersloh 1978), pp. 109–124.

[8] See the bibliography, below.

[9] For the late Reformation movements in the Alsatian imperial cities of Obernai, Sélestat and Turckheim, see below, p. 204.

[10] To my knowledge, the cities of Colmar, Haguenau, Aalen, Essen, Dortmund and Aachen were the only free and imperial cities in Germany where the Reformation was officially introduced after 1555, and

Since the beginning of this century, research on the city Reformation in Alsace has increasingly lapsed into a single-minded concentration on Strasbourg. Contrary to the situation in Swabia, where even small 16th century cities such as Isny, Wangen, Leutkirch and Biberach have since attracted the attention of Reformation historians, little research has been done during the last fifty years or more on the Reformation history of Alsatian cities other than Strasbourg.[11] I found it was time to rescue from general oblivion the Reformation history of at least one of the most prominent among these ten Alsatian imperial cities; one whose history often differed substantially from that of Strasbourg.

Unlike the Reformation in Strasbourg, the Colmar Reformation was entirely introduced "from above" by the ruling patriciate.[12] Furthermore, the introduction of the Reformation took place in the virtual absence of any competent urban reformer. These two aspects are only the most prominent differences between the Colmar and Strasbourg Reformations – Strasbourg being an example of an early city Reformation. The case of Colmar was not unique. As we shall see, it did not differ in any substantial way from the majority of other late city Reformations discussed in the present study. Consequently, there are striking differences between the patterns of the late and those of the early city Reformation in Germany as recently discussed by Bernd Moeller, Steven E. Ozment, A.G. Dickens, Thomas A. Brady and other scholars.[13]

Moeller investigated the impact of the early Reformation movement on about fifty-five imperial cities and, in particular, the impact this movement had on the complex dual relationships between city and church, urban community and city government. He observed an intrinsic connection between late medieval corporate urban ideology and the way the Reformation message was received by urban communities. This bond in-

where Protestant worship was not held during any significant length of time before the middle of the 16th century. A discussion of the Reformation in the imperial city of Wimpfen, for instance, was excluded from the present study because it was not really a "late" Reformation. Protestant worship was held in this city at least semi-officially and during some length of time before 1548 when the city council was forced to re-establish the Catholic status quo. See *Albrecht Endriss*, "Phasen der Konfessionsbildung: Aufgezeigt am Beispiel der Reichsstadt Wimpfen im Zeitraum von 1523 bis 1635," in Festgabe für Ernst Walter Zeeden, ed. by Horst Rabe, Hansgeorg Molitor and Hans-Christoph Rublack, RST, Supplemental Vol. II (Münster/Westphalia 1976), pp. 289–326.

[11] The only notable exception in this respect is Mulhouse. See the bibliography in *Philippe Mieg*, La Réforme à Mulhouse, 1518–1538, Strasbourg 1948.

[12] This observation is not meant to contradict Thomas A. Brady's recent re-assessment of Strasbourg's Reformation. Although Brady demonstrates that the impact of Strasbourg's ruling class on early and decisive ecclesiastical reforms in that city was much more significant than previous accounts led us to assume, he does not contend that the Strasbourg Reformation was the work of this ruling class alone. The latter, however, was essentially the case in Colmar. Cf. the discussion of Brady's account below, pp. 6–8, particularly nn. 27 and 31.

[13] The following historiographical and methodological discussion may be brief and selective. A critical outline of a few authors' significant findings will suffice to delineate the methodological parameters of the following study. Other comprehensive studies of the German city Reformation have recently been reviewed by *Hans-Christoph Rublack*, "Forschungsbericht Stadt und Reformation", in Stadt und Kirche im 16. Jahrhundert, ed. by Bernd Moeller, SVRG, No. 190 (Gütersloh 1978), pp. 9–26. There is no need to rehearse Rublack's succinct and virtually complete report. For a brief and illuminating survey of recent research, cf. also *Steven E. Ozment*, The Reformation in the Cities (New Haven and London 1975), pp. 5–14.

dicated, according to Moeller, that the continuity between the life of the late medieval and Reformation city was not restricted to the realm of anticlericalism. In essence, the Reformation movement revitalized the corporate-communal idea. This process of revitalization took place in the successful opposition of lower and middle strata burghers to the oligarchical tendencies of city government. The religious factor actively influenced urban social life by strengthening the corporate-communal spirit.[14]

In trying to understand the striking affinity between the religious message of the Reformation and the contemporary self-image of urban communities, Moeller found a "remarkable division" between the imperial free cities of the north and Franconia (i. e., Lübeck , Goslar, Hamburg, Nuremberg, and others) who all embraced Lutheranism, and the "so-called Upper German Cities of the Swabian or Alemannic region, from Esslingen in the north to Constance in the south, from Augsburg in the east to Strasbourg in the west, as well as the free Swiss cities, [who] all followed Zwingli and Bucer."[15] In observing that the corporate-communal ideology was much more pronounced in the city-life of the south and south-west than in the north and Franconia, Moeller pointed out that the urban Reformation movement in the north was less lively than in the south and south-west because Lutheranism, with its predominant emphasis on individual salvation (rather than on individual as part of collective salvation), could not provide as important a stimulus to the urban Reformation movement as Zwingli's and Bucer's teachings did. Moeller concluded that "the victory of the 'Reformed' Reformation in the Upper German imperial cities is finally explained by the encounter of the peculiarly 'urban' theology of Zwingli and Bucer with the particularly vital communal spirit in Upper Germany."[16] Thus, he stressed the continuity between the late medieval and the Reformation city not only in socio-political but also in spiritual terms. According to Moeller, these cities as "sacral corporations" (Brady) fulfilled a "pacemaker-function" (Rublack) for the early spread of the German Reformation in general.[17]

Valuable questions have since been raised regarding Moeller's evaluation of the restricted appeal of Lutheranism on the Upper German imperial cities. Ernst-Wilhelm Kohls countered this view with his argument for the early and lasting influence of Luther's concept of *Zwei Reiche* (two realms) in these cities. The weakness of Kohls' approach results from the nexus he constructs between the above argument and his distinction between an early, a-political, phase of the urban Reformation (the "evangelical movement") and a subsequent political phase (the "political Reformation").[18] The evidence does not support this distinction, as the present discussion and the following study will show. Furthermore, Kohls' criticism of Moeller is severely impaired by his

[14] See the summary of Moeller's argument by *Rublack*, ibid., p. 18.

[15] In this respect, the Lutheran city of Reutlingen was the single exception in Upper Germany. See *Moeller*, "Imperial Cities", p. 91.

[16] Ibid., p. 103. For the evolution of the entire argument, cf. ibid., pp. 95–103. See also *Heiko A. Oberman's* recent six theses on the differences between the north German and Upper German Reformation in idem," Werden und Wertung der Reformation (Tübingen 1977), pp. 372–6, especially p. 376.

[17] Since 1962, Bernd Moeller has substantiated his basic argument in several more recent publications; see *Rublack*, "Forschungsbericht", p. 17, n. 44.

[18] *Ernst-Wilhelm Kohls*, "Evangelische Bewegung und Kirchenordnung in oberdeutschen Reichstädten", ZSavRG, Kan. Abt. LIII (1967), 110–134. Cf. also below, p. 156, n. 146.

apologetically Lutheran bias, which leads him to view the influence of Zwinglian and Bucerian "Reformed" theology on the Upper German and Swiss reformers as an adulteration of these preachers' orginal commitment to Lutheranism caused by the adverse impact of Erasmus' "Biblical Theology."[19]

The debate initiated by Kohls has gained more substantial ground in Martin Brechts' assessment of the early Reformation politics of a number of mostly Upper German imperial cities, although Brecht seems to agree with Kohls' questionable periodization of urban reform in Upper German imperial cities. Brecht argues that before 1524 there was no difference to speak of between the Lutheran and Upper German city Reformation and concludes that further research will have to determine at which point such a difference began to surface in a politically effective form. He underpins this claim through a detailed analysis of so-called *Reformations-Ratschläge* from Nordhausen, Schwäbisch Hall, Nuremberg, Strasbourg and Constance. In further agreement with Kohls, he is thus led to state that the initial and chief motivating force of the city Reformation was religious rather than political or social. Yet, Brecht differs from Kohls by arguing that this motivation was primarily based on Luthers' theory of justification rather than simply on a commitment to the Reformation principle of *sola scriptura*. According to Brecht, only the case of Constance represents somewhat of an exception in this respect.[20] Brechts's argument lacks little in theological stringency, but the way in which he infers historical statements from it raises serious questions. How representative of the self-image of the early Reformation movement in the above cities were the respective theologically informed authors of *Reformations-Ratschläge*? Is it accurate to assume that their arguments were adopted in their purely religious context by the early Reformation politicians of these cities to whom Brecht attributes the crucial role in the process of the early urban Reformation? Brechts' assessment does not lack fruitful historical insights as, for instance, his emphasis on the decisive impact of urban politicians in favoring *or* opposing the early spread of the Reformation within their cities. This obervation has been substantiated by more recent research, as we shall see, and weakens Moeller's view of the Upper German city as a "sacral corporation" which "by virtue of its particularly vital communal spirit" was ideally suited for the early reception of the Reformation. However, both Kohls' and Brechts' arguments fall short of Moeller's level of interpretation in that they fail to challenge the latter's explanation of the appeal the Reformation message presented to urban communties *as a whole*.[21]

[19] idem, Die theologische Lebensaufgabe des Erasmus und die oberrheinischen Reformatoren: Zur Durchdringung von Humanismus und Reformation, Arbeiten zur Theologie, Reihe I, Heft 39 (Stuttgart 1969), pp. 27–8 et passim. For perceptive criticism of Kohls' argument, cf. also *Brady*, Ruling Class, Regime and Reformation,, pp. 7–8.

[20] *Martin Brecht*, "Die gemeinsame Politik der Reichsstädte und die Reformation", ZSavRG, Kan. Abt., LXII (1977), 180–263. For an abridged version of Brecht's article, cf. idem, "Die gemeinsame Politik der Reichsstädte und die Reformation", in Stadt und Kirche im 16. Jahrhundert, ed. by Moeller, pp. 87–90.

[21] How this could be done is indicated by Heinz Schilling in his examination of the case of Münster. Although Schilling does not share Moeller's idealized view of the corporate nature of the Reformation city, he demonstrates how the impact of Luther's concept of *Zwei Reiche* (two realms) within the urban environment was clearly ambivalent. It not only contributed to a strengthening of the position of a regime, but also

This is similarly the case with Steven E. Ozment's recent contribution to the present discussion, although it has rightly been argued that his book on *The Reformation in the Cities* "is a vast improvement on Moeller, in that it begins with the analytical concept of the 'original Protestant message' and asks why it appealed to the men of the sixteenth century."[22] In trying "to shed light on why so many people thought they wanted to be Protestants", Steven E. Ozment has argued that the initial popular breakthrough of the Reformation was based on the long cherished desire of the urban population to rid themselves of the psychological burden imposed on them by Catholic religious practice. As a result, Ozment observes that the city Reformation has to be viewed (contrary to Moeller's interpretation) as a process of de-sacralization and ultimately, as a kind of lay enlightenment. Ozment's thesis has the merit of introducing new and important psychological dimensions into the methodological discussions of urban Reformation historians, Yet, he does not live up to his self-confessed recent conversion to social history and, thus, fails to relate the process of de-sacralization he decribes to its roots within early 16th century urban society.[23]

Surely the most thought – provoking and weighty criticism has recently been mustered against Moeller's concept of the early city Reformation by Thomas A. Brady.[24] He does not quibble with Moeller's assertion of a particularly significant impact of Bucerian and Zwinglian theology on the Upper German imperial cities. Instead, his strong criticism concentrates on what social historians have long considered the weakest point in Moeller's argument–[25] the latter's idealistic view of the late medieval and Reformation city as a "sacral corporation".

Robert W. Scribner has suggested that the Reformation city, rather than cast in the role of a social body governed by corporate-communal consensus, could be viewed as a social system within which social control exerted by a ruling body assures the regulation

helped to enhance communal control over city government. See idem, "Aufstandsbewegungen in der stadtbürgerlichen Gesellschaft des Alten Reiches: Die Vorgeschichte des Münsteraner Täuferreichs, 1525 bis 1534", in Der deutsche Bauernkrieg, 1524–26, in Geschichte und Gesellschaft: Zeitschrift für Historische Sozialwissenschaft, special No. I (1975), 211, 225–6, and 235.

[22] *Bob Scribner*, "Is there a social history of the Reformation?", Social History, IV (January, 1977), 484.

[23] *Ozment*, The Reformation in the Cities. See the succinct summary of Ozment's contribution in *Rublack*, "Forschungsbericht", pp. 23–5. For critical comments on Ozment's book, see the review-article by *John M. Headley*, "The Reformation as lay enlightenment", Reviews in European History, III (No. 2, June 1977) 291–9; and *Brady*, Ruling Class, Regime and Reformation, pp. 9–10. Ozment seems unaware of the fact that his basic thesis has long been voiced by Jacob Burckhardt and Walter Koehler. See *Walter Koehler*, Zürcher Ehegericht und Genfer Konsistorium, Vol. I, Quellen und Abhandlungen zur schweizerischen Reformationsgeschichte, Vol. VII (Leipzig 1932), p. 447: "Man vergesse nicht, daß die Reformation als eine Befreiungstat für Unzählige zunächst eine sehr gefährliche Verführung zur Willkür war, daß die Massen, wie Jacob Burckhardt beißend, aber richtig charakterisierte, an erster Stelle das 'nicht mehr Müssen' empfanden und hier die ungeheure Anziehungskraft der Reformation erblickten."

[24] *Brady*, Ruling Class, Regime and Reformation. Brady summarizes part of his argument in idem, "Aristocratie et régime politique à Strasbourg à l'epoque de la réforme (1520–1555)", in Strasbourg au cœur religieux du XVIe siècle, ed. by Georges Livet and Francis Rapp, Société Savante d'Alsace et des régions de l'Est: Collection "Grandes Publications", Vol. XII (Strasbourg 1977), pp. 19–36.

[25] See *Schilling*, "Aufstandsbewegungen", 232; *Scribner*, "Is there a social history?", 484; and *Erdmann Weyrauch*, "Strasbourg et la réforme en Allemagne du Sud", in Strasbourg au cœur religieux du XVIe siècle, ibid, p. 362, n. 33.

of conflict between the ruling class and those being governed.[26] Brady uses a similar research strategy in his criticism of Moeller's approach. Yet, the strength of his argumentation lies not so much in this strategy but rather in that, unlike Moeller, he demonstrates the validity of his interpretative model through a concrete case study on the role of Strasbourg's ruling class during the first half of the 16th century. The paradigmatic character of this study results from the fact that the case of Strasbourg has so far been generally regarded as a typical example of an early city Reformation brought about above all by communal pressure exerted on a hesitating city government. Brady shows conclusively that Strasbourg's ruling class, anticipating rather than responding to mounting pressure "from below", implemented major ecclesiastical reforms before a majority of the men in power embraced the new faith in 1525. These reforms, according to Brady, were primarily the result of the ruling class' singleminded attempt to maintain public order and, thus, to safeguard its regime. Hence, he successfully illustrates his claim that, "stressing the corporate unity of the urban populations, Moeller can lay little weight on their internal structures . . . [and] therefore rejects the idea of an *independent* reforming role of the urban regimes, distinct from their succumbing to pressure from the *populus*, and therefore also the possibility of the regimes acting as instruments of certain parts of the social order."[27]

No one will want to deny the aesthetic appeal integrative approaches such as Moeller's exert upon historians who are faced with the difficult task of not only trying to understand but also of explaining the past. Much of Moeller's embattled concept has graciously weathered recent challenges. On the other hand, there can be not doubt that it has suffered significant modification through Brady's masterly analytical attempt to apply "modern canons of historical criticism" to a field "where their use is not self-understood".[28] Brady enhances our understanding of the early city Reformation and finally does justice to the work of a number of scholars who have long argued that the urban guild struggles of the 14th and 15th centuries were followed soon thereafter by a progressive oligarchization of urban regimes, which increasingly impaired the survival of corporate forms of urban life.[29] These observations have not been taken into due account

[26] *Robert W. Scribner*, "Sozialkontrolle und die Möglichkeit einer städtischen Reformation", in Stadt und Kirche im 16. Jahrhundert, ed. by Moeller, pp. 57–65.

[27] *Brady*, Ruling Class, Regime and Reformation, p. 5. Accordingly, Brady also modifies Moeller's view of the Reformation city as a "sacral corporation" in so far as he distinguishes between ideological expressions of the corporate ideal and the "proper social home" thereof: "The corporate ideal . . . was a typical expression of aristocratic political consciousness in Europe at the end of the Middle Ages and all through the early modern era". Compare with the following statement: "Most united and most militant in voicing the ideal of the civic 'sacral corporation' . . . were the Schöffen of those guilds that were ruled by small merchants and masters from relatively ordinary trades: butchers and cloth merchants, tanners and saddlers, tailors and furriers, bakers and masons. Here, one is pressed by the evidence to conclude, among these folk was the proper social home of the ideal of the commune as a religious corporation in its Reformation form". See ibid., pp. 16 and 269, respectively. It is important to note that Brady's revisionist evaluation of the reforming role of urban regimes does by no means entail a disclaimer of the equally important role of the corporate-communal forces in bringing about the early city Reformation. Cf. also below, p. 198.

[28] Ibid., p. viii.

[29] See *Erich Maschke*, "Verfassung und soziale Kräfte in der deutschen Stadt des Spätmittelalters vornehmlich in Oberdeutschland", VSWG, XLVI (1959), 289–349, 433–476; *Eberhard Naujoks*, Obrigkeitsgedanke, Zunftverfassung und Reformation: Studien zur Verfassungsgeschichte von Ulm,

by Moeller and A.G. Dickens. The latter has carried Moeller's emphasis on the urban corporate-communal spirit as the driving force of the early German Reformation to "panurbanistic" extremes.[30] It is important to note, however, that Brady does not intend to view the urban regime as the sole agent of the spread of the early urban Reformation. He modifies rather than dismisses the concept of the impact of communal and popular forces on this spread.[31] Only by the second half of the 16th century, as this book attempts to show, had the oligarchical structure of urban regimes become so pre-eminent that, in introducing the Reformation, city councils could act essentially on their own behalf, neither in response to popular pressure nor in anticipation of it through their own actions.

At no other time in European history was the concatenation of economic, social, political and religious factors as prominent as during the Reformation, particularly in its urban environment. In light of this, "the strength of Moeller's view of the urban reform . . . is his return to an historical interpretation of the theology of the Reformation era according to social principles of determination."[32] This historiographical and methodological discussion demonstrates that a comprehensive view of the urban Reformation can only be obtained through an intensification of interdisciplinary co-operation, last but not least between historical theology and social history.[33] The study of the Reformation in Colmar, forming the major section of this book, will further illustrate this need.

To date, although various aspects of Colmar's late medieval and 16th century history have been examined in a few substantial (and in a host of less than thorough or outdated) contributions, the extant literature on the Reformation in this city has remained scarce. Recently, Jürgen Bücking has dedicated a chapter of his biography of the 16th century churchman Johann Rasser to the Colmar events in the period 1571 to 1610.[34] He is the first historian to have used a wide variety of archival materials of different origin in an attempt to come to terms with the city's late 16th century history. Yet, in its brevity, Bücking's analysis is by no means exhaustive. Exhaustiveness was equally unintended by Gabriel Braeuner in his recent article on Colmar's pre-Reformation period (1522–1575). Braeuner presents a critical summary of the basic results of extant

Esslingen und Schwäbisch Gmünd, VKBW, Reihe B, Vol. III, Stuttgart 1958; idem, "Obrigkeit und Zunftverfassung in den südwestdeutschen Reichsstädten", ZWLG, XXXIII (1974), 53–93; and the case study by *Erich Meuthen*, "Der gesellschaftliche Hintergrund der Aachener Verfassungskämpfe an der Wende vom Mittelalter zur Neuzeit", Zs. Aachen, LXXIV/LXXV (1962/63), 299–392. Cf. also *Otto Brunner*, "Stadt und Bürgertum in der europäischen Geschichte", in idem, Neue Wege der Verfassungs- und Sozialgeschichte (Göttingen 1968), p. 213.

[30] *Dickens*, The German Nation. Cf. the discussion of Dickens' approach in *Rublack*, "Forschungsbericht", pp. 22–3.

[31] See below, p. 198, and above, n. 27.

[33] *Brady*, Ruling, Class, Regime and Reformation, p. 10.

[33] See *Bernd Moeller*, "Problems of Reformation Research", in idem, Imperial Cities and the Reformation: Three Essays, pp. 3–16; and the recent debate between Heiko A. Oberman and Leif Grane: *Heiko A. Oberman*, "Reformation: Epoche oder Episode", ARH, LXVIII (1977), 56–109; and *Leif Grane*, "Lutherforschung und Geistesgeschichte: Auseinandersetzung mit Heiko A. Oberman", ibid. 302–314.

[34] *Jürgen Bücking*, Johann Rasser (ca. 1535–1595) und die Gegenreformation im Oberelsass, RST, Vol. CI, Münster/Westphalia 1970. For a detailed discussion of some of the points raised by this author, cf. below, Chapters III–V.

research on the Colmar Reformation and formulates some useful questions for further research.[35] He also offers a brief discussion of extant monographical studies on the Colmar Reformation which, excepting some more recent brief accounts, were all published before the year 1876.

Two very recent results of work in progress on Colmar's medieval and 16th century history are currently in press. In a suggestive article, summarizing some aspects of his research to date on the relations between the city and church in Colmar during the late Middle Ages and the early 16th century, Dieter Demandt explores the various conflicts between Colmar's secular authorities and the church regarding the clergy's privileges from the 14th century to the 1520's. In an equally thorough article Erdmann Weyrauch examines the social composition and political authority of Colmar's ruling class in the years 1521 to 1575 and formulates significant theses concerning the impact of the city's oligarchy on the introduction of the Reformation in 1575.[36]

The first book-length study on the Colmar Reformation undertaken by the *Aufklärer* Franz Lerse, a friend of Goethe's during the latter's Strasbourg years, is based on only very rudimentary knowledge of the available source material – a kind of *roman historique* of highly conjectural quality. Also, the author does not maintain any critical distance to the few sources used. His work, like the even more unqualified monographical account of the Colmar Reformation by Xavier Mossmann published in 1853, more than sixty years after Lerse's study, focuses primarily on the period from 1575 to 1628, and leaves major questions unanswered as to how the Colmar Reformation came about.[37] A more recent attempt to come to terms with some salient aspects of Colmar's church history in the decades following the introduction of the Reformation in 1575, published by Joseph Schmidlin in 1934, is based on some new archival material, but is otherwise vitiated by the author's strongly confessionalist interpretation.[38] Only the two monographs on the Colmar pre-Reformation period written by the Lutheran minister Heinrich Rocholl in

[35] *Gabriel Braeuner*, "La Préréforme à Colmar (1522-1575)", Annuaire de Colmar (1975/76), 55–72.

[36] *Dieter Demandt*, "Konflikte um die geistlichen Standesprivilegien im spätmittelalterlichen Colmar", in Städtische Gesellschaft und Reformation, ed. by Ingrid Bátori, Spätmittelalter und Frühe Neuzeit: Tübinger Beiträge zur Geschichtsforschung, Kleine Schriften, Vol. II, Stuttgart 1979; and *Erdmann Weyrauch*, "Die politische Führungsgruppe in Colmar in der Zeit der Reformation", in Stadtbürgertum und Adel in der Reformation: Studien zur Sozialgeschichte der Reformation, ed. by Wolfgang J. Mommsen and Robert W. Scribner, Stuttgart 1979. See the discussion of some of Demandt's and Weyrauch's results below, especially pp. 21, n. 41; 44, n. 29; and 169, n. 21.

[37] *Franz Lerse*, Geschichte der Reformation der ehemaligen Reichsstadt Colmar und ihrer Folgen bis 1632, Second ed.; Mulhouse 1856. The first edition of this study was published in 1790. *Xavier Mossmann*, La réforme à Colmar, Colmar 1853. Both accounts have justly been subject to scathing, but not impartial, criticism by *C[harles] A. Hanauer*, "Les historiens de l'établissement du Protestantisme à Colmar", RCA, I (1859), 249–266, 406–415; II (1860), 169–181, 297–313. For more detail on Lerse and Mossmann, cf. *Braeuner*, "La Préréforme," 55–6. On Lerse, cf. also *Louis Kubler*, "François Christian Lerse et le patrimoine artistique du Haut-Rhin", Annuaire de Colmar (1953), 116–123.

[38] *Joseph Schmidlin*, Die katholische Restauration im Elsass am Vorabend des dreißigjährigen Krieges (Strasbourg-Neudorf 1934), pp. 125–154. Cf. also the criticism of this book by *Jürgen Bücking*, "Die Weihbischöfe von Basel Marcus Tettinger (1567–1599) und Franz Beer d. J. (1599–1611)", ZSKG, LXII (1968), 121.

1875 and 1876, deserve the respect of the modern historian.[39] Rocholl based his two studies on a thorough analysis of a great amount of archival material he discovered in the archives and city library of Colmar. He subjected his sources to critical scrutiny and quite successfully contrasted his local findings with the major Alsatian and German politico-religious events of the 16th century; notwithstanding their obvious merits, when scrutinized from a modern perspective, these contributions are not entirely without flaws. Due to his confessionalism, enhanced by the *Kulturkampf* of his day, Rocholl's interpretation is, occasionally, marred by his partisan outlook. Furthermore, he based his studies on Colmar evidence alone and thus missed some important insights he could have gained from using additional materials contained in archives situated outside of that city. In the meantime, the original value of Rocholl's monographs has experienced great depreciation through a complete reorganization of the Colmar city archives, rendering most of Rocholl's references entirely unusable. Johann Adam, in a brief chapter on the Colmar Reformation contained in his *Evangelische Kirchengeschichte*, sparingly added new insights to the above accounts: his assessment superseded the previous studies insofar as he was able to bring to bear his thorough knowledge of the archives of Strasbourg's chapter of St. Thomas.[40]

In short, there is no monographical account of Colmar's Reformation covering the entire period from the inception of the first Reformation movement in 1522 to the Counterreformation in 1628. Furthermore, none of the extant accounts covering parts thereof meet the standards of modern scholarship. This book tries to fulfill these needs. Its main body (Chapters I–V) focuses on Colmar's Reformation history in the period from 1522 to 1628. The analysis and interpretation presented is primarily based on the study of a range of archival materials supplemented by evidence contained in published sources and secondary literature. In presenting my findings, my primary intention was to write a monograph which will effectively serve further more specialized work on the Colmar Reformation and the city's history in the 16th and early 17th centuries. The realization of this plan has implied, above all, the exact identification of all primary and secondary sources used and, secondly, the comparison of my findings with local as well as more comprehensive studies on the city Reformation.[41] The concluding chapter, which transcends the confines of local history, is based largely on secondary literature.

The present study is divided into four parts. In the first chapter, I have tried to "set the stage" for the study of the Colmar Reformation. Because of the great variety of materials used in the main body of the text, I have outlined in a brief overview the

[39] *Heinrich Rocholl*, Anfänge der Reformationsgeschichte in Kolmar: Ein Beitrag zur Reformationsgeschichte des Elsass, Colmar 1876; and idem, Die Einführung der Reformation in der ehemaligen freien Reichsstadt Colmar: Ein Beitrag zur Reformationsgeschichte des Elsaß, Leipzig 1876. For Rocholl's articles used in this study, cf. the bibliography below.

[40] *Johann Adam*, Evangelische Kirchengeschichte der elsässischen Territorien bis zur Französischen Revolution (Strasbourg 1928), pp. 459–483.

[41] A technical comment is in order at this point. Wherever archival sources of Protestant origin dating from the period after 1582 (introduction of the Gregorian calendar) are cited in the following study, I have refrained from changing their original dates to modern style, in order to prevent the footnotes from becoming unreadable. The reader may note that the city of Colmar officially accepted the new calendar only as late as 1680.

economic, social, political and intellectual background prior to the introduction of the Reformation in 1575. The following parts of the study (Chapters II–IV) focus on Colmar's pre-Reformation period, i. e., the "blow by blow" account of events from 1522 to 1575. Based on the chronological course of events, these three chapters contain the analysis and interpretation of the three principle phases of the period. In Chapter V, I have attempted to portray the forces at work within Colmar's Protestant community during a period starting with the introduction of the Reformation in 1575 and ending with the climax of the Catholic Counterreformation in 1628. The first part of this chapter deals with the doctrinal development of the city's Protestant church, which (after a passionate eucharistic controversy in 1589–90) led to its gradual integration into the Calvinist camp – a process which was consolidated after 1600. The second part of the chapter is concerned with the communal institutionalization of the Reformation in the areas of public education, communal poor relief and matrimonial jurisdiction. In all of these chapters, the Reformation in Colmar is viewed as part of a broad movement spreading throughout Alsace, Germany and Switzerland. To my knowledge, there was no direct influence on the late Reformation in Colmar (1575) and Haguenau (1565) by the rise of Protestantism in France and by the French Wars of Religion. During the 16th century, the Vosges, especially of Upper Alsace, formed a natural frontier between France and Alsace.

In the final chapter, I have tried to set the case of Colmar in relation to the late city Reformation in Germany in general. This comparative chapter begins with an interpretative synopsis of my Colmar findings presented in the form of ten theses. It continues with a summary of extant research on the late Reformation in Essen, Dortmund, Aachen, Haguenau and Aalen, and is followed by a concluding discussion of the salient patterns of the late city Reformation in Germany, as gained from a comparison of my Colmar findings with the Reformation history of the above five cities.

This comparison concentrates primarily on the evolution, rather than the institutionalization, of the Reformation in the cities in question. Due to the scarcity of published evidence on some of these cities, a comparative analysis of their communal institutionalization of the Reformation is, as of yet, impossible. I have integrated into this comparative section a discussion of the prevailing interpretation of the most prominent aspects of the early German city Reformation as outlined in this introduction, and of its relevance to our understanding of the city Reformation in the second half of the 16th century.

CHAPTER I

SIXTEENTH CENTURY COLMAR

A. THE GEOGRAPHICAL LOCATION: ITS SIGNIFICANCE

In all respects, the Upper Rhine valley of the 15th and 16th centuries displayed a particularly lively atmosphere. Economically, the waters of the Rhine allowed the establishment of a widespread network of trade and exchange, mostly along the north-south axis of the river.[1] Upper Rhenish trade in this period admittedly never approached the volume and prestige of Upper Swabian commerce: the merchant families of Strasbourg and Basel, Haguenau and Colmar, never rivaled the fame and reputation of the Humpis and other families of Ravensburg, or of the Ehingers of Constance, not to mention the Fuggers, Welsers, and Höchstetters of Augsburg. But the Prechters and Ingolds of Strasbourg, the Botzheims of Haguenau, and the Vischers, Kriegelsteins and Wetzels of Colmar, to name only a few, were families which possessed considerable wealth and social weight.

Politically, the north-south orientation imposed by the Rhine made Alsatians the natural defenders of the cultural and political heritage of the German Empire against French influence. In the literature of the time, this situation provoked strong repercussions in the form of often rather crude German cultural nationalism, such as that propagated by the Alsatian humanists Jacob Wimpfeling and Thomas Wolf in the late 15th and early 16th centuries.[2]

Intellectually, the Rhine valley of the 14th and 15th centuries had proven a particularly fertile ground for the spread of mysticism between Cologne and Basel. On the eve of the Reformation, mystic spirituality was still alive in the thought of Alsatian humanists.[3] The Rhine also channelled a good deal of other influences which helped to

[1] *Hektor Ammann*, "Elsässisch-schweizerische Wirtschaftsbeziehungen im Mittelalter", Elsass-Lothringisches Jahrbuch, VII (1928), 42–43, has underlined this aspect of medieval Alsatian economic activities. Trade with the Upper German areas, east of Alsace, was secondary by comparison, and so was the rather uncommon commercial exchange with areas in the west of the Vosges. See also idem, "Von der Wirtschaftsgeltung des Elsass im Mittelalter", Alemannisches Jahrbuch (1955), 100. Through the river Ill, the Colmar merchants had access by boat to the Rhine; Lucien Sittler, "Le Ladhof et la navigation colmarienne", Annuaire de Colmar (1957), 13–23.

[2] *Joseph Knepper*, Nationaler Gedanke und Kaiseridee bei den elsässischen Humanisten: Ein Beitrag zur Geschichte des Deutschthums und der politischen Geschichte im Reichslande, Erläuterungen und Ergänzungen zu Janssens Geschichte des deutschen Volkes, Vol. I, Books 2 and 3, Freiburg i. Br. 1898.

[3] The eulogy on Jean Gerson, written by Peter Schott (1460–90), is a good illustration of the enthusiasm for the thought of Gerson shared by Alsatian humanists and learned clergymen of that time; cf. *Murray A. Cowie and Marian L. Cowie*, eds., The works of Peter Schott (1460–1490), Vol. I, University of North Carolina Studies in the Germanic Languages and Literatures, Vol. XLI (Chapel Hill 1963), pp. 258–266. Gerson's work also exerted a deep influence on Jacob Wimpfeling, Christoph von Utenheim,

give shape to Alsatian humanism. From the south, through Basel, important elements of Italian Renaissance humanism were brought to Sélestat and Strasbourg. Concurrently, ideas imported from the Netherlands, as generated by the *Devotio Moderna*, also exercised a certain influence on the Alsatian intellectual and religious climate.[4]

Today, it is the picturesque site of Alsatian towns in a landscape of widespread vineyards, rather than these cities' cultural heritage, that attracts the annual hosts of visitors. Similar qualities were eulogized as early as the 16th and 17th centuries: praise of the outstanding fertility of the land, amazement over the relatively dense urbanization, and memories of delicious wine are the tenor of early descriptions of Alsace and Colmar by Sebastian Franck (1534), Sebastian Münster (1544), and Matthäus Merian (1643).[5]

Considering these attractions, one would expect Colmar to have been rather overpopulated, which (however inconclusively) demographic accounts concerning its 16th century size indicate it was not.[6] One population estimate for the year 1495 numbers the city's inhabitants at 7,639.[7] This calculation has been challenged by A. Scherlen, who limits the figure to 3,489 inhabitants.[8] From a closer examination of these two accounts

and their mutual friend, Geiler von Kaysersberg; cf. *Joseph Knepper*, Jacob Wimpfeling (1450–1528): Sein Leben und seine Werke, (reprint of first edition, Freiburg 1902; Nieuwkoop 1965), pp. 133–4.

[4] On the roots of the *Devotio Moderna* and its spread, primarily in the Low Countries, see *R[egnerus] R. Post,* The Modern Devotion: Confrontation with Reformation and Humanism, SMRT, Vol. III (Leiden 1968). Post, however, limits his observations on the influence of the *Devotio Moderna* on the intellectual and religious life in Germany to a few pages only, dealing chiefly with its impact on Martin Luther and on humanism in Westphalia (Münster), and in the Lower Rhine area. In his revisionist approach, Post concedes only little influence exerted by the *Devotio Moderna* on the spread of Renaissance Humanism and on the Reformation. His view has justly been challenged by *Helmar Junghans* in his review-article on Post's study in Luther-Jahrbuch, XXXVII (1970), 120–124. In particular, Junghans has criticized the lack of any investigation, in Post's book, of the impact the *Devotio Moderna* had on the laity of its day. The present state of the debate over the influence of the *Devotio Moderna* on the devolopment of German humanism and on the spread of the Reformation is discussed by *Lewis W. Spitz*, "The course of German Humanism", in Itinerarium Italicum, ed. by *Heiko A. Oberman* and *Thomas A. Brady*, Jr., SMRT, Vol. XIV (Leiden 1975), pp. 371–436, especially pp. 373–4; and by *Heiko A. Oberman*, Werden und Wertung der Reformation (Tübingen 1977), pp. 56–71. For the influence of the *Devotio Moderna* on Alsatian humanism, see in particular, *Jean Rott*, "L'humanisme et la réforme pédagogique en Alsace", in L'Humanisme en Alsace, ed. by the Association Guillaume Budé (Paris 1939), pp. 67–8.

[5] The references to Sebastian Münster and to Matthäus Merian are given by *Jacques Betz* "Colmar à travers les textes du XVIe, XVIIe et XVIIIe siécles", Annuaire de Colmar (1959), 7–8. For the reference to Sebastian Franck, cf. *Luzian Sittler, „Das Elsaß im 16. Jahrhundert", in Geschichte des Elsaß, ed. by* idem, Vol. II (Third ed.; Colmar 1942), pp. 22–23.

[6] See the Colmar authorities' 1563-decree against the destruction of empty or abandoned houses: AMC, BB 44, p. 433; and *Lucien Sittler's* observations in *Roland Wertz* ed., Le livre des bourgeois de Colmar, 1512–1609, Publ. Arch. Colmar, Vol. II (Colmar 1961), pp. vi-xi.

[7] *Henri Fleurent*, "Essai sur la démographie et l'épidémiologie de la ville de Colmar", Bulletin de la Société d'Histoire Naturelle de Colmar, XV (1920–21), 45–111. The figures given by Fleurent should be contrasted with the estimate of approximately 5,000 inhabitants suggested by Johann Adam for early 16th century Sélestat, and with the figures indicated by Peter Eitel for the Upper Swabian imperial cities; cf. *Johann Adam*, Evangelische Kirchengeschichte der elsäßischen Territorien bis zur Französischen Revolution (Strasbourg 1928), pp. 414–415; and *Peter Eitel*, Die oberschwäbischen Reichsstädte im Zeitalter der Zunftherrschaft: Untersuchungen zu ihrer politischen und sozialen Struktur unter besonderer Berücksichtigung der Städte Lindau, Memmingen, Ravensburg und Ueberlingen, Schriften zur südwestdeutschen Landeskunde, Vol. VIII (Stuttgart 1970), p. 11.

[8] *Auguste Scherlen*, Colmar: Village et Ville (Colmar 1931), pp. 128–129.

one learns that notwithstanding a sorely lacking modern demographic analysis of the available source material the truth probably lies somewhere in the middle. With all due respect to the relative uncertainty of such estimates, we are therefore allowed to assume that 16th century Colmar was what A. G. Dickens has termed „the typical German city": "A little walled town with far less than 10,000 people"; bigger cities like Metz, Strasbourg, Nuremberg and Augsburg, with populations exceeding 20,000, definitely being exceptions to the rule.[9]

In comparison to the other imperial cities in Alsace (with the exception of Strasbourg), Colmar controlled by far the widest territory. North of Colmar, it extended approximately ten miles and ended just south of Guémar. To the south of the city, is was less far-reaching, but comprised some fertile lands and dense woods.

During the 16th century, Colmar succeeded on several occasions in expanding its territory. In 1536, it was able to buy from the widow of the imperial chancellor, Jacob Villinger of Schoenberg, the adjacent town of Heiligkreuz (Sainte-Croix en Plaine), the three now extinct villages of Blienschwyler, Woffenheim and Dingsheim, as well as the villages of Logelheim and Nambsheim.[10] These new possessions were administered by the Bailiff residing at Heiligkreuz. The position was appointed by, and represented, the Colmar government.

In 1543, the territorial possessions of the Colmar Franciscan monastery were added to the city's territory. Council and magistrate had purchased the property following the death of the last residing Franciscan brothers during the plague of 1541. In 1553, they were also able to buy, from the Cistercian Abbey of Pairis, its court of Widen situated just outside Colmar's ramparts. In 1575, in addition, came the acquisition of the considerable possessions of the city's Benedictine Priorate of St. Peter.

In considering the major divisions of Colmar's urban territory, we should mention the landed property belonging to the hospital which, in the 1520's and 1530's, fell under the city's control.[11] Its economic and political value was probably not unimportant. It has been shown that the landed property of many an imperial city's hospital often stretched beyond the territory under immediate control by the city itself.[12] However, the extensiveness of the property of the Colmar hospital still awaits examination.

Most of the city's land was used for wine-growing. The fame of Alsatian wine, considered one of the best German wines, originated as early as the High Middle Ages. During the 16th and 17th centuries, Colmar was the center of Alsatian wine production and trade. Its vineyards extended far beyond the territory held by the city. The bulk of them stretched through the foothills of the Vosges, between Turckheim and Riquewihr, where the ground was the most fertile. "In the old days, the vineyard constituted the

[9] *A. G. Dickens*, The German Nation and Martin Luther (London 1974), pp. 177–179.

[10] *Matthias Güntzer*, "Annales rerum memorabilium gestarum civitatis Colmariensis", in Miscellanae Alsatica, ed. by *A[rmand] M. P. Ingold*, Vol. III (Paris and Colmar 1897), pp. 55–68; cf. also *Lucien Sittler*, "Colmar au XVIe siècle", Annuaire de Colmar, (1975/76), pp. 21–22.

[11] See below, p. 43.

[12] *Friedrich Metz*, „Die Reichsstädte", in Beiträge zur Wirtschafts- und Stadtgeschichte: Festschrift für Hektor Amman, ed. by *Hermann Aubin*, et al. (Wiesbaden 1965), p. 34.

basis of bourgeois wealth in Colmar".[13] During the Late Middle Ages, the *Colmariens* had not yet developed their own regular wine trade outside their city. Only at the beginning of the 16th century, did some cloth-merchants (as well as iron and food-product dealers) turn over to a regional wine trade. Their business soon expanded from a regional level to an extended trade with the Netherlands and Switzerland and other equally distant areas, prospering continuously well into the 17th century, when it finally slowed down due to the Thirty Years War and hikes in customs and taxes levied along the trade route. Later in the 16th century, when a further expansion of the wine trade began to prove difficult, some well-to-do *Colmariens* specialized as brandy producers and dealers. Among these so-called *Brennherren,* who were mostly members of the guild *Zur Treue,* we encounter almost exclusively patrician names such as Barth, Birr, Buob, Dürninger, Goll, Graff, Hecker, Kriegelstein, Linck, Röttlin, Sandherr, Schultheiss, Wetzel, and other notable bourgeois families.[14]

As is shown by Leonhard Vischer's commercial success, the brandy trade was a very lucrative business. Here, as well as in the wine-trading business, we can observe a swift economic and social rise of a new merchant patriciate which soon superseded the old landed patriciate:[15] within only a few decades, the sons and successors of the early wine and brandy merchants became some of the most wealthy and influential citizens of Colmar, as is shown by the history of the Vischer, Kriegelstein, Sandherr, Wetzel and Birr families.[16] The majority of these families, as we shall see, played an active role in the introduction of the Reformation in 1575. Next to wine and brandy trade, commerce in cloth and drapery was important for Colmar's economy. In several Swiss towns, the Colmar merchants traded cloth for leather and hides. But they could not expand their network at will. Traditionally, the larger profits within their branch were claimed by the cloth-dealers of Strasbourg and Haguenau.[17]

Thus, the main economic role played by the 16th century *Colmariens* was agricultural. Agricultural occupations also dominated the economic spectrum of Haguenau, Sélestat, Obernai, and all other imperial cities of Alsace, excepting of course, Strasbourg.[18] Accor-

[13] *Lucien Sittler*, "Le commerce du vin de Colmar jusqu'en 1789", R d A, LXXXIX (1949), 40 and 46. Sittler's figures show a sharp rise in Colmar's wine production for the years 1542 through 1566, and, following twenty years of a relatively low level of production, again a distinctive rise for the period from 1586 to 1600; cf. also *Lucien Sittler*, La viticulture et le vin de Colmar à travers les siècles, Colmar 1956; *Willy Andreas*, Deutschland vor der Reformation: Eine Zeitenwende (Stuttgart and Berlin 1932), p. 363; and *Ammann*, "Von der Wirtschaftsgeltung", 101–153.

[14] *Eugène Waldner*, La distillation et le commerce de l'eau-de-vie à Colmar au seizième et au dix-septième siècle", Bulletin du Musée Historique de Mulhouse (1891), 3–12. The political power it held allowed this merchant oligarchy to monopolize its trade against justified protest voiced by the guild *Zum Riesen* (guild of coopers and related trades): ibid., 4–5.

[15] *Fritz Vischer-Ehinger*, Die Familie Vischer in Colmar und Basel (Basel 1933), pp. 26–28.

[16] *Sittler*, "Le commerce du vin de Colmar", 40–44; cf. also above, n. 13.

[17] *Lucien Sittler*, "Commerce et commerçants dans le vieux Colmar", Annuaire de Colmar (1966), 14–18; and *Hector Ammann*, "La place de l'Alsace dans l'industrie textile du moyen-âge", in La bourgeoisie alsacienne, ed. by La Société savante d'Alsace et des régions de l'Est (Strasbourg and Paris 1954), pp. 81–85.

[18] *Lucien Sittler's* observations in his article on „L'élevage à Colmar au Moyen Age et au début des temps modernes", BHP, I (1967), 49–59, are a case-in-point. Cf. also *Francis Rapp*, Réformes et Réforma-

dingly, among Colmar's ten guilds the vine-dressers' and the peasants' guilds were by far the largest in membership.[19]

B. THE SOCIAL STRUCTURE AND POLITICAL CONSTITUTION OF THE CITY COMMUNITY

Today we must consider social and constitutional history as correlative rather than divisible means of approaching the same historical process or problem. The constitutional development of any given community and the changes occurring within its social structure are therefore best considered under the same heading.[20]

The social and political development that led to Colmar's constitution of 1521 did not evolve harmoniously. At the time of the last Hohenstaufen emperors, Colmar

tion à Strasbourg: Eglise et Société dans le diocèse de Strasbourg (1450–1525), Collection de l'Institut des Hautes Etudes Alsaciennes, Vol. XXIII (Paris 1974), p. 19.

[19] For a list of the Colmar guilds, see *Lucien Sittler*, "La vie économique de Colmar (jusqu'en 1800)", Annuaire de Colmar (Numéro spécial, 1970), 29–30; cf. also: *Scherlen*, Colmar: Village et Ville, pp. 85–113. (Chapter entitled: "Les corporations de Colmar"). The guild-membership figures for 1554, listed by *Fleurent*, "Essai sur la démographie", 63, are the following: *Rebleute* (vine-dressers) 222; *Ackerleute* (peasants) 162; *Zum Haspel* (gardeners) 152; *Zum Holderbaum* (masons, carpenters, stone-masons, locksmiths and related crafts) 101; *Zur Treue* (tailors, merchants, glassmakers, ropemakers and related crafts) 76; *Zum Riesen* (overseers of baths, surgeon-barbers, pharmacists, inn-keepers and coopers) 65; *Zum Wohlleben* (shoemakers) 55; *Zum Adler* (weavers) 53; *Zum Kränzchen* (bakers and millers) 51; *Zum Löwen* (butchers and fishermen) 50.

[20] To date, the methodical problem of how to assess the social background of medieval and early modern constitutionality has been resolved only partially. *Hajo Holborn*, "The social basis of the German Reformation", Church History, V (1936), 330–339 (reprinted in *Lewis W. Spitz*, ed., The Reformation: Basic Interpretations [Second ed.: Lexington, Mass., Toronto and London 1972], pp. 75–84), has asserted that the social order of 16th century society „was in theory constructed not on the pattern of income and property but according to functional duties". Holborn thus clearly underestimates the thrust of economic power in an era of economic change: Nascent early capitalism unstabilized the functional self-image of 16th century society, especially within urban communities where this change was most apparent. However clearly a class structure approach is an insufficient basis for the assessment of early modern social order and constitutionality, it would be unwise, nevertheless, to disparage the analysis of income and property patterns as a correlative means of explaining this social order. A critical fusion of the "functional" and "economic" approaches discussed here will lead to more accurate results. Thomas Brady's recent study on Reformation Strasbourg makes an excellent case for such a combined approach. Brady largely heeds Wilfried Ehbrecht's repeated suggestion that the historian should examine his evaluation of the constitutional and economic situation of a given social group by contrasting his findings with that group's self-image and social status. See *Thomas A. Brady, Jr.*, Ruling Class, Regime and Reformation at Strasbourg, SMRT, Vol. XXII (Leiden 1978), Part One; *Wilfried Ehbrecht*, "Zu Ordnung und Selbstverständnis städtischer Gesellschaft im späten Mittelalter", Blätter für deutsche Landesgeschichte, CX (1974), 83–103; and idem, "Verlaufsformen innerstädtischer Konflikte in nord- und westdeutschen Städten im Reformationszeitalter", in Stadt und Kirche im 16. Jahrhundert, ed. by Bernd Moeller, SVRG, No. 190 (Gütersloh 1978), p. 29. Cf. also Brady's succinct analysis of the problems discussed here, ibid., pp. 19–41, particularly p. 33: "In the study of social structures of late medieval and Renaissance societies, the historian must work with estate and class categories simultaneously". For an interesting exploration of the range of clio-metric methods in the assessment of early modern social structure, cf. *Erdmann Weyrauch*, "Zur Auswertung von Steuerbüchern mit quantifizierenden Methoden", in Festgabe für Ernst Walter Zeeden, ed. by *Horst Rabe*, *Hansgeorg Molitor* and *Hans-Christoph Rublack*, RST, supplement-Vol. II (Münster/Westphalia 1976), pp. 97–127.

became a town with its own ramparts, market and seal of the *civitas.*[21] After the *Interregnum*, during which Colmar survived several assaults directed against its autonomy by the Bishop of Strasbourg, King Rudolf of Habsburg sanctioned the town's rise to independence by granting it the privileges of an imperial city in 1278[22]. During the early 14th century, when Ludwig the Bavarian and Friedrich of Habsburg disputed each other's claim to the imperial crown, the noble citizens of Colmar forfeited their hitherto undisputed rule of the city. They became deeply divided into supporters of one or the other pretender to the imperial throne. The bourgeoisie, organized in corporate guilds, in turn took over the major part of the city's administration. The change in the administrative structure, a result of the division of the noble patricians into "Reds" and "Blacks", did not remain undisputed. However, against the urban nobility's will, the bourgeois ascendancy was sanctioned by Emperor Charles IV in 1347/48, and again in 1358, following a last unsuccessful revolt by the noble patricians. Putting an end to almost half a century of constitutional struggle, the year 1358 marks the definitive victory of the *Zunftbürgertum* – of the burghers organized in merchant and craft guilds.[23]

The new authority of the guilded bourgeoisie was underlined and emphasized by the constitution of 1360. Certain modifications notwithstanding, this document was to remain in effect until 1521, throughout a period of rising hegemony of the bourgeois element which, in turn, increasingly limited the once considerable authority of Colmar's nobility.[24]

During the first half of the 14th century, like most other Southwest German imperial cities, Colmar had entered a new constitutional and social era of corporate rule – the era of the so-called *Zunftherrschaft.*[25] Unlike the Upper Swabian imperial cities of Memmingen, Kempten and Kaufbeuren, however, Colmar's community never experienced an entirely corporate rule, i. e. all burghers, including all patricians, organized exclusively in guilds. Beside being guild-members, Colmar's patricians of the 15th and 16th centuries commonly joined the *Gesellschaft zum Waagkeller*, an association resembling a guild in its organization. But, like the similar contemporaneous associations of Upper Swabian cities[26], and unlike corporate guilds, it did not play any role in the election of the city's council and court.

[21] See *Paul Wilhelm Finsterwalder*, ed., Colmarer Stadtrechte, Vol. I, Oberrheinische Stadtrechte, Abt. 3, Vol. III (Heidelberg 1938), No. 22, p. 26.

[22] Cf. ibid., No. 34, pp. 36–42.

[23] Through his interventions, Emperor Charles IV had assisted in the victory. He had a keen interest in furthering the bourgeois cause, for the rising bourgeois merchant class shared his concern for the establishment of public peace; cf. *Heinz Angermeier*, Königtum und Landfriede im Deutschen Spätmittelalter, Munich 1966; and *Lucien Sittler*, "Il y a six siècles: A Colmar en 1358", Annuaire de Colmar (1958), 18–27.

[24] The city was now governed by a council composed of thirty members and by the executive officials appointed by it. Of the thirty councillors, two-thirds were to be guilded burghers. Only eight noblemen were to be admitted to the council as well as two men from among their non-noble retainers; cf. *Sittler*, "Il y a six siècles", 25–27.

[25] *Eitel*, Die oberschwäbischen Reichsstädte, p. 3, has defined the *Zunftverfassung* as a form of urban régime "within which the corporate guilds had attained a majority of seats in the council, or, within which their vote was at least decisive in the elections leading to the composition of council and city court".

[26] *Eitel*, ibid., pp. 38–39, refers to the *Burgergesellschaft* in Biberach, the *Gesellschaft zum Sünfzen* in Lindau, and to similar associations in Ravensburg and Ueberlingen.

In 1539, the *Waagkeller*-society was comprised of 48 members, and 59 in 1579; eight among the latter were not citizens of Colmar but lived in adjacent towns and territories.[27] Most members of the city government probably belonged to this association. Yet, we cannot determine here how narrowly intertwined government and *Waagkeller*-society actually were. Like so many fascinating aspects of Colmar's early modern social and constitutional history, this question will have to await a special investigation of a considerably narrower focus than the present study.[28]

The growing influence on city affairs of a new generation of this patriciate originated at the beginning of the 16th century. This social political development coincided with the quick commercial success of some of the city's former cloth and leather merchants, grocers, craftsmen recently turned wine merchants and brandy dealers.

What were the social and economic attributes of this new patriciate? Pending a more detailed investigation, our sources suggest that:

a. generally, membership in the city council was a necessary prerequisite for joining the ranks of the patricians. This prerequisite had to be complemented by either one or both of the following:
b. membership in the patrician *Waagkeller*-association;
c. individual wealth based on ownership of land and real estate, trade, and/or on academic training.[29]

The ranks of Colmar's new indigenous merchant patricians were supplemented during the course of the Reformation century by various immigrant families such as the Heckers from Haguenau, the Barths from nearby Ammerschwihr, the Vischers and Sandherrs from Swabia, and the Lincks and Roettlins from neighboring Riquewihr.[30] It is characteristic of the restructuring of Colmar's upper class, which took place during the first half of the 16th century, that these newcomer families should be allowed to participate in the ongoing redistribution of socially and politically influential positions.

Inevitably, this rise of a new aristocracy intensified oligarchical tendencies already inherent in the city's bourgeois leadership since the 14th century.[31] As in Ulm and other

[27] [*Félix Chauffour*], "Notice sur la société du Waagkeller à Colmar", Curiosités d'Alsace, II (1863), 62–63; and *Lucien Sittler*, "Les bourgeois de Colmar: Essai d'une vue d'ensemble", in La bourgeoisie alsacienne, ed. by La Société savante d'Alsace et des régions de l'Est, p. 26. (Chauffour, ibid., fails to include Andreas Meyenbrunn among the outside members (*forains*). The association took its name from its assembly hall, called the *Waagkeller* – a cave arranged as a drinking hall and situated under a building which, before 1697, was the city hall. The *Waagkeller*-association owned some real estate and land in and outside of the city, and organized annual bathing expeditions for its well-to-do members and specially invited dignitaries; cf. *Chauffour*, ibid., 57; and *Vischer-Ehinger*, Die Familie Vischer, p. 11.

[28] We do not know why, for instance, the *Waagkeller* hall was bought up by the city in 1539; cf. *Andreas Waltz*, ed., Sigmund Billings kleine Chronik der Stadt Colmar (Colmar 1891), p. 63.

[29] For a further discussion of these points cf. *Ingrid Bátori*, "Das Patriziat der Deutschen Stadt: Zu den Forschungsergebnissen über das Patriziat besonders der süddeutschen Städte", Zeitschrift für Stadtgeschichte, Stadtsoziologie und Denkmalpflege, II (No. 1, 1975), 1–30; and *Carl-Hans Hauptmeyer*, "Probleme des Patriziats oberdeutscher Städte vom 14. bis zum 16. Jahrhundert", Zeitschrift für Bayerische Landesgeschichte, XL (1977), 39–58, especially 53–54.

[30] Cf. *Sittler*, "Les bourgeois de Colmar", pp. 26–27; and *Alfred Graf von Kageneck*, "Ueber das Patriziat im Elsaß und in der Schweiz", Genealogisches Jahrbuch, VIII (1968), 31–32.

[31] Lucien Sittler's characterization of Colmar's late medieval constitution and regime as having been "democratic" is thorougly mistaken. Cf. *Sittler*, "Il y a six siècles", 24. The case of Colmar was no exception

Swabian cities[32], the ruling families now increasingly tried to restrict the relative "openness" of Colmar's society. Although they owed their own positions in part to this "openness", they now tended to close off their ranks from the rest of the citizens.[33] The strike of the Colmar baker-journeymen and its aftermath in the late 15th and beginning of the 16th century, for instance, can be considered an early reaction against such tendencies.[34] These patrician inclinations also brought about a closer intertwining of the government with the patrician *Waagkeller* association. A decree of 1518 demonstrates the growing mutual entanglement by stating that the *Obristmeister* (mayor), the *Schultheiss* (provost or judge), the city-clerk, the court-clerk, as well as the *Usrichtermeister* (treasurer) and the *Umgelter* (collector of indirect taxes) should convene at the *Waagkeller* for at least one common meal per day in order to facilitate an effective administration of the city's affairs.[35]

The process of submission of Colmar's governmental institutions to the increasingly tight and authoritarian control executed by the merchant-patricians, foreshadowed by the decree of 1518, remained essentially undisputed throughout the Reformation and Counterreformation era (excepting the relatively short period of communal unrest in 1524/25). Also the noble patricians were no longer in a position to challenge the bourgeois patriciate's grasp for power. The once proud group of twenty or more noble families (in 1360) was now close to extinction.[36] In 1524, Hans von Rüst was their last representative to occupy the function of *Obristmeister*. Around the same time, the old noble association *Zur Krone*, first mentioned in 1348 and probably of an earlier origin, disappeared. The few remaining noble families joined the association *Zum Waagkeller*.[37]

The new constitution of 16th century Colmar clearly mirrors this decline in power of the city's noble patriciate: the extant documents report that on August 9, 1521, the imperial Bailiff changed the city's constitution, simultaneously reducing the number of

to the rule. This has recently been reconfirmed by Erdmann Weyrauch's evaluation, cited below, n. 41. In most German cities the late medieval guild struggles were followed by a progressive oligarchization of the regime. Cf. the literature cited below, n. 32; and Erich Meuthen's de-mythologization of tenets similar to those voiced by Sittler in "Der gesellschaftliche Hintergrund der Aachener Verfassungskämpfe an der Wende vom Mittelalter zur Neuzeit", Zs. Aachen, LXXIV/LXXV (1962/63), 299–392.

[32] *Eberhard Naujoks*, Obrigkeitsgedanke, Zunftverfassung und Reformation: Studien zur Verfassungsgeschichte von Ulm, Esslingen und Schwäbisch Gmünd, VKBW, Reihe B, Vol. III, Stuttgart 1958; and idem, "Obrigkeit und Zunftverfassung in den südwestdeutschen Reichsstädten", ZWLG, XXXIII (1974), 53–93. Cf. also *Otto Brunner*'s concise remarks regarding this problem in "Souveränitätsproblem und Sozialstruktur in den deutschen Reichsstädten der früheren Neuzeit", in idem, Neue Wege der Verfassungs- und Sozialgeschichte (Second ed.; Göttingen 1968), pp. 294–331.

[33] Cf. *Sittler*, "Les bourgeois de Colmar", pp. 26–27.

[34] *P[aul] A. Merklen*, Les boulangers de Colmar, 1495–1513 (Colmar and Mulhouse 1871). Merklen's analysis was summed up and expanded by *Georg Schanz* Zur Geschichte der deutschen Gesellenvereine im Mittelalter, (reprint of the first edition: Leipzig, 1876; Glashütten im Taunus 1973) pp. 78–91; cf. also *Eugen Waldner*, "Ein Konflikt zwischen dem Rate und der Bäckerzunft zu Colmar", ZGORh, XXXXVII (1893), pp. 616–625.

[35] "[. . .] taglich unnd Zum Wenigsten alle tag ein moll Zum wokeller Essen etc. Somit der statt unnd Bürgerschafft dester statlicher unnd fruchtbarer gewartett werde." AMC, BB 45 (1515–42), p. 20.

[36] *Sittler*, "Les bourgeois de Colmar", pp. 23–24; and *Alfred Graf von Kageneck*, "Ueber das Patriziat", 31.

[37] *Eugen Waldner*, Kurzer Ueberblick über die Geschichte der Stadt Colmar (Colmar 1914), pp. 30–31.

guilds from twenty to ten.[38] He thus sanctioned a request presented by the magistrate, council, council of jurors (*Schöffenrat*), and the entire community of Colmar citizens. While granting their request, he further stipulated that the city council henceforth consist of 24 members. Four of them were to be noblemen or their retainers chosen from among the members of the association *Zur Krone*. The remaining twenty councillors were to be elected among the burghers, i. e. two councillors from each guild, one of the two automatically becoming a member of the Committee of the XIII. In addition, all guildmasters were to take seats within the city council.

The election of a new council was to take place annually on the Sunday following Saint Laurent's day. On the preceding Friday, ten councillors, excepting the *Dreizehner* (Members of the XIII), and the ten guildmasters, as well as the retiring *Obristmeister*, would elect a new *Obristmeister* and later present him to the entire council. Then the council was to elect a new *Schultheiss* (provost, judge). On the following Sunday morning, all guilds were to nominate their new guildmasters. Subsequently, the retiring councillors and guildmasters, as well as the newly appointed guildmasters, should join the city council and elect the three *Stettmeister*. One of the latter should be taken from among the noblemen and their retainers. Then, to make matters even more complicated, the retiring councillors were to meet with the new guildmasters and appoint a *Dreizehner* from each of the ten guilds. Finally, the new *Obristmeister* and *Schultheiss* were to choose the remaining ten new councillors. In case of a disagreement between the two, the city-clerk was allowed to add his vote.

This constitution of 1521 essentially remained in effect until the final submission of Colmar to Louis XIV's French generals in 1673. In reconsidering briefly the main features of this constitution, it is important, first of all, to point out the corporate consensus leading to the drafting of this document: all elected members of the city's governmental institutions, as well as all guild members, had given their *placet* to this new law. It is thus difficult to see any other than economic reasons for the reduction of the number of guilds. During the 15th and early 16th centuries, some craft guilds had dwindled considerably both in membership and resources. A reduction of their number was the only way to improve this deplorable situation.[39] Only the corporations of the vine-dressers and peasants were not subject to changes in membership in 1521. The remaining eighteen guilds all seem to have needed a fusion with other corporations[40].

Secondly, the constitution of 1521 gave a fairly accurate rendition of the new social structure and of the resulting distribution of power within Colmar's urban community. While one-third of the seats within the council in 1360 had still been reserved for Colmar's noble patricians, their share was now reduced to a sixth of all seats. The constitution of 1521 acknowledged the guilded bourgeoisie, led by its patrician members, as the undisputed ruler of sixteenth century Colmar. It also conceded the bourgeois

[38] The document is printed in *Finsterwalder*, ed., Colmarer Stadtrechte, Vol. I, No. 200, pp. 253–256.

[39] *Xavier Mossmann*, Recherches sur l'ancienne constitution de la commune à Colmar (Colmar 1878), pp. 114–115.

[40] Cf. the table in *Sittler*, "La vie économique de Colmar", 29–30.

patriciate enough room for the expansion of its hegemony during decades yet to come.[41] When seen from this perspective, it is clear that a partial role of the Reformation of 1575 was to enlarge and preserve this specific condition provided by the constitution of 1521.

Let us now take a brief glance at the functioning of the different agencies of Colmar's government:[42]

Colmar's government of the 16th and 17th centuries acted on four different levels. The political and military leader of the city was the *Obristmeister*. Together with the *Schultheiss* and three *Stettmeister* he formed the magistrate (*Meisterschaft*). The function of *Schultheiss* was bought, in 1425, from Emperor Sigismund[43] and henceforth occupied by a citizen. The *Schultheiss* was the judge of Colmar. He presided over the lower court of jurors (*Schöffengericht*) and the higher court composed of the city councillors. He was normally assisted by the court-clerk (*Gerichtsschreiber*) who, next to the city-clerk, played a very influential role in the city's political and social life. The three *Stettmeister* shared among themselves the function of *Ausrichtermeister* (city-treasurer): each one was to occupy it for a third of his one-year term. Magistrate and council were assisted by the city-clerk (*Stadtschreiber*). Depending on the personality and zeal of the holder of this office, remarkable power and considerable influence could be united within this position: as a city-clerk, Andreas Sandherr, for instance, was instrumental in bringing about the Reformation in 1575.[44]

Further research is needed to pinpoint the exact function and amount of influence of the city council's most interesting partner, the Committee of the XIII, also referred to as the *Dreizehner*. In 1424, the lower-class guilds in opposition to the magistrate and council demanded the creation of this committee. Thus, the XIII became an additional decision-making body consulted in case of war or problems affecting the entire community. By 1521, the XIII had not only become part of the city council, but probably also constituted a governmental body meeting regularly on its own. Following the year 1521, it showed a remarkable continuity in its composition: Bartholomäus Dürninger was a member of the XIII uninterruptedly from 1528 to 1541; the patrician Oswalt Krus, Jr., from 1576 to 1587; and Hans Stumpf from 1547 to 1561. The patrician

[41] The first results of Erdmann Weyrauch's current research on Colmar's political leadership and the Reformation underline the accuracy of this observation. Weyrauch draws particular attention to the considerable authority accorded by this constitution to the members of the magistrate. In discussing how the constitution of 1521 favored the increasing oligarchization of the regime, he demonstrates that within the period 1540 to 1600 membership in the city's magistrate was the solid monopoly of about a fifth of Colmar's 100 politically leading families. Furthermore, from 1540 to 1630, only thirteen families controlled the key position of the *Obristmeister*. Cf. *Erdmann Weyrauch*, "Die politische Führungsgruppe in Colmar in der Zeit der Reformation", in Stadtbürgertum und Adel in der Reformation: Studien zur Sozialgeschichte der Reformation, ed. by Wolfgang J. Mommsen and Robert W. Scribner (Stuttgart 1979).

[42] Regarding the following, see the succinct analysis of research results to date in *Lucien Sittler*, ed., Membres du Magistrat, Conseillers et Maîtres des Corporations de Colmar: Listes de 1408–1600, Publ. Arch. Colmar, Vol. III (Colmar 1964), pp. iii-xiii; cf. also *Lucien Sittler*, "Colmar au XVIe siècle", Annuaire de Colmar (1975/76), 16–17; and *Finsterwalder*, ed., Colmarer Stadtrechte, No. 200, p. 254.

[43] *Finsterwalder*, ibid., No. 173, pp. 217–218.

[44] For this and the following, cf. *Sittler*, "Colmar au XVIe siècle", 16–17: the Colmar city-clerk was appointed by the magistrate.

Sebastian Wilhelm Linck was a *Dreizehner* from 1571 to 1583, and from 1582 through 1616, his term as *Stettmeister* always coincided with his membership in the XIII. For the years 1589 to 1595, the patrician Beat Henslin's political career reveals a similar pattern, and so do the careers of many others.[45] In the light of this evidence it is more than likely that the deliberations and decisions of the XIII had a considerable impact on Colmar's city government.[46] To date, the function of the government Committee of the Eight (*Echtwer*), which had not disappeared by the beginning of the 16th century as has been claimed by Lucien Sittler[47], remains even more obscure to us.

On the third level of government, the council of jurors (*Schöffenrat*) participated in the decision-making process. The role of the jurors was, however, far less important than that of magistrate and council. Participation by the council of jurors was limited, and only occurred by invitation from above, such invitation coming only when decisions of great importance for the entire community had to be taken. Accordingly, the *Schöffenrat* was consulted between December, 1524 and May, 1525, during a period of heightened agitation within the city. The more the ruling patricians strengthened their oligarchical authority, the less important the council of jurors became. It is interesting to note that the *Schöffenrat* was not consulted in 1575, prior to the introduction of Protestant worship in the city.[48]

The fourth level of government, finally was constituted by the citizen-burgher. In registering as a Colmar citizen, he had to pay a certain sum for his admission to the commune. In addition to owning a substantial fortune, he had to own or rent a house in town and prove that he had previously been residing in Colmar for a period of at least five years. He also had to be a member of a guild, and, as such, he annually executed his political rights in the city's elections.[49] Of course, there were also a fair number of people residing in Colmar who did not enjoy these rights and privileges. They comprised the so-called *Seldner* or *Hintersassen* – persons who had no particular rights beside the right to reside in town – among these, the clergy and its lay personnel.

C. COLMAR AS A MEMBER OF THE ALSATIAN DECAPOLIS

The well-known Austrian historian, Otto Brunner, once emphasized that "no city should be looked at in isolation", and that it should only be dealt with within the political and social framework it was related to at a given time.[50] In the case of 16th

[45] Cf. *Sittler*, ed., Membres du Magistrat, pp. 19–56.

[46] In 1528, the butcher's guild sought the approval of its new trade regulations by the XIII and the magistrate. In 1544, the XIII stipulated similar new regulations for the hotel- and inn-keepers: cf. ibid., p. x.

[47] The *Echtwer* are mentioned on several occasions im 1525: AMC, EE 7, 1, fol. 18 *et passim*; cf. also *Sittler*, ed., ibid., pp. vii-viii.

[48] Each guild elected and presented a number of jurors proportionate to its membership-size. Accordingly, the size of the council of jurors was subject to variations: there were 122 jurors in 1515, 138 in 1546, and 124 in 1622. Jurors were elected for lifetime service: *Sittler*, ed., ibid.; and *Mossmann*, Recherches sur l'ancienne constitution, p. 121.

[49] *Sittler*, "Les bourgeois de Colmar", pp. 27–29.

[50] *Otto Brunner*, "Stadt und Bürgertum in der europäischen Geschichte", in idem, Neue Wege der Verfassungs- und Sozialgeschichte, p. 215.

century Colmar, this framework was primarily provided by the town's relationship to the other Alsatian imperial cities. Excepting Strasbourg, all other ten Alsatian imperial cities were of a medium (Haguenau, Colmar, Sélestat and Wissembourg) or small size (Mulhouse, Munster, Obernai and Kaysersberg). The smallest among them were Rosheim and Colmar's neighbor, Turckheim.

Uniting against noble assaults, and encouraged to do so by Emperor Charles IV, they founded an urban alliance in 1354: the Alsatian ten-cities-league. This alliance was later called *Decapolis*.[51] The main purpose of the *Decapolis* was the defense of the free and imperial status of its members and the maintenance of their privileges.[52] The decisions of the league were met at diets which, following the 1520's, were usually held at Strasbourg. The member-cities were the ten towns mentioned above. After Mulhouse definitively joined the Swiss Confederation in 1515, the Palatine imperial city of Landau took its place as a new member of the *Decapolis*. Haguenau was the chief city within the alliance, distinguished from the other members by its primarily representative and administrative prerogatives. The 16th century policy of this leading city of the *Decapolis* was always closely, and often jealously, checked by the second-ranking city of the league: Colmar. At imperial diets in the 16th and 17th centuries, the cities of the *Decapolis* were usually represented by the delegates of Haguenau and Colmar.[53] Since the 14th century, the alliance had been regularly renewed by its members and was to play an important role as a stabilizing factor during the religious conflicts of the Reformation era. Depending on the nature of the conflict, the league either:

- defended Catholic tradition, while simultaneously warding off the orthodox excesses often advocated by the Habsburg or by their representatives;
- protected the Protestant party within one or more of its member-cities against Counterreformation interventions (commonly launched or backed by the Habsburg).

Thus, the main stimulus for the religious policy of the *Decapolis* during most of the 16th century was the ever increasing threat of Habsburg's ambitions for hegemony. In this respect, the ten cities remained on guard all the more because their political autonomy was limited by the authority of the imperial Bailiff (*Landvogt*) at Haguenau, whose office, during most of the 16th century, was in the hands of Habsburg-Austria. This was especially true in the case of the four Upper Alsatian imperial cities, i. e. Colmar and the three smaller towns of Munster, Turckheim and Kaysersberg, because in addition to containing the Bailiff's authority they constantly had to cope with the influence of the nearby Habsburg-Austrian Regency of Ensisheim. The constant Habsburg-Austrian check on Colmar and Haguenau was, as we shall see, a major reason for the late introduction of the Reformation in these cities.

[51] *Lucien Sittler*, La Décapole alsacienne des origines à la fin du moyen âge, Publications de l'Institut des hautes-études alsaciennes, Vol. XII, Strasbourg 1955; and idem, „Der elsässische Zehnstädtebund, seine geschichtliche Eigenheit und seine Organisation", Esslinger Studien, X (1964), 59–77.

[52] *Sittler*, La Décapole alsacienne, p. 90.

[53] Ibid., p. 91: "On ne peut pas se défaire l'impression, qu'entre Haguenau et Colmar il y eut constamment une certaine rivalité". Cf. also ***Lucien Sittler***, "Colmar et la Décapole: Une crise au sein de la ligue au XVIe siècle", Annuaire de Colmar (1954), 47–54.

In 1354, when the *Decapolis* was founded, Emperor Charles IV had named his Bailiff, his chief representative in Alsace, the protector of the city alliance.[54] The authority the Bailiff held over the *Decapolis* as a whole, as well as over its individual members, emerged from his personal authority rather than from the prerogatives officially and legally attached to his function.[55] Officially, his sole duty was to protect the city alliance and its members. This meant that he played the role of mediator when conflict arose involving one or several of the cities. He could also intervene as mediator when inner dissension struck one of the towns. (He did so, with great authority, in Colmar in 1358 and 1424.) Furthermore, he owed the cities his protection whenever they asked for it, and he commanded the contingents of the ten cities in the military operations of the Empire. As partner of the *Decapolis* during the Reformation and Counterreformation era, his role was predominantly limited to that of protector. From our evidence, it appears clear that his authority dwindled considerably in importance after the second half of the 15th century.[56] However, in the 16th century, he still held the right to intervene in the government of some of the smaller of the ten allied cities: no annual election in any of those towns could take its course without his, or his representative's, assistance. In Haguenau, Colmar and Obernai, his function was limited, on those occasions, to presiding over the elections. However, in other cities, such as Sélestat, and especially Kaysersberg, Munster and Turckheim, he was allowed an active role in the elections. Moreover, in the three latter cities, he alone held the right to appoint the new councillors each year.[57]

Several among the ten cities lacked other attributes of the entirely autonomous city. Kaysersberg, Munster and Turckheim, as well as the bigger cities of Wissembourg, Obernai, and even Haguenau, were not in charge of the administration of higher justice within their cities during the Reformation era; in their case, this prerogative was held by the Empire, and accordingly, their *Schultheiss* or *Vogt* was appointed by the Bailiff of Haguenau or by other Alsatian vassals of the Emperor.[58] When seen from this constitutional perspective, Colmar was the most autonomous of the imperial cities in Alsace, excepting proud Strasbourg, which, for reasons of its splendid size, never needed to join the Ten Cities League.[59]

[54] For the history of the imperial Bailiwick of Haguenau, see *Joseph Becker*, Geschichte der Reichslandvogtei im Elsaß: Von ihrer Einführung bis zu ihrem Übergang an Frankreich, 1273–1648, Strasbourg 1905.

[55] These observations only concern the Bailiff's prerogatives vis-à-vis the Decapolis as a whole. He did, however, have the right to be included in the electoral corps of some of the ten cities: cf. below.

[56] For a more detailed analysis, see *Sittler,* La décapole alsacienne, pp. 108–113; and idem, „Der elsäßische Zehnstädtebund", 73–5.

[57] Cf. *Becker*, Geschichte der Reichslandvogtei, pp. 215–221.

[58] *Joseph Becker*, "Die Reichslandvogtei Kaysersberg: Von ihrem Ursprung bis zur Französischen Revolution", Supplement added to Jahresbericht des bischöflichen Gymnasiums zu Strassburg (1906), Strasbourg 1906. Cf. also *Jean Gyss*, Histoire de la ville d'Obernai, Vol. I (Strasbourg 1866), pp. 323–358. In this respect, the city of Wissembourg was an exception because it controlled the administration of its own higher justice (*Vogtei*) only intermittantly, from 1518 to 1531, and following 1559; cf. *O. R. Landsmann*, Wissembourg: Un siècle de son histoire, 1480–1580, Rixheim 1903.

[59] However, during the 16th and 17th centuries, the radius of Colmar's political activity was often restricted by the influence exerted on the city by the neighboring Habsburg-Austrian Regency of Ensisheim.

In the light of all this it is evident that success or failure of the Reformation movement within one of the ten member-cities could be strongly influenced, in one way or another, by the Bailiff of Haguenau and by other holders of imperial offices institutionally connected with the *Decapolis*. The degree of this influence depended largely upon the amount of authority the Bailiff and those officeholders were granted by a given city's constitution or upon the amount of power they could exert on a city because of the relative defenselessness resulting from its small size.

For the members of the *Decapolis* it was, therefore, not unimportant who happened to be in charge of the Bailiwick of Haguenau, especially since the Emperor traditionally conferred the Bailiwick as a fief to a territorial prince. For the period of the 16th and 17th centuries we can distinguish three eras of rule in Haguenau:[60] from 1504 to 1530, the Bailiwick was in the hands of Habsburg-Austria. In the 1520's, it was Johann Jacob Baron of Morimont (Mörsberg) and Belfort, who, as a vassal of Habsburg-Austria, held the office of Imperial Bailiff. His stand in religious matters was traditional. Although he never wavered in his commitment to the Roman church, he did, on occasion, favor attempts by secular authorities to increase their control over the church and the Catholic clergy – as was the case with Colmar in 1527–28.[61]

From 1530 to 1558, the Palatine Prince-elector was the so-called *Oberlandvogt* of Alsace. Some of his representatives at Haguenau tolerated or even favored the growth of the Protestant movement within the member-cities of the *Decapolis*, particularly Heinrich von Fleckenstein, Bailiff from 1544 to 1555. When the Protestant Count Palatine Ottheinrich, Prince-elector from 1556 to his death in 1559, came to power, the Habsburg thought it wiser to regain control of the Bailiwick. In 1558, it fell again under their control, where it remained until its transition into the hands of the King of France in 1648. Habsburg-Austria's Bailiff from 1558 to 1589, the Baron Nicolaus of Bollwiller, was a fierce, uncompromising man and an earnest Catholic. He often tried quite openly to interfere with the cities' autonomy. It was during his rule that Colmar introduced the Reformation in 1575.

D. COLMAR'S ECCLESIASTICAL INSTITUTIONS

An imperial city of medium size, 16th century Colmar, in its number of churches and monasteries, could not rival such cities as Cologne with her eleven chapters, twenty parish churches, one hundred chapels and twelve monasteries; and, on the eve of the Reformation era, Colmar's clergy was certainly not as numerous as Worms' estimated 1,200 to 1,500 monks, nuns and priests, in relation to a total of five to six thousand inhabitants. A rough estimate for Colmar, a city of about the same size as Worms, would be about 250 clergymen, not including their servants and retainers. Exact figures are as of yet unknown.[62]

[60] Cf. *Becker*, Geschichte der Reichslandvogtei, pp. 80–102.

[61] *Heinrich Rocholl*, Anfänge der Reformationsgeschichte in Kolmar: Ein Beitrag zur Reformationsgeschichte des Elsaß (Colmar 1875), pp. 44 and 61.

[62] The figures for Cologne and Worms are listed in *Albert Werminghoff*, Verfassungsgeschichte der deutschen Kirche (Second ed.; Leipzig and Berlin 1913), p. 101. For further comparative purposes, see

At the beginning of the 16th century, the city walls enclosed three parish churches, seven monasteries and an undetermined number of chapels.[63] All of these ecclesiastical establishments fell under the spiritual authority of the Bishop of Basel, who did not hold, however, any jurisdictional power over Colmar's monasteries (which were, in this respect, subject to the superiors of the respective orders).[64] The amount of influence the Bishop, as *ordinarius loci*, exerted on Colmar's religious and ecclesiastical life differed with the character of the dignitaries entrusted with episcopal authority. While Bishop Christoph von Utenheim (1502–27) carried out a policy that was basically able and circumspect (although, on occasion, not vigorous enough), his successors, Jacob Philipp von Gundelsheim (1527–53) and Melchior von Lichtenfels (1554–75), exerted considerably less influence on their flock and clergy in Colmar. As far as the safeguarding of episcopal privileges and rights was concerned, their relatively detrimental policy was only reversed during the late 16th century by the vigorous reformer of the diocese, Bishop Jacob Christoph Blarer von Wartensee (1575–1608).[65] His access to episcopal authority and power marks the beginning of the Counterreformation and Catholic reform within the diocese of Basel.

The main church among Colmar's three late medieval parish churches was St. Martin's. It had been founded in the early Middle Ages hy the nearby Benedictine Abbey of Munster. In 1234, Pope Gregory IX transformed it into a collegial church. Attached to it was a chapter founded in 1237.[66] This chapter was headed by a Provost (*Probst*) appointed by the canons and invested by the Abbot of Munster, who also held the right to appoint the Dean of the chapter and could claim part of St. Martin's tithe. The Bishop of Basel was entitled to confirm the Provost and to confirm and invest the Dean following the latter's appointment. According to the *Liber Marcarum* of the diocese, he was also in charge of appointing the cantor of St. Martin.[67] Altogether, these were rather small episcopal prerogatives; some bishops, particularly the reformer, Bishop Jacob Christoph

also *Gerald Strauss*, Nuremberg in the Sixteenth Century, New dimensions in history (New York, London and Sidney 1966), p. 155; and *Bernd Moeller*, Deutschland im Zeitalter der Reformation, Vol. IV of Deutsche Geschichte, ed. by Joachim Leuschner (Göttingen 1977), p. 40.

[63] A comprehensive listing of Colmar's ecclesiastical institutions is presented by *Claude Laplatte*, Dictionnaire d'histoire et de géographie ecclésiastiques, Vol. XIII, cols. 258–272. Some of Laplatte's observations on Colmar's religious history are, however, erroneous. Joseph Trouillat's survey on Colmar's ecclesiastical establishments is incomplete: *Joseph Trouillat* and *Louis Vautrey*, eds. Monuments de l'histoire de l'ancien évêché de Bâle, Vol. V (Porrentruy 1867), pp. 85–8.

[64] Cf. *Trouillat* and *Vautrey*, ibid., pp. 87–88.

[65] For a concise survey of the history of the diocese of Basel, cf. *Georg Boner*, "Das Bistum Basel: Ein Überblick von den Anfängen bis zur Neuordnung, 1828", Freiburger Diözesan-Archiv, LXXXVIII (1968), 5–101. The handbook entitled Helvetia Sacra contains short biographies (incl. bibliographies) of the bishops of Basel: *Albert Bruckner*, general ed., Helvetia Sacra, Abt. I, Vol. I, Bern 1972.

[66] *François-Auguste Goehlinger*, Histoire du Chapitre de l'Eglise Saint-Martin de Colmar (Colmar 1951), p. 10; and *Louis Vautrey*, Histoire des Evêques de Bâle, Vol. I (Einsiedeln 1884), p. 201. The act of foundation is printed in *Trouillat* and *Vautrey*, eds., Monuments, Vol. V, No. 1237, pp. 141–3.

[67] *Trouillat* and *Vautrey*, eds., Monuments, Vol. V, p. 81. For the legal and economic aspects of the Dean's appointment, cf. also AMC, GC 27,4 (Statement by the Bishop of Basel, February 13, 1559).

Blarer von Wartensee, may often have wished to have disposed of stronger legal grounds for influencing the conduct of the Colmar canons.[68]

Originally, the chapter of St. Martin consisted of 16 members. Economically, the 13th century appears to have been the chapter's most prosperous period. During the following centuries, the Bishop was continually met with requests to reduce the number of canons: in 1440, a reduction to 12 canons, in 1548 to 9, and in 1583 to 7 canons. By 1590, and still in 1626, there were only three canons who resided in Colmar.[69] St. Martin's was comprised of regular prebendary canons, who alone enjoyed the right to vote during capitular assemblies (which commonly took place once a month), as well as canons in expectation of a prebend. At the bottom of the hierarchy were the chaplains, vicars and all lay personnel.[70] In addition to 16 canons listed in 1441–69 by the *Liber Marcarum* of the Basel diocese, 34 chaplains were employed at St. Martin's at that time.[71]

Who were these canons and chaplains and where did they come from? Trying to answer this question will help to explain why, during the last fifteen years or so preceding the Reformation of 1575, the relationship between the city's authorities and the secular clergy became increasingly precarious. While it is practically impossible to determine the geographical and social origin of a representative number of lower secular clergymen, valuable information is extant on a good number of St. Martin's canons.[72]

St. Martin's first Provost of the Reformation period was Gregorius Angeli, a native of Giengen near Ulm. Appointed as a canon and *scholasticus* of St. Martin's on May 9, 1514, he was shortly thereafter entrusted with the Provostship. A doctor of theology from Bologna University, a former adviser of Emperor Maximilian I in the Reuchlin affair, and, to all appearances, a friend of the Alsatian humanist Jacob Wimpfeling, Angeli was well versed in the worlds of politics and *lettres* alike. Like innumerable contemporaries, he was a pluralist and simultaneously held a fair number of benefices strewn between Giengen, Colmar, Wettolsheim, Strasbourg, and Wimpfen-im-Tal. This justifies the assumption that he rarely resided in Colmar. The last mention we have of him locates him in Naples and Rome in December, 1528, and April, 1529, respectively.[73] Relatively little is known about his successors Jacob Sagittarius (Schütz), Provost during the 1530's, and Andreas Koeltz, mentioned as Provost in 1541 and 1548. Sagittarius was a native of Heiligkreuz (Sainte-Croix-en-Plaine) near Colmar and was

[68] By comparison, the Bishop of Strasbourg held much more extensive prerogatives regarding the Strasbourg cathedral chapter: *Rapp*, Réformes et Réformation à Strasbourg, p. 59.

[69] *Goehlinger*, Histoire du Chapitre, pp. 15–16.

[70] Ibid., p. 24.

[71] *Trouillat* and *Vautrey*, eds., Monuments, Vol. V, pp. 8–10. It is uncertain whether any vicars are included in this list. The number of lay personnel is, as of yet, unknown.

[72] For the following, cf. also *Goehlinger*, Histoire du Chapitre, pp. 99–131, although it will in part go beyond Goehlinger's observations and, without explicit reference in each instance, correct his frequent mistakes.

[73] See *J. V. Pollet*, ed., Julius Pflug: Correspondence, Vol. I (Leiden 1969), pp. 151 and 166; Matr. Freiburg i. Br., Vol. I/1, p. 154 (No. 29); and *Gustav C. Knod*, ed., Deutsche Studenten in Bologna (1289–1562): Biographischer Index zu den Acta Nationis Germanicae Universitatis Bononiensis (Berlin 1899), p. 16 (No. 95). The information contained in *A[rmand] M. P. Ingold*, "Les prévôts du chapitre de Saint Martin de Colmar", in idem, Miscellanea Alsatica, Vol. I (Paris and Colmar 1894), p. 93, is now outdated.

enrolled as a student at the University of Heidelberg from 1507 to 1510, where he earned a master's degree.[74] The origin of Andreas Koeltz is unknown. The learned Franz von Apponex (from the town of Apponex in the Duchy of Savoy) was Colmar's Provost from 1551 to 1577. He only occasionally resided in Colmar, as is shown by the chapter's correspondence with him. Following the completion of his studies in Freiburg im Breisgau, he first stayed at Munster in the Vosges, where his brother, Petermann von Apponex, was the local Abbot from 1540 to about 1554. By virtue of his authority over the Colmar chapter, the latter undoubtedly assisted his brother in securing the Provostship at St. Martin's. In 1563, Franz von Apponex made the *Probstei* of Istein near Basel his headquarters.[75] In 1577, he became a canon and subsequently the Dean of the Basel cathedral chapter and moved to Freiburg im Breisgau. The Colmar Provostship he had resigned in 1577 remained vacant thereafter until 1611.[76]

The frequent, if not regular, absence of the Provosts from Colmar strengthened the position of the Dean who, during the Provost's absence, headed the chapter and personified its moral and spiritual authority. Yet, within the first half of the 16th century, not even the deans maintained permanent residence in Colmar, as is demonstrated by the case of the humanist and diplomat, Jacob Carpentarii (Zimmermann) from St. Hyppolite (St. Pilt) in the Vosges, – Colmar's Dean from 1502 to his death in 1541/42. He only established permanent residence at St. Martin's after 1526.[77] Georg Klein (d. 1551), master of arts and *baccalaureus biblicus*[78], was a native of Colmar. First mentioned as a canon of St. Martin's in 1521, he became Carpentarii's successor in about 1542.[79] The next Dean was again an outsider: Blasius Stoeritz, master of arts and Dean from 1551 to about 1553, was a native of Kirchheim near Stuttgart.[80] There is no extant evidence on the origin of his successor, Johannes Grüninger (d. 1556). It is unlikely, however, that he could have been a native of Colmar. His family name does not figure in Colmar's 16th century citizenship rolls.[81] Jacob Klein (d. 1563), a master of arts and priest from the diocese of Constance (probably from Kempten)[82], was originally hired by the chapter as a common priest (1553), but soon found appointment to the rank of

[74] Matr. Heidelberg, Vol. I, p. 464; and ibid., Vol. II, p. 432. Sagittarius can practically be considered a *Colmarien,* since his native Alsatian town was purchased by Colmar in 1536. Cf. above, p. 14.

[75] *Friedrich Schaub,* „Der Basler Domherr Franz von Apponex: Seine Studienstiftung und seine Bücher", Freiburger Diözesan-Archiv, LXIX (1950), 98–100; and STA Basel, Klosterarchiv C 1 (Istein), especially the correspondence from the years 1561–63.

[76] For biographical data, cf. *Schaub*, ibid., 92–110; and the short biography in *Bruckner*, general ed., Helvetia Sacra, Abt. I, Vol. I, p. 295.

[77] ADHR, 4 G, 3–11a (Presentation and investment by the Bishop of Basel in 1502, October 26 and 29). After 1525, Carpentarii was also the beneficiary of a prebend of Basel's cathedral chapter: *Konrad W. Hieronimus*, Das Hochstift Basel im ausgehenden Mittelalter (Quellen und Forschungen), (Basel 1938), pp. 317 and 419.

[78] Cf. Matr. Heidelberg, Vol. I, p. 413; and Matr. Freiburg i. Br., Vol. I/1, p. 125 (No. 2).

[79] *Isidore Beuchot*, "Die ehemalige Franziskaner-, jetzige Spitalkirche der Stadt Colmar", Colmarer Katholischer Kirchen-Kalender, VI (1912), 68; and AMC, BB 45 (1522–76), pp. 177–9.

[80] Matr. Freiburg i. Br., Vol. I/1, p. 296 (No. 16).

[81] Cf. AAEB, A 41, 26 (March 10, 1556); and *Wertz*, ed., Le livre des bourgeois.

[82] Cf. Matr. Freiburg i. Br., Vol. I/1, p. 241 (No. 3).

Dean in 1556. He appears to have maintained permanent residence in Colmar[83], as did his successor, Johann Rasser (*ca.* 1535–94), Dean from 1563 to 1565, – a native of nearby Ensisheim.[84] For a period of about ten years following Rasser's departure, the deanery was alternately administrated by different Vice-Deans, such as by the canon Christian Zanenbentz from Geislingen in Württemberg[85], the Suffragan Marcus Tettinger (1540–1600)[86] from Radolfzell, and in 1571–72, again by Johann Rasser. Only in the Spring of 1575 did the chapter finally prove successful in recruiting a new Dean just a few weeks before the introduction of the Reformation in the city. It entrusted the position to Matthias Theodorici, a native of Colmar and former Rector of the parish church of Molsheim in Lower Alsace.[87]

By virtue of their local origin, the canons of St. Martin's in the first half of the 16th century must have been more integrated in Colmar's urban community than the deans. The extant evidence accounts for a total of nineteen canons for the entire pre-Reformation period (1522–75). Eleven priests among them show up only in the records from the first half of the century. Five among the latter were, to all appearances, natives of Colmar:[88] Bartholomäus Wickram, Adolf Krus, Ambrosius Böschlin, Eusebius Kalbfleisch, and Michael Algewer. In addition, Wickram and Krus were sons of leading Colmar families. Furthermore, two other canons from this group of eleven priests both came from the Colmar area and were likewise closely related to members of Colmar's patriciate and elite: Theobald Klett from Rouffach and Augustin Güntzer from Châtenois near Sélestat.[89] An additional two or three canons from the same group were

[83] ADHR, 4 G, 5–1 (March 6, 1553); ADHR, 4 G, 3–11a (June 23, 1556); AMC, GG 27, 7 (April 28, 1563). See also below, pp. 99–102 and 111–4.

[84] *Jürgen Bücking*, Johann Rasser (ca. 1535–1594) und die Gegenreformation im Oberelsass, RST, Vol. CI (Münster/Westphalia 1970), pp. 13–4.

[85] Matr. Freiburg i. Br., Vol. I/1, p. 436 (No. 107). Zanenbentz is first mentioned as a cantor in 1565. In the same year, he served as Vice-Dean. In 1589, he is also referred to as a chaplain of the Basel cathedral chapter: ADHR, 4 G, 5–3 (December 12, 1565); and AMC, GG 20, 6 (March 6, 1589).

[86] *Jürgen Bücking*, "Die Weihbischöfe von Basel Marcus Tettinger (1567–1599) und Franz Beer d. J. (1599–1611)", ZSKG, LXII (1968), 121–141. Tegginger is mentioned as Colmar Vice-Dean in 1568: AMC, GG 26, 26. He was still a Colmar canon in 1575. Cf. below, p. 122, n. 134.

[87] ADHR, 4 G, 3–11b (March 20, 1575); and AMC, GG 151, 25 (March 20–21, 1575); and Matr. Freiburg i. Br., Vol. I/1, p. 443 (No. 78).

[88] Bartholomäus Wickram (d. 1532): AMC, GG 26, 81 (Appendix). He earned a Master of Arts at Paris University and studied at the University of Basel. See Auctarium Parisiensis VI, cols. 604, 606, 624, 627, 630. – Adolf Krus was in all likelihood a relative of the Colmar patrician familiy carrying the same name. He is mentioned last in 1534: *Wertz*, ed., Le livre des bourgeois, p. 43. – Ambrosius Böschlin: AMC, GG 24, 15 and 18; AMC, GG 25, 12 and 22 (May 29 – September 3, 1528); cf. also Matr. Basel, Vol. I, p. 339. He is mentioned last in 1538 in Matr. Heidelberg, Vol. I, p. 570. –Eusebius Kalbfleisch (d. 1558), perhaps originally from nearby Rouffach rather than from Colmar: Matr. Freiburg i. Br., Vol. I/1, p. 208 (No. 30); and Matr. Köln, Vol. II, p. 755 (No. 508,54). Cf. also AMC, BB 52 (1541–46), pp. 98–9 (September 4, 1542); and AMC, BB 52 (1554–66), (June 21, 1558). – Michael Algewer: Matr. Freiburg i. Br., Vol. I/1, p. 213 (No. 17); AMC, GG 147, 2 (1547). He is mentioned last as scholasticus in 1568: AMC, GG 26, 26.

[89] Theobald Klett: Matr. Basel, Vol. I, p. 356; Matr. Wien, Vol. III, p. 47, 1. 12. He is mentioned last as cantor in 1541: *Wertz*, ed., Le livre des bourgeois, p. 56 (No. 502). – Augustin Güntzer: *Philippe Mieg*, "Notes biographiques et généalogiques sur les Güntzer de Colmar, de Sélestat et de Riquewihr", Annuaire de Colmar (1974/75), 161. Augustin Güntzer was a brother of the influential Colmar city-councillor, Mathias Güntzer. Cf. below, pp. 82 and 87–8. For Theobald Klett's connections to Colmars's leadership, cf. below, ibid.

also natives of adjacent towns and villages and, as a result of their familiarity with Colmar's population, probably maintained a relatively harmonious relationship with the latter.[90] Yet, following the mid-century, this pattern changed considerably. Among the canons who figure in the extant records from the period following the reduction of St. Martin's prebends in 1548, Eusebius Kalbfleisch (d. 1558) was the only priest who still personified the old, relatively close relations between the city's laymen and the secular clergy. Nicolaus Zanenbentz and Marcus Tegginger, as we have seen, were "immigrants" from Swabia, and the remainder of their colleagues were outsiders as well. Michael Gasser (d. *ca.* 1563) was a native of Hohenems (south of Bregenz);[91] Leonhard Salzmann was a Swabian priest from a village named Rotwilen (?) in the diocese of Constance.[92] Finally, Nicolaus Wylman, although his origin is unknown, was surely no native of Colmar, since this name does not figure in the city's contemporary *Bürgerbuch*.[93]

Which insights can we gain from this lengthy survey?[94] For the first half of the 16th century it suggests a relatively close relationship particularly between the upper strata of Colmar's lay community and secular clergy, and it conveys the impression of a fairly harmonious relationship between the secular clergy and the city's population in general. It thus helps to explain the authorities' refusal of the Reformation message and, in turn, their dedicated pursuit of a policy of Catholic ecclesiastical reform during the 1530's and 1540's.[95] The generally good educational background of St. Martin's clergy in those days may have sustained the climate of humanist reformism which was, as we shall see, the backbone of this policy.[96] This situation changed during the 1540's and 1550's. After this period, the majority of St. Martin's deans and canons were outsiders. Most of them were Swabians who often encountered considerable xenophobia on the part of

[90] Bartholomäus Klug from Riquewihr: Matr. Basel, Vol. I, p. 170 (No. 17). He is mentioned last as Colmar canon in 1529: AMC, BB 45 (1515–42), p. 77. – Theobald Oiglin (Eugly) from Niedermorschwihr: Matr. Basel, Vol. I, p. 254 (No. 7). He resigned from his Colmar canonry in 1528. Cf. above, n. 88 (same sources as mentioned for A. Böschlin who was Oiglin's successor). – Heinrich Godel: he was perhaps a relative of Arbogast Godel from Rouffach, mentioned in Matr. Heidelberg, Vol. I, p. 561. Cf. also AMC, GG 25, 4, fol. 20r (1522); AMC, GG 25,9 and 10 (1528); Heinrich Godel is referred to as "licentiatus".

[91] Matr. Freiburg i. Br., Vol. I/1, p. 381 (no. 1); ADHR, 4 G, 2–4 (Notebook entitled "Volgt . . ."), fol. 12v.

[92] Matr. Freiburg i. Br., Vol. I/1, p. 421 (No. 26); mentioned as canon in 1565: ADHR, 4 G, 4–3c.

[93] First mention of Wylman as a Colmar canon in 1547: ADHR, 4 G, 5–2. Last mention in 1568: AMC, GG 26, 26.

[94] The extant information on Colmar's common priests (*plebani*) from the pre-Reformation period is too scarce and fragmentary to be included here. For a list of the common priests from 1547 to 1575, cf. below, p. 78, n. 33.

[95] This conclusion does not contradict *Klaus-Joachim Lorenzen-Schmidt*'s claim that in the cities of Schleswig-Holstein the relatively high percentage of natives among the secular clergy facilitated the introduction of the Reformation in these towns. Precisely those canons in Colmar who, through ties of kin and friendship maintained a close relationship with the city's leading families, showed, as far as we know to date, no sympathy for the Reformation movement. Cf. idem, "Die Geistlichen der Schleswig-holsteinischen Städte vor der Reformation und ihre Stellung in den Stadtgemeinden", in *Bernd Moeller*, ed., Stadt und Kirche im 16. Jahrhundert, SVRG, No. 190 (Gütersloh 1978), 125–7.

[96] Cf. below, Chapter III.

Alsatian laymen.[97] The old ties of kin and friendship engaged alike the canons and Colmar's leading families and, thus, assured a safe measure of mutual respect. As a result of their decline, anticlericalism could make important inroads into the ranks of the ruling patriciate. More importantly, with their decline disappeared a material interest in the preservation of the old church which could have thwarted the councillor's quasi unanimous decision to introduce Protestant worship in 1575.

The above survey has led us well beyond Goehlinger's vague observation that the canons of St. Martin's were "almost exclusively sons of rich Colmar citizens and of well-to-do inhabitants of Upper Alsace".[98] However, the question of the social origin of Colmar's canons of the pre-Reformation period (particularly difficult to answer in the case of non-*Colmariens*) must admittedly remain open, for no further evidence on the social recruitment of the canons of St. Martin's can be gained from other source material, such as the chapter's statutes. The conditions under which a new canon was admitted to the chapter contained no direct provisions for the desired social rank of the candidate other than the stipulation that he be of legitimate birth. Nevertheless, the chapter secured, albeit indirectly, that only sons of well-to-do families would find access to its prebends, since each candidate was supposed to submit the stately fee of fifty Rhenish florins for his admission, as well as an indemnity sum of 220 florins.[99]

The church of St. Martin was also Colmar's main parish church. St. Peter's and St. John's, the two other parishes of the community, ranked on a comparatively inferior level.[100] Scant information available for St. Peter's and St. John's makes it difficult to analyse in some depth the relationship between these three parish churches during the 16th century. St. Peter's had originally been an *Eigenkirche* of Colmar's Benedictine Priorate of St. Peter and had, as such, been controlled by the mother-monastery of Payerne (Peterlingen) in Switzerland.[101] However, in 1350, we find the city government, rather than the monastery, in charge of the construction of a choir at St. Peter's.[102] It appears that the city, at this point in time, had already established a fair amount of administrative control over this parish church. Up to the High Middle Ages – on an ecclesiastical and spiritual level – the church of St. Peter had been subject to the control of its mother church in the adjacent town of Horbourg. It is, nevertheless, the Dean of St. Martin's whom we find in charge of the cure of souls of both his as well as St. Peter's parish in 1524/25.[103] We do not know of any act of incorporation of St. Peter's church in St. Martin's. Dean Jacob Carpentarii had, therefore, simply been conferred the

[97] See *Rapp*, Réformes et Réformation à Strasbourg, pp. 306–318. The Bishop's observations regarding the proposed appointment of Matthias Theodorici as Dean of St. Martin's are a good case-in-point. He assumed that Theodorici, "da er zů Colmar vil Jar lang erzogen, doselbst als ein bekhantter verhoffenlich mehr vnd grössern, dan ein frembder, nutz mit fleissigem Catholischen Praedicieren schaffen möchte". Cf. ADHR, 4 G, 3–11b (Bishop of Basel to chapter of St. Martin, March 20, 1575).

[98] *Goehlinger*, Histoire du Chapitre, p. 22.

[99] ibid., pp. 24–6 (Summary of the conditions for admission).

[100] *Scherlen*, Colmar: Village et ville, p. 19.

[101] Ibid., pp. 11–12.

[102] *Trouillat* and *Vautrey*, eds., Monuments, Vol. V, p. 693.

[103] In 1524/25, the Dean employed a vicar at St. Peter's "... herr hans, so des dechants mietling zu Sant petter gewesen": AMC, EE 7, 1, fol. 3r. The same document clearly mentions the Saint Peter's parish ("kilchspyl"): ibid., fol. 6r.

pastoral care of both parishes. We do not know whether his successor was endowed with the same prerogative.

Although worship was still held at both St. Peter's and St. John's in 1539–40[104], these churches had ceased to play the role of actual *parish*-churches by the 1530's at the latest. Simon Iselin, the last residing Commander of the Commandery of the Knights of St. John, to which St. John's church was attached, died in 1530. Consequently, the "parish" of St. John's only comprised the servants and administrators of the Commandery and their families. The commanderies of Colmar and Soultz were henceforth headed by the same Commander who resided at Soultz. Only two chaplains of the order temporarily remained in Colmar, and by the end of the century the order was forced to hire a priest who continued celebrating the mass at St. John's. The church was no longer the center of a regular parish.[105]

After the city of Bern had conquered the Abbey of Payerne in 1536, – the Priorate of St. Peter's Swiss mother monastery –, the Prior Jean Cheurodi (Tscheurodi) and his servants remained the sole regular occupants of the Colmar Priorate. Following the death of Cheurodi in 1570, the Colmar authorities were able to buy the Priorate from Bern in 1575.[106] The parish of St. Peter's had lost its last raison d'être. This calls for the conclusion that by about 1540, Colmar's urban community and its parishes had amalgamated into one and the same political and ecclesiastical organism, insofar as the city's three *Kirchspiele*, – separate units throughout most of the Middle Ages –, had now merged into one parish (St. Martin's), which had grown identical in size to the *Gemeinde* (urban community). Henceforth, the regular communal cure of souls in Colmar was exclusively in the hands of the chapter of St. Martin.[107]

Meanwhile, the mendicant orders managed to maintain a lively influence on the city's religious and ecclesiastical life. The Dominicans had regained strength and authority at the end of the 14th century when Raymond of Capua, as master-general of the order, commissioned Conrad de Grossis (d. 1426) with the reform of the order in Germany. As Prior of the Colmar Dominicans since 1389, Conrad de Grossis first restored monastic observance in his own house, and then successfully completed the reform of the women's monasteries of Schoenensteinbach in 1397, and Unterlinden in Colmar in

[104] The preaching ordinance for the newly appointed preacher, Johann Fabri, stipulates: "Sub hora qua predicatur in ecclesia collegiata, in aliis ecclesijs et monasterijs non predicetur": AMC, GG 39, 24. Also, in a letter addressed to the Bailiff of Haguenau on April 28, 1568, the chapter emphasized that it was in charge of the entire Colmar ministry: AMC, GG 26, 38.

[105] See *Isidore Beuchot*, "Die ehemalige Johanniterkirche in Colmar", Colmarer Katholischer Kirchen-Kalender, VII (1913), 53; *Paul Huot*, La Commanderie de St-Jean à Colmar: Etude historique (1210–1870), (Colmar 1870), p. 5; and *August Scherlen*, Topographie von Alt-Colmar (Colmar 1922), pp. 11, 319–320.

[106] Cf. *Scherlen*, ibid., p. 142, and (for the original topographical extent within the city of St. Peter's parish) pp. 137–140. For the transfer of St. Peter's Priorate between 1570 and 1575, see AMC, BB 52 (Protocolla Missivarum/ 1570–75), pp. 14, and 20–21 (Letters from the Colmar authorities to Bern, August 29 and September 14, 1570), *et passim*. See also *André Waltz*, ed., Chronique de Colmar de Félix-Henri-Joseph Chauffour dit le Syndic (Colmar 1903), p. 86.

[107] Cf. *Gerhard Pfeiffer*'s observations on the formation of the early modern parish, in idem, "Das Verhältnis von politischer und kirchlicher Gemeinde in den deutschen Reichsstädten", in Staat und Kirche im Wandel der Jahrhunderte, ed. by *Walter Peter Fuchs* (Stuttgart, Berlin, Cologne and Mainz 1966), pp. 79–99.

1419, a well-known stronghold of Rhenish mysticism. From here the reform movement also reached Guebwiller and Basel. The observant tradition at St. Catherine's, Unterlinden's sister monastery in Colmar, was re-established with some difficulty in 1439.[108] Predominantly, these difficulties had to do with the fact that St. Catherine's convent, like the Unterlinden monastery, was a retreat frequently chosen by daughters of Colmar's patricians and the Alsatian landed nobility.[109] Many among these sisters of noble origin strongly resisted the reintroduction of observance into their convent. We do not know exactly how much of this fervent spirit of monastic renewal, which led to and made possible the monastic reform of the early 15th century, survived in Colmar's monasteries of the Reformation era. The Dominican sisters at Unterlinden and St. Catherine's maintained a relatively secluded life during most of the 16th century. During the 1540's and 1550's the Dominicans, however, as we shall be able to observe below, stimulated Colmar's ecclesiastical life with many important impulses. A similar role was played by the Augustinian friars during the 1530's and 1540's.[110]

Regarding the well-known signs of inner dissolution which characterized the German monastic life of the early Reformation years, we know of only a few individual cases of mendicant friars leaving their Colmar monasteries for religious reasons. The sources do not inform us, however, of how widespread this exodus *really* was in Colmar. Consequently, we are unable to explore the exact causes that lead to the downfall of the Franciscan monastery. We know that the few remaining brothers died during the plague of 1541, while their Guardian, Jacob Einfalt, was absent at Würzburg, where he had become a preacher at the local cathedral in 1536.[111] In 1543, the provincial Guardian, Bartholomeus Hermann, sold the Colmar monastery to the city of Colmar.[112] However, we lack any precise information on why the number of Franciscan friars was already down to four monks by 1525,considering the monastery had just gone through a relatively prosperous period under the guidance of Guardian Dr. Johannes Menzer.[113]

All semi-pelagian elements of late medieval theology and popular religiousness considered, we still cannot withstand the impression that the monastic ideal had lost some of its earlier appeal for the common man a while before the Reformation message reinforced this tendency. Humanism, for instance, had already contributed its fair share to discrediting the appeal of monasticism.[114] It is very likely that this factor was at the root

[108] *A[rmand] M. P. Ingold*, Notice sur l'église et le couvent des Dominicains de Colmar (Colmar and Paris 1894), pp. 36–44; and *Annette Barthelmé*, La Réforme dominicaine au XVe siècle en Alsace et dans l'ensemble de la province de Teutonie, Collection d'études sur l'histoire de droit et des institutions de l'Alsace, Vol. VII (Strasbourg 1931), especially pp. 23–37.

[109] Cf. AMC, GG 72, 3, and GG 73, 24; and *Philippe Dollinger*, "Strasbourg et Colmar, foyers de la mystique rhénane", in La Mystique rhénane, ed. by the Centre d'études supérieures spécialisé d'histoire des religions de Strasbourg (Paris 1963), p. 10.

[110] Cf. below, pp. 77–9 and 82–3.

[111] *August Hertzog*, „Die letzten Jahre des Colmarer Barfüsserklosters und Jakob Einfalt aus Geberschweier, dessen letzter Guardian", Jb. GSL, XVII (1901), 113–149.

[112] *August Hertzog*, "Inventare des früheren Franziskanerklosters von Colmar", Jb. GSL, XXI (1905), 23–44.

[113] *Hertzog*, "Die letzten Jahre", 118. For Johannes Menzer, cf. Matr. Freiburg, Vol. I/1, p. 107, (No. 11).

[114] See *Rudolf Wackernagel*, Geschichte der Stadt Basel, Vol. III (Basel 1924), pp. 247–8.

of the disintegration of the Colmar Franciscan order, preceding its ultimate fall in 1541. Thus, the slow but steady decomposition of beguine life on the eve of the Reformation and during the first Reformation years, as it took place in Cologne, Strasbourg, Sélestat and Colmar, comes as no surprise to us.[115] In medieval Colmar, there had once been ten beguine houses. By 1495, only one such house was left in town, inhabited by only three sisters.[116] The last mention of a Colmar beguine dates from 1525.[117] By that time, the social and religious unrest of the early Reformation years had not left the community untouched. Widespread discontent directed against clerical and secular authority shook the city between December, 1524 and May, 1525. The concomitant disturbances were, in good part, harbingers of a movement which would only find its definitive expression in the comparatively late introduction of the Reformation in 1575. We will turn to the vestiges and traces this movement left in Colmar's 16th century, following a brief glance at Colmar's intellectual life at the beginning of the 16th century, which will conclude this introductory overview.

E. THE INTELLECTUAL LIFE

As elsewhere in Alsace, Colmar's intellectual life on the eve of the Reformation era was narrowly linked to the life of the Roman church.[118] The fifty incunabula and numerous 16th century prints from the Colmar monastery libraries of the Dominican and Augustinian friars – today stacked in the Strasbourg City Library[119] – are a case-in-point, and an indication of the learnedness of some of the city's monks.

Theirs and the secular clergy's scholarship was embedded in the rules and intellectual schemata of traditional scholasticism. At the beginning of the 16th century, only very few of them had embraced humanism. It was in protest against the prevailing conservative scholastic outlook of Colmar's secular clergy that the humanist Matthias Ringmann Philesius proferred his slur of "*Kolbnarrenses*", alluding to the mace (*Kolben*) in Colmar's coat of arms.[120]

Colmar's most eminent scholar in those days was Sebastian Murrho (1452–94), a canon at St. Martin's. He had attended the humanist school of Sélestat, as a companion of the humanists Peter Schott of Strasbourg and Jodocus Gallus of Rouffach. Later, he was a student at the universities of Freiburg im Breisgau and Heidelberg. His private life as a Colmar canon, in the company of a mistress and the three children she had born him,

[115] *Jean-Claude Schmitt*, "Les dernières années d'un béguinage colmarien d'après ses comptes (1510–1531)", Annuaire de Colmar (1975/76), 31–42. For Sélestat, cf. *Paul Adam*, Histoire des hospices et hopitaux de Sélestat (Sélestat 1960), pp. 50–5.

[116] *Schmitt*, "Les dernières années", 33.

[117] AMC, FF 355, 45.

[118] Cf. *Francis Rapp*, "Die elsäßischen Humanisten und die geistliche Gesellschaft", in Die Humanisten in ihrer politischen und sozialen Umwelt, ed. by *Otto Herding* and *Robert Stupperich*, Mitteilung III of Deutsche Forschungsgemeinschaft, Kommission für Humanismusforschung (Bonn and Bad-Godesberg 1976), pp. 87–108.

[119] *François Ritter*, ed., Catalogue des Incunables et Livres du XVIe siècle de la Bibliothéque Municipale de Strasbourg (Strasbourg and Zürich 1948), pp. 1–81, *et passim.*

[120] *Charles Schmidt*, Histoire littéraire de l'Alsace, Vol II (reprint of first edition: 2 Vols.; Paris 1879; Hildesheim 1966), p. 93.

was a flagrant affront to contemporary humanist critics of clerical morals, but it did not discourage Wimpfeling, Reuchlin and the monk Conrad Leontorius, from entertaining a friendly rapport with Murrho, who was a humanist well versed in Latin, Greek, and even Hebrew.[121] Next to Conrad Pellicanus, Murrho was the first Alsatian humanist to devote himself to the study of Hebrew. Among his published works figure commentaries on the poetry of Baptista Mantuanus, and the *Epitome rerum Germanorum*, a history of Germany re-arranged and edited in 1505 (after Murrho's death) by his friend Jacob Wimpfeling.[122] One of Murrho's sons, Sebastian Jr., made promising progress in the intellectual footsteps of his father but died at a young age.[123]

At the beginning of the 16th century, humanist learning also found acclaim among the city's Augustinian friars. During the 1510's, their Prior Diepolt Vögelin devoted considerable interest to the collection of precious books and manuscripts, furthered the education of his subordinates, such as that of Thomas Gyerfalck, and may have also promoted the studies of Nicolaus Pruckner – the only direct witness to the scholarship of Colmar's Augustians in those days.[124]

Colmar's main school was originally in the hands of the chapter of St. Martin. However, in 1350 the chapter conceded a good measure of authority over this institution to the city government. Although the canons reserved the right to supervise the instruction given at the school, the magistrate was henceforth to recruit the teachers.[125]

[121] A letter from Conrad Leontorius addressed to his friend Bruno Amerbach in Basel on January 7, 1509, sheds more light on this friendship. Leontorius refers to the study of Hebrew "que quondam in vsu habuit non ignote scientie aut obscuri nominis dnus Sebastianus Murrho Colmariensis, qui maxima cura linguam Hebream senior et preter sacerdotis dignitatem jam tribus liberis genitis teste me et inspiciente studere voluit et apprehendere". He further recalls an unknown baptized Colmar Jew, named Paulus, who had introduced him (Leontorius) to Hebrew writing. The monk's letter also testifies to the liveliness of the correspondence Johannes Reuchlin used to entertain with the Colmar canon. See *Alfred Hartmann*, ed., Die Amerbachkorrespondenz, Vol. I (Basel 1942), No. 406, p. 370. For Leontorius' friendship with Murrho, cf. also *G. Wolff*, "Sebastian Murrhos Geburts- und Todestag", Anzeiger für Deutsches Alterthum und Deutsche Litteratur, XIV (September 4, 1888), 293–301. To date only one extant letter documents the correspondence between Murrho and Reuchlin; see *Ludwig Geiger*, ed., Johann Reuchlins Briefwechsel, Bibliothek des Litterarischen Vereins in Stuttgart, Vol. CXXVI (Tübingen 1875), No. 10, p. 13.

[122] Cf. Wimpfeling's letters to Johannes Amerbach: *Hartmann*, ibid., pp. 38, 50, 54, and 109. See also *Schmidt*, Histoire littéraire, Vol. I, pp. 177–8; Vol. II, pp. 4, 36–7, 323–4 (No. 20), and 391–2.

[123] For his epigram, "In laudem Conradi Celtis Protucii, poetae Germani", see *Hans Rupprich*, ed., Der Briefwechsel des Konrad Celtis, Veröffentlichungen der Kommission zur Erforschung der Geschichte der Reformation und Gegenreformation, Humanistenbriefe, Vol. III (Munich 1934), pp. 627-9. Sebastian Murrho, Jr. was a friend of Beatus Rhenanus, who, on February 2, 1513, sent greetings to him through the Strasbourg printer Matthias Schürer: *Adalbert Horawitz* and *Karl Hartfelder*, eds., Briefwechsel des Beatus Rhenanus (Leipzig 1886), p. 55. Cf. also *Schmidt*, ibid., Vol. II, pp. 39–40.

[124] For Vögelin, see Thomas Gyerfalck's later account in AMC, GG 99, 6 (n. d.[1538]); and *Isidore Beuchot*, "Die ehemalige Augustinerkirche zu Colmar", Colmarer Katholischer Kirchen-Kalender, IX (1915), 53. Nicolaus Pruckner's correspondence from 1518 with his friend Bruno Amerbach speaks for the former's humanist learning and informs us about Pruckner's acquaintance with the Basel printer Johannes Froben and with Beatus Rhenanus; see *Hartmann*, ed., Amerbachkorrespondenz, Vol. II (Basel 1943), Nos. 616, 620. Both Gyerfalck and Pruckner left the Colmar monastery during the late 1510's and, later, became reformers in Basel and Mulhouse, respectively; cf. below, p. 83 n. 61 (Gyerfalck), and *Timotheus W. Röhrich*, „Nicolaus Prugner, Reformator von Mühlhausen", in idem, Mittheilungen aus der Geschichte der evangelischen Kirche des Elsaßes, Vol. III (Strasbourg and Paris 1855), pp. 180–202.

[125] *Joseph Knepper*, Das Schul- und Unterrichtswesen im Elsass: Von den Anfängen bis gegen das Jahr 1530 (Strasbourg 1905), p. 233.

Judging from the little we know about the situation prevailing at the beginning of the 16th century, the secular authorities seemed to care little about the school's welfare. Only during the 1530's, as we shall see, did its desolate state begin to arouse their concern. Before that time, it was an "insignificant school"[126] with the possible exception of the days of Sebastian Murrho, who seems to have attracted pupils from far away.[127] In this connection, the difference between Colmar and the neighboring city of Sélestat, with its flourshing humanist school, could not have been more marked.[128]

The student of Wimpfeling and Lefèvre d'Etaples, Matthias Ringmann Philesius (1482–1511), tried in vain to introduce the spirit of humanist scholarship into the city's school. Probably talked into accepting the post of teacher in Colmar by the learned Strasbourg canon and Provost at St. Martin's in Colmar, Thomas Wolf (1475–1509), Ringmann quit his new job at the end of 1504, after a short stay of about one year, wishing his successor, the learned Augustin Sprung, the success he had been denied in trying to overcome the chapter's resistance to a reform of the curriculum of its school.[129] The extant evidence does not discuss any subsequent curricular reform or Sprung's successor.[130] It is thus safe to assume that up to the 1530's the teaching method and the curriculum in use at Colmar's city and monastic schools were still based upon the medieval scholastic heritage. Improvement of this situation, as we shall see, was brought about by laymen.[131]

[126] *Schmidt,* Histoire littéraire, Vol. I, p. XXI.

[127] This assumption is suggested by the fact that Peter Falck (d. 1519) from Freiburg in Switzerland, (later a staunch humanist, city politician and Swiss diplomat in Rome and Milan), attended the Colmar school in 1492–3. See *Adalbert Wagner,* „Peter Falcks Bibliothek und humanistische Bildung", Freiburger Geschichtsblätter, XXVIII (1925), 108–9, and 133–4.

[128] Cf. *Paul Adam,* L'humanisme à Sélestat, Sélestat 1962.

[129] See *Knepper*, Schul- und Unterrichtswesen, pp. 209–216, 233–4, 304–5; and *Schmidt*, Histoire littéraire, Vol. II, pp. 87–132, especially pp. 92–3. Ringmann was appointed to the position despite the Sélestat authorities' recommendation in favor of Paul Phrygio (1483–1543), addressed to the magistrate and chapter of Colmar on April 23, 1503: *Joseph Gény*, Die Reichsstadt Schlettstadt und ihr Anteil an den socialpolitischen und religiösen Bewegungen der Jahre 1490–1536, Erläuterungen und Ergänzungen zu Janssens Geschichte des deutschen Volkes, Vol. I, Books V and VI (Freiburg i. Br. 1900), p. 58. On Sprung, see Matr. Freiburg i. Br., Vol. I/1, p. 139 (No. 15): "Augustinus Sprong de Steinoug[= Steinach], clericus Argentinensis dioecesis, die 22. Junii", 1500. During the year 1503–1504, Sprung earned a master's degree at Freiburg University.

[130] The extant records on Colmar's teachers lack any information for the period 1504–1539, with the exception of a reference to Johannes Giger from Ehingen who was appointed on June 24, 1520: *Knepper,* ibid., p. 234.

[131] Cf. below, pp. 80–1.

CHAPTER II

FROM THE SOCIAL AND RELIGIOUS UNREST OF THE 1520's TO THE INTRODUCTION OF THE REFORMATION IN THE NEIGHBORING PRINCIPALITY OF HORBOURG-RIQUEWIHR IN 1535

A. COMMUNITY AND CHURCH AT THE BEGINNING OF THE 1520's

On the eve of the Reformation, popular religiosity found its most current and most important expressions in the worship of Saints, in religious processions and donations, in pious foundations, in pilgrimages, in the charity practiced by clerical and lay confraternities and in the indulgence trade. In recent historical research the place of so-called *Volksfrömmigkeit*, that is, popular religiosity in its pre-Reformation setting, has again been widely debated[1] and some historians have attempted to determine the relevance of early 16th century popular religiosity as an indirect cause or catalyst of the Reformation. It cannot be our intention in this study to compare the results of these often far-reaching scholarly inquiries with our local evidence; yet, we cannot disregard the topic altogether, as it is my conviction that the knowledge of the extent and intensity of 16th century popular religiosity greatly enhances our understanding of the anti-clericalism of the time. More often than not, religiosity and anticlericalism appeared as correlative forces, and – at least in the case of Colmar, as the following pages will show – it would be a mistake not to conclude that the bulk of 16th century anti-clerical protest was nur-

[1] See *A. G. Dickens*' justified remarks concerning the terminology used here, in idem, The German Nation and Martin Luther (London 1974), pp. 17–8. For the present state of research on 15th and 16th century popular religiosity, see *Bernd Moeller*, "Frömmigkeit in Deutschland um 1500", ARH, LVI (1965), 5–30; for a translation of Moeller's essay, cf. idem, "Piety in Germany around 1500", translated by Joyce Irwin, in The Reformation in Medieval Perspective, ed. with an introduction by Steven E. Ozment (Chicago 1971), pp. 50–75; *Steven E. Ozment*, The Reformation in the Cities (New Haven and London 1975), pp. 15–46; *Natalie Z. Davis*, "Some tasks and themes in the study of popular religion", in The pursuit of holiness in late medieval and Renaissance religion, ed. by Charles Trinkaus and Heiko A. Oberman, SMRT, Vol. X (Leiden 1974), pp. 307–336; *Francis Rapp*, "Réflexions sur la religion populaire au moyen âge", in La Religion populaire dans l'occident chrétien: Approches historiques, ed. by Bernard Plongeron, Bibliothèque Beauchesne: Religions, Société, Politique, Vol. II (Paris 1976), pp. 51–98; and *Hansgeorg Molitor*, "Frömmigkeit im Spätmittelalter und früher Neuzeit als historisch-methodisches Problem", in Festgabe für Ernst Walter Zeeden, ed. by Horst Rabe, Hansgeorg Molitor and Hans-Christoph Rublack, RST, Supplemental Vol. II (Münster/Westphalia 1976), pp. 1–20. For comparative purposes, see *Albrecht Endriss*, Die religiös-kirchlichen Verhältnisse in der Reichsstadt Wimpfen vor der Reformation, VKBW, Vol. XXXIX, Stuttgart 1967; *Gottfried Geiger*, Die Reichsstadt Ulm vor der Reformation: Städtisches und kirchliches Leben am Ausgang des Mittelalters, Forschungen zur Geschichte der Stadt Ulm, Vol. XI, Ulm 1971; and *Hans von Greyerz*, "Studien zur Kulturgeschichte der Stadt Bern am Ende des Mittelalters", Archiv des Historischen Vereins des Kantons Bern, Vol. XXXV, Book 2 (1940), pp. 173–491.

tured by a deep concern for the spiritual welfare of the church. I will therefore enter into a brief discussion of the religious confraternities or brotherhoods which, in the contemporary cities, supplied the institutional framework for popular religious activity. This discussion, however limited in scope, of the extent to which these brotherhoods existed in Colmar, will also help us to understand that Colmar's religious life on the eve of the Reformation era did not differ in any substantial way from what we know about its role in other contemporary German and Swiss cities.

Confraternities sponsored and maintained altars and prebends, worshipped their Saint-Protectors, organized religious processions and pilgrimages, and cared for their aging and ailing members, thus fulfilling an important aspect of social welfare. They also founded anniversary masses for the salvation of their deceased and held regular reunions reserved for common prayer. In pre-Reformation Colmar, as elsewhere, they embodied the most important institutional link between the corporate forms of communal association, such as the guild and the parish, and the more hierarchical and centralized body of the Catholic church.[2] In the case of Colmar, the number of fraternities, as well as their activities, suggest both the keen sense of communal responsibility and the deeply religious fervor shared by their members. Based on documents of the late 15th and early 16th centuries eighteen different Colmar confraternities of that period are known to me. Most of them were attached to the church of one of the mendicant orders in town, where they maintained their altars. The majority were confraternities of journeymen, such as the brotherhoods of the wool-weaver, the shoemaker and the tanner journeymen.[3]

Among the remaining confraternities, the Brotherhood of the Rosary was the most eminent. It was founded in 1484 by the Colmar Dominicans, based on the model of the famous Rosary confraternity of Cologne, and was open to both clerical and lay membership. Membership in this confraternity was not exclusively reserved for *Colmariens.* On the contrary, it spread over an extraordinarily large geographical area, reaching on the eve of the Reformation from the Upper Valais (Swiss alps) in the south, to the confines of Lower Alsace in the north. At this time, the Brotherhood of the Rosary had a total of 2,873 members in Colmar alone, of which 8.87 percent belonged to the city's clergy. Its lay members were predominantly, although not exclusively, the city's craftsmen.[4] On the basis of this evidence we can assume that the interchange between

[2] *P[aul] A. Merklen*, Les boulangers de Colmar, 1495–1513, Colmar 1871; and *Georg Schanz*, Zur Geschichte der deutschen Gesellenvereine im Mittelalter (reprint of the first edition: Leipzig, 1876; Glashütten im Taunus: 1973), pp. 69–92. For comparative purposes, see also *Nathalie Z. Davis,* „Strikes and salvation in Lyon", in idem, Society and culture in early modern France: Eight essays (Stanford, Cal. 1975), pp. 1–16.

[3] *Merklen*, Les boulangers de Colmar, p. 27, also mentions the brotherhoods of the journeymen bath-attendants and the journeymen coachmen. They entertained their altars at St. Martin's. For the 1470-foundation and the statutes of the brotherhood of the tanner journeymen, see [*Franz Joseph*] *Mone*, "Zunftorganisation", ZGORh, XVIII (1865), 20–24. For comparative purposes, in respect to craft-oriented brotherhoods, cf. *Endriss*, Die religiös-kirchlichen Verhältnisse, pp. 165–8; and *Geiger*, Die Reichsstadt Ulm, pp. 157–9.

[4] *Jean-Claude Schmitt*, "Apostolat mendiant et société: Une confrérie dominicaine à la veille de la Réforme", Annales ESC, XXVI (1971), 83–104; and idem, "La confrérie du Rosaire de Colmar (1485)", Archivum Fratrum Praedicatorum, XL (1970), 97–124. See also *Médard Barth*, "Die Rosenkranzbruderschaften des Elsass, geschichtlich gewürdigt," Arch. EA, XXXII (1968), 78. Concerning the other Colmar confraternities, cf. *Isidore Beuchot*, "Die ehemalige Augustinerkirche zu Colmar",

communal and ecclesiastical, lay and clerical life, taking place in early 16th century Colmar was extensive.

This brief glance at Colmar's religious brotherhoods suggests how closely interwoven the life of the 16th century burgher was with the life of the church, which monopolized all immanent means of absolution and salvation to a much greater degree than the church of the Reformation ever did. During the early 16th century, it was precisely this close amalgamation of ecclesiastical and communal life which greatly contributed to the rise of rampant anticlericalism. The Roman church of this period was much more than a charitable institution granting spiritual benefits. It was, at the same time, a powerful social and economic organism. As a member of the church, and often as a direct compensation for spiritual benefits received, the layman was bound to support the church through his material contributions. Whatever zeal he showed as a member of this or that particular confraternity, whatever fervor and generosity he demonstrated in his religious donations and pious foundations, and however often he was thus allowed to partake in the spiritual benefits of the church (such as in indulgences accorded to a particular church or monastery), he was never, or very rarely, spared the claim of the church on part of his income and possessions. Often this claim was substantial, and its legitimacy was, if needed, enforced by clerical courts. Faced with such financial obligations, the layman's eager and unconditional participation in the life of the church could turn into strong and occasionally violent feelings of anticlericalism. This was often catalysed by the daily sight of what many contemporaries considered the leisurely life of the clergy; by which they meant the frequent material ease of the higher secular and regular clergy, and widespread moral abuse, such as concubinage, practiced by many priests and monks of their day.

In early 16th century Colmar, the jurisdictional power of the church, as well as the clergy's legal privileges (such as the exemption from prosecution by secular courts, and their immunity vis-à-vis the material claims of a secular government, e. g. against taxation), were the most important targets of widespread anticlerical feelings. These privileges offended the urban layman's keen sense of corporate communality.[5] Furthermore, the not uncommon simony practiced by the pre-Reformation clergy, and their way of handling and renting out their own considerable real-estate, contravened the layman's sense of equity. Finally, wherever it occurred, the clergy's immoral life, considered incompatible with the *character indelebilis* of the priest, contributed to the layman's contempt. Another condition creating hostility was the so-called "*ewige Zinsen*". The exact amount of real-estate owned by this city's churches is not known, but there is no doubt that it must have been considerable. Only a small portion of this proper-

Colmarer Katholischer Kirchen-Kalender, IX (1915), 48; idem, „Die ehemalige Franziskaner-, jetzige Spitalkirche der Stadt Colmar", Colmarer Katholischer Kirchen-Kalender, VI (1912), 52–3; *Luzian Sittler*, "Landwirtschaft und Gartenbau im alten Colmar", Elsaß-Lothringisches Jahrbuch, XX (1942), 83; *August Hertzog*, "Die Bruderschaften am Minoritenkloster zu Colmar", Jb. GSL, XXV (1903), 39–53; and *Médard Barth*, "Die Sakramentsbruderschaften des Elsass", Arch. EA, XXXV (1971), pp. 211–223.

[5] *Bernd Moeller*, Imperial Cities and the Reformation: Three Essays, translated and ed. by H. C. Erik Midelfort and Mark U. Edwards, Jr. (Philadelphia: 1972), pp. 41–115; and idem, "Kleriker als Bürger", in Festschrift für Hermann Heimpel zum 70. Geburtstag, ed. by Mitarbeiter des Max-Planck-Instituts für Geschichte, Vol. II (Göttingen 1972), pp. 195–224.

ty was actually used by the clergy itself. Within contemporary German cities, as apparently also in Colmar, the bulk of it was nominally in the hands of laymen, who, in turn, owed the church the so-called "*ewige Zinsen*" – a kind of endless mortgage payment on this property. In late medieval Frankfurt and in Freiburg im Breisgau, one-third and two-fifths, respectively, of all bourgeois house owners had fallen into this kind of financial dependence on the church. Thus, many a peasant, vintner or merchant became heavily indebted to the church in years when the crops failed or in time of war, when the roads were unsafe for trade. In Alsace this situation led to open hostilities between burghers and clergy in Sélestat and Wissembourg in 1525. In Colmar, too, the problem was on many citizens' minds, for, in December, 1524, it figured on the list of communal grievances and in 1530, at the imperial diet of Augsburg, Colmar sought to gain imperial sanction for a general abolition of all "eternal" mortgages within its walls.[6]

Similarly widespread, and more prominent, was anticlerical resentment generated by the Colmar clergy's right of immunity, i. e. its exemption from local taxes and from the duties imposed upon every regular citizen, such as nightly watch and unpaid statute-labor. Equally unpopular was the clergy's exemption from prosecution by secular courts for their occasional misdeeds.[7]

Whereas the city government's support of most of the citizens' attack against clerical privileges was, in some cases, brought about by social pressure or by its keen interest in bolstering up the city's finances, the communal assault on clerical immunity, on the other hand, was usually nurtured by a sense of equity deeply rooted in the corporate-communal ideal as a widely accepted principle of urban social organization. As has been shown repeatedly by Bernd Moeller[8], the kind of collective corporate consciousness shared by the 16th century German burghers lent a powerful impetus to most communal action involving the church and the clergy: "Both social bodies, the clergy and the urban community of the late middle ages, mutually opposed each other in their tendency towards social exclusiveness."[9] All over Germany, the communal movement against clerical privilege gained momentum during the early 1520's. Strong anticlerical movements constituted themselves in the Alsatian cities of Strasbourg, Sélestat and

[6] *Heinrich Rocholl*, Anfänge der Reformationsgeschichte in Kolmar: Ein Beitrag zur Reformationsgeschichte des Elsaß (Colmar 1875), p. 24; cf. also *Günther Franz*, ed., Der deutsche Bauernkrieg: Aktenband (Munich and Berlin 1935), p. 188; and *Anton Störmann*, Die städtischen Gravamina gegen den Klerus am Ende des Mittelalters und in der Reformationszeit, RST, XXIV–XXVI (1 Vol.), (Münster/Westphalia 1916), pp. 65 and 76.

[7] Cf. below, pp. 43–4 and 51.

[8] *Moeller*, Imperial Cities and the Reformation; and idem, „Die Kirche in den evangelischen freien Städten Oberdeutschlands im Zeitalter der Reformation", ZGORh, s, LXXIII (1964), 147–162. However, the corporate homogeneity of the 15th and 16th century German city probably was not in all respects as tight as Bernd Moeller and A. G. Dickens would have it. Although the evidence of late medieval ritualistic solution of urban conflict (cf. *Wilfried Ehbrecht*, "Bürgertum und Obrigkeit in den hansischen Städten des Spätmittelalters", in Die Stadt am Ausgang des Mittelalters, ed. by Wilhelm Rausch [Linz 1974], pp. 275–294) tends to support their assessment, this process of ritualistic solution, based on a. corporate-communal consensus, often proved unsuccessful: the strike of the Colmar journeymen-bakers of 1495–1505, involving alike the constitutional and ecclesiastical life of the city, is a case in point; cf. *Merklen*, Les boulangers de Colmar.

[9] *Moeller*, "Kleriker als Bürger", p. 203.

Wissembourg [10]. In Colmar, where the debate over privilege became one of the basic issues during the urban city unrest of 1524/25, some *Colmariens* may have been able to recall that it had been hotly debated already a hundred years earlier: in 1424, the city council attempted to impose an indirect tax on the clergy and the nobility, but was prevented from implementing its plan by a rebellious *ad-hoc* coalition of noble patricians and agrarian groups in the population.[11]

In 1524/25, however, it was the community, rather than the authorities, which demanded the direct taxation of Colmar's clergy. Again, as in 1424, the bulk of the agitation originated within the vine-dresser and peasant guilds. Finally, under public pressure but not altogether unwillingly, the city government, as we shall see, carried through the anticlerical measures advocated by these malcontents.

B. THE CITY GOVERNMENT AND THE CHURCH IN THE EARLY 1520's[12]

In their attempt to curtail clerical privilege and gradually bring the city's ecclesiastical property under their control, the magistrate and council relied substantially on the institution of the *Pflegschaft*. In his outstanding book on the bourgeois society and the church in late medieval Augsburg, Rolf Kiessling has furnished us with abundant information on how the *Pflegschaft*, a kind of communal supervisory board, could be used by parish and city authorities to infringe upon ecclesiastical property and clerical exemption, thus curtailing the extent of the traditional rights and privileges of the church and the clergy.[13] The convents of Unterlinden and St. Catherine were, in all likelihood, the first monastic establishments to accept the control of their administration by city supervisors, i. e. by so-called *Pfleger*. They were followed by the Augustinian friars in 1464 and by the Franciscans in 1510. Among the mendicant orders in town, only the Dominicans refused this form of cooperation with the city government until August, 1525, when they, in turn, accepted a *Pfleger*.[14] Before 1525, the city had also imposed

[10] *Störmann*, Die städtischen Gravamina, pp. 174–5.

[11] *Eugen Waldner*, Kurzer Ueberblick über die Geschichte der Stadt Colmar (Colmar 1914), pp. 28–9; and *Xavier Mossmann*, Mémoire présenté au grand bailli d'Alsace sur une insurrection survenue à Colmar en 1424, Colmar 1882.

[12] Dr. Dieter Demandt of Tübingen University is presently preparing a study on the city and the church in Colmar during the late Middle Ages and on the eve of the Reformation. His detailed work will replace the weak study by *François-Auguste Goehlinger*, Histoire du Chapitre de l'Eglise Saint-Martin de Colmar, Colmar 1951, and will undoubtedly supersede the following comments. For the first results of Demandt's research, cf. idem, „Konflikte um die geistlichen Standesprivilegien im spätmittelalterlichen Colmar", in Städtische Gesellschaft und Reformation, ed. by Ingrid Bátori, Spätmittelalter und frühe Neuzeit: Tübinger Beiträge zur Geschichtsforschung, Kleine Schriften, Vol. II (Stuttgart 1979). For the following, cf. also Goehlinger, ibid., pp. 236–8.

[13] *Rolf Kiessling*, Bürgerliche Gesellschaft und Kirche in Augsburg im Spätmittelalter: Ein Beitrag zur Strukturanalyse der oberdeutschen Reichsstadt, Abhandlungen zur Geschichte der Stadt Augsburg, Vol. XIX, Augsburg 1971.

[14] For Unterlinden, a Pfleger is first mentioned in 1459: *Isidore Beuchot*, "Das frühere Unterlindenkloster zu Colmar im 15. und 16. Jahrhundert", Colmarer Katholischer Kirchen-Kalender, XII (1918), 62; idem, "Die ehemalige Augustinerkirche", 55; *August Hertzog*, "Die letzten Jahre des Colmarer Barfüsserklosters und Jakob Einfalt aus Geberschweier, dessen letzter Guardian", Jb. GSL, XVII (1901), 119; and for the supervision over the Dominican monastery: AMC, BB 44, p. 31.

its supervisors on the dwindling number of beguines and the city hospital.[15] However, we learn nothing of supervisors installed at St. Peter's or St. John's.

In Colmar, by the beginning of the 16th century, the *Pflegschaft*, perhaps originally a parish institution as in Augsburg, had fallen under the direct control of the city government, as is shown by the names of some of the citizens holding the office of ecclesiastical supervisor: in 1510, Ulrich Würmlin and *Stettmeister* Georg Ringlin were *Pfleger* of the Franciscan monastery. In 1525, we encounter *Stettmeister* Ludwig Hutsch and *Schultheiss* Conrad Wickram as supervisors of the Dominican monastery. These men were personally connected to the city government.[16] Their role documents the lively interest the authorities took in supervising the administration of the city's ecclesiastical institutions: through their ecclesiastical *Pfleger*, Colmar's authorities had continuous and regularly updated knowledge of the wealth, income and dues of a monastery, and could, accordingly, influence its administration considerably.[17]

Magistrate and council also controlled the *Pflegschaft* imposed on the so-called *Fabrik* or *Werk* of St. Martin's. The *Fabrik* of a parish church was an administrative institution, the formation of which had resulted from a medieval division of the church's prebendary property from its wealth accumulated through donations, foundations and similar gifts. Following this division, all of these latter sources of income henceforth constituted the property of the *Fabrik*. In Colmar, the *Fabrik* also owned all ceremonial and liturgical instruments used at St. Martin's.[18] In addition, the *Fabrik's* funds were bolstered by fines for swearing and blasphemy collected within the parish, and following the death of a parishioner, by the confiscation of his best garment, which traditionally the *Fabrik* was entitled to claim on such occasions.[19] The latter custom was also in effect at St. Peter's parish, although, as the scant evidence suggests, St. Peter's *Fabrik* was exempted from any lay control and, thus, firmly in the hands of the Benedictine Prior of St. Peter's.[20] Having direct influence on the administration of the main parish church was more important in terms of the objectives of the city's church policy than the supervision of the monasteries because it opened a way towards gradual curtailment of the Bishop's local prerogatives. Also, St. Martin's *Pflegschaft* was a considerably older institution than was the city's supervision of the monasteries. It existed as early as 1370, when the chapter of St. Martin recognized the right of the city authorities to institute two *Pfleger* as super-

[15] *Jean-Claude Schmitt*, "Les dernières années d'un béguinage colmarien d'après ses comptes", Annuaire de Colmar (1975/76), 33; cf. also: AMC, BB 44, p. 17 (1490).

[16] *Hertzog*, "Die letzten Jahre", 119; AMC, BB 44, p. 31; and *Lucien Sittler*, ed., Membres du Magistrat, Conseillers et Maîtres des Corporations de Colmar: Listes de 1408–1600, Publ. Arch. Colmar, Vol. III, Colmar 1964.

[17] *Beuchot*, "Die ehemalige Augustinerkirche", 55; and *Hertzog*, ibid.

[18] See *Karl Fröhlich*, "Kirche und städtisches Verfassungsleben im Mittelalter", ZSavRG, Kan. Abt., XXII, Vol. LIII (1933), 228; and *Lucien Pfleger*, Die elsäßische Pfarrei: Ihre Entstehung und Entwicklung, Forschungen zur Kirchengeschichte des Elsaß, Vol. III (Strasbourg 1936), p. 280.

[19] The latter custom called *Todfall*, first mentioned in 1372, was still in effect in 1521: AMC, GG 25, fol. 2r. Cf. also *Pfleger*, ibid., p. 371; and *Albrecht Werminghoff*, Verfassungsgeschichte der deutschen Kirche im Mittelalter (Second ed.; Leipzig and Berlin 1913), p. 109.

[20] AMC, BB 45 (1522–76), p. 76. I know of no extant information concerning St. John's 16th century *Fabrik*.

visors of St. Martin's *Fabrik*. But, in 1500, notwithstanding this 14th century agreement, one of the supervisors was taken from among the canons, thus leaving the city control over only one of the two posts.[21]

The city's control over these various *Pflegschaften* formed an important basis for its 16th century church policy in general. As of the 1520's, starting comparatively late, the magistrate and council increasingly used the institution of the *Pflegschaft* as a means of infringing upon ecclesiastical prerogatives in an attempt to buttress and expand their control over the clergy and their property. An extant report on the difficult negotiations regarding clerical prerogatives held between the city and the clergy of St. Martin in the years 1521–28, demonstrates the extent of the city's onslaught.[22] One of the major results of this policy was that, by the end of the 1520's, the city was firmly in control of the administration of the city hospital. Previously, the hospital had been administered by a brotherhood of prebendaries, supervised by a committee composed of the Dean of St. Martin and two representatives of the city council. During the early years of the 16th century, the city managed to strip this brotherhood, as well as the Dean, of their prerogatives. By about 1530, the administration of the hospital was in the hands of the secular authorities. This act of secularization would not have been possible had the authorities not been able to use the *Pflegschaft* over the hospital as a means of enforcing the intended shift in control.[23]

The magistrate's and council's onslaught against clerical privilege was not limited, however, to an attack on the traditional property rights of the church. The authorities also curtailed the Bishop's jurisdiction by restricting him to a mere competence in the regulation of strictly spiritual matters.[24] Thus, they strove against clerical immunity and exemption from taxation and civic duties. They tried to increase their active involvement in the appointment of priests, in the administration of pious foundations, anniversaries, and the handling of testamentary dispositions in favor of the parish church.[25] The city's attack on the extent of ecclesiastical jurisdiction was the constant and most important theme of the negotiations of the early 1520's, which were designed to settle differences between the city and the chapter of St. Martin's. Facing episcopal officials, Colmar's representatives referred to priestly slander, fraud and other unspecified offenses ("*Frevelkeiten*") allegedly committed by the Colmar clergy and prosecuted (or claimed to

[21] AMC, GG 28a, 6. A summary of this document may be found in *André Waltz*, ed., Chronique de Colmar de Félix-Henri-Joseph Chauffour dit le Syndic (1718–1806), (Colmar 1903), pp. 69–70. Pfleger's assumption that there was no lay supervisor at Colmar's St. Martin church is thus shown erroneous. Cf. *Pfleger*, Die elsäßische Pfarrei, p. 284.

[22] AMC, GG 25, 4.

[23] Cf. *Louis Vautrey*, Histoire des évêques de Bâle, Vol. I (Einsiedeln 1884), p. 224; See also *Isidore Beuchot*, "Das frühere Armenspital zum Heiligen Geist in Colmar", Colmarer Katholischer Kirchen-Kalender, XIV (1920), 39–44.

[24] I. e., a reduction of the Bishop's privileges to a competence restricted to the judgment of *delicta mere ecclesiastica* like apostasy, heresy and symony, while all *delicta mixta* like concubinage, sodomy, blasphemy, usury, duelling and the like were exclusively claimed for judgment by the city court; cf. *Störmann*, Die städtischen Gravamina, p. 194.

[25] AMC, GG 25, 4, *passim*. By the late 1520's, the city had secured the right under certain conditions to appoint additional Lent preachers. Cf. ibid., fol. 10v, 13v–14v.

have been prosecuted) under its own jurisdiction.[26] The logical extension of such usurpation of ecclesiastical prerogatives was that the authorities expected all clergy to assume the rights and duties of citizens. By the time this demand gained the support of the masses in 1525, the servants and all other lay retainers serving Colmar's clergy had already been forced to submit to Colmar's secular jurisdiction.[27]

While an urban ideal of corporate communality inspired the majority of such demands, there were also less idealistic interests dictated by the town's financial situation which, in the 1520's, motivated the city officials to intensify their attack on clerical exemption from taxes. In fact, in 1522/23, the magistrate and council, against stiff resistance from the Bishop and local clergy, managed to raise a contribution from St. Martin's clergy and from all the monasteries to subsidize the extensive repair of the city's fortifications.[28]

Both the onslaught on the extent of episcopal jurisdiction and the attack on the clerical exemption from taxation were traditional elements of late medieval urban church policy. It is interesting to note, however, how comparatively late the Colmar authorities began to implement this policy. While it experienced considerable intensification during the early 1520's, it was mainly the urban unrest of 1524/25 and the concomitant public pressure exerted on the authorities which added an entirely new dimension: whereas the massive public pressure radicalized official church policy, the Colmar authorities in turn used their success against clerical privilege to keep the unruly crowd in line.[29]

C. THE URBAN UNREST OF 1524/25

It is significant that the Alsatian peasant revolt of 1525 had its origin in a town: it was from the episcopal town of Saverne that the revolt spread into the rural areas of central Alsace at the beginning of 1525. However, although the revolt spread quickly in other areas of the German Empire during the early months of 1525, matters came to a head fairly slowly in Alsace.[30] In Lower Alsace, an army of peasants became active

[26] Cf. AMC, GG 24, 8 and 9 (Letters from the Bishop of Basel to the Colmar authorities, 1522); AAEB, A 41, 9 (Letter from the Bishop to the Bailiff of Haguenau, August 22, 1522); and AMC, GG 25, 4, especially fol. 1v–2v, 4r and 9r (Report on the differences between city and clergy from 1521–28).

[27] This right had been granted in 1516 by Emperor Maximilian I; cf. *Rocholl*, Anfänge der Reformationsgeschichte, pp. 36–7.

[28] AMC, GG 26, 3–8; cf. also *Goehlinger*, Histoire du Chapitre, pp. 237–8.

[29] The comparative lateness of Colmar's onslaught against clerical privileges is argued convincingly by *Demandt*, "Konflikte um die geistlichen Standesprivilegien". Demandt shows that conflicts between the city authorities and the clergy regarding the latter's *privilegium fori* (exemption from prosecution by secular courts) only really surfaced at the beginning of the Reformation era and that the late medieval disputes concerning the *privilegium immunitatis* (exemption from taxation by secular authorities) were far from being heated. For comparative purposes, see *Francis Rapp's* concise rendition of Strasbourg's late medieval ecclesiastical policy in idem, Réformes et Réformation à Strasbourg: Eglise et Société dans le diocèse de Strasbourg (1450–1525), Collection de l'Institut des Hautes Etudes Alsaciennes, Vol. XXIII (Paris 1974), pp. 108–114; and the comparative exploration in *Demandt*, ibid.

[30] For the general Alsatian background, see *Günther Franz*, Der deutsche Bauernkrieg (Tenth ed.; Darmstadt 1975), pp. 141–8. For two older renditions of the Colmar events, cf. *Rocholl*, Anfänge der Reformationsgeschichte; and *Karl Hartfelder*, Zur Geschichte des Bauernkriegs in Südwestdeutschland

around Easter (April 16, 1525) – that is, comparatively late. By May 17, its main division had occupied the town of Saverne. Consequently, the widespread revolt of the countryside peasants only reached Upper Alsace and the Austrian Sundgau by the beginning of May, 1525. While the Sundgau revolt continued well into the fall of the same year, the uprising within the remaining parts of Alsace was brutally put down by Duke Anthony of Lorraine's military expedition, culminating in the decisive battle of Scherwiler near Sélestat on May 20, 1525.

Several months before the peasant revolt spread across the countryside, religious and social unrest had seized the population of the Alsatian cities. In Colmar, unrest originated as early as December, 1524, in connection with the dismissal of a popular evangelical preacher by the council and the Dean of St. Martin.[31] While the impetus of this first phase of attempted revolt dwindled considerably during the first few months of 1525, the unrest burst out in a new and more tension-ridden phase on April 23 – to last, however, for only a few weeks before the magistrate and council decisively regained the upper hand. In its first phase, the Colmar inner city unrest of 1524/25 was a relatively autonomous movement. In its second phase, it was connected more closely (but never intimately) to the course of the revolt in the surrounding countryside.

The outbreak of unrest in Colmar in December, 1524, had a clearly religious undertone. The Dean's vicar at St. Peter's, named Hans, had created a considerable public for himself by preaching three or four "Lutheran" sermons. Unfortunately, we do not know their exact content.[32] On December 17, basing their decision on the imperial mandates condemning Luther and his followers, the secular authorities intervened and asked the Dean of St. Martin to dismiss the unruly preacher. As in Frankfurt at the end of 1524, where the authorities dismissed the preacher Sartorius, the similarly swift intervention of the Colmar city government in the case of the preacher Hans was undoubtedly motivated by the Emperor's penal mandate of Burgos of July 15, 1524.[33] There must have been an important number of adherents to the Reformation message among Hans' listeners, for in order to prevent a possible outbreak of unrest among the citizenry, the

(Stuttgart 1884), pp. 101–111. More recent research on the Colmar unrest has been presented by *Georges Bischoff*, "Colmar et la crise révolutionnaire de 1524–1525", Annuaire de Colmar (1975/76), 43–54; and by *Lina Baillet*, "Deux villes de la Moyenne Alsace: Sélestat et Colmar face aux conflits religieux et sociaux des paysans, 1525", in La guerre des paysans, 1525, ed. by Alphonse Wollbrett, Etudes Alsatiques édités par la Société d'histoire et d'archéologie de Saverne et Environs, Supplemental No. XCIII (Saverne 1975), pp. 93–102; for further background information, see also *Georges Bischoff*, "La Haute-Alsace et la Guerre des Paysans", in La guerre des paysans, 1525, ibid., pp. 111–120.

[31] Not the Dean of *St. Peter's*, as in *Hartfelder*, ibid., p. 102.

[32] There is only one document supporting the assumption that the preacher Hans was in fact a Benedictine monk. It is a letter addressed by the city of Sélestat to the Colmar authorities on January 5, 1525: AMC, EE 7,1. The letter is printed in *Joseph Gény*, Die Reichsstadt Schlettstadt und ihr Anteil an den socialpolitischen und religiösen Bewegungen der Jahre 1490–1536, Erläuterungen und Ergänzungen zu Janssens Geschichte des deutschen Volkes, Vol. I, Books 5 and 6 (Freiburg i. Br. 1900), p. 156, n. 1. It is difficult to see why the Dean would have employed a monk as his vicar.

[33] See *Sigrid Jahns*, Frankfurt, Reformation und Schmalkaldischer Bund: Die Reformations-, Reichs- und Bündnispolitik der Reichsstadt Frankfurt am Main 1525–1536, Studien zur Frankfurter Geschichte, Heft 9 (Frankfurt a.M. 1976), p. 36. The Burgos mandate is printed in *Heinrich Rocholl*, Die Einführung der Reformation in der ehemaligen freien Reichsstadt Colmar: Ein Beitrag zur Reformationsgeschichte des Elsass (Leipzig 1876), pp. 217–222.

magistrate and council decided to have their decision approved by both the chapter and the council of jurors before taking any action. Thus, following the authorities request, which he welcomed, Dean Jacob Carpentarii dismissed his vicar in the days immediately following December 18.[34]

However, the official attempt to prevent open unrest failed. On the evening of Saint Thomas' Day (December 21, 1524), some hundred or more men, under the leadership of Ludwig Kopp, Mathis Scherer, Mathis Reber and Hans Schedlin, assembled in front of the *Obristmeister*'s house requesting the re-installation of the preacher Hans. Johann Hummel, the city clerk and chronicler of these events, concedes in his report that their behavior was in no way hostile.

Who were these petitioners? They all claimed to represent concerned members of St. Peter's parish. Their leaders belonged to the agrarian guilds *Zum Haspel* (gardeners), *Ackerleute* (peasants), and *Rebleute* (vine-dressers).[35] Most of their followers probably belonged to the same guilds. Inevitably, three days later, the four leaders were cited by the magistrate and council and reprimanded for not having presented their request to their guildmasters or through a member of the XIII, rather than organizing a public protest rally. The response of the accused was to assemble their followers on the same day and to have the assembly formulate its various grievances and requests in the form of thirteen articles.[36]

The strongly religious motives of this unrest are evidenced by Articles One and Two of their Thirteen Articles of grievance addressed to the magistrate and council on the same day, December 24, 1524. Article One reads:

> First, it is our request addressed to you venerable and wise Lords, that our poor parish shall not be so sluggishly (*schlefferlich*) served by a common priest (*Leutpriester*) who has to preach to the liking of the chapter and who has especially to appear acceptable to the Dean. Thus, our souls are entirely misled; for we believe that the spreading of God's word should not be repressed because it is with the word of God that we want to live and through it that we want to grow well.[37]

Article Two asks for the promulgation in Colmar of the Ratisbon mandates and declares the astonishment of the community that these had hitherto been withheld from the population at large. This is followed, in Article Three, by a statement emphasizing

[34] A detailed account of the Colmar rebellion of 1524/25 can be found in Johann Hummel's, the contemporary city clerk's, detailed report entitled „Liber ortę seditionis": AMC, EE 7, 1. For the above, cf. especially, ibid., fol. 3r–5v. Regarding the preacher Hans, cf. n. 32, above. An undated letter, written most likely by the preacher Hans in the Spring of 1525, informs us of Hans' lack of sympathy for the rebellious peasants, but gives us no further clues as to the author's life and preaching: cf. AMC, EE 7, 7.

[35] "Liber ortę seditionis", ibid., fol. 6r, 8r, 20v–21r. The preacher Hans himself may have incited some of his followers to protest publicly on his behalf: cf. ibid., fol. 6v. In Basel, it was also the vine-dressers and gardeners, assisted by some weavers, who took the lead in the simultaneous urban unrest there: *Rudolf Wackernagel,* Geschichte der Stadt Basel, Vol. III (Basel 1924), p. 369.

[36] In a contemporary letter, the city-clerk of Sélestat refers to an assembly of about 600 *Colmariens: Gény,* Die Reichsstadt Schlettstadt, p. 155, n. 1.

[37] The articles are listed in the "Liber ortę seditionis": AMC, EE 7, 1, fol. 9r–11v, and printed in *Franz,* ed., Der deutsche Bauernkrieg: Aktenband, pp. 186–8. Regardning some striking parallels between these Colmar Articles and the Eight Sélestat Articles of October 6, 1524, cf. *Baillet,* „Deux villes de la Moyenne Alsace", p. 95.

that the Colmar city government should act according to the privileges it has received from kings and emperors.

Subsequently, Articles Four and Five voice some of the strong anticlerical feelings prevailing in the community. They state:

> Fourthly it is our request, that nuns and monks should also pay direct taxes and fulfill guard-, watch-, and statute-labor duties like all other citizens . . . Moreover, we ask that all people living in concubinage in Colmar should be driven from the city, . . . be they laymen or priests.

While Article Six, by demanding an alleviation of statute-labor, addresses social rather than religious or anticlerical concerns, the following article sums up the common man's disdain for the clerical courts and his preference to appear, if need be, before Colmar's own judges. Accordingly, the city authorities are asked to see to it that the citations of citizens by the episcopal officialate in Basel will cease and be abolished. The remaining articles, finally, relate to social and economic grievances of a rather local scope.

It would surely be wrong to intimate (as has been done in the past) a direct connection between the well-known Twelve Articles of the peasants of Swabia and the Thirteen Colmar Articles of December 24, 1524 – considering that the Twelve Articles date from February, 1525.[38] But it is nevertheless noteworthy that both documents postulate in Article One an increase in the influence of the community on the appointment of their common priest or minister, even though this demand was voiced more conspicuously in the Twelve Articles. Another similarity is that both documents combine – throughout – religious and political demands with grievances of a social and economic nature. This aspect is further emphasized by the catchword list containing "unofficially" registered communal grievances which the city clerk, Johann Hummel, included in his "Liber ortę seditionis".[39] The catchwords point to grievances related to rents and tithes, to unlawful exemption from guard-duty for certain privileged *Colmariens*, to a needed reform of indirect taxes on flour and other goods and to the non-residence of the Dean[40], to name only the most important ones.

But let us briefly return to the Thirteen Articles. While most of the articles cited above speak for themselves, it is not easy to understand the motivations leading to the formulation of Articles Two and Three. The Ratisbon assembly of June 1524 was a meeting of Catholic princes and bishops under the leadership of Archduke Ferdinand of Austria. Its function was the enforcement of the Edict of Worms of 1521, outlawing Luther and his partisans. It is not clear, at first sight, why members of a movement favoring evangelical preaching should complain about the non-promulgation of these Ratisbon decisions. However, when one takes into account that the Dean of Colmar, Jacob Carpentarii, at-

[38] See *Günther Franz*, "Die Entstehung der 'Zwölf Artikel' der deutschen Bauernschaft", ARH, XXXVI (1939), 195–213.

[39] *Franz*, ed., Der deutsche Bauernkrieg: Aktenband, p. 188.

[40] At that time, apparently, the Dean did not reside in Colmar all too frequently: *Emil Dürr* and *Paul Roth*, eds., Aktensammlung zur Geschichte der Basler Reformation in den Jahren 1519 bis Anfang 1534, Vol. II (Basel 1933), No. 491, pp. 388–389 (Letter from the Bishop of Basel addressed to the Basel authorities, 1526, September 23).

tended the Ratisbon convention as Bishop Christoph's representative[41], one strongly senses that the authors of the Thirteen Articles attempted to reveal some kind of unofficially acknowledged understanding between the Colmar authorities and the clergy, and/or the Habsburg then in charge of the Bailiwick of Haguenau.

Article Three, therefore, must be considered a direct consequence of these suspicions: the authors request the city government to give up its unacknowledged commitment to the Bishop's and/or Ferdinand I's Anti-Lutheranism and to base its future decisions on the rights and privileges of Colmar as an imperial city subject to none other than the Emperor. Between the lines, this grievance possibly implied that the magistrate and council should adhere to the recent decisions of the Nuremberg diet of 1523.[42]

The community's use of the term "*Mandata*" issued at Ratisbon facilitated the authorities' answer to Articles Two and Three. They were quick to point out that the Ratisbon convention had *not* been an assembly convocated in the name of the Emperor and thus succeeded in giving some rhetorical weight to their subsequent declaration that, hitherto, they had never intentionally disregarded Colmar's special rights and privileges. As to their response to Article Four, the authorities chose to temporize and declared that they would prefer to conform to the measures taken by other imperial cities. In response to the request voiced in Article Five that all practicants of concubinage be banned from town, the magistrate and council first referred to all corresponding ordinances issued in the recent past, which apparently had not had the desired effect, and then stated theirs and the council of juror's agreement that henceforth all laymen and clergy living in concubinage be prosecuted and punished by the city court.[43] Concerning the reform of statute-labor demanded in Article Six, the government conceded that from now on all citizens would have to serve "with their body". Thus, in the future, there should be no possibility for well-off citizens to "buy" their statute-labor replacement. As in their response to Article Four, the authorities also chose to temporize regarding Article Seven. They claimed not to be aware of grievances caused by citations of *Colmariens* issued by the episcopal officialate and added the rather evasive promise that: "if, as a result of the course the events took withing the Holy Roman Empire regarding these and other matters, change in this matter became permissible, they would be ready to abolish the cause of these kinds of grievances."[44] The official response to the remaining articles carefully emphasized the position that the city government was obliged to act in the interest of the *whole* community. Through the use of such catchwords as *gemein Nutz* (common

[41] *Walter Friedensburg*, "Der Regensburger Konvent von 1524", in Historische Aufsätze dem Andenken an Georg Waitz gewidmet (Hannover 1886), pp. 502–539, especially p. 516, n. 5 (Participation of the Colmar Dean).

[42] It is noteworthy in this repect, that the Colmar printer Amandus Farckall issued a pamphlet containing the decrees of the Nuremberg diet of 1523: *Lina Bailet*, „Un complément à la ‚Bibliographie de la ville de Colmar' d'André Waltz (1902)", Annuaire de Colmar (1975/76), 77. Cf. also below, pp. 58–9. Regarding the ambivalence in religious matters of the Nuremberg decrees of 1523: *Bernd Moeller*, Deutschland im Zeitalter der Reformation, Vol. IV of Deutsche Geschichte, ed. by Joachim Leuschner (Göttingen 1977), p. 126.

[43] "Liber ortę seditionis", AMC, EE 7. 1, fol. 12v–13v. Cf. the comments on the lifestyle of canon Sebastian Murrho, above, pp. 34–5.

[44] The authorities launched minor attempts to do so in 1527 and 1528, and again after 1548: cf. below, p. 101, n. 30.

interest), the authorities tried to weaken the frequent accusation contained in the Thirteen Articles that they accorded preferential treatment to the rich and to people of superior social standing.[45]

Although half of the Thirteen Articles dealt with the clergy and the church, they were all directed at the oligarchic governmental practices of the ruling patricians. If the account given by the Sélestat city clerk is accurate[46], the Colmar authorities were facing an important opposition movement composed of approximately one-tenth or more of the entire population at the end of 1524. Given the council's toleration of Farckall's printing activities in Colmar from 1522 to 1524[47], it seems more than likely that at the beginning of 1525 there was a group of substantial size among the councillors, which, although not daring to embrace the new faith openly, was not directly opposed to the Reformation movement. In this respect, it is typical that the authorities, in their response to Article One, decided to "pass the buck" to the Dean of St. Martin's – they did not want to take an official stand on evangelical preaching. The dismissal of the preacher Hans, they may have argued, had been dictated by their obedience to imperial mandates rather than by their religious conviction. The authorities' reaction to religious and anticlerical demands voiced in the Thirteen Articles is best summed up by the temporizing statement (cited above) made as a response to Article Seven. Obviously, the city government did not want to take the lead in clarifying the controversial religious and ecclesiastical issues at stake. In short, it was waiting to see which way the wind would blow.

In promulgating its response to the Thirteen Articles, the city government wisely chose to follow the old principle of *Divide et impera*; during their meeting on New Year's Day, 1525, the magistrate and council decided to submit their response personally to each of the ten guilds, one by one. Thus, they expected to learn "who adhered to the unruly crowd, and to find out whether anyone wanted to add something to the Thirteen Articles, extend their number or improve their wording."[48] The result of the ensuing consultation with the different guilds shows that the opposition to the city's régime must have been of a fairly moderate kind. Through their clever maneuver of consulting the guilds one by one, the authorities clearly managed to discourage the population from further manifestations of discontent.

As was foreseeable, they encountered the most resistance in the guilds of the vinedressers and peasants and perhaps also among the gardeners, although the record is am-

[45] "Liber ortę seditionis": AMC, EE 7, 1, fol. 13v–16v. *Hans-Christoph Rublack*", Politische Situation und reformatorische Politik in der Frühphase der Reformation in Konstanz", in Kontinuität und Umbruch, ed. by Josef Nolte, Hella Tompert and Christof Windhorst, Spätmittelalter und frühe Neuzeit: Tübinger Beiträge zur Geschichtsforschung, Vol. II (Stuttgart 1978), pp. 324–5, accurately stresses the flexible function of such integrative norms as "gemeiner Nutzen". In his observations on "gemein nutz", *Ernst-Wilhelm Kohls*, Die Schule bei Martin Bucer in ihrem Verhältnis zu Kirche und Obrigkeit, Pädagogische Forschungen: Veröffentlichungen des Comenius-Instituts, Vol. XXII (Heidelberg 1963), pp. 121–9, fails to recognize that within the socio-political context of the 15th and 16th centuries the function of this norm was often ideologically tinged – as in the case in point referred to above.

[46] Cf. above, n. 36

[47] Cf. below, pp. 58 -9.

[48] „Liber ortę seditionis", AMC, EE 7, 1, fol. 18r.

biguous in this last respect. However, no opposition at all was encountered in the guilds *Zum Kränzlein* (bakers and millers), *Zum Holderbaum* (masons, carpenters, stonemasons, etc.) and *Zum Löwen* (butchers and fishermen). Thus, an important segment of the city's artisans had remained loyal to their superiors. Within the remaining four guilds, only a few individual opponents dared to present their complaints, although several members of the guild *Zum Adler* (weavers, hatmakers, ropemakers, etc.) voiced their support for Articles One and Five.

As a result of these consultations, the magistrate and council had regained firm control of the community, and only then did they decide to inform the Bailiff of Haguenau of what had taken place within their city.[49] They next turned to prosecuting the four leaders of the movement and the twelve members of the committee, composed of gardeners, peasants and vine-dressers, who had collectively authored the Thirteen Articles. We hear of no actual punishment that resulted from this prosecution.

Following the events of December, 1524, there was no renewed open agitation in Colmar for a period of almost four months, until suddenly, as the bands of peasants from the countryside approached the Colmar area, renewed unrest – this time more radical – broke out on April 23, 1525.

On Sunday, April 23, 1525, at nearby Ribeauvillé and Riquewihr, rebellious peasants were up in arms. Simultaneously, in Colmar, the news of this uprising added to the circulation of uncertain rumors that a hundred knights on horseback were approaching the city to reinforce it against a possible attack by the revolting peasants. The rumors, in turn, brought about a spontaneous gathering of *Colmariens* at the vine-dressers' guild.[50] The unruly spirit of those present at this gathering, combined with their collective anti-Jewish feelings led, on the next morning, to their confiscating all Jewish possessions and to the lynching of a Jew named Jacob;[51] (the Jews, who were not allowed to reside in town themselves, had deposited their possessions within the city walls at the outbreak of the countryside revolt). Overnight, the rumors about the knights expected in town gained much in concreteness – those gathered at the vine-dressers' guild and at other guilds now believed that the authorities, on request of the Bailiff of Haguenau, were ready to allow several hundred mounted knights to enter the city. This

[49] Ibid., fol. 18r–22r.

[50] Cf. *Lina Baillet*, "La Guerre des Paysans, un cas de conscience dans la famille de Ribeaupierre", BHP, I (1976), 357–437, especially 380–2 (a passage from a contemporary chronicle describing the situation prevailing at Ribeauvillé on April 23, 1525): "... Do hat Vrban Heidelberg angeffangen zu sagen, [dass] ein schenck in seim husz seig gesein, vnd [do] hab er gehert von vil burgeren: es sey die r[ed], der lantfock wel dis nachgt mit XVc perden komen vnd die Stat iber fallen vnd die do[rin] alle vmbringen vnd schedigen ...." For the concurrent Colmar events: AMC, FF 358, 48 (Proceedings of Ulrich Singer's trial); and AMC, FF 96, 26 (Proceedings of Jacob Bader's, Sr., trial).

[51] AMC, FF 96, 26 (Jacob Bader's, Sr., later testimony): „Sig ... der schocher vnd andre in Jacob Baders hus kommen, anklopfent vnd gsagt, der Schultheis hab erloupt, wo oder hinder wem mann Juden gutter wuß, die solle mann nemenn, etc. Daruff er, Jacob, geantwurt, so disen beuelch, mögent si nachgen ..." Later, the same morning, when Bader, as he recalls, was back at the vine-dressers' guild-hall, "habent si Jacob Juden gfencklich pracht vnd ersticht". Four days later, these Jewish goods were in turn confiscated by the council in view of their eventual restoration to their owners: AMC, EE 7, 1, fol. 46v.

not entirely unsubstantiated rumor[52] drove them all to the city gardens, where during the course of Monday morning a crowd of considerable size had converged.[53]

A council-delegation, dispatched to learn about the purpose of the gathering, was presented the following grievances by the crowd's leader, the inn-keeper Jacob Bader, Sr.: The Council should have the city's monasteries destroyed and their goods confiscated. Jacob Bader, Sr., is also said to have referred to the great riches of the nuns of Unterlinden and the Dean of St. Martin's, and to have claimed that even a small fraction of their stocked-up wheat would help many a poor companion among those present to nourish his family.[54] The crowd also reiterated the old demand that the town's clergy become regular citizens, pay taxes and fulfill the nightly watch and all other civic duties as any other citizen does.[55] Furthermore, it requested an amnesty for the four leaders of the unauthorized gatherings of December, 1524. The council had threatened these men with punishment for their unruly conduct.[56]

Meanwhile, rumors about the imminent arrival of the knights dispatched by the Bailiff so aroused the crowd that they rushed to take the defense of the town into their own hands. Between 3 and 5 p. m. on the same day, they armed themselves at home and in the city's arsenals, and under the battlecry "We have been sold out and betrayed by our authorities", they rushed to the ramparts. One Conrad Singer allegedly even shouted that only rendering rich peasants poor would solve the crowd's problems.[57] The set objective of their spontaneous attempt to defend the town was to prevent any more than the Bailiff, accompanied by a maximum of twenty knights, from entering the city.[58] Their realization, however, that the rumors about the arrival of the dreaded knights had been unfounded, brought their unauthorized act of self-defense to an end almost as quickly as it had started.[59]

[52] The imperial Bailiff had in effect offered to the magistrate and council on April 21, 1525, to appear in Colmar in the company of 300 to 400 knights to assist in an eventual defense of the city, but the Colmar authorities refused his offer: *Hartfelder*, Zur Geschichte des Bauernkriegs, p. 105. Compare with *Baillet*, "La Guerre des Paysans", 381, n.6 who, in the case of Ribeauvillé, mentions a similar offer by the Bailiff of Upper Alsace leading to the said rumors.

[53] There is no evidence revealing the size of this crowd. In his "Liber ortę seditionis" Johann Hummel refers to a substantial crowd ("*grosse menge*"): AMC, EE 7, 1, fol. 35v–36v. Conrad Singer's deposition in court gives a good impression of how the rumor spread across town: AMC, FF 358, 47.

[54] Court testimony of *Stettmeister* Hans Ruch against Jacob Bader, Sr., in 1528: AMC. FF 96, 32.

[55] Court testimony of the fisherman Ulrich Singer: AMC, FF 358, 48. In Sélestat, the same communal demand was voiced as early as October, 1524: *Gény*, Die Reichsstadt Schlettstadt, p. 144.

[56] "Liber ortę seditionis": AMC, EE 7, 1, fol. 34r and 36v. The four were readmitted into the Council's grace after a solemn apology and payment of a fine on May 1, 1525: cf. ibid., fol. 52r.

[57] AMC, FF 355,6 Regarding the rush to the ramparts, cf. AMC, EE 7,1 fol. 37v–38v; and the testimonies of Conrad Singer and Lux Schuelin: AMC, FF 355,6; FF 355,69; FF 15,7.

[58] AMC, FF 358,48 (Deposition made by Ulrich Singer).

[59] In the case of Würzburg we can observe that on April 11, 1525, the very same fears and rumors led to a similar spontaneous communal act of defense. See *Hans-Christoph Rublack*, "Die Stadt Würzburg im Bauernkrieg", ARH, LXVI (1976), 76–99, especially 79–80. For a brief attempt at explaining this kind of spontaneous action in terms of social psychology: cf. *Jürgen Bücking* and *Hans-Christoph Rublack*, "Der Bauernkrieg in den vorder- und oberösterreichischen Ländern und in der Stadt Würzburg: Ansätze zu einer Theorie des Bauernkriegs", in Bauernkriegs-Studien, ed. by Bernd Moeller, SVRG. No. 189 (Gütersloh 1975), pp. 60–62.

Nevertheless, events repeated themselves as a similar rush to the ramparts took place on the following Tuesday afternoon. This second *Auflauf* occurred just hours after the vine-dressers' guild had presented the XIII (who had been sent to the guild by the magistrate) with apologies for the last uproar. At this meeting, the delegates of the council were once again presented the crowd's grievances. Now the crowd demanded that a part of the copious provisions of the monasteries and secular clergy be alotted to them by the council. They also requested that the authorities install a skilled and qualified preacher – "one who will preach the word of God".

In response to these new demands, the council decided to temporize and promised the crowd that it would start immediate negotiations with the secular clergy. It also begged the crowd to refrain from any acts of open hostility against the clergy and the monasteries, and reminded the assembly that the present preacher's sermons contained nothing which was contrary to the Evangile; however, should the preacher choose to leave town, the council would not prevent him from doing so. At least temporarily, this rather evasive response from the council had its intended effect: it took some important momentum out of the general commotion.[60] The council further enhanced its momentary success by promising to find a solution to the problems regarding Colmar's clergy and monasteries. In doing so, the council drew attention away from the more threatening issues of the religious and social claims of the opposition.

On the following Thursday morning, April 27, 1525, when a delegation of the chapter appeared in front of the council to find out what the clergy could expect from the authorities in these troubled times, the council promised them its further protection, but made no bones about the community's intention to oblige the clergy to pay taxes and fulfill the normal duties of citizens.[61] In this situation, the clerical delegation had no other choice but to offer the clergy's submission to such measures.

At this point, the council could slowly catch up with the opposition. Without encountering resistance, it admonished a newly gathered group of disgruntled burghers assembled on the same morning at Jacob Bader's inn *Zum Schlüssel* to be patient and to leave the clergy and the monasteries unharmed.[62] Determined to prevent further riots and come to terms with what they chose to consider the backbone of the commotion – "the grievances against the clergy"[63] – the authorities (including the council of jurors) decided to run the relatively calculable risk of assembling the entire community on the following Friday.

On that day, the authorities finally gained the upper hand. Acting on the *Obristmeister's* proposition, a communal committee (*Ausschuss*) was formed. It was to assist the council and the jurors in their joint decisions. Furthermore, the entire community had to swear that in the future they would adhere to all majority-decisions taken joint-

[60] "Liber ortę seditionis", AMC, EE 7,1, fol. 41r–42r.

[61] Ibid., fol. 43r: "Man welte aber Jnen nit vorhalten, das der gemeinen Ernstlich vorhaben, sie zu bürgerlichen bswerden zupringen".

[62] Ibid., fol. 43v.

[63] Thus the semi-official explanation offered by the city-clerk Johann Hummel in his "Liber ortę seditionis": ibid., fol. 44r. Hummel states that it was "eins Rhads gut beduncken, das vff morn ein gantze gmeindt versamlet, vnd wie disen vffruren vnd vrsachen derselben, beswerdt der geistlichen halben, zu begegnen sig, gehandelt vnd beslossen [werde]".

ly by these three bodies. This procedure decisively exposed the relative weakness of the opposition movement. Even among the committee members elected within the vine-dressers' and the peasants' guild, where the commotion had started, only Peter Nunnenmacher is known to us as a leader of the discontented.[64] Thus, by Friday afternoon, April 28, 1525, when a delegation of Colmar's monks and nuns offered all services and contributions that could reasonably be levied from them, so that the city would continue to include them in its protection, the authorities were again in firm control of the city's affairs. Together with the council of jurors and the newly formed communal committee, they not only prohibited all further harassment of the clergy and the monasteries by individual citizens, but also outlawed all further unauthorized gatherings.[65]

Looking back on the events of late April, 1525, it appears that because of the comparative moderation of the discontented crowd and, in all likelihood, due to the limited spread of discontent throughout the agrarian section of the population, the commotion did not turn into a fullfledged revolt against the city government. In neighboring Sélestat, where, by comparison, the plutocratic character of the ruling oligarchy was more pronounced than in Colmar, the concurrent social and political opposition to the ruling patricians was far more significant.[66] In Colmar, given the lack of a determined spirit of opposition, the basic force of the April movement, as the authorities had recognized in time, remained the anticlericalism directed at the clergy of St. Martin's and, especially, the monasteries.

As early as the beginning of February, rumors had circulated in town that some *Colmariens* were willing to launch an attack against the city's monasteries.[67] Later, on April 16, the council had to deal with rumors that 600 men, from among three guilds (probably the vine-dressers', peasants' and gardeners' guilds), were planning to sack the Franciscan monastery.[68] Neither attack took place, and we do not know if they had ever been planned. We only know of individual cases of molestation of the clergy. However, the seriousness with which such rumors were dealt with by the authorities shows how dangerous a threat to public peace, and thus to the council's authority, the rampant anticlericalism was regarded. Accordingly, all such threats uttered by the movement's leader, Jacob Bader, were not taken lightly by the authorities.[69]

We can further observe that by April, 1525, the primarily religious demands of the December movement had become slightly overshadowed by increasingly widespread anticlericalism. Nevertheless, the old demand for evangelical preaching had not been dropped from the list of grievances, although (surely due to the lack of support through open evangelical predication within the city at that time) it was no longer

[64] Ibid., fol. 44v–45v, *et passim*.

[65] Ibid., fol. 47v; and AMC, EE 7, 12.

[66] This is an interesting comparative and interpretative element unfortunately missing in *Lina Baillet's* predominantly narrative account: cf. idem, "Deux villes de la Moyenne Alsace". Thus, in Sélestat, where the guilds forced the city government to cooperate with a communal committee, the temperary solution of the pending „monastic problem" was initiated by the urban community, rather than by the authorities, as was ultimately the case in Colmar; see *Gény,* Die Reichsstadt Schlettstadt, pp. 168–171.

[67] "Liber ortę seditionis": AMC, EE 7,1, fol. 27v.

[68] Ibid., fol. 33r; cf. also *Hartfelder*, Zur Geschichte des Bauernkriegs, p. 105.

[69] AMC, EE 7,12; and AMC, FF 96,32; FF 96,26 (Trial proceedings of Jacob Bader, Sr.).

voiced as unequivocally as before.[70] Thus, the unrest of December, 1524, and April, 1525, appear as parts of one and the same religious, anticlerical and political movement. This impression is further substantiated by a look at the role played by the thirty leaders involved in the movement. Seventeen among them played a role of leadership in both open commotions.

Who were these leaders? Fourteen of them were burghers in 1525, and five more acquired citizenship between 1525 and 1530. Like most of their followers, the majority of them belonged to one of the three agrarian guilds of Colmar.[71] In political terms, they represented a group without direct access to city government; only four among them had, at one time or another, served as a member of the city council and among these four, only Jacob Bader, Sr. was a councillor during the crucial year, 1524/25.[72]

The little we know about the composition of the crowd of malcontents does not suggest that it was comprised of a significant number of persons likely to insure a continuing contact between the movement within the city and the bands of peasants roaming the surrounding countryside.[73] In this respect, the Colmar movement of April, 1525, was clearly autonomous, although elements of ideological identification with the peasants in rebellion outside the city were not lacking. We find this, for instance, in the planned resistance against the imaginary knights sent to defend Colmar against the countryside peasants. However, at the beginning of May, 1525, when such a peasant attack on Colmar became more likely than ever before, the magistrate and council were firmly back in control of their town[74] and could turn to the task of restoring public peace by extending their authority over the clergy.

Around mid-May, 1525, the peasant war reached its climax in Alsace. Five days before the decisive battle of Scherwiler near Sélestat (lost by the revolting peasants, and ending the revolt in Lower and Middle Alsace), the Colmar authorities (magistrate, council, jurors and the communal committee) threatened severe punishment to any *Colmarien* who dared to continue entertaining contacts with the revolting peasants outside of town. Wisely enough, the council combined this threat with the declaration of a general amnesty for those who had been involved in the recent agitation. Thus, although labelling the unruly countryside peasants Colmar's enemies, the council encountered no real opposition from the citizenry.[75]

Undoubtedly, the vigour with which they had adopted the community's anticlerical demands and sought a solution to the clerical and monastic problem during the first half

[70] "Liber ortę seditionis": AMC, EE 7,1, fol. 57r.

[71] Regarding the social status of the malcontent Colmar peasants, it has not been established as of yet, whether such peasants as the relatively well-to-do *Meier*, (described by Luzian Sittler, "Landwirtschaft und Gartenbau im alten Colmar", Elsaß-lothringisches Jahrbuch, XX (1942), 76–7), were also involved in the oppositional movement.

[72] For more details on Jacob Bader, Sr., cf. *Bischoff*, "Colmar et la crise révolutionnaire", 48.

[73] Cf. „Liber ortę seditionis": AMC, EE 7, 1, fol. 40r. Only in the cases of Jacob Bader, Sr., and the painter Lux Schuelin we have evidence proving that they joined the revolting peasants outside the city: AMC, FF 96, 10; and FF 15, 7.

[74] Notwithstanding this development, much latent discontent about the city government prevailed. On May 1, 1525, for instance, the authorities had to threaten punishment for all further open slander directed against them by Colmar women: "Liber ortę seditionis": ibid., fol. 53r.

[75] Ibid., fol. 61v–64v; and AMC, EE 7, 10.

of May, must have rehabilitated the authorities' image for many previously disgruntled *Colmariens*. Following the receipt of information on the annual income of the canons and priests of St. Martin's and upon recommendation submitted to them by a specially constituted commission, the council, jurors and communal committee came to the following joint conclusions. In a common meeting on May 5, 1525, they decided that each priest should swear the citizen's oath and, therefore, join a guild and fulfill the same duties as other guild-members (except for minor provisions). On Monday, May 8, the clergy of St. Martin's had to swear their citizen's oath and were told to join a guild within the next eight days. This was done by all of the canons and priests present, with a provision for their allegiance to the Bishop of Basel and to their foundation of St. Martin.[76]

Finding a solution to the monastic problem was simplified by letters addressed to the authorities at the beginning of May, 1525, from Unterlinden and St. Catherine's.[77] In light of the ongoing commotion and the increasing frequency of reproaches about the material self-enrichment of the monasteries, both convents offered to submit themselves and their belongings entirely to secular control – under the condition that the city assure them its continuous protection. On May 6, all monasteries had to submit their detailed income lists to the council. These lists were to constitute one of several grounds for the steps taken by the joint body of council, jurors and communal committee five days later: primarily implementing tendencies inherent in their own *Pflegschaft*-policy (and only secondarily responding to the anticlerical call from the community) the authorities decided to infringe substantially on the traditional rights and privileges of the monasteries.

On May 11, they stipulated the following points.[78]

1. All foreign monks will be sent back to their mother monasteries.
2. Those among the younger nuns wishing to leave their convent, or those requested to leave by their families ("*von Iren fründen*"), will be allowed to do so and be restored their personal belongings in due process.
3. Whether the monks and nuns should, in turn, be housed in one specific place will be decided later, upon receipt of information about how this problem is handled in Strasbourg and other cities.

[76] "Liber ortę seditionis": ibid., fol. 49v–57v. A very similar development took place in Haguenau. Like Colmar, Haguenau did not get directly involved in the peasant war: cf. *C[harles] A. Hanauer*, Le protestantisme à Haguenau (Strasbourg and Colmar 1905), pp. 55–6. On May 2, 1525, the same process also came to an end in Basel: *Wackernagel*, Geschichte der Stadt Basel, Vol. III, p. 389. In Sélestat, a few weeks earlier, it had been decided by the authorities to subjugate all secular clergy and monks, including all previously exempted laymen, to statute-labor duties; cf. *Gény*, Die Reichsstadt Schlettstadt, p. 163. In all these cases the decisions taken were influenced by the example of Strasbourg where clerical citizenship had been openly debated since 1523. Among the Upper Rhenish cities, Strasbourg took the lead in subjugating its clergy to citizenship through a mandate issued on January 16, 1525: cf. *Moeller*, "Kleriker als Bürger", pp. 211–214.

[77] A transcription of the two very similar letters is presented by *Isidore Beuchot*, "Das ehemalige Katharinenkloster zu Colmar", Colmarer Katholischer Kirchen-Kalender, VIII (1914), 58; and idem, "Das frühere Unterlindenkloster: Niedergang und Auflösung", ibid., XIII (1919), 43–44.

[78] AMC, EE 7, 4. Same text also in "Liber ortę seditionis": AMC, EE 7, 1, fol. 59v–60r. According to *Rocholl*, Anfänge der Reformationsgeschichte, pp. 54–5, these stipulations were based on the contemporary monastic mandate of Strasbourg.

4. All monasteries and convents will henceforth take in novices solely with the previous knowledge of, and approval by, the council.
5. The father-confessor will no longer live at Unterlinden but with his own order.
6. All harvest provisions of the monasteries will be kept locked up, with the key in the city's possession.
7. "Several hundred quarters" will be taken from the above provisions and, whenever needed, distributed among the community. Such contributions to individual citizens, however, must be recorded.
8. Since the city will have control of all monastic goods, each monastery will be provided with a secular administrator appointed by the council.
   If the monasteries should henceforth die out and become abandoned, all of their goods shall be confiscated at that point by the city for the benefit of the community.[79]

The authorities' adjustment to the general anticlericalism pervading the community could not be expressed more clearly. Furthermore, some points of contact between this mandate and contemporary Protestant monastic policy are undeniable, especially in regard to articles Three and Eight.[80] Yet, to all appearances, even the phrasing of these two articles rather expressed additional concessions the authorities were willing to make in order to appease the radical ,elements withing the community than the result of evangelical tendencies shared by a majority of the mandate's authors.

Through a swift dealing with the most important anticlerical grievances of the community, the city government greatly enhanced its authority. A few days later, on May 20, the decisive defeat of the peasants at Scherwiler must have further discouraged whatever unruly elements still existed in the population. By mid-May, 1525, five months of inner-city agitation were brought to an end.

D. THE CONDITIONS AND CAUSES OF THE UNREST

What were the conditions facilitating the religious unrest of 1524/25? The most immediate occasion for the outbreak of the agitation was the effect of the spread of the Reformation message within the community.[81] Unfortunately, Colmar's early Reforma-

[79] Several of these stipulations were reiterated in the Colmar authorities' monastic mandate of 1538. This proves that the magistrate and council did not succeed in actually implementing all measures outlined in the presend document. Cf. below, pp. 75–7.

[80] "Zum dritten, ob man die wi[b]s personen zusamen vnd die Munch ouch an ein ort thun, ist bedacht, noch zur zit still ston, bis man sich erfart, wie es zu strospurg vnd andern enden gehalten. . . . Zum achten ist verlassen, diwil der geistlichen gütter zu der Stat hand[en] genom[men], das ein jedes kloster durch ein weltlichen schaffner, so ein Rhat setzen, versehen vnd jrs jnnemens vnd vßgebens rechnung von jm entpfahen.
Vnd so demnach die kloster vßgestorben, vnd abgethan, das dan[n] all derselben gutter zu der Stat vnd gemein handen genom[men]". AMC, EE 7, 1, "Liber ortę seditionis". fol. 59v-60r.

[81] There can be no doubt about the impact of the Reformation on the Colmar unrest of 1524/25. The same has been stated for the Alsatian peasant revolt in general. Cf. *Franz*, Der deutsche Bauernkrieg, p. 144: "Kein Zweifel, der Aufstand im Elsaß wurzelte im Evangelium. Bürger und Bauern erhoben sich zur Verteidigung der neuen Lehre und zur Züchtigung des Klerus". In opposition to Günther Franz's conclusion, Hans Hillerbrand has argued that the impact of the Reformation on the peasant revolt of 1525 was

tion years are not well documented; as a result, some of our interpretation of this period remains conjectural. On the basis of Johann Hummel's report on the inner-city struggle of 1524/25[82], however, we are led to the conclusion that by the end of 1524, the Reformation message had found an important number of adherents in Colmar.

On July 6, 1522, a Colmar Franciscan monk, arrested and bound, was led to Basel by episcopal officials because he had tried to get married in Colmar.[83] Later, on May 6, 1525, one Wilhelm Wölflin was tried and banished from the city for secretely having married a beguine sister named Susanna.[84] Considering that during the early Reformation years clerical marriage symbolized, as a rule, an open break with the old church, this evidence tends to show that Luther's message had found some open adherents among Colmar's clergy.

More important, the Reformation message had also made an inroad into the lay community. In June, 1524, one Heinrich Zimmermann was expulsed from town for having slandered the Holy Sacrament.[85] By 1525, the citizens Thomas Müller, Stephan Drübein and several members of the guild *Zum Adler* (weavers, hat- and ropemakers and related crafts) appear to have embraced the Reformation message.[86] It is very likely that even some city councillors openly adhered to the new faith: all evidence points to the inn-keeper Jacob Bader's conversion. When he became the leader of the malcontent crowd in April, 1525, he was serving his first term as a councillor. A further adherent of Lutheranism among the councillors, and supporter of the printing press of Amandus Farckall, was Peter Nuwgart[87], who was later, in the 1530's, to occupy important functions in the city government.

one of a mere "catalyst". Thus, in interpreting the influence of the Reformation on the contemporary popular attitude toward the clergy and the Catholic church as being a "catalyst" of anticlerical feelings, Hillerbrand, in a sense, follows the tradition established by *Alfred Schultze*, Stadtgemeinde und Reformation, Tübingen 1918, who tended to explain the Reformation as a primarily anticlerical popular reaction against the Catholic church. However, the Reformation message certainly also "caused" the outbreak of unrest in 1525, wherever it added a new religious dimension to the traditional anticlerical issues. Obviously, the latter was the case in Colmar, as well as in Alsace in general. Cf. *Hans J. Hillerbrand*, "The German Reformation and the Peasants' War", in The social history of the Reformation: Festschrift in honor of Harold J. Grimm, ed. by Lawrence P. Buck and Jonathan W. Zophy (Columbus Ohio 1972), pp. 106–136, especially p. 126.

[82] "Liber ortę seditionis": AMC, EE 7, 1.

[83] See AMC, GG 139, 16 (Bishop of Basel to Colmar authorities, Mai 25, 1522): "... Wir werdenn bericht, wie ein Barfüsser Munch jm closter by vch zu Colmar sig, so verganngner tagenn mit einer vwer Inwonerin sich jnn vermenttenn eelichem stanndt verpflichtet. ... Wir [haben] vnnsern viscal mit eim beuelch hinab zu vch abgefertiget, vch den ze erscheinen, vnnd besonners, das vnnser fruntlich beger an vch sig, Ir wellenn jnn vnnserm vnnd sins prouincials namenn den gedachten munch fencklich[en] lassenn annemen vnnd jnn gefenncknuss by vch bytz vff weyter bescheidt also enthaltenn ...,; See also *Jgnaz Chauffour*, ed., „Aus der Ensisheimer Chronik, 1471–1527: Nach Sigismund Billing's Abschrift mitgeteilt" Alsatia (1873/74), 281–297, especially 292. On the tradition of this source, cf. *Rocholl*, Anfänge der Reformationsgeschichte, p. 32, n. 1; and *Hertzog*, "Die letzten Jahre", 121.

[84] AMC, FF 355, 45.

[85] AMC, BB 44, p. 28: "... so er den achtend tag corporis christi gerett, Nemlich das er lieber Zwen hundt mitt einander gesehen handeln alss das hochwirdig sacrament sehen gehalten thun".

[86] This follows from comments made by them to councillors: "Liber ortes seditionis": AMC, EE 7, 1, fol. 21v; and below, pp. 69–70.

[87] Ibid., fol. 1v (Testimony by Jacob Bader, Jr. and four other witnesses): „... die fünff habent kuntschaffts wis gesagt, das si also byenander zecht, hab Jacob bader [Sr.] zu petter Nuwgart geret, wie

The quick spread of the Reformation message throughout Germany in the early 1520's would not have been possible without the help of the printing press.[88] During the 16th century, Colmar could call only two printers its own – Amandus Farckall and Bartholomäus Grüninger, who worked in Colmar from 1522 to 1524, and from 1539 to 1545, respectively. The unorthodox among Colmar's clergy, combined with the printer Amandus Farckall, must have had an important effect on the development of the religious climate in Colmar between 1522 and 1525.[89] It is very telling that Farckall chose to establish himself in Colmar during the early Reformation years: he must obviously have had reason to expect a profitable turnover in Colmar for at least part of his work. Except for a short note dated March 3, 1523, showing that Farckall was involved in a legal dispute for having insulted the priest of neighboring Kientzheim,[90] the only additional evidence about his Colmar activity – from the end of 1522 to the Spring of 1524, when he established himself in Haguenau – are his publications. These are very revealing and establish beyond any doubt that during his Colmar years, like most German printers of the early 1520's, Farckall "violently favored Luther and his allies".[91]

In Colmar, Farckall published seventeen major and minor works, the bulk of them evangelical pamphlets, such as two tracts attributed, respectively, to Melanchthon and Hermann von dem Busche. They dealt with clerical marriage and with "Martin Luther's suffering". Farckall also printed Erhard Hegenwald's report on the Zürich disputation of January 29, 1523. Among his major works figure an „*Außlegung der Epistelen vnd Euangelien* . . ." by Martin Luther, and Erasmus' "*Novi Testamenti totius aeditio* . . .". Excepting this Erasmus edition and a Latin translation of Herodianus, all

meinstu, du bist ouch ein lutterer, vnd hast die truckery vnderhalten, du mechtest wol ein gutt sach haben, wann du der puren houptmann würdest". Thus, it is clearly wrong to presume, as Lina Baillet does, that Peter Nuwgart allegedly intended to become the rebellious peasants' leader. Cf. *Lina Baillet*, "Amandus Farckall, le premier imprimeur de Colmar (Fin 1522? – Ier semestre 1524)", Gutenberg-Jahrbuch (1968), 170; and idem, "Deux villes de la Moyenne Alsace", p. 95.

[88] On the impact of printing on the spread of the Reformation message, cf. *Elizabeth L. Eisenstein*, "L'avènement de l'imprimerie et la Réforme", Annales ESC, VI (1971), 1355–1382; *Richard G. Cole*, "The Reformation in print: German pamphlets and propaganda", ARH, LXVI (1975), 93–102. For a more comprehensive appraisal, see *Rudolf Hirsch*, Printing, Selling and Reading 1450–1550 (Wiesbaden 1967), especially pp. 78–103. For the specifically Alsatian dimensions of the problem: *François Ritter*, Histoire de l'imprimerie alsacienne aux XVe et XVIe siècles, Publications de l'Institut des Hautes Etudes alsaciennes, Vol. XVI, Strasbourg 1955.

[89] The activity of Farckall in Colmar has been the object of several thorough studies by *Lina Baillet*. The previous results of her research, published in the Annuaire de Colmar, in the years 1960 through 1963, are summarized in idem, "Amandus Farckall, le premier imprimeur de Colmar"; and in idem, "Un complément". On 16th century printing in Colmar, cf. *Ritter*, Histoire de l'imprimerie, pp. 411-420; and on Colmar's 16th century book-trade in general: *Heinrich Grimm*, „Die Buchführer des deutschen Kulturbereiches und ihre Niederlassungen in der Zeitspanne 1490–1550", Archiv für Geschichte des deutschen Buchwesens, VII (1967), cols. 1414–1416.

[90] AMC, BB 45 (1522–76), p. 16.

[91] *Dickens*, The German Nation, pp. 111–2. Dickens, ibid., attributes to Farckall of the Haguenau period (following May, 1524), a compromising attitude in religious matters, possibly caused by financial incentives. As for Farckall's Colmar period, the evidence does not allow for any such qualification. Regarding Farckall's Haguenau publications, cf. *Ritter*, Histoire de l'imprimerie. p. 585, and appendix No. 466.

remaining fifteen publications among Farckall's Colmar production "are of a Lutheran tendency".[92] There is therefore no doubt as to Farckall's important influence on the spread of the Reformation message in Colmar on the eve of the attempted revolt of 1524/25. Farckall's unequivocal stand in religious matters also sheds some more light on the role of the authorities in these early years of the Reformation era: given Farckall's religious attitude and the material investment necessary to establish and run his two presses, it is unlikely that Peter Nuwgart was the only councillor to materially and/or ideologically support Farckall's undertaking.

If clerical and lay proselytizing, as well as Farckall's activity, prepared the religious grounds for the agitation occurring in 1524/25, it was finally the preacher Hans, who, through his sermons, helped to bring about the outbreak of open unrest. As cause and catalyst alike, Hans' sermons and his subsequent dismissal brought about the open adherence to the preaching of the Evangile of an important number of citizens. As a catalyst, Hans' preaching helped to trigger a number of reactions based on the social, economic and political experiences and frustations of the rebels. These were primarily directed against:

a) the ruling patriciate's privileged economic situation and social position within the community. In the Thirteen Articles, the rebels opposed the distribution of free wood to the doctor, pharmacist and other favored dignitaries. They also demanded that the *Allmend* (common pasture) be re-opened to all burghers, and that every citizen, excepting councillors, personally fulfill statute-labor duties.

b) against the social privileges and economic advantages of the clergy: In December, 1524, this reaction was still relatively moderate and primarily directed against such alleged nuisances as the Dean's influence on preaching, his frequent non-residence, clerical and lay concubinage and summons by the episcopal court in Basel. In Spring, 1525, this reaction expanded into a more general and more violent anticlericalism, underlined by occasional verbal threats against the monasteries. It finally found its most concrete expression in strong complaints voiced by the rebels about the exclusive economic advantages of the Dean and the city's convents, leading to the ultimate request that the community be allowed to share the riches of the clergy.

c) the alleged economic privileges of the Jews, by whose usury the malcontents felt victimized.[93]

Having summarized the major influences on the spread of the Reformation message as a major condition, partial cause and catalyst of the 1524/25 agitation, we must now turn to the question of whether there were any important outside influences which brought about the inner-city rebellion. The agitation which immediately followed the

[92] *Baillet,* "Amandus Farckall, le premier imprimeur de Colmar", 182. For an updated list of Farckall's Colmar publications, see idem; "Un complément", 77–8.

[93] It is undeniable that many of the complaints cited here were also directed against the city authorities. In the end, however, what remained were clearly the complaints aimed at the church and the clergy, since the council had succeeded in involving the community in the further decision-making process, and in making most communal anticlerical demands its own, thus critically weakening all criticism directed against its oligarchic position.

preacher Hans' dismissal did not have any roots outside the city.[94] However, four months later, in April and May, 1525, there were some obvious outside influences intensifying the inner-city commotion already in progress, such as the rumor about the imminent arrival of mounted knights (a rumor apparently imported from Ribeauvillé) and the fear inspired by the possibility of agrarian losses outside the city.[95] But one gains the general impression from these events that this outside influence never became really important and that the majority of the malcontents among the citizens had in view, at all times, the defense of their city's independence against outside intruders.[96] Between December, 1524, and June, 1525, the revolt never came close enough to Colmar to represent a real threat to the town: if it had, Colmar might have gone through much severer inner dissension.[97]

In debating the roots of the urban agitation of 1524/25, we must also turn our attention to the primarily non-religious, ideological roots of the crisis. The so-called *Bundschuh* conspiracies of Sélestat (1493), Speyer (1502) and Lehen near Freiburg im Breisgau (1513) may have expressed and established a tendency among the agrarian population of the Upper Rhine area to become involved with revolutionary and social rebellion, with the aim of remediating the shortcomings of their economic and social situation. Yet, by reason of their conspiratorial nature, the several attempted *Bundschuh* uprisings only involved a limited group of peasants.[98] However, a wide section of the population were aware of the *Bundschuh*'s basic objectives, derived from the ideal of the reign of divine justice – such as the abolition of serfdom, free hunting and fishing, free access to water-currents and common pastures for all. Even though it is impossible to determine the concrete influence of the *Bundschuh* objectives on the stand of the discontented

[94] This falsifies Peter Blickle's thesis that urban unrest in 1524/25 was commonly imported from the countryside. *Peter Blickle*, Die Revolution von 1525 (Munich and Vienna 1975), p. 171. The case of Sélestat, too, ist not easily subsumed under Blickle's thesis. Cf. *Gény*, Die Reichstadt Schlettstadt.

[95] "Liber ortę seditionis": AMC, EE 7, 1, fol. 60v and 62r.

[96] As is visible, for instance, in the rebels' reponse to the council's inquiry regarding obscure outside elements among them: ibid.. fol. 40r (April 25, 1525). Also, the prevailing differences between the respective social and political constitution of the countryside and of even small imperial cities may have enhanced the difficulties of communication between the two sides. Cf. the pertinent remarks by *Bischoff*, „Colmar et la crise", pp. 51–2; and by *Heiko A. Oberman*, „Tumultus rusticorum: Vom ‚Klosterkrieg' zum Fürstensieg", in Deutscher Bauernkrieg, ed. by idem, ZKG, LXXXV (No. 2, 1974), 161. For some correlative observations on the economic and social relationship between small cities and the surrounding countryside: *Volker Press*, "Der Bauernkrieg in der deutschen Geschichte", Nassauische Annalen, LXXXVI (1975), 174–5.

[97] See Blickle's pertinent observations regarding the correlation between the "Legitimationszwang" and the readiness of a crowd to unleash open rebellion. In Colmar, this "Legitimationszwang" was considerable throughout. Cf. *Blickle*, Die Revolution von 1525, pp. 137–8. Regarding the peculiarities of the Alsatian situation in 1525, cf. ibid., pp. 167–8, and below, pp. 62–3. For information on the development of the revolt in the countryside surrounding Colmar in April and May, 1525, see *Bischoff*, „La Haute-Alsace", 111–2, and the map contained in this article.

[98] *Albert Rosenkranz*, Der Bundschuh: Die Erhebungen des südwestdeutschen Bauernstandes in den Jahren 1493–1517, Schriften des Wissenschaftlichen Instituts der Elsaß-Lothringer im Reich, 2 vols., Heidelberg 1927. For an English translation of the *Bundschuh*-articles of 1502 (Speyer) and for a contemporary description of the 1513 – *Bundschuh* revolt in Breisgau, cf. *Gerald Strauss*, translator and ed; Manifestations of discontent in Germany on the eve of the Reformation (Bloomington, Ind. 1971), pp. 144–150.

Colmariens in 1524/25, these objectives deserve mention in this connection because in early 16th century Alsace they definitely influenced the agrarian class's ideological horizon and climate of opinion.

In determining the extent of other outside ideological influences on the Colmar rebellion, it would be clearly erroneous to assume an influence on the contemporary Alsatian peasant *mentalité* by such 15th century pamphlets as the well-known "*Reformatio Sigismundi*" or by the Upper Rhine Revolutionary's "*Book of a Hundred Chapters and Forty Statutes*". Regarding the *Reformatio Sigismundi*, recent research has convincingly established its exclusively urban and profoundly non-agrarian position.[99] As for the "*Book of a Hundred Chapters*", it was unpublished and existed only as a manuscript.[100] If at all, the social criticism of these *Reformschriften* may "be regarded as a symptom rather than a cause of unrest and anticlericalism" in the early Reformation years.[101] Moreover, in the case of the urban unrest in Colmar, there is no evidence of the spread of socially programmatic or of eschatological and millenarian ideas so prominent in the "*Book of a Hundred Chapters*" or in the objectives of the *Bundschuh* conspiracies. Other than the demand for evangelical preaching, the objectives of the discontented vine-dressers and peasants of Colmar reveal no link to any more widerspread contemporary ideas of social and political reform which might have transcended the range of their predominantly local grievances. During the five months of commotion, the opposition movement in Colmar lacked any revolutionary leader or program. Compared to other concurrent urban rebellions, the attempts at revolt in Colmar were of a very moderate nature.[102]

In this connection, it is important to state that both Günther Franz and, more recently, Peter Blickle, were mistaken in pointing out that the Colmar grievances did not "differ much from the Twelve Articles" of the Swabian peasants.[103] Although, as pointed

[99] Nonetheless, Upper Rhenish seigneurial authorities were on guard regarding the pamphlet's further dispersion. In 1521, Wilhelm von Rappoltstein emprisoned his retainer, Nicolaus Weibel, for having arranged the printing of the *Reformatio Sigismundi* at Strasbourg. Cf. *Baillet*, "La Guerre des Paysans", 359. See also *Lothar Graf zu Dohna*, Reformatio Sigismundi: Beiträge zum Verständnis einer Reformschrift des 15. Jahrhunderts, Veröffentlichungen des Max-Planck-Instituts für Geschichte, Vol. IV, Göttingen 1968; and *Hartmut Boockmann*. "Zu den geistigen und religiösen Voraussetzungen des Bauernkriegs", in Bauernkriegs-Studien, ed. by Bernd Moeller, SVRG, No. 189 (Gütersloh 1975), pp. 11–15. A short description of the contents of the *Reformatio Sigismundi* is presented by *Dickens*, The German Nation, p. 11. For an English translation of a substantial portion of the pamphlet, see *Strauss*, ibid., pp. 3–31.

[100] *Gerhard Zschäbitz*, "Historisches zum Buch der Hundert Kapitel", in Das Buch der Hundert Kapitel und der Vierzig Statuten des sogenannten Oberrheinischen Revolutionärs, ed. by Annelore Franke with an introduction by Gerhard Zschäbitz, Leipziger Uebersetzungen und Abhandlungen zum Mittelalter, Series A, Vol. IV (Berlin 1967), pp. 11–162. For an English translation of a few salient passages from this document, see *Strauss*, ed., Manifestations of discontent, pp. 233–247.

[101] *A. G. Dickens*, The German Nation, p. 16.

[102] *Otthein Rammstedt*, "Stadtunruhen 1525", in Der deutsche Bauernkrieg, 1524–1526, ed. by Hans-Ulrich Wehler, Geschichte und Gesellschaft: Zeitschrift für Historische Sozialwissenschaft, Special No. I (1975), 239–276, especially 240. Further research, particularly on the Colmar revolts of the 14th and 15th centuries, will have to determine to what degree the conflict of 1524/25 was solved within traditional and ritualized forms of solution of conflict: See above, n. 8.

[103] *Blickle*, Die Revolution von 1525, p. 158. Blickle's argument is based on *Franz*, Der deutsche Bauernkrieg, p. 232. An English translation of the Twelve Articles may be found in *Kyle C. Sessions*, ed., Reformation and Authority: The meaning of the Peasants' Revolt, Problems in European Civilisation (Lexington, Mass. 1968), pp. 17–19. For the Thirteen Colmar Articles, cf. above, n. 37.

out above, some obvious similarities do exist between the two documents, it is important to emphasize that the Thirteen Articles of December 24, 1524, contain neither a direct demand for the communal election of preachers nor a complaint about tithes. Furthermore, except for what might be regarded as a biblicist statement in Article One, the Thirteen Articles contain no explicit claim that the Word of God should become the new principle of social organization. Yet, it is precisely on these elements (and on the demand for the abolition of serfdom which, for obvious reasons, may be omitted from this comparison) that Peter Blickle bases his interpretation of the "revolutionary contents of the Twelve Articles".[104] A close comparison of the two documents reveals that there is little substantial similarity between them. Affinities mostly occur in articles of minor importance for Blickle's interpretation. Since his assessment of the contents of the Twelve Articles is his stepping stone toward a new interpretation of the German peasant revolt of 1525 as a revolution of the "common man" (*Gemeiner Mann*), it is important to underline here the basic differences between the Colmar and the Swabian grievances.[105] The Colmar Articles were not, by any means, a revolutionary program. Thus, and also because of the lack of significant interaction between the Colmar rebels and the revolting peasants of the countryside, the Colmar events from December, 1524 to May, 1525, can in no way be regarded as an integral part of a more widespread revolutionary movement.

In recent research, the necessity of a more intensive study of the socio-economic factors in connection with the German peasant revolt of 1525 has justly been emphasized.[106] This also applies to further research on the concurrent Colmar events. Francis Rapp has attempted to present a new explanation of the intricate web of social and economic causes of the peasant revolt in Lower Alsace. In the light of my own analysis of the conditions and causes of the Colmar rebellion, it is remarkable how well my local findings appear to support Rapp's explanation – which I will therefore summarize briefly.

In a preliminary analysis of the possible preconditions of revolt in Alsace, Rapp excludes "demographic pressure", i. e. the effects of overpopulation, as a possible incite-

[104] *Blickle*, ibid., pp. 21–27. For a different assessment of the meaning of the Twelve Articles: cf. *Martin Brecht*, „Der theologische Hintergrund der Zwölf Artikel der Bauernschaft in Schwaben von 1525", in Deutscher Bauernkrieg, ed. by Heiko A. Oberman, ZKG, LXXXV (No. 2, 1974), 174–208.

[105] For Blickle's interpretation, see idem, Die Revolution von 1525, pp. 156–213; and idem, "Thesen zum Thema – Der 'Bauernkrieg' als Revolution des 'Gemeinen Mannes'", in Revolte und Revolution in Europa, HZ, Beiheft 4, ed. by idem (Munich 1975), pp. 127–131. A discussion of Blickle's fascinating but not unproblematic thesis would go far beyond the purpose of this study. For general criticism of his assessment, cf. *Franklin Kopitzsch* and *Rainer Wohlfeil*, "Neue Forschungen zur Geschichte des Deutschen Bauernkrieges", in Der deutsche Bauernkrieg, 1524–1526, ed. by Hans-Ulrich Wehler, Geschichte und Gesellschaft: Zeitschrift für Historische Sozialwissenschaft, Special No. I (1975), 312–314. For salient criticism of Blickle's thesis from the perspective of the urban historian: *Heinz Schilling*, "Aufstandsbewegungen in der stadtbürgerlichen Gesellschaft des Alten Reiches: Die Vorgeschichte des Münsteraner Täuferreichs, 1525 bis 1534", in Der deutsche Bauernkrieg. 1524–1526, ibid., 237–238.

[106] *Blickle*, ibid., p. 11; and *Volker Press*, "Der Bauernkrieg in der deutschen Geschichte", 170. For a comprehensive discussion of the lacunae of modern research on the German peasants revolt of 1525, cf. *Rainer Wohlfeil*, ed., Der Bauernkrieg 1524–26: Bauernkrieg und Reformation. Neun Beiträge, Nymphenburger Texte zur Wissenschaft, No. 21, Munich 1975; especially the articles by *Franklin Kopitzsch*, *Rainer Wohlfeil* and *Heide Wunder*.

ment to revolt. He concludes that early 16th century Alsace was rather underpopulated.[107] He then argues that in 15th and 16th century Alsace, most fields and vineyards were not cultivated by their owners but usually by a tenant.[108] A tenant would sign a lease of nine to twenty years duration, wherein a fixed amount of annual rent payable to the owner was stipulated. In addition to this rent, the tenant annually paid various kinds of taxes, tithes and the like. Consequently, he was only able to earn a fraction of the actual yield of his fields or vineyards. Since, according to Rapp, most lower Alsatian peasants produced their goods for the market rather than exclusively for their own consumption, they inevitably fell prey to the increasing fluctuation of prices during the second half of the 15th century. As a result, the peasants lived in an increasingly unstable economic situation. A few rich peasants, but mainly monasteries, chapter-foundations and hospitals, had the means to stock wheat and wine during abundant years and were able to sell their stock when the harvest had been bad and prices were high. This, of course, did not help curtail the rampant anticlericalism among the peasants and vine-dressers; they saw their disadvantageous market situation worsened still further by clerical competition.[109]

Since these peasants and vine-dressers had to pay their rent, taxes, tithes and the like, independently of the yield and quality of their annual harvest, they often received credit from Jews, whose frequent usurious policy of charging interest created hatred and resentment among their clients.[110] When a debtor as it often happened was not able to pay his back-rent to the owner of a field or vineyard, he was usually cited and often punished by the episcopal court because most leases, according to Rapp, were drawn up in the presence of a clerical notary.[111] Again, such a turn of events could, and did, enhance the spread of anticlerical resentment. Francis Rapp has determined that the general indebtedness of peasants and vine-dressers was a major cause of the peasant revolt in Alsace. In the case of Colmar, future research will have to determine whether further

[107] *Francis Rapp*, "Die soziale und wirtschaftliche Vorgeschichte des Bauernkriegs im Unterelsaß", in Bauernkriegs-Studien, ed. by Bernd Moeller. SVRG, No. 189 (Gütersloh 1975), 29–45; for further, more comprehensive discussion of the same argument, cf. idem, "La guerre des paysans dans la vallée du Rhin supérieur: Quelques problèmes d'interpretations", in Charles Quint, le Rhin et la France: Droit savant et droit pénal à l'époque de Charles-Quint, ed. by Centre de Recherches Rhénanes et Régionales de l'Université des Sciences Humaines de Strasbourg, Publications de la Société Savante d'Alsace et des Régions de l'Est: Collection "Recherches et Documents", Vol. XVII (Strasbourg 1973), pp. 135–156. For Colmar, too, we have been able to observe a complete lack of demographic pressure and, for the second half of the 16th century, even a pattern of demographic decline, cf. above, p. 13, n. 6.

[108] For Colmar, cf. the reference above, n. 71.

[109] See the complaints about the rich provisions of the Colmar clergy, and the propositions on how these should be made accessible to the lay community (cf. above, pp. 51–2) and the vine-dressers' great apprehension in view of possible losses inflicted to their vineyards by the revolting peasants: AMC, EE 7, 1, fol. 60v and 62 r.

[110] For these reasons, anti-semitism ran high within the Colmar area at the beginning of the 16th century. In 1521, Ulrich von Rappoltstein was forced to assuage general anti-semitic discontent among his peasants by limiting the range of Jewish pawn-broking to include only moveable goods. See *Baillet*, "La Guerre des Paysans", 358. Yet, the continued legal seizure by Jews of vineyards owned or leased by Colmar burghers who failed to pay back their credit, suggests that such a limitation did not exist in Colmar. See, for instance, AMC, BB 52, "Protocollum Missivarum" (1526–29), pp. 113 and 120, *et passim*. Regarding the anti-semitic aspects of the Colmar agitation, cf. above, p. 50.

[111] See Article Seven of the Thirteen Colmar Articles of December 24, 1524: above, pp. 47–8.

social and economic evidence substantiates my impression that Rapp's explanation of the economic causes of the peasants' revolt contributes significantly to our understanding of events in Colmar in 1524/25.

E. COLMAR'S ECCLESIASTICAL, RELIGIOUS AND SOCIAL POLICY FOLLOWING MAY, 1525

Following May, 1525, for a duration of more than two years, no clearly discernable dissension between the Colmar authorities and the clergy disrupted the city's life. The Bishop of Basel was now an old man, fairly resigned to the fate of not having been able to withstand the tide of the Reformation within his diocese. His once so vigorous coadjutor, Niklaus von Diesbach, now had to devote most of his time and energy to the problems raised by the introduction of the Reformation in the city of Basel.[112]

Only in November, 1527, after the election of Jacob Philipp von Gundelsheim to the See of Basel[113], do we hear of new negotiations being held between the canons and priests of St. Martin's and Colmar's city council. The ecclesiastics asked to be freed from statute-labor and guard-duties. They did not, however, refuse to fulfill all other obligations of their citizen's oath. Based on the excuse that the troubled political situation years.[116] The edict threatened „concubinaries" who did not comply with its stipulations with severe punishment or expulsion from town. It was officially addressed quest.[114] But, early in the year 1528 – when Bishop Jacob Philipp began interfering in favor of an integral re-establishment of all traditional privileges of Colmar's secular clergy – the council was much less amenable. The Bishop demanded that the clergy be freed from their citizen's oath, which he considered a flagrant infringement on his own prerogatives.[115]

Toward the end of July, 1528, the council countered and once more re-asserted its jurisdictional claim over the clergy by issuing a mandate designed to repress all notorious concubinage in town. The authorities thus fulfilled a demand contained in the Thirteen Articles of December, 1524 – a not uncommon communal request in the early Reformation years.[116] The edict threatened "concubinaries" who did not comply with its stipulations with severe punishment or expulsion from town. It was officially addressed to both laymen and clergy, but was, in fact, mainly designed as an attack on the latter. A week after its promulgation, the mandate was solemnly presented to the canons and

[112] See *Georg Boner*, "Das Bistum Basel: Ein Ueberblick von den Anfängen bis zur Neuordnung, 1828", Freiburger Diözesan-Archiv, LXXXVIII (1968), 73–76; and *Wackernagel*, Geschichte der Stadt Basel, Vol. III, pp. 93–94.

[113] In July, 1528, in view of the imminent introduction of the Reformation in Basel, Bishop Jacob Philipp established his and his successors' residence at Porrentruy in the Jura: *Boner*, ibid., 77–79; for the following, see also *Goehlinger*, Histoire du Chapitre, pp. 238–239.

[114] AMC, EE 7, 25; the same events are also recorded in the "Liber ortę seditionis": AMC, EE 7, 1, fol. 66v–67r.

[115] AMC, GG 25, 23; GG 25, 4; GG 24, 19 (Transactions of January 6 through May 26, 1528, in respective chronological order).

[116] AMC, BB 44, p. 42 (Mandate of July 26, 1528); cf. also *Störmann*, Die städtischen Gravamina, p. 270.

priests of St. Martin's, and they were requested to adjure it. They all complied, excepting Dean Jacob Carpentarii, who thus forfeited his citizen's oath. As was to be expected, the Bishop immediately and violently protested against this procedure.[117] Emphatically, he reiterated his earlier demand that the clergy be released from their citizen's oath.

Thus, open conflict was unavoidable when at the end of August the canons and chaplains of St. Martin's were invited by the magistrate and council to renew their citizen's oath. As they refused to do so, they were granted only eight days for reflection. In the meantime, upon the Dean's initiative, two episcopal delegates appeared in town to officially present their superior's demand that the clergy be spared the renewal of their citizenship. The magistrate, however, vigorously disputed the Bishop's right to oppose the oathtaking, whereupon the two delegates, as a last resort, had their solemn protest registered by a local notary. In its counter-protest the council referred to the decisions of the recent imperial diet of Speyer and emphasized that it intended to adhere to all stipulations issued by the forth-coming national council planned to take place at Speyer.[118] It obviously expected the sanction of clerical citizenship from such a national council.

The open confrontation between the council's expansionist jurisdictional claims and the Bishop's attempt to safeguard his traditional prerogatives was underway. Following intense deliberations, the council finally decided to circumvent the clergy's obstinacy by diversion: on September 9, 1528, the authorities demanded that the canons store their entire church treasure in a secure place and turn over the keys to the magistrate.[119] At the same time, unabashed by the Bishop's determined stand on the issue, the council proceeded three days later to force the clergy to renew their oath. This happened in the absence of the Dean and three canons. However, although the chaplains swore the oath, there was only one canon who also agreed to comply with the procedure – his four colleagues preferred to abstain.[120]

Despite a mandate issued by the Imperial Supreme Court (instigated against the council by the Bishop), and although during negotiations held in Basel a few days later the Bishop left no question as to his determination not to allow the clergy's civic oath, the Colmar authorities did not waver.[121] But when the Bailiff of Haguenau (as mediator in the negotiations between the council and the Bishop) finally gave up his hitherto continuous support of Colmar's position, the council's defeat in the negotiations was sealed: it was not powerful enough to carry on the struggle all by itself. The councillors probably also feared the expense of a lengthy trial in the Imperial Supreme Court. In a treaty

[117] AMC, BB 44, p. 42; and AMC, GG 24, 13 (Bishop to Colmar authorities, August 4, 1528); AAEB, A 41, 17 (Colmar authorities to Bishop, August 14, 1528: Copy of this letter in AMC, GG 25, 4, fol. 33r). We have no clear evidence as to whether the mandate was ever really applied. However, the banishment of the maids of seven canons and chaplains on July 6, 1529, for disobedience to the secular authorities may have been based on it: cf. AMC, BB 45 (1515–42), p. 77.

[118] AMC, GG 25, 4, fol. 38v–45v.

[119] AMC, GG 25, fol. 1r–3v, especially fol. 3r–3v; and AMC, GG 25, 9 (Advice by Dr. Pludenz, the city's legal advisor, dated September 8, 1528).

[120] AMC, GG 25, 9, fol. 4r–5v; and GG 25, 10, fol. 1r–2v.

[121] AAEB, A 41, 18 (Mandate issued by the Imperial Supreme Court, dated September 16, 1528); and AMC, GG 25, 10, fol. 3r–6v.

agreed upon on September 27, 1528, it released the clergy from their oath and received in turn sixty guilders as protection-money. The council also had to restore the clergy with the key to their treasures.[122]

The wheel of political fortune had come around full circle and the Colmar authorities had lost most of the advantages over clergy and Bishop gained during the agitation of 1524/25. The agreement of September, 1528, re-established, in effect, the *status quo* as far as the council's control over the secular clergy was concerned. Concurrently, as we shall see[123], the authorities also lost some recently acquired advantages over the city's monasteries. Only the two convents remained firmly under their control after 1525.

In re-establishing and furthering their authority vis-à-vis the community during the period following May, 1525, the magistrate and council did not suffer any comparable set-backs. As early as mid-May, 1525, the council was firmly back in control of the situation; its major concession to the opposition having been to adopt most of the movement's anticlerical demands. Colmar's situation on the fringe of the countryside revolt did not force the authorities to make any further concessions to the unruly elements within the community in order to keep them in line, except that they promised the community communal responsibility for any possible damage inflicted on the outside property of Colmar citizens. Likewise, after they overcame the oppositional danger, they did not need or want to rule by threat of inflicting draconic punishment on the rebels, as was done in neighboring Ensisheim.[124] In Colmar, the most common punishment imposed on the offenders of April and May, 1525 – for outsiders and burghers alike – was banishment from town for a certain period of time.[125] Other forms of punishment in such cases were rare. For example, one Hans Belmer, a baker, was prohibited from carrying arms, except for a blunt knife.[126] The case of the inn-keeper Welfflin from Hirtzfelden in the Sundgau, was the only case of corporeal punishment we are aware of: he had his tongue cout out for slandering the Colmar authorities.[127] In December, 1528, after a long period of imprisonment, Jacob Bader, Sr., the leader of the Spring, 1525, movement, was finally pardoned by the Bailiff of Haguenau and, consecutively, by the magistrate and council. The intervention of his relatives and friends, among them Count George of Württemberg, played an important role in bringing about this peaceful settlement.[128]

[122] AMC, GG 25, 20; and GG 25, 10, fol. 7r–9v. We do not know the outcome of the ensuing quarrel between the chapter and the city council concerning the ratification of the treaty; yet, given the lack of evidence going beyond December 13, 1528, we may safely assume that the conflict was probably resolved by the end of that year: cf. AMC, GG 25, 1; GG 25, 7; GG 25, 6; GG 25, 5 (in chronological order), as well as AAEB, A 41, 9.

[123] Cf. below, pp. 75–7.

[124] *Bischoff*, „La Haute Alsace", 118; and *Rocholl*, Anfänge der Reformationsgeschichte, p. 29.

[125] AMC, BB 45 (1515–42), pp. 54–55 (Expulsion of Heinrich Hug, Michael Belmer, Bartholomäus Weibel and of the servant Hans Ros; the first three of them were outsiders); AMC, FF 355, 43 (Expulsion of Claus Linsen); AMC. BB 45 (1515–42), p. 73 (Punishment of Wilhelm Schur); AMC. FF 358, 47 (Punishment of the fisherman and *Seldner* Conrad Singer); cf. also AMC, FF 355, 69; and AMC, FF 15, 6–39 (The case of the painter Lux Schuelin).

[126] AMC, BB 45 (1515–42), p. 61.

[127] AMC, FF 95, 1–7.

[128] AMC, FF 96, 1–40, especially 26 („Jacob Baders Handlung").

Notwithstanding the relative moderation of these judgments, the authorities did not hesitate in strengthening their authority through a policy of mandates designed to enhance their control over communal life. In January, 1526, the council re-issued its old mandate suppressing blasphemy and excessive drinking.[129] Three weeks later, through another mandate, it restricted its traditional welfare policy by forcing all able-bodied beggars to work[130], and two years later it announced the previously mentioned mandate against clerical and lay concubinage. In 1532, finally, it renewed all former mandates suppressing blasphemy, excessive drinking, adultery, concubinage, public dances and gambling. In an official declaration, this mandate was justified by the observation that the prevailing Turkish threat had been brought about "by us Christians, through our apostasy [i. e. the Reformation] and our transgression against God's commands with blasphemy and other sinful vices". It concluded that the Christian soldiers, facing the Turks, would only stand a chance if "we desist from our error in faith and from our sinful vices, and beg the Almighty for His Grace and forgiveness of our evil".[131]

In the light of these mandates, there can be no doubt that, following the events of 1524/25, the Colmar council, like the authorities of Sélestat[132], tended to identify the evangelical movement with the threat of social unrest. Similar official reactions to the social and religious turmoil of the early Reformation years have also been observed in the cases of Memmingen and Cologne.[133] As a result, the evangelical movement within Colmar was increasingly forced into concealment and anonymity. If, more for social than genuinely religious reasons, the evangelical movement in Colmar was thus gradually suppressed, it is not untypical that a measure of genuine religious uncertainty prevailed among the city councillors. As for the clarification of their uncertainty, they anxiously awaited the decisions of a national council convocated by the Emperor.[134]

Accordingly, the loyalty vis-à-vis the Emperor was the main theme of a joint letter which Colmar, Haguenau and others from among the Alsatian Ten Cities sent to Obernai in 1527, imploring its authorities not to embrace the new faith.[135] This development in Colmar's official position, with respect to the increasing politico-religious "con-

[129] AMC, FF 621, 1.

[130] AMC, BB 44, p. 38; cf. also below, pp. 161–2.

[131] AMC, FF 600, 7: „... Dwil dan solichs von vns christen durch den abfal vnsers gloubens vnd vbertretung der gebot gottes, als mit gotzlesterung vnd andernn süntlichen lastern verursacht ...". During the following years, this policy of increasing social control from "above" also led to the suppression of traditional manifestations of popular culture. On December 29 and 30, 1537, the magistrate prohibited the Day. See AMC, BB 44, pp. 353–4.

[132] For Sélestat's "policy of mandates" foolowing the year 1525, see *Gény*, Die Reichsstadt Schlettstadt, p. 193, and for interesting supplemental information: *Paul Adam*, Histoire réligieuse de Sélestat, Publications de la Société des Amis de la Bibliothèque de Sélestat, Vol. I (Sélestat 1967), p. 200.

[133] For Memmingen, cf. *Peter Eitel*, Die oberschwäbischen Reichsstädte im Zeitalter der Zunftherrschaft: Untersuchungen zu ihrer politischen und sozialen Struktur unter besonderer Berücksichtigung der Städte Lindau, Memmingen, Ravensburg und Ueberlingen, Schriften zur südwestdeutschen Landeskunde, Vol. VIII (Stuttgart 1970), p. 104; for Cologne, cf. *Robert Scribner*, "Why was there no Reformation at Cologne?", Bulletin of the Royal Institute for Historical Research, XLIX (1976), 217–241, especially 218 and 233–234.

[134] Cf. AMC, GG 25, 4, fol. 45v.

[135] *Joseph Gyss*, Histoire de la ville d'Obernai, Vol. I (Strasbourg 1866). pp. 472–473.

fessionalization" taking place all over the German Empire in the late 1520's and early 1530's, was vigorously sustained by important outside influences. These were chiefly exerted by the Regency of Ensisheim and the Bailiff of Haguenau, both representing the interests of Habsburg-Austria in Alsace. In 1526, upon request by Archduke Ferdinand of Austria, Colmar, like all other member-cities of the Decapolis, had to assure the Bailiff of its continuing adherence to the Roman church.[136] Later, in 1528, the Archduke had his Bailiff distribute anti-Lutheran mandates among the Alsatian Ten Cities.[137]

Meanwhile, the vigorous persecution of Protestants and the unmerciful slaughtering of rebellious peasants by the Regency of Ensisheim must have contributed to the strengthening of Colmar's commitment to Catholic orthodoxy. Had the Colmar authorities wavered in this commitment, they would have given Habsburg-Austria a welcome pretense to interfere with Colmar's autonomy as an imperial city.[138] Colmar ostensibly tried to stay aloof of Ensisheim's policy of repression, although the Regency launched several attempts to involve the neighboring city in the pursuit of its own schemes.[139]

In 1530, Colmar's cautious policy in religious matters was re-enforced by the following experience. At the imperial diet of Augsburg, where the Emperor was re-asserting his authority vis-à-vis the Protestant estates, Colmar's representative, Hieronymus Boner, unexpectedly saw himself denounced at the imperial court as the prime mover of the Protestant cause in Colmar; in particular, he was criticized for his alleged contacts with Basel's city clerk.[140] In a swiftly elaborated defense, the magistrate and council thoroughly refuted these unfounded accusations and solemnly denied any association of Colmar with either the Swiss or Lutheranism.[141] There is no doubt that

[136] TLA, Pestarchiv, XVIII, 45 (Letter dated September 29, 1526).

[137] AMC, GG 144, 7 (Letter dated January 20, 1528).

[138] There is abundant evidence documenting the despotism of the Regency of Ensisheim. One very significant source is a letter from the Basel burgomaster addressed to the Margrave of Baden and Hochberg, dated November 28, 1525, cf. *Dürr* and *Roth*, eds., Aktensammlung, Vol. II, pp. 152–153. For comparative purposes, regarding the simultaneous repression unleashed by Habsburg-Austria in other areas of South and Southwest Germany, see *Karl Friedrich Vierordt*, Geschichte der Reformation im Grossherzogthum Baden (Karlsruhe 1847), p. 252; and *Hans-Georg Hofacker*, "Die Reformation in der Reichsstadt Ravensburg", ZWLG, XXIX (1970), 83 and 90.

[139] For instance, Colmar did not comply in 1525 with Ensisheim's requests for military reinforcement: AMC, EE 7, 1, fol. 54r and 65r/v. This was done despite a mutual promise of assistance: *Hartfelder*, Zur Geschichte des Bauernkriegs, pp. 143–150.

[140] See Boner's letter written from Augsburg on August 27, 1530 (AMC, AA 74, 68), printed in *Gustaf Wethly*, Hieronymus Boner; Leben, Werke und Sprache: Ein Beitrag zur elsäßischen Literaturgeschichte (Strasbourg 1892), pp. 9–12; cf. also *Fernand J. Heitz*, "Messire Jérôme Boner, humaniste, diplomate et maire de Colmar", Annuaire de Colmar (1938), 119; and *Jacques Betz*, "Jérôme Boner, un humaniste colmarien devenu maire, diplomate et traducteur", Annuaire de Colmar (1975/76), 84.

[141] H. H. St. A., Kleinere Reichsstände, fasc. 84 (Letter dated September 2, 1530). The court's fear that Colmar could associate itself with the Swiss was not entirely unfounded: in 1529/30, the Zürich reformer Ulrich Zwingli indeed contemplated a possible alliance between Colmar and the Swiss and Alsatian cities recently joined together in the Protestant alliance called "Christliches Burgrecht": cf. Amtliche Sammlung der ältern eidgenössischen Abschiede, Vol. IV, Section Ib, ed. by Johannes Strickler (Zürich: 1876), p. 309. Cf. also *René Hauswirth*, Landgraf Philipp von Hessen und Zwingli, Schriften zur Kirchen- und Rechtsgeschichte, Vol. XXXV (Tübingen 1968), pp. 89–90. Although delegates of the Protestant Swiss cities travelled through Colmar in January, 1530, apparently no negotiations took place on that occa-

Colmar's indignation about these accusations was genuine, and that the denunciation had been entirely unfounded. Nevertheless, the incident deserves mention because it also contributed to strengthening Colmar's loyalty to the Emperor's religious policy.

F. THE REFORMATION MOVEMENT IN COLMAR, 1525–1535

Whereas in 1524/25 an important number of *Colmariens* had rallied in opposition to the council's religious policy and in support of evangelical preaching, no direct trace of their activity as a group can be delineated for the period following May, 1525. Faced with the council's hostility toward religious change, many among them must have retreated from their intention of bringing about the preaching of the Word of God. Other members of their group, however, were forced into concealment, where several of them joined groups of Anabaptists.[142] Judging by the religious attitude of the authorities during those years, there is good reason to suspect that several among those who, in 1524/25, had joined the group of malcontents for primarily religious reasons, now joined the growing ranks of Anabaptists.

A citizen named Thomas Müller was one of them. In May, 1525, he was cited by the council for having criticized the common priests' sermons and for having encouraged the latter to go right ahead and "preach the truth". Under questioning, however, Thomas Müller denied having done so.[143] Shortly after this incident he became an Anabaptist. Between 1530 and 1535, on at least two occasions, he preached to fellow Anabaptists from the pulpit of St. Martin's. The record is not clear as to whether or not he did this by interrupting the regular worship being held at that church. We are also left uninformed about the contents of his preaching, except that he appears to have said that the Holy Sacrament contained "neither blood nor the body [of Christ]", and that it was all void. Under questioning, in 1535, he also admitted to having baptized others. In the same year he recanted but later broke his promise of adherence to the old faith.[144] Apparently, the leniency extended to Anabaptists and religious non-conformists in general, as demonstrated by the Strasbourg authorities of the early Reformation period, was likewise practiced by the Colmar city government, for, in 1545, Thomas Müller was still

sion: Amtliche Sammlung, Vol. IV, Section Ib, ibid., p. 499. Cf. also *Jean-Paul Tardent*, Niklaus Manuel als Staatsmann (Bern 1968), pp. 53–4. However, according to Boner's own testimony (see his letter from Augsburg of August 31, 1530: AMC, AA 74, 63), the denunciation of himself and of his city at the imperial court was based on the role Colmar played in the March 1530 negotiations between the city and the Bishop of Basel, and in the restitution to Basel's secular authorities of rents belonging to ecclesiastics who had fled the city of Basel during the introduction of the Reformation there.

[142] There is, as of yet, no comprehensive work on the early spread of Anabaptism in Upper Alsace. For Colmar, an uncritical accumulation of the evidence contained in AMC, GG 168 is presented by *Xavier Mossmann*, Les Anabaptistes à Colmar, 1534–1535, Colmar 1869. Since, as far as I can judge, Anabaptism was more a result of, than an influence on, the spread of the Reformation in Colmar, I will exclude further references to it from the present account.

[143] "Liber ortę seditionis", AMC, EE 7, 1, fol. 53v.

[144] AMC, GG 158, 8. For Thomas Müller's first preaching in 1530: AMC, BB 45 (1515–42), p. 80 (Expulsion of Hans Cuntz). An undated letter written by Thomas Müller (probably from the year 1535), in which he implores the authorities to treat him with forbearance, is in AMC, GG 168, 11.

alive and well and perhaps even continued to proselytize, as is suggested by the alleged adherence to Anabaptism of his neighbor Claus Giger.[145]

The locksmith Hans Cuntz and one Bernhard Widichem were among Thomas Müller's early fellow Anabaptists[146], but under questioning by the authorities they both recanted. On April 24, 1535, Jacob Stedli and five companions (four women and one man) were expelled from town for their Anabaptist activities.[147] By then, the establishment of a millenarian Anabaptist "kingdom" in the city of Münster in Westphalia, and the ensuing turmoil within that city, had rendered all German authorities much more watchful for the alleged conspirative activities and gatherings of Anabaptists. Thus, the Colmar records for the years 1534 and 1535 inform us about important Anabaptist gatherings in the surrounding countryside, involving several Colmar burghers, and about secret get-togethers of Anabaptists in the city itself. But we remain again uninformed about the nature of the creed shared by these men and women.[148] Despite the heightened watchfulness of the magistrate and council, Anabaptist circles continued to exist in and around Colmar well up to the first half of the following century.

As for the Colmar clergy's susceptibility to the new faith within the period in question, the extant evidence only accounts for one Augustinian monk's conversion to Protestantism. Leonhard Verula's later testimony from 1538 recounts how, when his Protestant leanings became known, he was imprisoned by the city government, questioned by the canon Georg Klein and by several city councillors, and subsequently sent back to his monastery. However, shortly thereafter the Prior of the Augustinians had him re-imprisoned. For fear he might be taken to nearby Ensisheim and severely punished for hersey, he broke out of prison and fled to Basel. Verula does not relate the exact date of this episode. It probably took place in the late 1520's or early 1530's.[149]

[145] See AMC, FF 346, pp. 53–4.

[146] AMC, BB 45 (1515–42), p. 80; and AMC, FF 355, 88.

[147] AMC, BB 45 (1515–42), p. 32; and AMC, GG 168, 2.

[148] AMC, GG 158, 4–10. Cf. also Amtliche Sammlung der ältern Eidgenössischen Abschiede, Vol. IV, Section Ic, ed. by Karl Deschwanden (Lucerne 1878), p. 495 (No. 274).

[149] AMC, GG 99, 8 and 10. For the circumstances which led to Verula's testimony of 1538, cf. below, p. 83.

CHAPTER III

FROM 1535 TO THE PEACE OF AUGSBURG, 1555[1]

A. THE INTRODUCTION OF THE REFORMATION INTO THE NEIGHBORING TERRITORY OF HORBOURG-RIQUEWIHR: ITS SIGNIFICANCE FOR COLMAR

During the years 1522–25, the city of Colmar, as we have seen, did not stay abreast of the rising tide caused by the quick spread of the Reformation movement throughout Germany. The city's relatively broad Reformation movement, advocating religious, social and political reform alike, culminated in the social unrest lasting from December, 1524, through May, 1525. Following these events, the Colmar movement appears to have lost its considerable impetus almost from one day to the next, caused, in part, by the city government's increasingly hostile attitude and by Habsburg-Austria's vigorous repression of the Reformation in Upper Alsace. Likewise, the city authorities did not succeed in safeguarding the political windfall profits achieved in May, 1525: in 1528, they saw themselves constrained to release the secular clergy from the citizen's oath and to restore most of their old rights of immunity. Although this setback did not discourage the city councillors in their continued pursuit of the main objective of their ecclesiastical policy, which was the reduction and eventual abolition of all clerical jurisdiction within their town, they experienced yet another defeat in the same area: in 1535, at the Imperial Supreme Court in Speyer, the council lost a trial initiated against it by the Order of the Knights of St. John and was, as a result, forced to refrain from any attempt to collect an extra-ordinary tax from the Colmar commandery (a tax levied on all other city monasteries).[2]

The situation prevailing in 1535 could hardly invoke any remembrance of the religious and social climate of the years 1522–1525. However, within the same year, a new source of religious influence established itself within Colmar's close proximity, which during the following decades was to have an increasing and long-lasting effect on the religious attitude of the *Colmariens*. In 1535, the Reformation was introduced into the neighboring principalities of Horbourg-Riquewihr, which immediately bordered Colmar in the northwest, north and east.

[1] The following chapter is in part a revised version of my article "La Préréforme à Colmar, 1535–1555: Continuité ou rupture?" BHPF, CXXII (1976), 551–566.

[2] Cf. ADHR, Ordre de Malte, Colmar, 20 (Letter addressed to the Supreme Court by Johann von Hattstein, Commander of the order in Germany, dated September, 1532; and judgment of June 2, 1535). See also *Heinrich Rocholl*, Die Einführung der Reformation in der ehemaligen freien Reichsstadt Colmar: Ein Beitrag zur Reformationsgeschichte des Elsaß (Leipzig 1876), pp. 25–27. In 1565, the city council lost another trial initiated by the same order on similar grounds: *Paul Huot*, La Commanderie de St.-Jean à Colmar: Etude historique (1210–1870), (Colmar 1870), p. 70.

Since the first half of the 14th century, the county of Horbourg and the principality of Riquewihr had been ruled by the Dukes of Württemberg.[3] During the 16th century these lands formed an administrative unity with the principality of Montbéliard in the south, which was also in the hands of Württemberg. In 1519, when the unruly Duke Ulrich of Württemberg lost his major possessions through a penal expedition of the Empire and the Swabian League, he was allowed to remain in charge of ruling these territories situated on the left bank of the Upper Rhine. In 1535, following Duke Ulrich's re-possession of his homelands from the hands of King Ferdinand, he charged the administration of his Alsatian possessions, including that of Montbéliard, to his brother, Count George (1498–1558). With the exception of Montbéliard, these territories were to be governed uninterruptedly by Count George until his death on July 17, 1558.

During his rule, the county of Horbourg consisted of Horbourg and the villages of Algolsheim, Appenwihr, Bischwihr, Durrenentzen, Fortschwihr, Muntzenheim, Sundhoffen, Volgelsheim and Wolfganzen, while the *Herrschaft* Riquewihr was composed of the small town of Riquewihr and the villages of Altwihr, Bebelnheim, Hunawihr, Mittelwihr and Ostheim.[4] The treaty of Kaaden in Bohemia, concluded on June 29, 1534, confirmed Ulrich's re-conquest of his lands and sanctioned the introduction of the Reformation in his territories;[5] Ulrich and his brother George had openly embraced the Reformation message long before.

Thus, following the treaty of Kaaden, evangelical worship was established in most of the villages surrounding Colmar, with whose inhabitants the *Colmariens* found themselves in daily contact, be it out in the fields or at their city market.[6] Count George, who had been in close contact with several Swiss reformers, chose to give his new territorial church a decidedly Reformed imprint. He commissioned the Zürich archdeacon Erasmus Fabritius (Schmid), and following Fabritius' return to Switzerland, the schoolmaster of the small imperial city of Gengenbach, Matthias Erb (1494–1571).[7]

[3] For the territorial history of Württemberg's lands situated in Alsace and in the region of Montbéliard, see *John Viénot*, Histoire de la Réforme dans le pays de Montbéliard depuis les origines jusqu'à la mort de P. Toussain, 1524–1573, Vol. I, Montbéliard 1900. Specifically for the history of Horbourg-Riquewihr during the first half of the 16th century, see *Heinrich Rocholl*, "Herzog Georg von Württemberg und die Reformation im Ober-Elsaß", Kirchliche Monatsschrift, XIX (1900), 513–522; and for a more comprehensive account: *Henri Strohl*, Le protestantisme en Alsace (Strasbourg 1950), pp. 146–162.

[4] *Johann Adam*, Evangelische Kirchengeschichte der elsäßischen Territorien bis zur Französischen Revolution (Strasbourg 1928), p. 293.

[5] Cf. *Rocholl*, "Herzog Georg von Württemberg", 522.

[6] For the following, see ibid., 561–578; and *Adam*, Evangelische Kirchengeschichte, pp. 292–348.

[7] Research to date has neglected the role played by this interesting and important exponent of the Swiss-Reformed and Bucerian tradition in the Upper Rhine area. Matthias Erb entertained an intensive correspondence with such men as his old friend Caspar Hedio of Strasbourg, Peter Tossanus (Toussain), the reformer of Montbéliard, the Basel *Antistes* Simon Sulzer, and with many other contemporaries. Most important was his continued correspondence with Heinrich Bullinger, Zwingli's successor in Zürich. It has recently been investigated by *Beat-Rudolf Jenny*, "Bullingers Briefwechsel mit dem Elsaesser Reformator Matthias Erb (1539–1571)", in Heinrich Bullinger, 1504–1575: Gesammelte Aufsätze zum 400. Todestag, ed. by Ulrich Gäbler and Erland Herkenrath, Vol. II, ZBRG, Vol. VIII (Zürich 1975), pp. 57–86. Jenny's account corrects several biographical errors contained in the older articles on Erb by

Matthias Erb, the superintendent of the church of Horbourg-Riquewihr from 1538 to 1560, and his friend, the minister of Hunawihr, Niklaus Regius (König), closely aligned their new territorial church with Bullinger's church of Zürich and Bucer's of Strasbourg. This essentially Reformed orientation only ceded to Lutheran influence after the death of Count Georg in 1558. At that time, Count George's son and successor, Prince Frederic, was still a minor. His tutors – among them Duke Christopf of Württemberg – however, were all staunch Lutherans. Thus, in 1560, Matthias Erb and Niklaus Regius were forced into retirement, and Erb's sucessor, the superintendent Nicolaus Cancerinus, successfully strove to impose upon his church an orthodox Lutheran stance in accordance with the two Württemberg church ordinances of 1536 and 1559.[8] This new theological orientation of the church of Horbourg-Riquewihr was to prevail well into the period of the Thirty Years War.

The introduction of the Reformation into this area was to have important effects both on Colmar's ecclesiastical politics and on the city's religious climate. Its far-reaching political effect was to counter-balance much of the growing anti-Lutheran influence exerted by the nearby Habsburg-Austrian Regency of Ensisheim and, later, to mitigate part of the influence of the Habsburg vassals established as Bailiffs of Haguenau following the year 1558.[9] Thus, the Colmar authorities could exercise more autonomy in their ecclesiastical policy.

On the doctrinal level, the effect of the Reformation in Horbourg-Riquewihr was more direct. Following the year 1535, the Württemberg ministers of the neighboring villages began to convert a growing number of *Colmariens* to Protestantism or at least succeeded in awakening their interest in evangelical worship. This influence, as we shall see, greatly increased when, in 1552, the immediately adjacent town of Horbourg became an independent parish administered by Bartholomäus Westheimer (1499–1567). Furthermore, the specifically Reformed doctrinal influence exerted by Matthias Erb, Bartholomäus Westheimer and others on Colmar's population during the years before 1560 helped to spread the seeds of the later conversion of Colmar's Protestants from Lutheranism to Calvinism.[10]

Timotheus W. Röhrich, "Matthias Erb: Reformator von Reichenweier", in idem, Mitteilungen aus der Geschichte der evangelischen Kirche des Elsaßes, Vol. III (Strasbourg and Paris 1855), pp. 275–297; and *Heinrich Rocholl*, Matthias Erb: Ein elsässischer Glaubenszeuge aus der Reformationszeit, Beiträge zur Landes- und Volkskunde von Elsaß-Lothringen, Vol. VI, No. 26, Strasbourg 1900. However, Rocholl's appraisal still merits our interest because he draws attention to Erb's theological position. In this respect, see also *Ernst-Wilhelm Kohls*, ed., Die evangelischen Katechismen von Ravensburg (1546/1733) und Reichenweier (1547/1559), VKBW, series A, Vol. X (Stuttgart 1963), pp. 101–128.

[8] Cf. *Adam*, Evangelische Kirchengeschichte, pp. 306–315; and *Rocholl*, ibid., pp. 17–20.

[9] Around 1535, this counter-balancing effect was enhanced by the fact that in 1530, for a period to last twenty-eight years, the imperial Bailiwick of Haguenau had changed hands from Habsburg-Austria to the Palatinate. Cf. *Joseph Becker*, Geschichte der Reichslandvogtei im Elsaß von ihrer Einrichtung bis zu ihrem Übergang an Frankreich, 1273–1648 (Strasbourg 1905), pp. 85–90. Both Count Palatine Ludwig V, the *Oberlandvogt* from 1530–1544, and his successor's, Prince Elector Friedrich II's representative at Haguenau, Heinrich von Fleckenstein, Bailiff from 1544 to 1555, turned out in favor of the Reformation: see *Rocholl*, Die Einführung, p. 22.

[10] Cf. below, Chapter V.

B. THE ECCLESIASTICAL POLITICS OF THE CITY GOVERNMENT

The Reformation in Horbourg-Riquewihr was to have important consequences in the course of the Reformation movement in Colmar. It is no exaggeration to claim that it opened a new phase in the city's Reformation history.As far as the spread of the evangelical message is concerned, this new phase distinguished itself from the preceding one by a surprising lack of popular initiatives supporting evangelical preaching. Initially this was, as we have seen, mainly due to the Dean of St. Martin's and the council's hostility vis-à-vis the social and political under-currents of the Colmar Reformation movement.[11] As the years progressed (in fact up to the very year of the introduction of the Reformation) this lull in activity continued, largely because of the absence of a distinguished lay or clerical reformer who might have mobilized the parishioners in the city. Thus, the establishment of Protestant worship in 1575 was chiefly the work of the Protestant majority within the magistrate and council.[12]

My research suggests, as we shall see in more detail later, that long before the year 1575, more secretly than openly at first, a growing number of leading *Colmariens* already adhered to the Protestant faith.[13] These men were not more actively supportive of the Reformation before 1575, primarily because of the unambiguous religious policy of Emperor Ferdinand, particularly his vigilance as holder of the imperial Bailiwick of Haguenau from 1558 until his death in 1564. In 1558, Habsburg-Austria, with the manifest intention of intensifying its control over the religious politics of the ten Alsatian imperial cities organized within the *Decapolis*[14], recalled the Bailiwick from Ottheinrich, Prince-elector of the Palatinate, who had embraced Protestantism.[15], If, following the treaty of Nuremberg of 1532[16] and the take-over of the Bailiwick of Haguenau by the Palatine Prince-electors in 1530, all these later pressures were as of yet largely nonexistent, then we must ask the question: Why did religious change not occur between 1535 and 1555, when there were ostensibly less obstacles which might have prevented the Colmar authorities from introducing the Reformation?

Since 1528, the magistrate and council had shown themselves exceedingly loyal to the religious mandates issued by the Emperor regarding Protestantism. They had expulsed both obstinate Protestants and Anabaptists[17] and, through a series of municipal mandates, had threatened stiff prosecution for blasphemy and swearing. But the leading *Colmariens* were not content with the effects of these measures alone: in fact, they

[11] Cf. above, p. 67.

[12] I agree, in this respect, with the analysis of *Jürgen Bücking*, Johann Rasser (ca. 1535–1594) und die Gegenreformation im Oberelsaß, RST, Vol. CI (Münster/Westphalia 1970), pp. 18–35.

[13] The first indication to this effect is dated February 12, 1560: AAEB, A 41, 31b (Letter addressed to the Bishop of Basel by the chapter of St. Martin).

[14] Cf. the two letters addressed to the Colmar authorities by the Regency of Ensisheim in 1556, menacing grave consequences should Colmar undertake any change in religious matters: AMC, GG 29a, 18 and 19.

[15] See *Barbara Kurze*, Kurfürst Ott Heinrich: Politik und Religion in der Pfalz, 1556–1559, SVRG, No. 174 (Gütersloh 1956), pp. 11–14, 67–72.

[16] For the meaning of the Nuremberg "religious peace" of 1532, cf. *Stephan Skalweit*, Reich und Reformation, Propyläen Bibliothek der Geschichte (Berlin 1967), pp. 262–3.

[17] Cf. above , pp. 69–70.

thought at this juncture that an inner reform of the city church should supplement these secular actions. When the debauchery of one Hans Fritsch – an Augustinian friar – was discovered in 1537, they reacted with severity and concern:[18] among other injunctions, the authorities forbid the Augustinian friars to leave their premises and ordered them to entrust all outside transactions to a lay administrator.[19] Ensuing protests by Hans Fritsch himself, as well as by the Prior Johannes Hoffmeister and the head of the order's province, Conrad Treger, proved of no avail. The magistrate and council showed little willingness to modify their order. On the contrary, they were determined to profit from the monks' embarrassment by elaborating their grievances concerning monastic life in the city in a series of articles.

In the introduction of this document, the city government emphasized that it had so far enforced all imperial mandates against Lutherans and Anabaptists and, thus, in reforming lay discipline, had expected to influence the city's regular clergy to improve their conduct as well. Quite inversely, however, the monks not only continued to violate their rules and vows but also went on opposing their own superiors. In addition, the government reproached them for their neglect in the celebration of worship and for their slander of doctrinal adversaries in their predication. Furthermore, the monks were reprimanded for not restricting their constant strolling-about in town, which highly displeased the authorities. Magistrate and council, when asked to explain this series of accusations, responded that a reform of lay discipline necessarily corresponded to a reform of clerical conduct. They were, thus, not content to confine their rule to an enforcement of morality merely within the lay community. Consequently, they decided to issue the following decree:[20]

1. The monks are advised to live a life in honor of God, i. e., in chastity, by singing, reading, praying and by observing the fast.
2. In prohibiting their strolling around town, the magistrate and council order the monks to entrust their financial transactions to their city supervisors (*Pfleger*) or to a lay administrator.
3. The city government refrains from a wholesale prohibition of masses and sermons celebrated and preached by monks outside their monasteries; however, it demands that these take place before lunch-time and that, on such occasions, the monks leave their premises in groups of two or more.
4. In order to suppress another impropriety, the authorities stipulate that the father-confessors of the city's nuns should be elderly and pious friars and they should lodge with their fellow friars rather than at the convents.
5. As for the continued concubinage practiced by certain monks, these friars should stay in their monasteries and cease to meet their mistresses.[21]

[18] Regarding the "Hans Fritsch affair", see *Adeodatus Vermeulen*, Der Augustiner Konrad Treger: Die Jahre seines Provinzialates (1518–1542), (Rome 1962), pp. 123–5.

[19] AMC, GG 98, 2–5.

[20] AMC, GG 146, 1 (July 19, 1538).

[21] The municipal mandate against concubinage issued on July 26, 1528, (AMC, BB 44, p. 42) apparently had not had the success originally intended: cf. also above, pp. 64–5. Next to the concubinage practiced by the Augustinian friar Hans Fritsch, cited above, another *cause célèbre* of Colmar's 1530's was the

6. As for the slandering of adversaries in sermons and writings, the authorities consider it an offense against the extant imperial mandates and disadvantageous to their good reputation.[22] They therefore order that all preachers in town are to preach the Word of God clearly, according to the Holy Scripture and in agreement with the imperial mandates. In doing so, the preachers are "to refrain from further unnecessary babbling".[23]
7. Although the city government has already instructed the monasteries years ago not to admit novices without previously having informed the secular authorities, this order has been ignored by them. Thus, the government repeats its old demand.

The last Article of the monastic mandate of July 19, 1538, contained the only written reference to similar earlier stipulations. Indeed, thirteen years before, on May 11, 1525, several grievances listed in 1538 were voiced jointly by the council, council of jurors and by the temporary communal commitee constituted around that time. The mandate of 1525 also contained stipulations regarding the nuns' father-confessors, the recruitment policy of the monasteries and secular administrators to be imposed upon the religious establishments, as reiterated in Articles Two, Four and Seven of the mandate of 1538.[24]

The fact that in 1538 the authorities saw themselves compelled to repeat their old demands indicates that following the events of 1525, the friars, like Colmar's secular clergy, had been able to redress most of the infringements upon their autonomy decreed on May 11, 1525. Yet, the significant lack of complaints about the convents in the grievances of 1538 indicates that the city government had at least been successful in preserving the whole extent of its authority established over the city's nuns in 1525.

Thus, the link between the two monastic mandates of 1525 and 1538 evidences the government's continued efforts and its determination to increase and expand its control over the religious orders established in town, even though in 1538 no manifest popular pressure from below forced it to assume this role. Moreover, the differences between the two mandates delineate the traditional position of the council's monastic policy which, in 1525, had been radicalized by public pressure. Significantly enough, the mandate of

relationship entertained by the Franciscan Guardian Jacob Einfalt with the wife of Jörg Bartenstein, and whose denouncement may have contributed to Einfalt's decision to leave Colmar for Würzburg: cf. AMC, FF 355, 94 and 95. See also *August Hertzog*, „Die letzten Jahre des Colmarer Barfüsserklosters und Jakob Einfalt aus Geberschweier, dessen letzter Guardian", Jb. GSL, XVII (1901), 113–149. Hertzog was unaware of this affair.

[22] AMC, GG 146, 1: " ... "Zum sechsten. Als ouch ettlich ordens lut, zuzitten si das predig Ampt versehen, jn ein solichen mispruch komen, das si es nit zufriden, die laster vnd das vnrecht (wie dann jr Ampt erfordert), jn gemein zu stroffen, sonder düttendt mit Namenn vff sonders personen mit so groben schmechlichen worten vnd schrifften, die vns nit allein zu nochteil, sonder wider allen Inhalt keiserlichen Mandaten vund des heiligen Richs vsgangen Abschiden". This is, in all likelihood, a reference to the "Dialogorum libri duo ... ", published in 1538 by the Augustinian Prior Johannes Hoffmeister: see *Nikolaus Paulus*, Der Augustinermönch Johannes Hoffmeister: Ein Lebensbild aus der Reformationszeit (Freiburg i. Br. 1891), p. 384.

[23] AMC, GG 146, 1: "Deshalb .... will ein Erbarer Rhat fürtherhin von allen predicanten alhie das wort gotes lüter clar nach dem text, vnd wie das die key [serlichen] Mandaten vnnd Abschid vermegen gepredigt, vnd damit alle vnutze vnotwendige geschwetz abgestelt haben".

[24] The articles of the monastic mandate of May 11, 1525, are listed in the Liber orte seditionis: AMC, EE 7, 1, fol. 94v–60r. The same text is also contained in: AMC, EE 7, 4. Cf. also above, pp. 55–6.

1538, unlike the earlier document, does not comprise any speculative considerations on an eventual dissolution of the monasteries. It also lacks any call for a confiscation of monastic goods, although in 1538 the authorities continued to insist on an extension of their control over the regular clergy's economic transactions, which it had apparently been unable to enforce through earlier stipulations.

The Seven Articles summarized above were presented to the city's monasteries in July, 1538. The demands contained therein were immediately accepted by the Franciscans and in part by the Dominicans, although they refused to subscribe to Articles Two and Seven. The Prior and the head of the province of the Augustinian friars, however, responded with a wholesale rejection of the mandate.[25] Unfortunately, we do not know how and if the conflict thus created was resolved.

The authorities' ecclesiastical intervention of 1538 was only the beginning of a series of similar reform acts. In the following year, the magistrate and council turned their interest toward the preaching at the collegial church of St. Martin with the intention of improving its standard through the creation of an endowed preachership.[26] Based on negotiations with the chapter of St. Martin's, they came up with the following plan: the preacher to be entrusted with the new preachership was to be chosen by a committee composed jointly of canons and councillors; he was to be salaried jointly by the chapter and the council on the basis of a four to six years' contract; he was to be absolved, by the general of his order, of the obligation of wearing the cowl; and was to be permitted to lodge in a preacher's house furnished by the city, rather than at the monastery of his order.[27] These very specific arrangements reveal that the choice had already been made: it had fallen on Johann Fabri, preacher of the Dominican order in the imperial city of Wimpfen.[28]

[25] AMC, GG 146 (Reverse side).

[26] It is rather surprising that the *Colmariens* came up with this idea as comparatively late as that. In Strasbourg, the endowed preachership of the eloquent and influential preacher Geiler von Kaysersberg (1445–1510) had been created many decades ago, in 1479: *Miriam U. Chrisman*, Strasbourg and the Reform: A study in the process of change (New Haven and London 1967), pp. 68–73; and *Francis Rapp*, Réformes et Réformation à Strasbourg (1450–1525), Collection de l'Institut des Hautes Etudes Alsaciennes, Vol. XXIII (Paris 1974), pp. 150–160. Gerhard Pfeiffer reports that by the end of the 15th century only two imperial cities in Swabia had not created an endowed preachership: cf. idem, "Das Verhältnis von politischer und kirchlicher Gemeinde in den deutschen Reichsstädten", in Staat und Kirche im Wandel der Jahrhunderte, ed. by Walter P. Fuchs (Stuttgart, Berlin, Cologne and Mainz 1966), p. 86.

[27] Cf. AMC, GG 39, 28 and 29.

[28] See the biography of Johann Fabri in *Nikolaus Paulus*, Die deutschen Dominikaner im Kampfe gegen Luther (1518–1563), Erläuterungen und Ergänzungen zu Janssens Geschichte des deutschen Volkes, Vol. IV, Books 1 and 2 (Freiburg i. Br. 1903), pp. 232–266. The reason Fabri was to be dispensated from having to wear his cowl is explained by *Ammann* Hans Vogler of Riquewihr in one of his letters addressed to Joachim Vadianus of Saint Gall: Johann Fabri "ist zwaymal vertriben worden des evangeliums halb und offenlich geredt: werd er noch 1-mal vertriben, so well er die kutten an ain boum hencken. Also wirbt der rath gen Rom umb ain dispensation; kompt bald. Ist im von predicanten geraten worden, gůtter hoffnung, Schletstatt und ander stett och hernach komen": Vadianische Briefsammlung, Vol. V, ed. by Emil Arbenz and Hermann Wartmann, Mitteilungen zur Vaterländischen Geschichte, Vol. XXIX (St. Gall 1903), p. 568 (Letter dated August 9, 1538). The chancellor of the Bishop of Basel, Dr. Lucas Klett, helped to secure the desired dispensation: cf. AMC, GG 39, Nos. 22, 18, 10, 9, 5, 11, 30, 20 and 16 (in chronological order). A preaching schedule for Johann Fabri is contained in: AMC, GG 39, 24 (Patri Lectoris Joannis fabrj status et ordo contionandj).

Johann Fabri began preaching in Colmar in the Summer of 1539. Through his eloquence, he quickly gained a considerable reputation.[29] As early as February, 1540, the Bishop of Strasbourg requested the loan of Fabri's service as a preacher during a religious colloquium held at Saverne.[30] Fabri preached in Colmar until about 1545, after which he left for the neighboring city of Sélestat, where he was entrusted with the function of Prior and preacher of the Dominicans.[31]

By creating Fabri's preachership in 1539, the authorities simultaneously pursued two objectives. They intended to remediate the "damage" already caused by the increasing outside Protestant influence, and they wanted to assist the chapter in restoring some of its lost income – knowing full well that the reform of worship and the reform of lay discipline were concomitant factors in the pursuit of this second goal.[32]

After 1545, the preachership created in 1539 seems to have ceased to exist. In any case, following about 1547 the magistrate and council seem not to have dealt regularly with the salary of any preacher. Therefore, we can assume that after Fabri's departure, the pulpit of St. Martin's again belonged to the regular *Leutpriester* (common priest), who owed his income exclusively to the yield of a prebend furnished by the chapter.[33] However, the authorities' interest in the preaching at St. Martin's continued. In 1549, they intervened with the chapter's allegedly insufficient provisions for the preaching during Lenten fast.Facing the chapter's unwillingness to cover the cost resulting from their demand for the preaching of additional sermons, the authorities decided to pay an additional salary to the Lent preachers.[34]

[29] *Ammann* Hans Vogler of Riquewihr reports: "Zů Colmar ist ain gwaltiger Predigermünch, der Christum trülich prediget. Ich hab in gehörtt zu Rappoltzschwihr [Ribeauvillé] .... Der ganz rath handhapt in. Hatt drümal zů Enßheim [Ensisheim] vorm regiment gepredigt.":Vadianische Briefsammlung, Vol. V, ibid.

[30] AMC, GG 39, 21 (Letter dated February 5, 1540). The Colmar government responded by saying that it would agree to send Fabri, but that the Bishop should allow Fabri to return at the earliest possible date because the *Colmariens* were much inclined to listen to his sermons: *Paulus*, Die deutschen Dominikaner, p. 236.

[31] Cf. the letter addressed to Fabri in Sélestat on St. Ambrose's Day (April 4, 1547) by Barbara Stör, the Subprioress of the Unterlinden convent: AMC, GG 72, 5. A transcription of this letter is offered by *Isidore Beuchot*, "Das frühere Kloster Unterlinden zu Colmar im 15. und 16. Jahrhundert", Colmarer Katholischer Kirchen-Kalender, XII (1918), pp. 67–8.

[32] In a letter addressed to the General of the Dominican order on May 6, 1539, the Colmar authorities observed that the spread of the Reformation in Colmar's neighborhood had created heresy and discord among the population. They hoped that the creation of the endowed preachership would help remediate this situation: "... Conantes diutius ... eiusmodi pestes a Republica nostra declinare, atque arcere: qui quasi in medio pugnę, inter Basileam heluetię, ac Argentinam Alsatię vrbes, germanię siti: Preterea Comitatu Wirtenbergensium contigui": AMC, GG 39, 22.

[33] From 1547 to 1569, when the authorities inaugurated a new endowed preachership at the hospital church (see below, p. 120), the common priests or *plebani* at St. Martin's were: Vitus Gessler (1547 to ca. 1549.: ADHR, 4G, 3-IIb [1547]; AMC, GG 26, 19); Christian Schwager (1549 to ca. 1550: ADHR, 4G, 2–4 [Notebook entitled "Volgt ..."], fol. 7v; AMC, FF 336a, p. 1); Jacob Babę (1551; d. about October, 1551: ADHR, 4G, 5–1 [September 6, 1551]; AMC, GG 20, 5); Magister Jacob Klein (1553 to 1555; in 1556 he was appointed Dean: ADHR, 4G, 5–1 [March 5, 1553]; ADHR, 4G, 3–11a [June 23, 1556]); and Theobald Vogel (1555 to ca. 1569?: ADHR, 4G, 2–4 [Notebook entitled "Volgt ..."] fol. 8v; ADHR, 4G, 5–2 [March 13 and July, 1559]; ADHR, 4G 3–11b [December 12, 1562]; AMC, GG 26, 26 (AGJanuary 29, 1568]). See also above, pp. 28–30.

[34] ADHR, 4G, 5–1 (Capitulum Kalendae Februarii, 1549). They repeated a similar intervention in 1557: AMC, GG 26, 5.

In 1540, the politics of intervention practiced by the magistrate and council vis-à-vis the local church culminated in the "Hoffmeister Affair". Through his publications and sermons, Johannes Hoffmeister (*ca.* 1509–1547), the Prior of the Colmar Augustinians and head of the order's province, had won a solid reputation in Alsace and beyond.[35] Frequently involved in theological controversy, he always handled his task very conscientiously: a loyal Catholic, he nevertheless demonstrated no interest in ignoring the abuses plaguing the Roman church of his day, nor did he lack certain traits of the mediator.[36] But, as a theologian of controversy, Hoffmeister was never ready to compromise in his attack against doctrinal adversaries. It is therefore not too surprising that in 1538, Hoffmeister and his work "*Dialogorum libri duo* ..." seem to have attracted the authorities's criticism.[37] In 1539, Hoffmeister felt urged to reply to Martin Luther's "*Articles of Smalkald*" through a pamphlet entitled "*Warhaftige Endeckung* ..."[38] where he showed himself rather too zealous in his attack against Luther and his party. The result was open conflict between the Augustinian Prior and the Colmar authorities, who, in the Spring of 1540, had Hoffmeister's book confiscated. The Prior's request to have his pamphlet released and restored to him went unanswered; likewise the series of repeated angry requests which continued until 1543.[39]

The intervention of 1540 marks the climax of the city government's politics of ecclesiastical reform inaugurated in 1537. From 1540 through 1555 and beyond, no similar initiatives took place. This development does not, however, point to an abrupt change in the religious attitude of Colmar's leadership: in 1547, upon request of the chapter, the authorities severely reproached the parishioners for their negligence in attending Catholic worship[40], and in 1554, they showed no qualms in decreeing a general prohibition (for all *Colmariens*) on attendance of Lutheran worship in the neighboring towns and villages.[41] Although, in these ecclesiastic interventions in the period following 1540, their function was more of a passively preventionist rather than actively reformist kind, the authorities' continued and lively interest in the quality of preaching offered at St. Martin's demonstrates that they had not entirely abandoned their old policy of

[35] *Paulus*, Der Augustinermönch, p. 17. See also Caspar Hedio's letter addressed to Matthias Erb on May 9, 1540: "De Colmariensi monacho idem sentio quod tu. Is est apud quem Episcopus Argenti consilia capit contra concionatores Argenti". See BNUS/Th. B., 671, fol. 154.

[36] In this respect, more precisely on the doctrinal level, *August von Druffel*, Der Elsäßer Augustinermönch Johannes Hoffmeister und seine Korrespondenz mit dem Ordensgeneral Hieronymus Seripando, Abhandlungen der königlichen bayerischen Akademie der Wissenschaften, III. Historische Klasse, Vol. XIV, Abteilung I (Munich 1878), p. 141, has observed a certain parenthood between Hoffmeister's interpretation of the dogma of justification and the position advocated by the Catholic reformer, Cardinal G. Contarini. The refutation of von Druffel by *Paulus*, ibid., pp. 208–4, is not definitive, since it is rather formalistic and thus fails to deal more than peremptorily with the actual substance of Hoffmeister's doctrine. Therefore, the question needs further investigation.

[37] Cf. above, n. 22.

[38] Warhafftige endeckung unnd widerlegung deren artickel, die M. Luther auff das concilium zu schicken vnd darauff beharren furgenommen, republished by *Hans Volz*, ed., Drei Schriften gegen Luthers Schmalkaldische Artikel von Cochläus, Witzel und Hoffmeister, Corpus Catholicorum, Vol. XVIII (Münster/Westphalia 1932), pp. 116–187.

[39] AMC, GG 100, 2–6, Hoffmeister's letters are printed in *Volz*, ed., ibid., pp. 190–7.

[40] ADHR, 4 G, 5–1 (Capitulum Kalendae Martii, 1547).

[41] ibid., (Capitulum Kalendae Augusti, 1554).

reform. If the implementation of this policy now ceased to appear in the old form, this was also very likely due to the disastrous plague of 1541, and to the wars of 1546/7 and 1552, which preoccupied Colmar's leadership.

As for the authorities' willingness to further the improvement of both lay and clerical conduct, they once more expressed their determination to do so around 1545, by voicing their particular concern about the decrease in attendance at the city's Latin school. In their view, this regrettable development was due either to some parents' ignorance of the benefits in honor, utility and welfare for the entire community (as well as for their own families) resulting from their childrens' attendance at the Latin school, or, it was caused by some families' incapability of furnishing the mandatory tuition for their boys, whom they therefore preferred to send to the less expensive German school. In order to remedy this deplorable situation, the government decreed that henceforth all tuition should be abolished at the Latin school and that the schoolmaster should be compensated for the loss of income thus incurred by a raise in salary. The decree concluded with the observation that "from now on no city boy should be prevented from achieving the highest honor – that of being able to speak Latin".[42]

This uncommon measure was the outcome of more than a decade's increased attention to the welfare of the city's schools. Before 1530, Colmar's school had been a rather insignificant choir-school, closely attached to the chapter, which seems to have done nothing to raise the standard of teaching.[43] Thus, in 1530, for the first time in that century, the magistrate and council interfered with the chapter's authority over the school to improve the schoolmaster's salary. Hand in hand with this and similar subsequent interventions went a growing secularization of the school. This tendency is clearly visible in the different contemporaneous listings of the teacher's salary: the city's, as compared to the chapter's, contribution to the schoolmaster's pay significantly increased from 1530 to 1545.[44]

[42] AMC, BB 51 (Eidbuch 1545–63), pp. 264–6, especially p. 266: "... Das nun hinfüro eins jeden bürgers kindt die latinisch schul for sonder gelt vnd holtz, vnd also vergebens vnd vmb sonst besuchen, vnd nit zur vrsach nemen, Ire kinder obgehorter bswerden halben den tutschen lermeistern zu befelhen, das wenigst bj demselben zubegriffen, vnd das höchst, als latin reden, fallen lassen". The dating of this decree as "ca. 1545" is an estimate.

[43] Cf. above, pp. 35–6.

[44] Cf. AMC, GG 190, 5 (School negotiations of June, 1530); AMC, GG 190, 6 and 4 (School negotiations of January, 1536, and concurrent list of schoolmaster's pay); AMC, GG 190, 3 (List of April, 1538); AMC, GG 190, 19 (List of July, 1538); AMC, BB 51 (Eidbuch 1545–63), p. 266 (List of ca. 1545).

[45] AMC, GG 190, 3 (April 6, 1538): "Vnser fruntschaft vnd alle getreuckeit beuor, Hochgelerter gunstiger herr vnd fründt. Vß vrsachen, wir diser zit eins geschickgten schulmeisters jn mangel, habent wir vnsern mitrathfündt Mathiam gintzer ... abgefertigt, vnd buelch vch pitlich anzukeren, vns vff jemanden, so der schul mit kunst vnd gutten sitten vorsein mog, zu dutten. Deshalb vnd dwil wir vch für den gelertsten vnd berumbsten haben vnd erkennen, so langt vmb gemeines nutzes willen vnser gantz fründlich pit, dem vnsern ... anleitung geben, wo er vns einen solchen Mann bekumen ... mochte ...". Undoubtedly, the foundation of a humanist Gymnasium at Strasbourg in the same year must have increased the Colmar authorities' concern for their own city schools. Cf. *Anton Schindling*, Humanistische Hochschule und freie Reichsstadt: Gymnasium und Akademie in Strasbourg, 1538–1621, Veröffentlichungen des Instituts für Europäische Geschichte Mainz, Vol. LXXVII (Wiesbaden 1977), pp. 30–3.

Based on this development, the city government also gradually strove to laicize the education offered at the Latin school. In 1538, in an attempt to improve the standard of teaching, it freed the schoolmaster from further attendance of St. Martin's choir during weekdays. At the same time, in search of a learned and qualified new teacher, it consulted the Freiburg humanist, Heinrich Loriti (Glareanus).[45] He may have been responsible for sending the council's delegate, Matthias Güntzer, on to Rottenburg on the Neckar and to Rottweil, where Güntzer managed to recruit Master Valentin Tengen of Mettern (Valentin Meternus) as Colmar's new schoolmaster.[46] Meternus, who remained im Colmar from 1538 to 1542, was in turn successful in urging the council to carry through the overdue separation of the German from the Latin school.[47] In the following year, therefore, the Latin school was moved to a new building – an event proudly praised by a slogan akin to humanist and Lutheran concerns alike.[48] The evidence regarding the authorities' involvement with the city's schools in the period after 1545 is scarce: from the chapter's growing reluctance to acknowledge its own obligation to contribute to the Latin teacher's salary, however, one may reasonably assume that during this period, the secular government's control over the Latin school was still increasing.[49] Thus, in 1575, following the introduction of the Reformation, when the Latin school was ultimately taken away from the chapter, the secular clergy's repeated attempts to regain control of this school stood on rather shaky grounds.[50]

A brief analysis of the magistrate's and council's ecclesiastical policies for the period from 1535 to 1547[51] calls for the following observations:

1. An important principle in these policies is the authorities' conviction that the morality of the clergy should correspond to that of the laymen, and both should be enforced by the secular power. This idea resulted from the perception of spiritual duties that the leading *Colmariens* shared. They regarded their city as a corporate commonalty, within which all estates should live in honor of God. Consequently, in their monastic mandate of 1538, the magistrate and council declared that they considered it their proper responsibility to watch over the daily discipline and morality of the community. They shared the citizenry's claim, voiced so unequivocally in 1525, that the clergy was an integral part of their community.[52] Important elements of laicization can thus be

[46] In chronological order: AMC, GG 193, 7; GG 193, 19; GG 193, 12; GG 193, 8. (The name of "Meternus" may refer to Metternich near Koblenz).

[47] AMC. BB 45 (1515–42), pp. 100–1 (September 14, 1538); also AMC, GG 190, 20.

[48] The epigram on the new school building read: "Aedes has pueris cvr [a patrum pia] foecundi ingenii condidit incolis discendi [linguam] Lati[n]am, palladium et viam plantanda est etenim posteritas bona aediles fuerant mvst [?] Georgius cognomen cvi erat parvo Ieronomo et Consul Fabius Nostrae Hieronymus vrbis dulce decus summa tenens loca. M[D] XXXIX": *Andreas Waltz*, ed., Sigmund Billings kleine Chronik der Stadt Colmar (Colmar 1891), p. 63. (Waltz's rendition probably distorted some of the original spelling).

[49] Cf. ADHR, 4 G, 5–1 (Capitulum Kalendae Julii, 1548; Kalendae Septembris, 1552; Kalendae Decembris, 1553); and ADHR, 4 G, 5–2 (Capitulum Kalendae Augusti, 1550).

[50] cf. below. pp. 159–160.

[51] The year 1547 marks the end of the era of active reforms. It is Hieronymus Boner's last term as *Obristmeister*. As we shall see, Boner was the prime author of the policy of reform in question. 1546–47 is also the year of death of the influential city-clerk Johannes Hummel, and of his friend Johannes Hoffmeister, Colmar's last qualified preacher before the installation of Jacob Klein, 1553.

[52] This ideal and its implementation in ecclesiastic politics was not new: cf. above, pp. 51 and 54–5.

found both in the monastic ordinance of 1538 and in the school reform decisions of the late 1530's.

2. Because of the apparent coherency and discipline displayed by the chapter of St. Martin under Jacob Carpentarii's leadership (Dean from 1502 to his death in 1541/2) and taking into consideration the new political power of the chapter, (as experienced by the secular government in the late 1520's), the magistrate and council did not dare to impose an ordinance upon the secular clergy similar to the one of 1538, even though during the late 1540's and early 1550's such a measure clearly would have been justified. They attempted, however, to influence the preaching of the secular clergy, and the evidence demonstrates that from 1539 to the end of the 1550's, they continuously considered preaching the chief duty of the clergy.[53]

3. Let us emphasize, therefore, the great importance and value the authorities attached to the preaching of the Gospel. Their attitude reveals somewhat of a withdrawal from the mystery of the eucharistic sacrament and the assumption of a rather "rationalist" view.

4. The obedience to the religious mandates issued by the Emperor, which defined the framework and limits of evangelical preaching (recommended in the ordinance of 1538), also served as justification for other attempts of the city government to bring about ecclesiastical reform. On the one hand, the pronounced commitment to this loyalty mirrors the problems attached to any resistance against the superior authority – then regarded as instituted directly by God. Only the Peace of Augsburg of 1555 was to untangle some of these problems.[54] On the other hand, the preoccupation of Colmar's leaders with their declamatory loyalty toward the Emperor's religious mandates was a cautionary maneuver, brought about by the vigilance of the Regency of Ensisheim.

5. The chief consequence of this loyalty was the authorities' continued attachment to the old faith. During the 1530's and 1540's, this was, in turn, reinforced by:

a. the frequent close cooperation between the city government and the secular clergy, as, for instance, in the creation of the endowed preachership in 1539;
b. the ties of kin and friendship existing between part of the clergy and the lay leadership, as in the case of Johannes Hoffmeister and the city-clerk Johannes Hummel[55], or the canon Augustin Güntzer and his brother, the councillor Matthias Güntzer;[56] or the cantor Theobald Klett and his brother-in-law, the city physician Sebastian Austrius;[57]
c. the influence of Johann Fabri as a resourceful preacher;

[53] Cf., for instance, the transactions of 1556–58, documenting the concurrent negotiations concerning the income of the Dean: ADHR, 4 G, 3–11a; and AMC, GG 27, 2.

[54] Cf. below, pp. 94–5.

[55] *Eugen Waldner*, ed., „Vier Briefe von Johannes Hoffmeister", ZGORh, XLV (1891), 172–7. Furthermore, Johannes Hoffmeister, the canon Diepolt Klett and the city councillor Hieronymus Boner all belonged to the circle of friends grouped around the powerful Abbot of Murbach, Johannes Rudolf Stör: Cf. *A. Gatrio*, Die Abtei Murbach im Elsaß, Vol. II (Strasbourg 1895), pp. 192–201. The canon Diepolt Klett was in turn a relative of the influential city physician Sebastian Austrius (Oesterricher): cf. below, p. 88.

[56] *Philippe Mieg*, "Notes biographiques et généalogiques sur les Güntzer de Colmar, de Sélestat et de Riquewihr", Annuaire de Colmar (1974/75), 161.

[57] Cf. below, p. 88.

d. the considerable authority of such clergymen as the Dean Jacob Carpentarii (d. 1541/42), the Prior Johannes Hoffmeister, or the learned Dominicans Balthasar Werlin (1521–65) and Wilhelm Hammer (d. *ca.* 1564);[58]

6. A seemingly new element introduced itself in the ecclesiastical policy of the authorities through their confiscation of the anti-Lutheran pamphlet authored by the Prior Johannes Hoffmeister. Why did they intervene in this case?

It is unlikely that they would have confiscated the book in question simply on the grounds that the author attacked Luther and his partisans, although prevention of further discord among the citizens may have played a role in their decision.[59] Based on the evidence analyzed above, I am convinced that the act of confiscation does not prove that many councillors were on their way to embracing the Protestant faith, as was claimed by Heinrich Rocholl.[60] Had this been the case, the magistrate and council would have taken a less reserved position in the negotiations in 1538 with Thomas Gyerfalck and Leonhard Verula of Basel, who, as former Colmar friars now turned Protestant, demanded financial support from Colmar's Augustinian monastery.[61] It is also improbable that personal motives should have incited the authorities to sabotage the publication of Hoffmeister's work, as was supposed by Nikolaus Paulus.[62] The only aspect reasonably evidenced by the authorities' action was their willingness and determination to play the role of mediator.

This determination to mediate was not a new element in Colmar's ecclesiastical policy. It is, in fact, possible to find its early traces in Article Six of the monastic ordinance of 1538, which outlined the officially sanctioned way of preaching the Gospel. During the phase of the Colmar pre-Reformation period in question, we can observe the gradual growth in prominence of a tendency toward mediation, which increasingly determined the official church policy. The magistrate and council saw nothing in this role that was incompatible with the other pre-eminent factor of their ecclesiastical actions – the loyalty vis-à-vis the imperial religious mandates. This tendency towards mediation also clearly points to a certain amount of influence exerted by humanist thought on the attitude of the leading *Colmariens*, as is, for instance, evidenced by their school-reform politics of the 1530's and 1540's. It was most prominent in the case of Hieronymus Boner, whom I consider to have been the prime author of this policy of mediation. In order to have become promoted into his leading position, Boner's stand and, thus, his humanist commitment, must have found a favorable resonance among his

[58] See *Paulus*, Die deutschen Dominikaner, pp. 181–6.

[59] A reference to such discord is contained in the Colmar letter addressed to the General of the Dominican order, cited above, n. 32.

[60] *Rocholl*, Die Einführung, p. 75. The same erroneous point was also made by *C[harles]-A[uguste] Hanauer*, „Les Historiens de l'établissement du Protestantisme à Colmar", RCA, I (1859), 257.

[61] Regarding these negotiations, cf. *Vermeulen*, Der Augustiner Konrad Treger, pp. 32–38. On Thomas Gyerfalck's early career in Freiburg (Switzerland) and following the year 1524 in Basel, as a colleague of the reformer Johannes Oecolampadius, cf. *Vermeulen*, ibid., pp. 71–73; and *Rudolf Wackernagel, Geschichte der Stadt Basel, Vol. III (Basel 1924), p. 340. There is no extant additional information on* Leonhard Verula. While, in the late 1510's, Gyerfalck never returned to Colmar from his university studies in Cologne and Basel, Leonhard Verula, in turn, must have fled from Colmar in the late 1520's or early 1530's. Cf. above, p. 70.

[62] *Paulus*, Der Augustinermönch, p. 15.

colleagues in the city government. Therefore, if we now direct our attention to Boner's career, we will simultaneously gain an awareness of the general intellectual climate reigning in the Colmar of his day. Some additional observations on Matthias Güntzer, Boner's successor as a humanist member of the city's magistrate, will delineate the extent to which Boner's policy of mediation found its continuation in the years 1547 to 1555.

C. HIERONYMUS BONER AND MATTHIAS GÜNTZER: THEIR INFLUENCE ON CITY POLITICS

We have seen above how, during the first decades ot the 16th century, the pursuit of humanist studies in Colmar was largely the domain of the clergy. The learned physician, Lorenz Fries (Phrysius), who practiced medicine in Colmar around 1518, before leaving the town for Strasbourg in the following year, was clearly an exception in this respect.[63] During the following decade, the main exponent of humanist scholarship in Colmar was again a man of the church and, as of yet, there seemed to be no layman who fully shared his enthusiasm for the "revival of antiquity" (P. Joachimsen). This man was Jacob Carpentarii, Dean of St. Martin's from 1502 to 1541/42, the treasures of whose library found the praise of Erasmus' disciple Beatus Rhenanus.[64]

More significant lay learnedness only took root in Colmar around 1530, as is shown, for instance, by the awakening of a growing lay interest in the quality of the city's public education. The historian will not encounter any notable humanists among the *Colmariens* of the following decades. However, as local personalities of some weight, such men as Hieronymus Boner and Matthias Güntzer were simultaneously and strongly influenced by humanist thought. Participating in city government during the religious conflict of the era, they played an instrumental role in Colmar's ecclesiastical politics. During the entire period from 1535 to 1555, Boner and Güntzer were members of the magistrate. Their humanist education led them to call for moderation in the religious dispute and motivated them to turn their energy toward the reform of the local Catholic church.[65]

[63] Cf. *Ernest Wickersheimer*'s article on Lorenz Fries in NDB, Vol. V, pp. 609–610.

[64] See *Adalbert Horawitz* and *Karl Hartfelder*, eds., Briefwechsel des Beatus Rhenanus (Leipzig 1886), pp. 282–3. Jacob Carpentarii (Zimmermann) was a student at Paris University from 1483 to 1485, where he graduated as M. A. In 1485, he entered the Faculty of Arts of Basel University "ad doctrinandum in via antiquorum". In 1489, he became a canon at St. Peter's in Basel, and was a professor of poetry there from 1489 to 1492. In 1491–92, he was Rector of Basel University. In 1502, he was appointed Dean of St. Martin's in Colmar, However, he only took personal residence in Colmar after 1526. A diplomat well versed in German, French and Latin, he served on several missions in the service of the city of Basel, of Duke Charles of Savoy and of the Bishop of Basel. In particular, he was dispatched by the latter to the Ratisbon convention in 1524 (cf. above, pp. 47–8), and to the important disputation of Baden (Switzerland) in 1526. He apparently died during, or shortly after, the plague of 1541. See Auctarium Parisiensis VI, col. 599, 1.21; col. 619, l.9; col. 620, l. 27; Matr. Basel, Vol. I, p. 186; *Wackernagel*, Geschichte der Stadt Basel, Vol. III, p. 194; Amtliche Sammlung der älteren eidgenössischen Abschiede, Vol. IV, Abt. Ia, ed. by Johannes Strickler (Brugg 1873), No. 362 ("Disputation zu Baden"), p. 931; and AMC, BB 45 (1522–76), p. 177–9. Cf. also above, pp. 28 and 47, n. 40.

[65] According to *Ern(e)st Staebelin,* „Bâle et l'Alsace", in L'Humanisme en Alsace, ed. by the Association Guillaume Budé (Paris 1939), p. 33, the humanist movement in Basel and in Alsace was situated "within the Christian church, and was a movement of Christian disposition and tendencies".

We are left uninformed about the year Hieronymus Boner was born.[66] In the city transactions he is mentioned for the first time in 1525, when he assumed the function of court clerk. From 1527 to 1551, he was a member of the magistrate and, as such, fulfilled the function of *Obristmeister* for a total of eleven annual terms.[67] During all these years, Boner's role was "one of a mediator and temporizer".[68] His reputation as a scholar rested upon his translation into the vernacular of such classics as Herodian, Plutarch, Justinus and Orosius.[69] Hieronymus Boner never wavered in his commitment to the Catholic faith; yet he was not opposed to contradicting the Pope and the Roman court in matters related to his cherished vision of the restoration of Christian unity. As is suggested unequivocally by the church politics implemented under his leadership, Boner was a typical representative of the so-called "*Via Media*".

What was the "*Via Media*"? The notion defines a position of mediation and conciliation assumed by those 16th century humanists who preferred not to align themselves with one or the other religious party. According to the Swiss historian Kurt Maeder[70], the *Via Media* position can best be circumscribed by the following three criteria:

1. The embracement of the great humanist vision of the "*Christianismus renascens*";[71]
2. The refutation of extremely partisan confessional positions because they could threaten the Christian peace;[72]
3. The conviction that a reconciliation of the confessional parties remained a real possibility – under the condition, however, that the willingness to keep the channels of communication open prevailed on both sides.[73]

[66] On Hieronymus Boner, cf. *Gustaf Wethly*, Hieronymus Boner: Leben, Werke und Sprache: Ein Beitrag zur elsäßischen Literaturgeschichte, Strasbourg 1892; *Fernand J. Heitz*, "Messire Jérôme Boner: Humaniste, diplomate et maire de Colmar", Annuaire de Colmar (1938), 111–134; and *Jacques Betz*, "Jérôme Boner, un humaniste colmarien devenu maire, diplomate et traducteur", Annuaire de Colmar (1975/76), 81–90; (1976/77), 57–66.

[67] *Lucien Sittler*, ed., Membres du Magistrat, Conseillers et maîtres des corporations de Colmar: Listes de 1408–1600, Publ. Arch. Colmar, Vol. III (Colmar 1964), p. 22.

[68] *Heitz*, "Messire Jérôme Boner", 115.

[69] *Lawrence S. Thompson*, "German Translations of the Classics between 1450 and 1550", Journal of English and Germanic Philology, XLII (1943), 355–360.

[70] *Kurt Maeder*, Die Via Media in der Schweizerischen Reformation: Studien zum Problem der Kontinuität im Zeitalter der Glaubensspaltung, ZBRG, Vol. II (Zürich 1970), p. 98.

[71] Cf. the salient summary of this vision given by *Augustin Renaudet*, Humanisme et Renaissance, Travaux d'Humanisme et Renaissance, Vol. XXX (Geneva 1958), pp. 168–169.

[72] Avoidance of *tumultus* was a major tenet of *Via Media* and Erasmian proposals for religious and ecclesiastical reform. In Colmar, it found its explicit expression in Article Six of the monastic mandate of 1538, directed in part against the offensive preaching of the regular clergy, which was regarded as a danger to public peace.

[73] This third aspect of the *Via Media* position came close to the concurrent attitude of Italian "Nicodemites", as described by *Delio Cantimori*, "Submission and conformity: 'Nicodemism' and the expectations of a conciliar solution to the religious question", in The Late Italian Renaissance, ed. by Eric Cochrane, Harper Torchbooks, No. 1481 (New York, Evanston, Ill., and London 1970) pp. 244–265, although, in general, "Nicodemism" involved a secret commitment to the Protestant cause, which the northern *Via Media* was not ready to make. To my knowledge, only the historiography of the English Reformation operates with the concept of a Protestant *Via Media*: see, for instance, *John K. Yost*, "Protestant Reformers and the Humanist Via Media in the Early English Reformation", Journal of Medieval and Renaissance Studies, V (1975), 187–202. However, in ascertaining "that the via media of the official religious Reformation consisted of a Protestant humanism formulated in the distinctive spiritual and moral teaching of the English reformers" (especially of Richard Taverner), and in emphasizing that "the humanists

The representatives of the *Via Media* were cultivated men, influenced in one way or another by Renaissance humanism, and particularly by the thought of Erasmus of Rotterdam. The Upper Rhenish humanists Bonifacius Amerbach and Beatus Rhenanus, and the Lower Rhenish humanist politicians Johann von Vlatten and Conrad von Heresbach, were some of its more illustrious exponents.[74] But, beneath the rank and file of these celebrities, there were a fair number of personalities, less well known today, who all played an important role in the politics of different German cities while at the same time adhering to the vision and position of the *Via Media*.

Formally, these representatives of the *Via Media* were all Catholics. Nevertheless, the preservation of the Catholic church, in its existing form, was never one of their objectives. They preferred to envisage a *Restitutio Ecclesiae*, a restitution of the early Christian church, which had not yet experienced the excesses plaguing the Roman church of that time. Yet their vision, clearly evinced in Erasmus' popular work „*De amabili ecclesiae concordiae*" of 1533[75], did not allow them at any time to sanction the rupture between the old and new church. On the contrary, it kept alive in them a deep hope for reconciliation.[76]

Within the cultivated *milieu* of the Upper Rhine area, Erasmian humanism – as expounded by many disciples of Erasmus, such as Beatus Rhenanus (to name only the most eminent) – must have produced more intensive repercussions than extant sources suggest to the twentieth century historian.[77] The latter has often been misinformed by partisan confessional historiography which, by its nature, tends to underestimate the role played by men committed to the *Via Media*.[78] Rhenish mysticism in the 14th and 15th centuries, so prominent in Colmar and Strasbourg, as well as the influence of the *Devotio Moderna* on the Alsatian humanist circles[79] had helped to prepare the ground for a fertile reception of Erasmus' Christian humanism in Alsace.[80]

who served the government in the Reformation of the 1530's followed the reformers in that respect and thus promoted a via media which was essentially the result of a Protestant humanism", Yost fails to present a conclusive definition of his concept of *Via Media*. Cf. *Yost*, ibid., 187 and 202.

[74] *Maeder*, Die Via Media; and *Anton Gail*, "Johann von Vlatten und der Einfluss des Erasmus von Rotterdam auf die Kirchenpolitik der vereinigten Herzogtümer", Düsseldorfer Jahrbuch, XVL (1951), 1–109.

[75] See *Robert Stupperich*, Der Humanismus und die Wiedervereinigung der Konfessionen, SVRG, No. 160 (Leipzig 1936), pp. 27–30; and *Bernd Moeller*, Deutschland im Zeitalter der Reformation, Vol. IV of Deutsche Geschichte, ed. by Joachim Leuschner (Göttingen 1977), pp. 108–9.

[76] It is very telling, in this respect, that the Montbéliard court chaplain should write to Joachim Vadianus on August 9, 1539, that the persecuted Lutherans of the Austrian town of Breisach on the Rhine could still find refuge in nearby Colmar: Vadianische Briefsammlung, Vol. V, ed. by Arbenz and Wartmann, p. 569.

[77] In Colmar, strong repercussions of this humanism show up, for instance, in the attempts at school reform of the 1530's and 1540's, as summarized above.

[78] See, for instance, August Franzen's justified criticism of the traditional historical assessment of the ecclesiastical policy pursued by the 16th century Dukes Johann and Wilhelm of Jülich-Cleves and their advisers: idem, "Das Schicksal des Erasmianismus am Niederrhein im 16. Jahrhundert", Historisches Jahrbuch, LXXXIII (1964), 84–7.

[79] Cf. *Lewis W. Spitz*, The Religious Renaissance of the German Humanists (Cambridge, Mass. 1963), pp. 8–9; and *M. Vansteenberghe*, "Influences Rhénanes", in L'Humanisme en Alsace, ed. by the Association Guillaume Budé (Paris 1939), pp. 10–27. For a further discussion of the impact of the *Devotio Moderna* on German humanism, cf. above, p. 13.

It was only later, in the course of increasing "confessionalization", originating toward the middle of the 16th century[81], that the *Via Media* gradually lost its *raison d'être*. Concomitantly, its representatives saw themselves progressively constrained to alignment with one or the other religious party. This move toward alignment is probably best exemplified by the case of Matthias Güntzer (1502–1564), Hieronymus Boner's partner and successor. He was a member of the city magistrate from 1543 to 1563. In his youth an outstanding pupil at the humanist school of Sélestat, he acquired the post of assistant to his teacher Sapidus.[82] Later, in 1521, he completed his studies at the University of Wittenberg.[83] In 1529, he became a Colmar citizen and, like Hieronymus Boner, was entrusted with many diplomatic missions, representing Colmar's authorities at imperial diets and meetings of the *Decapolis*. Unfortunately, we have only scant information on the remainder of his life as a leading Colmar politican and scholar.[84] He played an instrumental role in the recruitment of a skilled schoolmaster in 1538, thus entering into contact with the humanist Glareanus.[85] A contemporary letter also shows him in contact with Beatus Rhenanus.[86] We are lacking the supplemental evidence, however, that would be necessary for an interpretation of Martin Bucer's letter to "Guntzero, Colmariae" of 1546[87], and cannot ascertain whether the two men knew each other personally.

Similarly, our knowledge of Güntzer's religious position remains rather fragmentary. In 1566, in a letter addressed to Bucer's former secretary, Conrad Hubert of Strasbourg, the Horbourg minister Bartholomäus Westheimer, refers to Güntzer as an apostate.[88] It seems that Güntzer privately confessed his Protestant inclinations to Westheimer without subsequently taking a public stand in favor of the Reformation. Thus, it is very likely that Matthias Güntzer was one of Colmar's "secret Nicodemites" mentioned by the Basel chronicler Christian Wurstisen.[89] In 1554, the Dean of St.

[80] See *Gerhard Ritter*, Erasmus und der deutsche Humanistenkreis am Oberrhein, Freiburger Universitätsreden, XXIII, Freiburg i. Br. 1937.

[81] *Ernst Walter Zeeden*, Die Entstehung der Konfessionen: Grundlagen und Formen der Konfessionsbildung im Zeitalter der Glaubenskämpfe (Munich and Vienna 1965), pp. 33–34.

[82] Letter from the Horbourg minister Bartholomäus Westheimer addressed to Conrad Hubert of Strasbourg on June 13, 1566: AMS/AST, 162, III, pp. 455–457.

[83] *Philippe Mieg*, "Notes biographiques", 161.

[84] The extant proofs of his literary and historical activities are scarce. There is a fragment of his *Annales rerum memorabilium gestarum civitatis Colmariensis*, in *A[rmand] M. P. Ingold*, ed., Miscellanea Alsatica, Vol. III (Paris and Colmar 1897), pp. 55–68; and a citation from Horace on the cover of Güntzer's report from the diet of Speyer, 1544: AMC, AA 76, 77.

[85] Cf. above, p. 81.

[86] Letter of May 9, 1540: *Horawitz* and *Hartfelder*, eds., Briefwechsel des Beatus Rhenanus, No. 336, p. 464.

[87] The same goes for the best wishes to Andreas Boner presented in the same letter. Bucer must have confused Boner's Christian name with that of the one-time city-clerk of Sélestat: AMS/AST, 153, III, pp. 375–378.

[88] Cf. above, n. 82.

[89] *Christian Wurstisen*, Basler Chronick, darinn alles was sich in Oberen Teutschen Landen gedenckwürdiges zugetragen (Basel 1580), p. dclii. See also *Philippe Mieg*, "Barthélemy Westheimer, pasteur à Mulhouse et à Horbourg, 1499–1567", "Annuaire de Colmar (1956), p. 46. On the concept of 16th century "Nicodemism", cf. Delio Cantimori's article cited above, n. 73; and, for a more recent assess-

Martin's praised Güntzer as a sincere and prudent man, capable of giving the chapter good advice.[90] This praise would hardly have been registered if Güntzer had openly adhered to Protestantism at that time and suggests that Güntzer remained, at least outwardly, faithful to Catholicism up to at least 1554. There is no indication that he actively continued the politics of reform inaugurated by Hieronymus Boner, but it is certain that, under his leadership, the magistrate and council kept alive and frequently re-stated their old interest in the quality and the standard of the preaching offered at St. Martin's.

In order to implement his ecclesiastical policy, Hieronymus Boner must have found important allies among Colmar's leadership. In concluding the present discussion I will add, therefore, a few remarks on the role played by such men as Sebastian Austrius, Johannes Hummel, Conrad Wickram and Peter Nuwgart.

A brother-in-law of the episcopal chancellor Lucas Klett, of the Provost of the collegial chapters of Thann and Lautenbach Gallus Klett, and of the Colmar cantor Theobald Klett[91], the physician Sebastian Austrius (Oesterricher) was (by virtue of these "good connections") instrumental in bringing about the foundation of the endowed preachership in 1539.[92] It is certain that as a student of grammar and medicine at the University of Freiburg im Breisgau, and subsequently as Beatus Rhenanus' personal physician, he did not remain uninfluenced by Upper Rhenish Erasmianism. In 1539, the Bailiff of Riquewihr, Hans Vogler, described him as an admirer of Joachim Vadianus and as one who hoped „that the city of Colmar would soon embrace Christ".[93] Coming from the pen of a Protestant, this characterization is nonetheless ambiguous: did Austrius hope for a *Restitutio Ecclesiae*, as described above, or did he actually envisage a wholesale adherence to Protestantism? In any case, there is no doubt that any open sympathy on his part for the new faith would have been incompatible with the role he played in Colmar's ecclesiastical politics in 1539. He may have been one of Colmar's early "Nicodemites", but his later career as a professor at the orthodox Catholic University of nearby Freiburg suggests that his reported hopes referred, in fact, to his and other *Colmariens'* plans for a thorough reform of the church under humanist auspices.

The possible commitment of the city-clerk Johannes Hummel to humanist learning must remain questionable, although it is suggested by the energy he invested in the

ment, *Carlo Ginzburg*, Il nicodemismo: Simulazione e dissimulazione religiosa nell' Europa del' 500, Turin 1970.

[90] ADHR, 4 G, 5–1 (Capitulum Kalendae Junii, 1554).

[91] AMC, GG 39, 17 (Dr. Lucas Klett to Johannes Hummel, October 24, 1539); and AMC, GG 39. 15 (Dr. Lucas Klett to his brother Theobald Klett, n. d. [1539]). For Lucas and Gallus Klett, cf. also Matr. Basel, Vol. I, p. 295; and *Hans Winterberg*, Die Schüler von Ulrich Zasius, VKBW, Vol. XVIII (Stuttgart 1961), p. 48. Gallus Klett was also a friend of the Colmar Augustinian Prior Johannes Hoffmeister: cf. *Paulus,* Der Augustinermönch, p. 385 (No. 5). For Theobald Klett, cf. above, p. 29.

[92] AMC, ibid. All four men were natives of Rouffach in Upper Alsace. On Sebastian Austrius, see Die Amerbachkorrespondenz, Vol. VI, ed. by Beat Rudolf Jenny (Basel 1967), P. 175, n. 3; and ibid., Vol. VIII, ed. by Jenny (Basel 1974), p. xxv; and Vadianische Briefsammlung, Vol. V, ed. by Arbenz and Wartmann, pp. 580–1 (No. 1081); and ibid., Vol. VI, ed. by Arbenz and Wartmann, Mitteilungen zur Vaterländischen Geschichte, Vol. XXX (St. Gall 1908), pp. 108–9 (No. 1225); and Briefwechsel des Beatus Rhenanus, ed. by Horawitz and Hartfelder, pp. 510 and 538.

[93] Letter addressed to Joachim Vadianus of St. Gall by *Ammann* Hans Vogler of Riquewihr, dated December 8, 1539: Vadianische Briefsammlung, Vol. V, ibid., No. 1081, pp. 580–581.

education of his son Hieronymus.[94] In this context, however, we need to underline that Hummel's role during the 1530's and 1540's until his death in 1546, must have been influential in strengthening the Colmar authorities' commitment to Catholicism. This is strongly suggested by the friendship he entertained with the Prior Johannes Hoffmeister, and by the family ties connecting him to Ensisheim's patriciate

The investigation of Conrad Wickram's and Peter Nuwgart's religious stand and of their role in Colmar's church politics, remains a *desideratum* for further research. However, the two men deserve to be mentioned here because their impact on city politics must have been considerable. The one-time city-clerk Conrad Wickram was a member of the city council from 1503 onwards, and from 1517 to 1545 (possibly the year of his death) he continuously served his town as one of the five members of the magistrate.[95] Peter Nuwgart appears to have belonged to Colmar's Lutherans during the early Reformation years.[96] Unfortunately, we do not know what became of his convictions during the 1530's, although his vote must have carried considerable weight: having served four terms as councillor from 1522 to 1528, he became a member of the magistrate in 1530 and kept this function until 1539.[97]

Concluding, we are able to observe that the ecclesiastical policy of Colmar's authorities in the years 1535 to 1555 consisted of two different phases. While, in 1537, the city government inaugurated a policy of ecclesiastical reform, which it actively pursued until about 1547, it later confined its activity in this area to the mere prevention of outside Protestant influence. After 1555, as we shall see, this vigilance gradually gave way to a growing climate of indifference among Colmar's leading men. Some of them joined the ranks of the city's "Nicodemites". Beyond 1555, the only permanent element of the government's church policy was the authorities' keen interest in the quality of the Catholic preaching offered within their city. The thorough defeat of Emperor Charles V's policy of religious concord must have been a deeply discouraging event for men committed to the *Via Media* ideals, when the defeat became known in 1552. Together with the strongly increasing process of "confessionalization", it sealed the eventual ruin of the *Via Media*.

In Colmar, this turn of events must have progressively split the ranks of the leadership into mutually opposed factions. Under these new auspices, a return to the old policy of church reform was out of the question. Also, most of Colmar's prominent political and ecclesiastical leaders of the 1530's and 1540's who had survived the plague of 1541, died or left the city shortly thereafter. The new men in power from 1555 onwards, largely belonged to a younger generation of politicians who, in many ways, related dif-

[94] On Johannes Hummel, see Die Amerbachkorrespondenz, Vol. VI, ed. by Jenny, p. 17, n. 3; and ibid., Vol. VIII, ed. by Jenny, pp. xix–xx. He died on November 25, 1546: *Andreas Waltz* ed., Chronik des Colmarer Kaufhauses (Colmar 1897), p. 10.

[95] *Lucien Sittler*, "Colmar au XVIe siècle", Annuaire de Colmar (1975/76), 16; and idem, ed., Membres du Magistrat, p. 53. The date of Conrad Wickram's death given by *Waltz*, ibid., (November 8, 1540), does not agree with the other evidence cited here; the most likely date of death is November 8, 1545.

[96] Cf. above, pp. 57–8.

[97] *Sittler*, ed., Membres du Magistrat, p. 43.

ferently to the ongoing religious conflict of their age, not in the least because they had not experienced the threatening religious and social turbulence of the early Reformation years.

D. THE REFORMATION MOVEMENT, 1535–1555

Due to its relatively slow institutionalization, particularly with regard to the recruitment of new Protestant ministers, the introduction of the Reformation into the neighboring territory of Horbourg-Riquewihr did not provoke immediate repercussions in Colmar; although, as early as April, 1536, Veltin Mülin and his wife were banished from town for their attendance of Lutheran sermons at Horbourg, and, in 1538, Martin Mülin and his family were forced to leave the city for the same reason and for having dared to proselytize among their fellow citizens.[98] The plight of these families was, at that time, the solitary harbinger of an urban movement quite soon to reach more representative proportions. A sure sign to this effect is the fact that similar expulsions stopped after 1538.

As early as the following year, as we have seen, the authorities' fear of the growing impact of the outside Protestant influence significantly contributed to their decision to attempt a stemming of the tide by establishing Johann Fabri's preachership. A contemporary memorandum contained the following observations:[99]

> Most of the neighbors of the imperial city of Colmar are Lutherans. Nevertheless, the community and Colmar's citizens and inhabitants, now swamped by this plague, desire to remain within the old faith and obedient to the sacrosanct . . . Roman church. Now, they greatly fear that if there is no post provided at the parish church for a learned, pious and diligent preacher, who will preach the Word of God against the Lutherans and dissuade the citizens from their adherence to Lutheranism, . . . these citizens will soon begin to defect from the old church.

After 1539, the Lutheran "plague" did not stop short of affecting the homogeneity of the city's clergy as well. In February, 1545, two nuns attempted to flee from St. Catherine's convent, but their action was foiled by the authorities' vigilance.[100] Within Colmar's lay community, the first widespread effect of the Reformation in Horbourg-Riquewihr was the progressive laxness within important parts of the population in their attendance of worship at St. Martin's. Thus, in 1544, the city government felt obliged to threaten punishment to those encountered at home or out in the streets while worship

[98] AMC, BB 45 (1515–42), p. 87 (Banishment of Veltin Mülin and his wife on April 29, 1536); and ibid., p. 88 (Expulsion of Martin Mülin and family on May 7, 1538).

[99] AMC, GG 39, 6 ("Memoriale ad urbem"): "Ciuitas Jmperialis Columbariensis, cuius vicini fere vndique et exeunti parte sunt Lutheranj, ipsa tamen dicta ciuitas cum suis ciuibus et incolis an huiusmodi lepra adhuc inunda, cupiens in Veteri sancta religione et obedienta sacrosancte Romane eclesie et sanctę apostolice persistere, timet vehementer, si in parochiali sua ecclesia docto, religioso, et diligenti Concionatore dictę veteris religionis non continuo provisa sit, qui verbum Dominj contra virus Lutheranum proponat, ciues a Lutheranismo dehortetos et vicinòs debita fide atque sedulitate in melius reuocare studeat, netandem et ipsi ciues deficere incipiant . . .".

[100] AMC, GG 83, 4–6.

was being held at the parish church.[101] But this intervention was to prove to no avail: three years later, the chapter bitterly chastized their flock's outrageous neglect of the fast laws and their non-attendance and frequent condemnation of confession and eucharist. The Dean and his fellow canons particularly emphasized that "many, nay, innumerable" citizens were now guilty of such behavior. Again, the authorities intervened by ordering the entire population to attend confession and eucharist and by threatening all offenders with punishment.[102] They were compelled to reiterate their order in February, 1549.[103] Neither of these ordinances were severe enough and, very likely, were not enforced vigorously enough to produce the desired results.

A second effect of the new Protestant outside influence, simultaneously taking root within the community, was the growing indifference and even hostility with which many *Colmariens* viewed pious donations and ecclesiastical contributions. The income of a 16th century parish church was based on three different sources: on the so-called *Wittum*, i. e. the church's endowment (such as its glebe-lands and real-estate), on the tithes collected from all parishioners and on the oblations and fees collected for clerical services. In 1547, St. Martin's chapter complained about palpable losses and decreases of income in all three areas at once. In particular, it appeared discontented about the noticeable decrease in the number of lay anniversary foundations and in the amount of the so-called "four offerings", traditionally collected from the parishioners on the four principal holidays – Christmas, Easter, Whitsun and All Saints.[104] These complaints unmistakingly implied that the progressive reluctance of a growing number of *Colmariens* to continue their traditional support of the old church and its clergy was largely responsible for St. Martin's increasing financial crisis. However, the Reformation in the surrounding Württemberg territory, where the chapter owned much land, and the incessant rise in prices, accompanied by a constant inflation of the value of currency, must also have contributed to the clergy's economic plight.

In his outstanding book on pre-Reformation reform attempts in the diocese of Strasbourg, Francis Rapp pertinently describes the *circulus vitiosus* encountered by the pre-Reformation clergy. He discusses the continued loss in value of prebendary en-

[101] AMC, FF 626, 1 (1544): "Mine herren Meister vnd Rhat werdent vß teglicher verkündung des wort gottes gewisen, das man dasselbig heren, behalten, vnd dardurch selig werden solle. Dwil dann gar bj mencklich durch den gebruch des Sonteglichen vskündens deren verhindert . . . vnd was durch den obristen weibel verkünt zuhoren, vnd also vsserthalb der kirch vnd den gotlichen Emptern zupliben, vrsach genommen wirt . . . Solichem vorzesein, habent myne herren . . . erkant, das sich hinfüro, vnd derzit, so mann das predigt Ampt vnd andere gotzdienst vollpringt, weder burger, burgerin, noch derselben kinder, vff dem platz noch den gassen, sonder einstweders in der Kirchen, welichs got am gefelligsten vnd Jnen selbst zu Jrer selen selikeit am fürderlichsten sein, oder in ihren husern finden lassen . . .."

[102] ADHR, 4 G, 5–2 (Transactions of the chapter on March 13, 1547).

[103] ADHR, 4 G, 5–1 (Capitulum Kalendae Februarii, 1549). A similar situation prevailed at neighboring Breisach where a visitation of the church on April 16, 1550, recorded the following observation: "So bald das Volck am Sonntag die Predig hör, so lauf es uß der kirchen und blyb nit by der Meß". See *Günter Haselier*, Geschichte der Stadt Breisach am Rhein, Vol. I/1 (Breisach 1969), pp. 292–3.

[104] A list of all of the chapter's complaints was presented to the magistrate and council in 1547: AMC, GG 26, 19. For the different categories of ecclesiastical income here referred to, see *Lucien Pfleger*, Die elsäßische Pfarrei, ihre Entstehung und Entwicklung, Forschungen zur Kirchengeschichte des Elsaß, Vol. III (Strasbourg 1936), pp. 222–223, 342–343. St. Martin's economic crisis was far from unique in 16th century Alsace: cf. ibid., pp. 235–236.

dowments, resulting in the cumulation of benefices creating ever larger numbers of impoverished chaplains and vicars. This situation led to clerical greediness and, simultaneously, to a continuous deterioration of the standard of worship, thus preventing *a priori* any substantial success for attempts at internal reform – as were repeatedly called for by the mighty preacher Geiler von Keysersberg, or by the humanist Jacob Wimpfeling, as well as by numerous other contemporaries.[105]

Although, in 1540, the Bishop of Basel reduced the number of St. Martin's prebends in order to consolidate the Dean's and other canons' income[106], it remains an easy task to imagine how the impact of the Reformation in, and outside of, Colmar rapidly increased the chapter's problems in recruiting skilled and qualified priests, and how, as a result, the chapter could not keep up with the traditional standard and quality of worship.[107] All this, in turn, had adverse effects on the discipline and morality of Colmar's secular clergy, whom the Dean had to admonish acrimoniously on more than one occasion.[108]

It is also easy to imagine that the decline in the quality and frequency of worship was not taken lightly by the lay community. The shoemakers' guild was probably not particularly enchanted when its complaint, presented to the chapter in 1548, merely evoked the canons' response that nothing could be done about restoring the previous frequency of the celebration of the guild's St. Andrew's mass.[109] In fact, the deplorable situation of the church of St. Martin, and particularly the desolate state of some of its clergy, must have further discouraged the *Colmariens* in their loyalty to Roman Catholicism and heightened their readiness to embrace the new faith.

Thus, the regular Sunday "*exodus*" of parishioners, including "*plures ex Ciuibus non infimi*" (many well situated citizens), who attended Protestant worship in adjacent towns and villages, grew to such proportion as to incite the chapter to present the matter to the authorities in August, 1554. The city government's response was to threaten all those who continued to attend Protestant worship in Horbourg or elsewhere outside Colmar, with a fine of ten crowns.[110] However, like similar earlier interventions, this measure

105 *Rapp*, Réformes et Réformation, *passim*.

106 ADHR, 4 G, 3–7 (Act of February 28, 1540).

107 All these problems are disclosed by the chapter in the grievances it voiced in 1547: AMC, GG 147, 1; and GG 26, 19.

108 Cf., for instance, ADHR, 4 G, 5–1 (Capitulum Kalendae Maij, 1550; and Capitulum Kalendae Septembris, 1551).

109 ADHR, 4 G, 5–2 (Transactions of the chapter on July 30-August 1, 1548). Another complaint about the chapter's sluggishness in administrating pious foundations was presented as early as 1535 by the Freiburg patrician and son of a former Colmar *Obristmeister*, Ambrosius Kempf, regarding his ancestor's foundation of alimonies for the poor. In the same letter, Kempf complains about the adverse effect the chapter's carelessness has on the citizens' inclination to create new pious foundations: AMC, GG 18, 25. Kempf's decision, based on this situation, was to transfer his ancestors' foundation from control by the clergy to the direct authority of the city government.

110 ADHR, 4 G, 5–1 (Capitulum Kalendae Augusti, 1554): "Vltimo deliberatum est, quonam consilio ac via res aggredienda sit, quinquidem subditi seu parrochiani et plures ex Ciuibus non infimi, cum multa eorum familia diebus Dominicis atque festiuis relicta et spręta eorum parrochiali Ecclesia neglectaque Euangelica prędicatione ac diuino cultu, Sequntur quendam Wirtenbergensem prędicatorem [= Bartholomäus Westheimer] in pago Horburg, qui sua sana scilicet et noua doctrina calumpniosa nempe simplicem populum seducens [. . . sentence interrupted]. Ad precavenda igitur multa hic sequentia incommoda communi omnium consensu statuit Capitulum hanc rem ad Senatum esse deferendam, quod factum est per Decanum, Scolasticum et Nicolaum Wilman. Vnde die Dominica sequenti, quę erat quinta dies Augusti,

was not to have any long-lasting effect. The *conditio sine qua non* of its success would have been a thorough inner reform of Colmar's Catholic church. In 1555, the prospects for such a reform looked rather bleak, and, when it was finally initiated during the 1580's, it came too late.

in omnibus tribubus publice proclamatum est, et sub pęna decem Coronatorum interdictum, ne quis amplius quocumque loco hijs contionibus seditiosis uelit interesse".

CHAPTER IV

FROM THE PEACE OF AUGSBURG OF 1555 TO THE INTRODUCTION OF THE REFORMATION IN 1575

A. THE IMPACT OF THE AUGSBURG TREATY ON URBAN CHURCH POLITICS IN ALSACE AND IN COLMAR

Although the Peace of Augsburg of 1555 was not an immediate consequence of the revolt of the German princes in 1552, entailing the defeat of Emperor Charles V, it is nevertheless linked to these events because it sealed Charles V's débâcle in the area of religious politics. "The whole political development from the Augsburg Diet of 1518 to that of 1555 can best be understood as the advances coupled with strategic retreats, of Charles toward the goal on which he was determined – the restoration of the unity of the church under the aegis of a universal empire".[1] The Treaty of Passau of 1552 put an end to the Emperor's political universalism and brought to the fore princely and territorial particularism. Three years later, in the Peace of Augsburg, the principle of religious pacification was found precisely in this particularism. The treaty thus destroyed all hopes – cherished by Charles V – for the restoration of religious unity within the boundaries of the old church. By sanctioning politico-religious particularism, the events of 1552–55 helped to enhance the tendency towards territorial absolutism in Germany. In the long run, this development, along with the concomitant weakening of the Emperor's authority, was to constitute a serious threat to the autonomy of the free imperial cities.[2]

As a result, those imperial cities which felt threatened in their autonomy by neighboring princes sought to counter this adverse influence by assuring their allegiance to the Emperor. In Alsace, in 1564, the protectorate over the ten imperial cities allied within the *Decapolis*, the Bailiwick of Haguenau, was pledged by the Emperor to Archduke Ferdinand of Tyrol, who was to control the Bailiwick until his death in 1595. Ferdinand II strove hard to subject the pawned fief to the authority of his princely family. Faced with this situation, the Ten Alsatian Cities hoped to gain a measure of imperial protection against Ferdinand's expansive whims through the maintenance of a strict loyalty toward the Emperor. Before 1555 this loyalty, especially in the case of the smaller and strategically relatively exposed cities such as Colmar, automatically implied those cities' continued adherence to the Emperor's religious faith – that is, to Catholicism.[3]

[1] *Lewis W. Spitz*, "Particularism and Peace: Augsburg – 1555", Church History, XXV (1956), 111.

[2] *Gerald Strauss*, Nuremberg in the Sixteenth Century, New Dimensions in History: Historical Cities, ed. by Norman F. Cantor (New York, London and Sydney 1966), p. 46.

[3] *Heinrich Rocholl*, Die Einführung der Reformation in der ehemaligen freien Reichsstadt Colmar: Ein Beitrag zur Reformationsgeschichte des Elsass (Leipzig 1876), p. 5, is right to point out that "during

This situation changed through the legal recognition of Lutheranism by the Peace of Augsburg. Henceforth an imperial city's loyalty was no longer bound to its commitment to Catholicism. This must have greatly encouraged those *Colmariens* who sympathized with the Reformation movement especially because, as later sources testify, there was no one in Colmar who seriously doubted that the Peace of Augsburg implicitly sanctioned the imperial cities' right to reform, as it did in the case of all other imperial estates.[4] The example of the action taken by two neighboring princes must have increased the speculations of Colmar's open and secret Protestants on an eventual victory of their cause: in 1555, based on their *ius reformandi*, corroborated by the Peace of Augsburg, both Egenolph von Rappoltstein and Margrave Karl II of Baden-Durlach openly embraced the Protestant message and began to introduce the Reformation into their territories.[5]

However, the fourteenth article of the Augsburg edict of 1555 did not explicitly specify an urban right to reform. It only ruled that Lutheranism and Catholicism should remain intact in those free and imperial cities where they had existed jointly for some time, and that Lutherans and Catholics in these cities should leave each other unencumbered in their respective practice of worship and ecclesiastical ceremonies.[6] In fact, the treaty left the old question unanswered as to whether the free and imperial cities were entitled to a seat and vote at imperial diets and, therefore, whether they were to enjoy the same privileges as all other imperial estates whose *ius reformandi* was ascertained at Augsburg. Consequently, it was also left to further debate whether or not these cities were entitled to the same "right to reform".[7] In Alsace, the problems relating to the constitutional status of the free and imperial cities and to their *ius reformandi*, as raised by the so-called city article of the Augsburg treaty, were to play an important role soon after 1555. The occasion arose through the introduction of the Reformation in Haguenau in 1565.

B. THE INFLUENCE OF THE REFORMATION IN HAGUENAU ON THE RELIGIOUS CLIMATE IN COLMAR, 1565–1574.

In 1562, when Emperor Ferdinand I visited their town, the Haguenau jurors and city councillors promised their superior that they were dedicated to continuing their

several decades of the 16th century, in the eyes of the Colmar authorities, allegiance to the Emperor and the adherence to the Catholic faith were practically identical". Compare also the more comprehensive approach to the same problem by *Gerhard Pfeiffer*, "Der Augsburger Religionsfrieden und die Reichsstädte", Zeitschrift des historischen Vereins für Schwaben, LXI (1955), 226–227.

[4] Cf. the later testimonies from 1574 and 1575 mentioned below, pp. 109–110. The only extant testimony to this effect from the pre-Reformation period dates from March 26, 1568: AMC, GG 26, 34 (Letter from the Bailiff of Sainte-Croix (Heiligkreuz), Johann Kotschareuter, to the city-clerk Beat Henslin).

[5] On the Reformation of the Ribeaupierre, cf. *Louis Süss*, Geschichte der Reformation in der Herrschaft Rappoltstein, I. Teil: Bis 1648, Saverne 1914; and *Johann Adam*, Evangelische Kirchengeschichte der elsässischen Territorien bis zur Französischen Revolution (Strasbourg 1928), pp. 348–370. On the Reformation in Baden-Durlach, cf. *Karl Friedrich Vierordt*, Geschichte der Reformation im Grossherzogthum Baden (Karlsruhe 1847), pp. 416–423; and *Friedemann Merkel*, Geschichte des evangelischen Bekenntnisses in Baden von der Reformation bis zur Union, VVKB, Vol. XX (Karlsruhe: 1960), pp. 16–21.

[6] *Karl Brandi*, ed., Der Augsburger Religionsfriede vom 25. September 1555 (Göttingen 1927), pp. 49–50.

[7] Cf. the discussion by *Pfeiffer*, "Der Augsburger Religionsfrieden", 274–275.

adherence to the Catholic faith. Yet, only about two years later, in 1564–65, the council let itself be persuaded by the Protestant party and its influential exponents, such as the *Stettmeister* Rochius of Botzheim and the city-clerk Dr. Cornelius Fürstein, that the Franciscan church – unadministered since 1545, and therefore at the council's disposal – should be provided with an evangelical preacher. Upon the council's request, the Duke of Württemberg sent his court chaplain and chancellor of the University of Tübingen, Dr. Jacob Andreae, with orders to introduce Protestant worship into the Lower Alsatian city. Andreae arrived in Haguenau in late November, 1565, and was accorded a "princely reception".[8] During the few weeks of his presence in town he installed Philipp Heerbrand, the former pastor of Lauffen in Württemberg, as the first minister of the quickly growing Protestant parish.

Four aspects, in particular, facilitated the introduction of the Reformation in Haguenau. They gain in importance once we consider that the act of reform in this city was largely the result of the efforts of a relatively small group of influential citizens.[9] The first two aspects were a result of Emperor Ferdinand I's death in 1564:

1. Unlike Ferdinand I, his successor Maximilian II was generally known for his irenic stand in religious matters. It appears that deputees of the Haguenau city council, while visiting the imperial court in Vienna, had been able to witness Maximilian's moderation.[10]
2. From 1559 to 1564, Emperor Ferdinand I controlled the Bailiwick of Haguenau. Maximilian II was to pledge it to his brother, Archduke Ferdinand II of Tyrol. As long as the Ten Alsatian Cities organized within the *Decapolis* had not sworn their customary oath of allegiance vis-à-vis the new *Oberlandvogt*, Archduke Ferdinand II's officials within the Bailiwick were not legally in any position to influence the ecclesiastical politics practiced by the council of Haguenau. Yet, in 1564 and 1565, the cautious cities of the *Decapolis* refused to take their oath vis-à-vis the Archduke (as their new protector) without simultaneously being reassured of the safeguard of their imperial privileges by the Emperor himself. Thus, between 1564 and 1566, a kind of *interregnum* was created within the Bailiwick which facilitated the religious change in Haguenau.[11]
3. In addition, in 1565, Haguenau suffered a severe onslaught of the plague. The town was thus temporarily freed from the presence of the officials of the Bailiwick and

[8] *Adam*, Evangelische Kirchengeschichte, pp. 442–443. Regarding the Haguenau Reformation, see also: ibid., pp. 436–459; and *[Charles] A[uguste] Hanauer*, Le protestantisme à Haguenau, Strasbourg and Colmar 1905. A modern rendition of Haguenau's 16th century history is sorely missing.

[9] *Charles A. Hanauer*, ed., Cartulaire de l'Eglise S. George de Haguenau, Quellenschriften der Elsässischen Kirchengeschichte, Vol. V (Strasbourg 1898), p. 508; cf. also *Timotheus W. Röhrich*, "Die evangelische Gemeinde in Hagenau", in idem, Mittheilungen aus der Geschichte der evangelischen Kirche des Elsasses, Vol. II (Paris and Strasbourg 1855), pp. 450–511.

[10] ADBR, C 5, 7 (Letter from the Bailiff of Haguenau to Archduke Ferdinand II, November 11, 1565); and TLA, Kopialbücher der Regierung, 1565, fol. 657v–659r (Letter from the Upper Austrian government at Innsbruck to Archduke Ferdinand II).

[11] Cf. TLA, Kopialbücher der Regierung, 1565, *passim*. Regarding the final oath-taking procedure, cf. ibid., fol. 301r–302v (Letter from Archduke Ferdinand II to Upper Austrian government, December 12, 1565); and ibid., Kopialbücher der Regierung; 1566, fol. 122r–119v (Letter from the Upper Austrian government to the Archduke, May 14, 1566). The Bailiff Nicolaus of Bollwiller's counterbond for Colmar is dated March 18, 1566: ADBR, C 11, 75 (copy).

from the influence these men, as residents of Haguenau, customarily exerted on the decisions of the city government. The officials had all fled the plague.[12]

4. Finally, it is likely that the cathartic experience of the plague, seen as a divine punishment, enhanced the Protestants' determination to act.[13]

From the start, the Haguenau Reformation[14] captured the undivided interest of Archduke Ferdinand II and his advisers. In fact, the first time a reference to the imminent introduction of Protestant worship into the Lower Alsatian city appeared in the correspondence of the Innsbruck government was as early as November 15, 1564[15] – a fact revealing the long period of hesitation which preceded the decisive step of Haguenau's authorities. In the Innsbruck letter of November 15, 1564, the prince's advisers warned the Archduke about wasting any serious considerations on the Bailiff of Haguenau's alleged assertions pertaining to the legal and constitutional status of the Ten Alsatian Cities. Apparently, the Bailiff Nicolaus of Bollwiller had claimed that the member-cities of the *Decapolis* were not really imperial cities, considering their subjection to the Bailiff's protection. Bollwiller allegedly concluded from this premise that the cities' legal status would thus justify an Austrian intervention in religious matters. The Innsbruck councillors warned their prince that such an intervention could easily find an undesirable, quasi- unanimous disapproval at a future imperial diet because, considering these cities' *actual* status, such interference would constitute a flagrant offense against the very substance of the Peace of Augsburg of 1555.

The councillors advised their superior to confine his actions to requesting his Bailiff to influence, by means of persuasion and intrigue, the outcome of the upcoming city-elections in Haguenau and the other member cities of the *Decapolis*. The Bailiff's objective was the election of as many loyal Catholics as possible. As is shown by their subsequent correspondence, the Innsbruck government, driven by the fear that Nicolaus of Bollwiller's rashness might gain the upper hand, was dedicated to preventing any forceful interference by the Archduke in the course of Haguenau's religious change. In November, 1565, they also appealed to their prince to remember the recent case of the Reformation at Munster (Alsace), where all attempted interventions instigated by the impulsive Bailiff of Haguenau had failed because Munster, like Haguenau, was an imperial city and thus immediately subject to the Emperor.[16] In April, 1564, the

[12] ADBR, C 5, 4 (Letter from the Upper Austrian government at Innsbruck to the Archduke, November 15, 1564 (copy); also in TLA, Kopialbücher der Regierung, 1564, fol. 164v–175r.

[13] A letter of apology from the magistrate and council of Haguenau addressed to the Emperor on March 18, 1566, touches upon this point in arguing that the plague thwarted the Haguenau Protestants' possibility to be administered, as before, by Protestant pastors in the service of adjacent principalities: AMC, AA 84, 2 (copy).

[14] The Protestant church of Haguenau, created in 1565, never reached an age of maturity. Toward the end of the 16th century, for various reasons, Protestantism progressively lost its support within the city's community. As a result, it did not successfully, in any organized form, survive the 1620's. However, this later development is without direct importance to what concerns the immediate effects the introduction of the Reformation in Haguenau had on the course of events in Colmar. Cf. below, pp. 195–6.

[15] Cf. above, n. 12.

[16] TLA, Kopialbücher der Regierung, 1564, fol. 164v–175v; ibid., 1565, fol. 657v–659r; and ibid., 1566, fol. 112r–119v; (Letters from the Upper Austrian government to the Archduke of November 15, 1564; November 23, 1565; May 14, 1566). The councillors of the Innsbruck government shared no

Imperial Supreme Court, based on the Augsburg Peace of 1555, forbade Nicolaus of Bollwiller any further molestation of this city.[17]

However, by May, 1566, it had occurred to the Innsbruck government that it was quite questionable whether, based on the Augsburg treaty, imperial cities had to be granted any *ius reformandi* at all. The cautious advisers were by no means ready to adopt the opinion of the subordinate Austrian officials at Ensisheim, who flatly denied any such urban prerogative. They preferred to propose to the Archduke that he leave any decision in this matter up to his brother, the Emperor.[18]

Maximilian II, who was preoccupied by the revolt of the Low Countries, did not devote any immediate attention to this problem, although, in two successive mandates, he forbid the Haguenau authorities the religious change they had undertaken. The two imperial letters provoked no palpable effect. Thus, Archduke Ferdinand II urged the Emperor to dispatch an imperial commission to Haguenau to abolish without delay the Protestant worship established in this city.[19] The Emperor complied. However, for various reasons, including Maximilian's reluctance to escalate his interference in this case, the planned imperial mission only materialized eight years later in 1574.

At this time the politico-religious situation in Alsace, and particularly in the *Decapolis*, was no longer comparable to the climate prevailing in 1567. In the meantime, facing the repeated challenge to their imperial privileges by the Habsburg-Austrian officials of Haguenau and Ensisheim, the Alsatian Ten Cities, notwithstanding their religious differences, all supported Haguenau.[20] Moreover, in Haguenau the Protestant church had been able to enlist and organize popular support. By now, Haguenau's Protestants could also fully rely upon the Colmar authorities' unrestrained patronage. It is doubtful whether the Lower Alsatian town could have expected such support from its sister city eight years earlier. In 1574, however, Colmar's leadership was itself on the verge of introducing Protestant worship into its town. The constantly recurrent fear, so prominent in the contemporary Habsburg-Austrian correspondence, now proved entirely justified: the Austrian officials in Haguenau, Ensisheim and Innsbruck all suspected that, following the introduction of the Reformation in Haguenau, other member cities of the Alsatian *Decapolis* might soon feel inclined to follow Haguenau's example.

It is obvious that the fact that the establishment of Haguenau's Protestant church did not meet any serious outside encumbrance during the first decade of its existence must have fostered new hope among Colmar's Protestants. Yet, by 1567, it became apparent

doubts about the right of "immediacy" of the Ten Alsatian Cities. Cf. their letter addressed to the Archduke on July 21, 1565: "Ob gleich E.fl.dt. Inn ettlichen Stetten das Malefitz vnd ettwa mer speties Jurisdictionis furnemblichen Jnn der Statt Hagenaw zustendig, das doch disfalls von Rechts wegen ad alias species Jurisdictionis ... nit Jnferiert, vnnd sonderlich solliche speties vil weniger ad omnimodam & universalem Jurisdictionem extiert werden mögen": TLA, Kopialbücher der Regierung, 1565, fol. 465r–483v.

[17] Cf. *Xavier Mossmann*, "Diètes de la décapole de 1563 à 1566: La décapole à Munster", in idem, Notes et documents tirés des Archives de Colmar (Colmar 1872), Chap. III (no page nos.). For comprehensive accounts of the Reformation in Munster, see *Ludwig Ohl*, Geschichte der Stadt Münster und ihrer Abtei, Vorbruck-Schirmeck 1897; and *Adam*, Evangelische Kirchengeschichte, pp. 396–410.

[18] TLA, Kopialbücher der Regierung, 1566, 112r–119v (Letter dated May 14, 1566).

[19] Cf. *Röhrich*, Mittheilungen, Vol. II, p. 464; and *Hanauer*, Le protestantisme, pp. 146–157.

[20] See the correspondence from the years 1566–67 contained in AMC, AA 84, 9, 11 and 13.

that they still needed to strengthen their foothold within the ranks of the city's leadership. On January 15, 1567 (?), the latter, in unison with colleagues from Sélestat, Kaysersberg and Turckheim, appealed to Haguenau's city government to reconsider its recent decision in favor of the Reformation.[21] This evidence demonstrates that the rallying of an open majority within Colmar's leadership came about relatively late, considering that the growing laxity of the community in ecclesiastical matters had already reached significant proportions in the late 1540's. This comparatively slow development was clearly mirrored in the concurrent ecclesiastical politics of the magistrate and council.

C. GRADUAL SHIFTS IN THE OFFICIAL CHURCH POLICY, 1555–1575.

In the years immediately following 1555, the relationship between the Colmar authorities and the secular clergy continued in the relatively good spirit of cooperation prevailing throughout the 1540's. However, toward the end of the decade, growing dissension marred this cooperation and the year 1560 was to mark the beginning of a new phase in this relationship. It was increasingly characterized by mutual suspicion and distrust, inevitably leading to a climate of progressive alienation, and, from there, to the secular authorities' mounting hostility toward the old church and its clergy. A major factor in the change in climate around 1560 was the concurrent shift in the composition of the magistrate.[22] In addition, the contemporaneous, tedious and overlengthy negotiations between the Abbot of nearby Munster and the chapter of St. Martin's regarding the income of the Dean, must have deeply hurt the reputation of the canons in the eyes of Colmar's leadership; and a number of simultaneous controversial issues helped to overshadow the memory of the relative concord of earlier years.

Thus, the years of fairly unencumbered cooperation were short-lived. Following the year 1552, the chapter willingly paid a contribution levied by the authorities to cover the costs of the extensive fortification of the city walls and ramparts, undertaken in that year because of the threat of a possible siege of Colmar by the King of France. In 1557, the authorities in turn complied with the canons' request for a reduction of the installment payments designed to cover this contribution.[23] Furthermore, the brief quarrel in March, 1556, between the city government and Philipp Blunder, the episcopal *Offizial*

[21] However, especially regarding the late introduction of Protestant worship in Colmar, it is noteworthy that this appeal contained no religious argumentation and was based solely on political considerations about Haguenau's provocation of the Habsburg: "... Erstlich, das die vier Catholische ... stett nitt gern gehörtt, das sich diese Jrrungen zugetragen; besonder viel lieber gesehen, das bey dieser unrhuwigen Zeitt, do one das gegen E. stetten der Landvogtey, wie kundlich, allerhand newerungen gesucht werden, alles das jhenig vnderlassen plieben, was yemanden zu vnrhue vrsach hette geben. Bis Gott der Herr gelegenheitt vnd Mittel geschickt, das man jnn Religion vnd prophan sachen zu besserer vergleichung khommen mögen ... :" AMC, AA 84, 19.

[22] Cf. below, pp. 114–7.

[23] AMC, GG 26, 1 and 5. Yet, I am referring to a gradually more uneasy relationship between city government and clergy. On July 25, 1557, when Dean Jacob Klein requested the Bishop to support the chapter's demand that the Colmar authorities assist the clergy in remediating the community's laxity in religious matters, Klein insisted that the ordinary should not let the *Colmariens* know that the support in question was based on St. Martin's request: AAEB, A 41, 31a.

at Altkirch, did not have any long-lasting consequences: the bone of contention was the inventarization of Dean Johannes Grüninger's estate by Colmar officials. This was done because Grüninger had left debts to some of Colmar's citizens.[24] The short-lived dispute found no immediate continuation. It was more than a decade later, in a considerably more heated phase of the jurisdictional dispute between city and Bishop, that the same debate was resumed. However, in 1557, when asked again to contribute their share toward the imposition levied on Colmar by the Empire for the financing of the imperial war against the Turks, the canons raised no objections.[25]

Between 1556 and 1560, a dispute over the refusal of a few dozen *Colmariens* to pay their tithes, and the simultaneous negotiations between the chapter and the Abbot of Munster over the Dean's income, contributed to a significant deterioration of the hitherto prevailing climate of cooperation. The dispute regarding the tithes was foreshadowed, when, in October, 1556, the Dean of St. Martin's established an impressive list of eighty-five alleged "tithe-rebels".[26] What these "rebels" objected to was the imposition of the manorial rather than the ecclesiastical tithe.[27] Economic reasons, as well as biblicism, seem to have nurtured their refusal, although there is no clue as to the actual weight of these motives. Their obstinacy had no immediate repercussions until, in 1560, there was a trial before the episcopal *Offizial* at Altkirch: the chapter of St. Martin's and the Abbot of Munster, in alliance with the landed noblemen Johann Heinrich von Landeck and Nicolaus von Hattstatt, had indicted a number of *Colmariens* for their continued refusal to deliver their tithes. The Colmar authorities grasped the occasion to challenge the legitimacy of episcopal jurisdiction in this matter and demanded that the chapter disassociate itself from the other plaintiffs and bring the case before Colmar's city court. To lend more weight to their demand, they threatened to harass the canons, should they not comply. But the clergy did not bow to this intimidation. Finally, against the clergy's will, and possibly instigated by the magistrate, the Regency of Ensisheim stepped in and settled the dispute between all parties concerned during a meeting held in Colmar in November, 1560. The settlement included the following points:

1. The titheholders agreed to retract their pending litigation at the episcopal court;
2. Since some of the old treatises were lost, the Colmar authorities were to interrogate all alleged offenders in order to determine whether their refusal was legitimate or not;

[24] AAEB, A 41, 26 (Letter from Colmar authorities to Bishop, March 10, 1556); also in AMC, BB 52, "Protocollum Missivarum", (1554–66), pp. 187–190; and AAEB, A 41, 30 (Letter from the episcopal *Offizial* to the Bishop, March 23, 1556).

[25] Cf. *Rocholl*, Die Einführung, p. 109.

[26] ADHR, 4 G, 5–1 (Convocatio feria 5 ante Mathej [September 16] 1556).

[27] For the different forms of tithes, see *Anton Störmann*, Die städtischen Gravamina gegen den Klerus am Ausgang des Mittelalters und in der Reformationszeit, RST, XXIV–XXVI (1 Vol.), Münster/Westphalia 1916), pp. 80–81; and for more detailed information: *Lucien Pfleger*, Die elsaessische Pfarrei: Ihre Entstehung und Entwicklung, Forschungen zur Kirchengeschichte des Elsass, Vol. III (Strasbourg 1936), pp. 310–313.

[28] A report on the negotiations by Dean Jacob Klein is contained in: ADHR, 4 G, 5–2 (Capitulum Calendae Nouembris, 1560). In this connection, see also ibid., Assumptionis, 1560; transactions of December 30, 1560; and transactions of September 2, 1561; and AMC, CC 77.

3. The Colmar city government was to force all accused citizens who failed to show cause to deliver their dues.[28]

The tithe negotiations of 1560 deserve our attention in this connection primarily because they occasioned the first full-scale attack by the Colmar authorities on citations of citizens by the episcopal court at Altkirch; (the court was transferred to this small town in Sundgau from its previous location in Basel in 1529). In 1524–25, as we have seen, the authorities' response to the community's complaints about these citations was fairly dilatorial[29] and in subsequent years they only occasionally opposed such episcopal citations.[30] Thus, in its comparatively more significant scope, the assault upon episcopal citations launched in 1560 marks an escalation of their campaign for jurisdictional autonomy. Moreover, during the negotiations of 1560, the representatives of the Colmar magistrate shocked the clergy with an aggressive self-assertion hitherto unknown. The outspoken determination of these representatives documented the authorities' full intention to profit from the chapter's increasing material and spiritual problems in their attempt to come to terms with the clerical and episcopal privileges they considered obsolete.

Simultaneously, the magistrate and council tested the weight of their vote in ecclesiastical matters in the influence they successfully exerted on the outcome of the quarrel over the Dean's income, which preoccupied and divided the chapter of St. Martin's and the Abbot of Munster between 1556 and 1559.[31] During these negotiations it was largely due to the repeated interventions of Colmar's lay leadership that the chapter was reassured of the continued service of the Dean Jacob Klein, even though, on several occasions, the latter complied very reluctantly with the canons' request not to leave them 'in these troubled times'. Colmar's councillors greatly appreciated the preaching and the cure of souls extended to them and their community by this qualified and eloquent priest.[32] While pleading strongly for Klein's continued employment by the chapter, the authorities did not refrain from using harsh language when they thought it necessary: In 1558, for instance, following the renewed renunciation of the deanery by Klein, they pointed out that Klein had done so because "the Provost and the chapter of St. Martin's who, as of old, together with the Abbot of Munster in St. Gregory's valley are responsible for providing us with a minister, not only charge the latter with all the preaching but, at the same time, overburden him with too much work and too many administrative duties. Yet, they are not willing to remunerate him with more than a very scarce salary".[33] With unmistakable insistance the authorities thus tied a good part of the

[29] Cf. above, pp. 47–8.

[30] Cf. AMC, BB 52, "Protocollum Missivarum", (1526–29), p. 38 (January 8, 1527); AMC, GG 25, 19 (April 23, 1528); AMC, BB 52, "Protocollum Missivarum", (1529–41), (December 2, 1538); AAEB, A 41, 22 and 24 (February-July, 1548); AMC, GG 29d, 6 (September 22, 1550); AMC, BB 52, "Protocollum Missivarum", (1554–66), pp. 80–3 (February 17, 1555); AMC, GG 29d, 7 (February 19, 1555).

[31] AMC, GG 27, 4 (Report from the Bishop of Basel recapitulating the past negotiations and the new agreement reached on February 10, 1559, dated February 13, 1559). For the treaty concluded on Ash-Wednesday (February 10), 1559, see AMC, GG 27, 8.

[32] AMC, GG27, 2 (Letter from magistrate and council of Colmar to Bishop of Basel, February 16, 1558).

[33] Ibid.

growing financial problem, often apologetically referred to by the chapter, to the canons' moral, rather than their material, incapability to furnish Colmar's parishioners with adequate preaching and cure of souls. Jacob Klein's last entry in the transactions ledger of the chapter in January, 1562, shortly before his death, at least in part reconfirmed the authorities' complaint. He wrote: "I have resigned the deanery because of the troublesomeness of its administration and in considering my bad health".[34]

Facing the general shortage of qualified priests in these years, it must not have been easy to recruit a successor for Klein who could match the latter's authority, eloquence and learnedness. But although the chapter succeeded in solving this difficult task by enlisting Johannes Rasser (the son of a well-respected Ensisheim family who served as Dean from November, 1563 to January, 1565), the canons did not alleviate the Dean's administrative workload in any tangible manner. As a result, the industrious Rasser soon resigned his post, primarily because he, too, felt overburdened with the management of the chapter's economic affairs.[35] Following his departure and during a period of almost two and a half decades, the canons' progressively more feeble attempts to recruit a new Dean of a similar stature were continuously thwarted. The resulting depreciation in the quality of Catholic worship weighed heavily on the chapter's relations with the council, considering the councillors' often demonstrated concern with the standard of the preaching offered at the church of St. Martin. Furthermore, it was no secret that much of the canons' lack of success in the continued recruitment of qualified deans was due to their sluggishness and unwillingness to share some of the Dean's administrative duties.[36] Faced with this unsatisfactory situation, the authorities increasingly chose to go their own way in their church policy.

Their new strategy became apparent in 1560. In the Spring of this year, following the colorful illumination of the church of St. Martin carried out under their supervision, the magistrate and council, without prior notification to the canons, destroyed seven of the church's altars and proceeded to put pews in their place. They had obtained the Bishop's sanction for this procedure three years earlier, but now chose to disregard the Bishop's stipulation that the altars be de-sacralized prior to their destruction. The ensuing violent objections by the canons were rejected by the councillors. They allegedly countered with the traditional argument that the council alone was in charge of the

[34] ADHR, 4 G, 5-2 (Capitulum Calendae Januarii, 1562). Apparently, the chapter did not keep the following promise made to Jacob Klein: "Zum Vierdten So uil Curam Collegij betrifft mit taeglicher execution vnd fürfallenden geschefften, die Jme bis her in studijs verhinderlich gewesen, [dass] nun fürtherhin alle Jar vngeuerlich acht tag vor oder nach Johannis baptistae ein Executor ... aus vns gesetzt werd ..., derselbig soll schuldig sein, die taeglich fürfallenden geschaeffte ... mit fleissigem anhalten zu exiquieren": ADHR, 4 G, 2-4 (Notebook beginning: "Volgt ..."), fol. 18v–19v. Apparently, Jacob Klein's resignation was not definitive: he still held the rank of the Dean in December, 1562, but died shortly thereafter during Lenten fast, 1563. See ADHR, 4 G, 3–11b (December 12, 1562); and AMC, GG 27, 7 (Bishop to chapter of St. Martin, April 28, 1563).

[35] *Jürgen Bücking*, Johann Rasser (ca. 1535–1595) und die Gegenreformation im Oberelsass, RST, Vol. CI (Münster/Westphalia 1970), pp. 13–14.

[36] Cf. ibid.

Fabrik of St. Martin's and added that the destruction of the altars was intended as a "revival rather than an abolition of religious practice".[37]

The authorities' progressively restless quest for undisputed hegemony in the city's ecclesiastical affairs became even more apparent in their next action – the transformation of a mass-foundation endowed by the noble family von Hattstatt. In 1560–61, with the consent of Nicolaus von Hattstatt, but against the manifest will of the canons, the magistrate transformed the foundation into an endowment for St. Martin's organist. In doing so, Colmar's secular leadership demonstrated a growing disrespect for the traditional values of the Catholic church.[38] In light of this evidence, it is not surprising that, following the disputes of the late 1550's, relations between Colmar's patricians and councillors and the secular clergy continuously deteriorated. The subsequent controversy over the chapter's tax duties marked the last decade before the introduction of the Reformation in 1575 with a previously unknown degree of disharmony between the two camps which finally led to open anticlerical defiance on the part of the councillors.

The initial occasion for this dispute was the authorities' imposition on all secular and regular clergy of a contribution toward the imperial war-tax designed to finance the ongoing campaign against the Turks. The city's monasteries all complied without voicing much disapprobation.[39] The chapter of St. Martin's, however, pleaded inability to provide the requested funds because the Bishop of Basel insisted that contributions be paid to him. As a result, the city government first tried to persuade the Bishop that, based on old tradition, it was the city that was entitled to levy this kind of tax.[40] In reality, this was a questionable assumption and the Bishop knew it. He only obliged in so far as he allowed the Colmar canons to deliver the sum against a written receipt stating that the clergy's contribution was given freely and voluntarily and by no means because the

[37] Cf. AAEB, A 41, 31b (Letter from Provost and chapter of St. Martin to Bishop, February 12, 1560): "Es habenn die Ersamenn Weysenn Meister vnd Rath der statt Colmar in verschienem lix. Jar in vnser Pfarkirchen, darinn wier den teglichen Gottsdienst verrichtenn, die wend oben her ausserhalb dem chor angefangen zů illuminierenn; neben dem selben werck aber, dieweyl inenn die fabric zůgehörig, auch an die handt genommenn, die besatzung der kirche . . . auffzůhebenn, wie dan grössers theils beschehenn mit abreissung vnnd wegraumung siben conferierter Altar, on einiche vorgende degradation, zu welchen . . . noch ettlich mer conferierte altar in kurtzer Zeytt abgeworffen vnd weggeraumbt sollen werden vnder dem schein, die kirchen eben zůbesitzenn vnd mitt einem neüwen gestüel zů zieren, etc. Da hetten wier vnns wol versechenn, sy wurden vnns als iere kirchendiener zuuor . . ., auch gemeine burgerschaft auff den Zünffttenn iers fürnemmens gnugsamm und grundtlich verstendiget habenn, das sy hiemitt nit abschaffung sonder auffung der Religion fürwendtenn, welchs doch bis hieher anderst dan ad partem nie beschechen". Additional sources: ADHR, 4 G, 11 (Letter from Bishop to Colmar authorities, September 1, 1557, and letters from magistrate and council to Bishop, dated August 18 and September 11, 1557); ADHR, 4 G, 5–2 (Transactions of the chapter from February to April, 1560). See also AMC, BB 52, "Protocollum Missivarum", (1554–66), pp. 448–9 (Colmar authorities to burgomaster and council of Breisach, April 21, 1559).

[38] ADHR, 4 G, 5-2 (Transactions of January 30, 1560); and BMC, Fonds Chauffour, I. Ch. 74 bis, No. 9.

[39] The only extant supplication regarding this imposition is dated April, 1567, and was written by the Dominicans: AMC, GG 39, 14.

[40] AMC, GG 26, 22-24. For the following, see also *François-Auguste Goehlinger*, Histoire du chapitre de l'Eglise Saint-Martin de Colmar (Colmar 1951), pp. 247–258. In 1549, the city of Essen attempted a similar maneuver regarding the taxation of its clergy: cf. *Störmann*, Die städtischen Gravamina, pp. 163–164.

city was legally entitled to it.[41] Earlier, in 1565, in the case of the clergy's contribution toward the restoration of Colmar's fortifications, the magistrate and council agreed to seal such a receipt.[42] However, in 1568, in the case of the so-called Turkish tax, they categorically refused to repeat the same procedure. The clergy's offer to pay only fifty instead of the 125 guilders requested by the authorities may have provoked their uncompromising attitude.[43]

In demanding the clergy's unconditional payment of the imposed sum, they referred to the secular clergy's obligations as inhabitants of Colmar, which, in their eyes, differed in no way from "any other citizen's" duties. This argument, of course, brought the controversy close to a renewal of the old dispute over the clergy's citizenship fought in the late 1520's.[44] As in the altar controversy of 1560, the magistrate and council argued that, based on their supervision (*Pflegschaft*) over the church of St. Martin, the church's clergy was implicitly subject in worldly affairs to their, rather than the Bishop's, authority. They added that the Augsburg decree of 1566 entitled them to levy such a contribution from the canons.

The clergy, however, remained obstinate. The city government's next move was to escalate hostilities by subjecting all of the chapter's income to confiscation, pending the clergy's payment of the tax. The canons countered with a plea to outside allies and succeed in involving the princely councils of Haguenau and Ensisheim in the ongoing controversy. This not only considerably raised the ill-humour of the city's leading men, but, in opposing the Colmar authorities to Habsburg-Austria's officials, the chapter's measure added an entirely new dimension to the dispute.[45] In an attempt to unlock the stalemate, the Bailiff of Haguenau proposed to the two parties a day of settlement to be held on June 16, 1568. However, the Colmar magistrate and council, worried about the possible adverse political consequences of their compliance with such outside interference, did not seriously consider honoring the Bailiff's request.[46] While the Colmar authorities continued their confiscation of the canons' income, Archduke Ferdinand II finally answered the Colmar clergy's earlier plea by extending his official protection to the canons and their foundation.[47] This step, however, did not result in a resolution of the chapter's problems and only increased the leading *Colmariens*' defiance.

[41] "... dergestalt, das solche erlegung aus kheiner schuldiger pflicht noch gerechtigkheit, so Sie [the authorities] darzue hetten, sonder allein aus guetem freyem willen geschehe": AMC, GG 26, 25 (Letter from the Bishop to the chapter of St. Martin, September 17, 1567).

[42] Cf. AMC, GG 26, 1.

[43] AMC, GG 26, 26 (Letter from the chapter to the magistrate and council, January 29, 1568). Cf. also ibid., 54 (Letter from the chapter to the Bailiff of Haguenau, June 12, 1568); and regarding the following: ibid., 38 (Letter from the chapter to the Bailiff of Haguenau, April 28, 1568.

[44] Cf. above, pp. 64–6.

[45] AMC, GG 26, 28 and 29. See also the grievances of the chapter addressed to the councillors of the Bailiwick of Haguenau: AMC, GG 26, 30 (March 3, 1568).

[46] AMC, GG 26, 32, 14 and 33 (Letters from the Bailiff of Haguenau and his councillors to Colmar, March 11–16, 1568). Cf. also the advice of Colmar's legal counsel, Prof. Jacob Streit of nearby Freiburg: AMC, GG 26, 21. Streit underlined that Colmar's participation in the proposed settlement could very likely entail Habsburg-Austria's continued intervention in all subsequent controversies occurring between council and clergy. For Colmar's refusal to participate at the diet: AMC, GG 26, 48. Cf. also ibid., 38 and 20. For the Bishop's instructions for the planned settlement, cf. AAEB, A 41, 57 (June 4, 1568).

[47] AMC, GG 150, 3 (Protection-letter of January 2, 1571 [copy]).

Another day of settlement, initiated by the Archduke himself, went by unattended by their deputees.[48] Ultimately, it was a harsh letter addressed to Colmar's authorities by Emperor Maximilian, who had been asked to intervene by his offended brother, which moved the *Colmariens* to attend a settlement meeting held at Ensisheim on July 10, 1572.[49]

The settlement proposed to the two parties by the councillors of the Regency of Ensisheim primarily concerned the following point: the chapter was to agree to pay the thirty-third part of the Turkish tax imposed on Colmar. The authorities, in turn, were to honor the clergy's gesture by delivering the receipt they requested.[50]

Although the Colmar deputees present at the meeting accepted this proposal, the city's magistrate and council flatly refused to ratify the agreement: a few days later, when the canons, represented by their temporary Vice-Dean Johann Rasser, and by Christian Zanenbentz and Theobald Vogel, attempted to pay their dues under the conditions proposed at Ensisheim, the city councillors refused to accept the clergy's money under the said conditions and added that "even if the city walls should crumble over all this, they would never consent to accepting the chapter's contribution nor refrain from the continued confiscation of the clergy's income, unless the sum was paid without condition". This rash argumentation finally brought about their victory: on July 20, 1572, the canons reluctantly agreed to pay their dues without claiming the hitherto hotly disputed proviso clause.[51]

Thus, in the period of 1566 to 1571, the relationship between Colmar's councillors and the city's secular clergy reached a state of almost permanent tension, with hostility prevailing on both sides. Since, during these years, the councillors obstinately stuck to their anticlerical defiance, the relationship had reached a phase in which every issue rapidly became an angrily debated bone of contention. So it was, for instance, in the case of the chaplain Marx Pfeiffer, who, in 1568, found himself in some undefined legal dispute with a Colmar burgher named Georg Ulmer.[52] One evening in the Spring of 1568,

[48] The correspondence regarding this new attempt to bring about a settlement is contained in: AMC, GG 26, Nos. 56, 56a, 55b, 58, 57a, 61, 63, 65b (In chronological order: Letters exchanged by Colmar and the chapter with the Bailiff of Haguenau and his councillors between November 13, 1570 and July 3, 1571). Cf. also AMC, GG 27, 57b (Letter from the Bailiff of Haguenau to Colmar, November 13, 1570).

[49] Cf. TLA, Kopialbücher der Regierung, 1572 (Letter from the Upper Austrian government to Archduke Ferdinand II, January 19, 1572); and AMC, GG 26, 72 (Letter from Emperor Maximilian to Colmar, February 12, 1572): Referring to Colmar's flat refusal to cooperate with Archduke Ferdinand's attempt to mediate, Maximilian states, "wann vns nun solches von Euch nit wenig frembdt fürkumbt, wir auch, (da Jr nochmals by solcher mainung bestehn soltet, das wir vnns aber mit nichten versehen), dannenhero vns kain andere gedanken machen konten, als ob Jr sondern lust truget, mit derendts geistligkeit in vnwillen zuuerfarren, vnd als die sterckern Ewer vorhabens one Zulassung einiges güetlichen gleichmessigen Mittels mit der that und gewalt durchzutringen . . .". He adds that he requested his brother, the Archduke, to launch a renewed attempt at mediation and that he firmly expects the Colmar authorities to respond to it. Cf. also AMC, GG 26, 73 and 76 (Ensisheim Regency to Colmar, May 6 and June 7, 1572).

[50] AMC, GG 26, 78 (Record of the Ensisheim diet of July 10, 1571). Also in: AAEB, A 41, 103.

[51] AMC, GG 26, 69 (Letters exchanged between the chapter and the Bailiff of Haguenau, July 16–18, 1571); and AAEB, A 41, 83 (Magistrate and council to chapter, June 26, 1571). Cf. also, *Bücking*, Johann Rasser, p. 22.

[52] AMC, GG 26, 26 (Letter from chapter of St. Martin to Colmar authorities, January 29, 1568).

the two quarreled with each other in the street, whereupon Ulmer hit the chaplain in the face. Informed of Ulmer's misdeed, the authorities insisted that the case be tried in their own court – a procedure the chapter, clinging to the clergy's privileges of exemption, refused to condone.[53] The matter was still pending when, at the beginning of May, the chaplain got involved in another verbal difference with the former custodian of St. Martin's. The latter had him cited by the council, whereupon the chapter formally forbid the chaplain to comply with the citation. Subsequently, when the council sent its sergeants to arrest Pfeiffer, he only narrowly escaped certain imprisonment and had to flee the town.[54]

In some aspects, the conflict thus created was a radicalized extension of the controversy over episcopal citations fought in 1560. The repeated bitter protests of the chapter about this open incursion in the area of clerical exemption from legal prosecution by secular authorities, and the several remonstrances of the Bishop of Basel against this flagrant attack on his jurisdictional prerogatives, proved of no avail. The city government did not allow the chaplain to return to Colmar and the case of citizen Georg Ulmer probably remained unexpiated – much to the disgrace of the canons, who justly feared that such an outcome would greatly encourage other citizens to vent their own hostile feelings toward the clergy.[55]

Simultaneously, following the death of the common priest Johannes Schuler, who had left debts, the renewal of the old issue of whether the city government had a right to dispose of priestly heritage, aggravated the rapidly deteriorating relations between Colmar and the Bishop of Basel. Like most other concurrent ecclesiastical disputes between the city authorities and the clergy and Bishop, the problem remained unsettled.[56] The Ensisheim diet of July 10, 1572, failed to bring about a lasting settlement of the issues at stake. The contention continued to take its course and further widened the gap between Colmar's leadership and the city's secular clergy.[57] In 1571, when the magistrate and council attempted to force the canons to marry their mistresses and maids, their action revealed how close to adopting genuinely evangelical issues they had come.[58]

[53] AMC, GG 26, 29 (Letter from the Colmar authorities to the Bailiff of Haguenau, March 3, 1568); AMC, GG 26, 30 (Chapter of St. Martin to Bailiff of Haguenau, March 8, 1568); and AMC, GG 26, 20 (Report from the magistrate and council on the dispute in April, 1568).

[54] AMC, GG 26, 40 (Chapter to Bishop, May 15, 1568).

[55] AMC, GG 26, 41 (Bishop to Colmar authorities, May 26, 1568); and AMC, GG 26, 54 (Chapter to Bailiff of Haguenau, [ca. June 12], 1568). A later and similar brawl involved three Colmar priests and a burgher from nearby Thann. Subsequently, the Colmar authorities fined two among the three priests for allegedly having provoked the dispute. The incident is referred to in AMC, BB 52, "Protocollum Missivarum", (1570–75), pp. 390-2 (Colmar to the Bailiff, Administrator and city-council of Thann, March 13, 1574).

[56] AAEB, A 41, 93 (Letter from the episcopal *Offizial* to magistrate and council, September 11, 1571); ibid., 98 (Magistrate and council to Bishop, February 15, 1572); AMC, GG 26, 81 (Magistrate and council to Regency of Ensisheim, October 21, 1572). A survey of the occurrences of the problem to date and a discussion of the legal technicalities involved were presented by the chapter in two contemporaneous memoranda: AMC, GG 26, 17; and AAEB, A 41, 31 (The latter source is largely identical with ibid., 100). Regarding this controversy, cf. also *Störmann*, Die städtischen Gravamina, pp. 113–4.

[57] Cf. AMC, GG 26, 86 (Letter from the magistrate and council of Colmar to the Regency of Ensisheim, January 5, 1573); and AAEB, A 41, 113 (Bishop to Regency of Ensisheim, October 9, 1574).

[58] AMC, GG 26, 10 (Report by the chapter, n.d. [August, 1571]).

Yet political circumstances led the *Colmariens* to proceed with the utmost caution. Even though there was a growing number among them who had overcome their "Nicodemism" and now showed open sympathy for the Reformation, the continued and growing vigilance of Habsburg-Austria's officials in Alsace, who, with constant scrutiny, watched over the religious politics of the Alsatian cities, limited the autonomy of their ecclesiastical and religious decisions. The period following the year 1558 is a case-in-point, when Emperor Ferdinand I resumed control over the Bailiwick of Haguenau, and especially so, the period after 1564, following Archduke Ferdinand II's promotion to the position of *Oberlandvogt*. From 1564 onwards, Ferdinand II could, at any given time, (using his Regency at Ensisheim and his Bailiff and councillors at Haguenau as instruments of his policy) exert considerable pressure on the Colmar city government. As early as May and June, 1556, preceding the take-over of the Bailiwick by Emperor Ferdinand I, Colmar's councillors were warned by the Ensisheim officials to refrain from any rash action in religious matters.[59] Ferdinand I's visit to Colmar in December, 1562, must have reminded the *Colmariens* of these earlier warnings.[60] Simultaneously, the Habsburg inclination to reduce the imperial Bailiwick of Haguenau to the status of an hereditary Austrian territorial possession, dictated the use of a significant degreee of caution by Colmar's authorities in order not to give the Habsburg any easy pretext to interfere with their city's autonomy.[61] Colmar's leadership knew from its own observations what such interference could be: this became apparent when Egenolph von Rappoltstein (d. 1585) began introducing the Reformation into his territories in 1555.[62] Also, Colmar had been a front row spectator when the Bailiff Nicolaus of Bollwiller attempted his vigorous (although ultimately unsuccessful) intervention in Munster, in 1563 and, in alliance with the Abbot of Munster, again from 1569 to 1575. In the years immediately preceding the decisive events of 1575, Colmar's cautious policy was further legitimized by the threat of the Counterreformation imposed upon the neighboring Margraviate of Baden by Count Ottheinrich of Schwarzenberg.[63] Thus, in the early 1570's the factor of utmost importance to the growing number of Protestants among the city councillors was the politico-religious attitude ultimately assumed by Emperor Maximilian II in the yet unresolved issue of the Reformation in Haguenau.

[59] AMC, GG 29a, 18 and 19 (Letters from the Regency of Ensisheim to Colmar of May 29, and June 25, 1556). In the second letter the Ensisheim councillors informed Colmar that, in view of taking possession of the Bailiwick by the end of the current year, Ferdinand had requested the Palatine Prince-elector, "das [er] mittler weil in der Landuogtey Hagnaw mit der Religion vnnd sonst kein ordnung vnd neuwerung fürnemen, noch solches zu thun anndern gestatten wellen . . .", and that Ferdinand had ordered them, "das wir hierinn ein vleissig vffmerckhen haben, Euch vvnd anndere Euwere mitverwandten hieriber von Irer Kön[iglichen] M[ajestä]t wegen fleissig vermanen sollen, jm fhal, das dergleichen neuwerungen an Euch vnnd sy gelangt, das Jr vnd sy darein keins wegs sich begeben . . .".

[60] On the Emperor's visit, cf. the following reports: AMC, BB 44, p. 75; and ADHR, 4 G, 5-2 (transactions of the chapter of December, 1562).

[61] See *Lucien Sittler*, La décapole alsacienne des origines à la fin du moyen-âge, Publications de l'Institut des Hautes-Etudes Alsaciennes, Vol. XII (Strasbourg 1955), p. 128.

[62] *Röhrich*, Mittheilungen, Vol. II, pp. 103–8.

[63] *Karl Franz Reinking*, Die Vormundschaften der Herzöge von Bayern in der Markgrafschaft Baden-Baden im 16. Jahrhundert: Eine Studie zur Geschichte der Gegenreformation, Historische Studien, Heft CCLXXIV (Berlin 1935), pp. 127–168.

D. THE JOINT MISSION OF HAGUENAU AND COLMAR DEPUTEES TO THE IMPERIAL COURT IN VIENNA, NOVEMBER, 1574 – JANUARY, 1575.

Shortly before May, 1575, the religious affairs of Haguenau once more captured the interest of the *Colmariens* and, finally, helped the Protestants among the city councillors to bring about the long awaited break-through for their cause. Primarily, this was a political attainment because it appears that, as early as 1565, there must have been a majority of Protestants among Colmar's leadership who, however, feared the political consequences of introducing the Reformation at that time.[64] The political outcome of the "Haguenau affair" was of the utmost importance for Colmar's Protestant party.

The increasing gravity of the Haguenau matter was foreshadowed by the difficulties faced by the council and the community of Munster, discussed by a diet of the Alsatian *Decapolis* in December, 1569. The renewed assault on the community's adherence to Lutheranism and the repeated challenge to the city's status as an imperial and "immediate" city launched by the recently elected Abbot of Munster Heinrich of Jestetten, in alliance with the Bailiff of Haguenau Nicolaus of Bollwiller, once more demonstrated the serious dimensions of the threat to the Ten Cities' autonomy presented by Habsburg-Austria's vassals and officials. The natural reaction of the Ten Cities was to intensify their interaction and solidarity as members of the *Decapolis.*[65] Meanwhile, in Haguenau the conflict with the officials of the imperial Bailiwick had increased considerably in tension and gravity.[66] There was great apprehension in Haguenau and among the sister cities of the *Decapolis*, when, on May 17, 1574, the imperial commission (conceived in 1567) finally visited the Lower Alsatian city. The commission was composed of Count Ottheinrich of Schwarzenberg, the uncompromising *spiritus rector* of the contemporaneous Counterreformation in the Margraviate of Baden, and deputees of the Bishop of Strasbourg. In their attempt to settle the conflict created by the Haguenau Reformation, the commissaries proposed the following points to the city's authorities:

1. They argued that no positive answer could be given on whether imperial cities were provided with a right to reform (i. e. with an *ius reformandi*) as long as it remained up to debate whether imperial cities were entitled to "session and vote" at imperial diets.
2. They stipulated that the so-called city article of the Augsburg treaty of 1555[67] only allowed for the existence of a Lutheran church within imperial cities where it had already existed before 1555.

[64] See Matthias Erb's letter to Heinrich Bullinger of December 23, 1565: "... Ingens spes Selestad, Colmarienses et reliquas civitates decem, quae domuj Austriacae oppignoratae sunt, Christum recepturos. Hagenouae q[uae] primaria est, ex actis sacrificis Concionatorem substituerunt, quam sequuta est Obernehem [Obernai]. Colmariae totus senatus conspirarunt in Christum, excepto uno et altero. Oramus strenue ut Christi regnum propagetur. Et uos orate pro nobis ...": AMS/AST, No. 139, fol. 184. Matthias Erb is a fairly reliable witness, for his friend and personal physician, Thomas Schoepf, kept him well informed about the religious situation prevailing in the neigboring imperial city. On Schoepf, cf. below, p. 116.

[65] Regarding the Reformation in Munster, cf. above, n. 17. As for the legal status of the Protestant church of Munster, it is important to note that unlike the Protestant church of Haguenau it was established before 1555. Cf. also *Xavier Mossmann*, "Diète de la décapole à l'occasion de nouveaux griefs de la ville de Munster contre l'abbé Henri de Jestetten: Mémoires et correspondance, 1569–1670", in idem, Notes et documents, Chap. iii (no page nos.).

[66] Cf. *Hanauer*, Le protestantisme, pp. 161–163.

[67] Cf. above, n. 6.

3. Finally, they concluded that the cities of the *Decapolis* were not entitled to base their religious policy on the city article of the Augsburg treaty because, as subjects of Habsburg-Austria, they could not claim any status of "immediacy" (*Reichsunmittelbarkeit*).[68]

The tone thus struck so forcefully by the commissaries was, of course, ill-designed to render Haguenau's leadership more amenable. On the contrary, the commissaries' full scale attack on the city's major prerogatives and autonomy stiffened the city council's uncompromising attitude. No negotiations took place, and the imperial deputees were forced to leave the city under protest and empty-handed.[69]

The far-reaching propositions of the commission made it an easy task for Haguenau to submit the matter to the next diet of the *Decapolis*, whose members' sense of solidarity had been aroused by the problems encountered by the city of Munster in 1569. Thus, on June 24, 1574, the matter was presented to the deputees of the Ten Cities, who judged it grave enough to be submitted to the next diet of imperial cities (*Städtetag*) held at Speyer on August 22, 1574. There the majority of urban delegates decided to dispatch the deputees of the *Decapolis* to Vienna to submit their grievances (along with other urban *gravamina* presented by the deputees of Strasbourg and Nuremberg) directly to the Emperor.[70]

Haguenau's *Stettmeister* Rochius of Botzheim, together with two Colmar deputees, the city-clerk Beat Henslin and the councillor Sebastian Wilhelm Linck, were put in charge of presenting the matter to the head of the Empire. They sojourned to Vienna from December 2–30, 1574, in the company of the Strasbourg and Nuremberg delegates.[71] In their supplication, they appealed to Maximilian II to recall the Ten Cities' obedience and allegiance demonstrated hitherto, and to recognize these cities, therefore, "as common, although small, but nonetheless goodhearted and obedient members [of the Empire], subject directly to Your Majesty and to the Holy Empire". In addition, they petitioned the Emperor to protect and govern them in such a way as "to let them enjoy all of the Holy Empire's constitutions, benefices and edicts established by the said common estates".[72] In his answer to their appeal, Maximilian II emphasized that he intended no reduction of the privileges commonly shared by imperial cities, and underlined that the propositions presented to Haguenau by the imperial commission in 1574 should not be understood as resulting from such intentions. However, he struck a very cautious note as he referred to the question of whether imperial cities were entitled to an *ius reformandi*:

[68] Cf. *Xavier Mossmann*, "La réforme à Haguenau; Difficultés qu'elle soulève; interventions des villes impériales, 1574–1576", in idem, Notes et documents, Chap. iv (no page nos.).

[69] *Hanauer*, Le protestantisme, p. 161.

[70] Cf. ibid.; and *Mossmann*, Notes et documents, Chap. iv; and *Rocholl*, Die Einführung, pp. 167–169.

[71] Cf. their reports from Vienna: AMC, AA 86, 37 and 39.

[72] AMC, AA 86, 33: "... vnnd demnach sy [the Ten Cities] jnn gemein als E[urer] M[ajestä]t vnnd des hayligen Reychs vnmittelbare, gleychwol geringe, doch guethertzige, gehorsambste Mitglider erkhennen ... schützen vnnd handthaben, sy alle des hay[ligen] Reychs Constitutionen, Benefitien vnd Ordnungen, souyl dieselben gemeinen Stennden zum besten vffgericht, nicht wheniger als anndere Stennd vnnd Stett jm Reych geniessen lassen ...".

> In what concerns the wholesome constitution of the religious peace [of Augsburg, 1555] and who should or should not be entitled to its benefits, His Majesty prefers not to debate the understanding of the said constitution, but leaves it standing in its intrinsic value.[73]

The indecisiveness of the Emperor thus evidenced, and undoubtedly reiterated in the report of the two Colmar deputees (back in their town on February 2, 1575) appears to have brought about the crucial shift in the attitude of Colmar's authorities in their evaluation of the political chances of a Colmar Reformation.[74] Their change of opinion was further encouraged a month later by the settlement of the six year old controversy over the city of Munster's *ius reformandi* created by the Abbot of Munster and the Bailiff of Haguenau: in the Kientzheim treaty of March 15, 1575, the differences ended in a compromise favoring the consolidation of Protestantism in Munster.[75] This treaty was, above all, the achievement of Baron Lazarus von Schwendi, the close confident of Emperor Maximilian II. Since 1573, Schwendi had been in charge of the *Reichsvogtei* of Kaysersberg, assuring the protection of the cities of Kaysersberg, Turckheim and Munster. In 1568, in taking over the dominion of Hohlandsberg, Schwendi became an immediate neighbor of Colmar. It is, therefore, not impossible that Schwendi, officially a Catholic, as a man of unusual religious tolerance, may have had an indirect influence on the determination, shared by a majority of Colmar councillors by the Spring of 1575, to tackle the task of establishing a Protestant church.[76]

[73] Maximilian II observed: "... wie auch diße gantze sach, vnndt der Statt Hagenauw wegen beschehen verordnung nit dahin zu verstehen seind, daß Jhr Kay[serliche] May[estät] dardurch den Frey- und Reichstetten an berüerten jhren im Reich hergebrachten, Stand habenden Freyheiten, Rechten vnndt gerechtigkeiten yederzit praiudicieren wellen. Waß aber sonsten die Hailsambe Constitution deß Religionfridenß betrifft, vnndt wer derselbig fähig sey oder nit, wellen Ihr Kay[serliche] May[estät] den verstand solcher Constitution nicht disputirn, sondern lassen dieselbige in jhrem werth bleiben ...:" AMC, AA 86, 34 (copy); and also AAEB, A 41, 112 (copy).

[74] See the report from the Vice-Dean and Suffragan, Marcus Tettinger, sent to the Bishop of Basel on March 14, 1575, in AMC, GG 151, 24: "... Den sonsten auch ein Geschrey aussgangen, die von Collmar haben durch jhre Gesandten, so sie bey der Kay[serlichen] May[estät] gehabt, angehalten, die augspurgisch Confehsion in ihrer Statt vermög viller Reichstäges abscheidt ahn und in das werkh zuerichten. Was die aber diss ordts erhalten, ist noch ungewiss ...".

[75] *Ohl*, Geschichte der Stadt Münster, pp. 256–283 (includes the text of the treaty); and *Adam*, Evangelische Kirchengeschichte, p. 400.

[76] On Schwendi's irenic attitude, cf. *Rudolf Krone*, Lazarus von Schwendi, Kaiserlicher General und Geheimer Rat: Seine kirchenpolitische Tätigkeit und seine Stellung zur Reformation, SVRG, Hefte 106–107 (Leipzig 1912), pp. 125–167. The most recent biography of Schwendi is *Johann König*, Lazarus von Schwendi, Römisch-Kaiserlicher Majestät Rat und Feldoberst, 1522–1583: Beitrag zur Geschichte der Gegenreformation, Schwendi (Württemberg) 1934. The several official contacts between Schwendi and the Colmar councillor Sebastian Wilhelm Linck I am aware of, however, all date from the period after the introduction of the Reformation in Colmar: "Ex Analibus Linckianis", in "Kirchners Elsaessische Chronik", fol. 324–325. Yet, through his close relationship with Johann Jacob Wecker (1528–86), Colmar's city-physician from 1566 to 1586, Schwendi must have had an intimate knowledge of Colmar's ecclesiastical politics in those days. For Schwendi's friendship with Wecker, see the latter's correspondence with his brother-in-law, the Basel professor of medicine Theodor Zwinger, UB Basel, Hs., Fr. G. Ms., I and II, *passim*. Unfortunately, this extensive correspondence contains no clues as to Colmar's contemporary religious situation. Regarding the composition of Colmar's elite during the last decade preceding the Reformation of 1575, it is interesting to note that Wecker, a member of Colmar's patrician association *Zum Waagkeller* and a former student at the universities of Basel and Wittenberg, was undoubtedly committed to the cause of Protestantism. On Johann Jacob Wecker, cf. also Matr. Basel, Vol. II, p. 37 (No. 30); and *Valentin Lötscher*, ed., Felix Platter: Tagebuch (Lebensbeschreibung, 1536–67), Basler Chroniken, Vol. X (Basel and Stuttgart 1976), p. 253, n. 788.

E. THE REFORMATION MOVEMENT, 1555–1575.

The introduction of the Reformation in Colmar on May 15, 1575, was the result of the continuous consolidation of the city's Protestant community during the two preceding decades. There is no concrete evidence pointing to the existence of an organized group of Protestants within the community in 1550. However, the city's religious life was pervaded by increasing anticlericalism[77], and, more important in this respect, by many burghers' progressive laxity and indifference to Catholic worship and to the continuance of their traditional material support for the old church and its clergy.[78] Also, the authorities' first mandate (1554) against the attendance of Protestant worship in the adjacent villages testifies to the fact that a growing number of *Colmariens* shared an interest in the Protestant message. At that time, however, sympathies with Protestantism had not yet significantly penetrated the ranks of Colmar's political leadership.[79]

As for the situation prevailing around 1560, the Dean's passionate report to the magistrate and council regarding the numerous improprieties and abuses which had gained ground among the parishioners, provides us with a relatively clear picture of the growth of the Reformation movement at that time.[80] Dean Jacob Klein opened his report with the following information: "For several years now, during Lenten fast, heated controversy and disunity in matters of faith have brought great disorder to Colmar's community". He went on to explain that the chapter of St. Martin had expected this situation to be reversed, but that despite these hopes, the religious attitude of the community had become more aggravated. Within all strata of Colmar's society, Christian regulations and the statutes of the church were now subjects of contempt and rejected by many as useless. Klein went on:

> Doubtlessly, the fact that, for several years now, various well-known booklets and sectarian, slanderous pamphlets have been sold openly and still continue to be sold on the market is an important cause of this. The common people are as anxious to get hold of them as the child is eager to play with knives ... By reasons of their ardent wish for reform, or because of their immaturity, they thus harm themselves and take offense and, as a result, try to separate themselves from the remainder of the community. They leave the

[77] Regarding acts of violence committed between citizens and clergy in 1555, cf. AMC, GG 29a, 7.

[78] In 1555, some citizens did not refrain from breaking Catholic custom by getting married during Lent. Furthermore, despite repeated exhortations of the parishioners by the clergy and the magistrate, their refusal annually to pay the so-called four offerings (cf. above, p. 91) became more and more common: cf. ADHR, 4 G, 5–1 (Capitulum Calendę Decembris, 1556); AMC, GG 26, 5; and *Rocholl,* Die Einführung, pp. 107–108.

[79] In 1557, the Protestant minister of Horbourg Bartholomäus Westheimer repeatedly regretted that the "cause of the Evangile" in Colmar was, as of yet, in a deplorable state: AMS/AST, No. 162/III, pp. 433 and 439 (Letters addressed to Conrad Hubert). In the same year, the Jesuit Peter Canisius reported from a visit to Alsace: "In reditu Ducatum Wirtenbergensem transij, ubi Dominus Israelis reliquias, sicut et in Alsatia, multas reliquit, praesertim Brisachij, Colmariae, Sletstadij, Friburgi, Rubachij, ubi magnam mihi consolationem attulerunt viri Catholici, et antiquae pietati ex animo addicti": *Otto Braunsberger*, ed., Beati Petri Canisii societatis Iesu Epistulae et acta, Voll. II (Freiburg i. Br. 1898), pp. 183–4; cf. also ibid., p. 190.

[80] AMC, GG 145, 3. Same text (without the last paragraph) also in: AMC, GG 149, 1. For the publication of the original text of this source, see above, p. ix, n. 1.

old parish church, go to Horbourg or, as several (we are told) do, run to the dark woods at night, where they hold their *conventicula*, without having any bad conscience or feelings of aversion about their transgression of Christian obedience. Consequently, matters have worsened such that, although several thousand annually attend the Holy Sacrament and join the Lord's table, only a few hundred prepare themselves through penitence, contrition and confession.

In addition, the Dean also complained bitterly about the increasingly frequent offenses against fast laws. In general, he feared that the *Colmariens* would "continue widening the hole in the fence until, ultimately, the whole hedge will be torn down". His report ended with an urgent appeal to the authorities to remediate such confusion and disorder before it was too late.

The picture drawn by Jacob Klein of a progressive indifference in the community in its attendance of Catholic worship, and of a growing laxity in the performance of Catholic rituals, is further substantiated by the increasing occurrence of tithe-refusals during the late 1550's.[81] The fact that well-to-do citizens can be found among these "tithe rebels" indicates that economic motives were, most likely, not the only cause of this phenomenon: anticlericalism and biblical considerations may also have contributed their share to the spread of collective refusal. Utterances to this effect by the landed nobleman Hans Heinrich von Landeck and by the Colmar court-clerk Anton Ortlieb are cases-in-point.[82]

Around 1560, the number of *Colmariens* who regularly kept in touch with Horbourg's Protestant minister Bartholomäus Westheimer was significant. In writing that "ciues multi Colmarienses me adeunt", Westheimer confirmed the Dean's assessment.[83] In 1566, Westheimer informed his Strasbourg correspondent Conrad Hubert, that his Sunday sermons were primarily attended by Colmar's unmarried craft journeymen – the attendance of his sermons having been forbidden to all citizens of Colmar, and punishable by a fine of ten crowns.[84] But, as we shall see, the prohibition referred to by the Horbourg pastor was not particularly effective.

Thus, from 1560 onward, in trying to assert their spiritual authority vis-à-vis the lay community, the clergy of St. Martin's met with the growing indifference and distrust of parishioners from all different levels of Colmar's urban society. By 1560, it became evident that even the magistrate and council had failed in their attempt to ward off Protestant influence from their own ranks. The increasing impact of the Reformation message on some of their members was, in many ways, mirrored in their changing church policy. However, in so far as major elements of this policy (e. g., the challenge to clerical exemp-

[81] Cf. above, pp. 100–101.

[82] AMC, FF 16, 56 (Litigation between the Colmar authorities and the nobleman Hans Heinrich von Landeck, July, 1561): Hans Heinrich von Landeck allegedly criticized the increasingly widespread opinion that tithes were an iniquitous and ungodly institution. Anton Ortlieb, in turn, allegedly cited Sebastian Franck's arguments against tithe-giving.

[83] AMS/AST, No. 162/III, pp. 479–480 (Letter to Conrad Hubert, August, 1560 [?]).

[84] Ibid., pp. 455–457 (Letter dated June 13, 1566). Westheimer's observations coincide with Christian Wurstisen's rendition of Colmar's pre-Reformation history in idem, Basler Chronick, darinn alles was sich in Oberen Teutschen Landen gedenckwürdigs zugetragen (Basel 1580), p. dclii. Wurstisen's account is based on a report sent to him by an unknown Colmar author: AMC, GG 151, 3. For the publication of this report, see above, p. ix, n. 1.

tion from taxation, or the assault upon the local episcopal jurisdiction) were of a distinctly traditional quality, it would be a mistake to consider this changing mode at its face value – that is, as unambiguous proof of growing Protestant sympathies among the city councillors. This sympathy was evidenced more unequivocally by the progressive indifference and lack of dedication to the Catholic cause, and in the authorities' weakening cooperation with the secular clergy in the suppression of the spread of Protestantism within the community.

The authorities' reaction to the chapter's grievances presented by the Dean in 1560 is an example of the deterioration of these ties. Their response in this matter was almost indecently evasive: they claimed they could not forbid travelling tradesmen from presenting their wares (i. e. Lutheran pamphlets) and only promised to admonish the burghers not to buy the "slanderous booklets" so violently criticized by the Dean. They half-heartedly promised to see to it that the parishioners did not continue severing their ties with the local church, but added that they had no means to impose similar measures upon travelling tradesmen and craftsmen. In addition, they declared their willingness to uphold the prosecution of Anabaptists and to enforce the parishioners' attendance of confession and penitence prior to their participation in the celebration of the eucharist. Yet, the magistrate and council refused to present the canons with a copy of the mandate promised, and it is telling that they refrained from the customary posting of their decree in public: they confined their action to an official reading of their mandate to the different guilds.[85] Undoubtedly, the opinion of the authorities on what to do about the growing incursion of Protestantism must have been strongly divided at this time. Their wavering position is caught in the Dean's remark, "magistratus favor hinc totus quasi extinctus est".[86]

To be sure, their half-hearted interventions did not result in the curtailment of the spread of the Protestant message within the population of their town. On April 28, 1563, following the death of Jacob Klein, Bishop Melchior of Lichtenfels ordered the Colmar chapter not to lose time installing an apt successor for Klein "so that the common, pious ... Christians there will be kept within the well-established Catholic religion ... and will steadfastly adhere to it".[87] But, at the time, the number of active Protestants among Colmar's councillors must have been a minority, for in 1564, the authorities renewed their decree prohibiting the attendance of outside Protestant services. This measure was probably a result of corresponding remonstrances made by Johann Rasser, who, from November, 1563, to January, 1565, administered the Deanery of St. Martin's.[88] The renewal of this prohibition coincided with a devastating outbreak of the

[85] ADHR, 4 G, 11: Copy of the chapter's grievances, n.d. [March 3] 1560, including the following report on the authorities' reaction to the Dean's exhortations: "Rhats mundtliche antwurt ... kurtzer inhalt: Das die hoch Oberkeyt Kayserlicher Mayestät zů diesen gefarlichen Zeytten in Religions sachen selbs nit iers gefallens ordnung machen vnd vnordnung abstellen möcht, etc; dernhalben ainem Rath dester weniger zu uerargen, etc. Wolt aber doch mittel fürnemen, vnd nechsten Sontag vff allen Zünften durch geschriben edict mass geben ... Sölch gschriben edict, demnach wier [the canons] copias daruon begert, ist allain vff den Zünften fürgelesen, aber nit angeschlagen worden, vns aber copey zu geben abgeschlagen". For the publication of the full text of this source, see above, p. ix, n. 1. Cf. also below, n. 121.

[86] ADHR, 4 G, 5–2 (Capitulum Kalendae Nouembris, 1560).

[87] AMC, GG 27, 7.

[88] *Bücking*, Johann Rasser, pp. 13–14.

plague, which did not spare the ranks of Colmar's leadership, and, thus, necessitated a redistribution of the council seats. In the following year, Matthias Erb estimated that a majority of Colmar's councillors now "conspired in Christ".[89]

Looking back, it becomes evident that the noticeable shift which occurred between Bartholomäus Westheimer's "negative" assessment of the religious situation of Colmar in 1557 [90], and Matthias Erb's hopeful observation of 1565, is accounted for by two major factors:

1. changes in the personal composition of Colmar's magistrate and council;
2. the outside influence of Protestant ministers, particularly of Bartholomäus Westheimer.

As to a third, comparatively minor factor, which, however, grew in importance after Johann Rasser resigned from the deanery in 1565, we must point to the questionable morality of some of the city's canons and priests. The daily confrontation with their worldly lifestyle enhanced the widespread anticlericalism shared by Colmar's leadership and, thus, the councillors' sympathetic disposition toward the Reformation message.

As to the changing composition of the city's magistrate[91], it is striking to note that within a period of seven years (1557 to 1564), its formation underwent a fundamental change. With the exception of Matthias Be(e)r, a member from 1544 to 1575, all of its members first elected before 1557 died within these seven years. An important result of the consecutive redistribution of seats was that the evangelical cause, so far defended within the magistrate by Jörg Vogel[92], now found two advocates who soon turned out in favor of introducing the Reformation: Michael Buob and Hans Goll, members of the magistrate from 1558 (Buob) and 1560 (Goll) to 1587. To date, very little is known about Michael Buob's life and career. Hans Goll was a second-generation descendant of a (probably) Swabian immigrant family whose father, a baker, managed to accumulate a considerable fortune within a relatively short time. Hans Goll became a citizen in 1546, and, seven years later, initiated an astounding political career by becoming guildmaster of the *Zunft zur Treue*; (thus, he cannot be regarded as one certain Hans Goll, who, according to Rocholl, was expulsed from Sélestat in 1556 for religious reasons).[93] In 1568, Hans Goll and Michael Buob found a third ally in Gregor Berger, a member of the magistrate from 1568 to 1587. From 1568 onward, the magistrate was clearly in

[89] Cf. above, n. 64.

[90] Cf. above, n. 79.

[91] On its place within the city's constitutional life and on the function of its five members, cf. above, p. 21. For the following, see *Lucien Sittler*, ed., Membres du Magistrat, Conseillers et Maîtres des Corporations de Colmar: Listes de 1408–1600, Publ. Arch. Colmar, Vol. III, Colmar 1964; and *Roland Wertz*, ed., Le livre des bourgeois de Colmar, 1512–1609, Publ. Arch. Colmar, Vol. II, Colmar 1961.

[92] In 1560, Dean Jacob Klein claimed that Jörg Vogel was "part Zwinglian and part Lutheran": ADHR, 4 G, 5-2 (Capitulum Calendae Nouembris, 1560). Jörg Vogel died on September 30, 1564: "Kirchners Elsaessische Chronik", fol. 219r.

[93] *Rocholl*, Die Einführung, p. 128. Rocholl's source is *A[ntoine] Dorlan*, Notices historiques sur l'Alsace et principalement sur la ville de Schlestadt, Vol. I (Colmar 1843), pp. 156–157, who in turn does not indicate his archival source. On Hans Goll, cf. also *Philippe Mieg*, "Généalogie de la famille Goll de Colmar", Annuaire de Colmar (1955), 68–72; and *Edouard Metzenthin*, "Anciennes familles colmariennes: Les Goll et leur origine", Annuaire de Colmar (1955), 56–68.

the hands of the future Protestant leaders; in 1575, only two of its five members did not turn out in favor of the Reformation: Matthias Be(e)r and Hans Henckel.[94]

At about the same time, important changes also occurred within the group of administrative officers who exercised great authority in their participation at the magistrate's daily meetings. In 1556, the former court-clerk Beat Henslin (d. 1595) was promoted to the post of city-clerk, which he occupied until 1575. Thereafter, he continued his political career as a member of the magistrate[95] and in 1564, Andreas Sandherr, the administrator of the hospital, succeeded Anton Ortlieb as court-clerk. Shortly after the introduction of the Reformation in 1575, he became Beat Henslin's successor as city-clerk, a position he held until his death in 1600. While the attendance of Protestant universities was prohibited to all subjects of the Austrian Sundgau, Sandherr studied at the Protestant University of Tübingen, where he married the daughter of a local family in 1557. The importance of the instrumental role played by both Sandherr and Henslin in the establishment of Protestant worship in Colmar cannot be underestimated.[96]

Regarding the composition of the city council, the Plague year of 1564 brought the demise of four councilmen and, for reasons unknown, the end of the careers of a few other councillors. They were replaced by seven new and generally younger councillors. Among the latter, Balthasar Berner, Jacob Riefflin, Michael Schuster, Hans von Embs and Michael Wydmann thus began political careers which were to last at least for a decade, or, as in the case of Michael Schuster, twice as long.[97] During the last four years preceding the introduction of the Reformation, the role of a leading promoter of Protestantism among them was played by the noble patrician Sebastian Wilhelm Linck, who served as a member of the so-called Thirteen before he entered the magistrate in 1582. The stature and influence of this man is indicated by the frequency with which he was commissioned with Colmar's diplomatic missions – as, for instance, to the imperial court in Vienna in 1574.[98] He was a son of the wealthy Colmar patrician Sebastian Linck. From 1550 to 1555, he studied at the University of Bologna. In 1565, he married Martha, the daughter of the influential clothmaker and patrician Georg Kesselring. Four years later he acquired citizenship. His death, in 1617, ended an outstandingly successful political career.[99]

[94] For Matthias Be(e)r, see the (partisan) characterization by Bartholomäus Westheimer, who depicts Be(e)r as a "Juratus hostis evangelij", as a great persecutor of Protestants, and as a "bachus nec valet consilijs sed tantum vino deditus", whose father, Franz Be(e)r, had been an enemy of Protestantism in Basel: AMS/-AST, No. 162/II, pp. 455-457 (Letter to Conrad Hubert of June 13, 1566). Matthias Be(e)r was the brother of Franz Be(e)r, Jr., the administrator of the chapter-foundation at Thann: cf. *Jürgen Bücking*, "Die Weihbischöfe von Basel Markus Tettinger (1567–1599) und Franz Beer d. J. (1599–1611)", ZSKG, LXII (1968), 132. For Hans Henckel's continued adherence to Catholicism: cf. idem, Johann Rasser, p. 26, n. 39.

[95] *Lucien Sittler*, "Colmar au XVIe siècle", Annuaire de Colmar (1975/76), 16.

[96] On Andreas Sandherr, cf. *Lucien Sittler*, "Notice sur la famille Sandherr", Annuaire de Colmar (1950), 57–66; and *Christian Wolff*, "André Sandherr, greffier-syndic de Colmar (1533–1600)", Annuaire de Colmar (1963), 68–79.

[97] Same source (also for the following) as above, n. 91.

[98] Cf. above, p. 109.

[99] *Eugen Waldner*, Allerlei aus dem alten Colmar (Colmar 1894), pp. 56–71. See also the excerpts from a now lost family chronicle in "Kirchners Elsaessische Chronik", fol. 316r–326r (Paragraph entitled "Ex

In fact, as is shown by the case of Thomas Schoepf, the restructuring of Colmar's leadership in progress during those years also included those sections of the elite, which did not directly participate in city government. Whereas Colmar's city-physician of the 1540's, Sebastian Austrius, was yet an exponent of humanist-Catholic ecclesiastical reform[100], his (indirect) successor, Thomas Schoepf (1520–77), was a convinced Protestant.[101] A former teacher in Basel and a student at the universities of Wittenberg, Basel, Montpellier and Valence, Thomas Schoepf was appointed to the position of Colmar's city-physician in 1554. During the eleven years of his stay in Colmar, he established an intimate friendship with the reformer Matthias Erb[102] and corresponded with the Zürich *Antistes* Heinrich Bullinger, with whom he shared his hopes for the victory of the Reformation in Colmar.[103] Thomas Schoepf's successor, Johann Jacob Wecker (1528–86), Colmar's city-physician from 1566 to 1586, likewise was a Protestant.[104]

This brief prosopographical survey substantiates the conclusion that, within the decade from about 1556 to 1565, a change of great consequence altered the formation of Colmar's political leadership: the majority of the new men in power were second and third generation members of a new, predominantly trade-oriented bourgeois patriciate of merchants and craftsmen. Composed of many immigrants, it began establishing itself in Colmar during the first decades of the 16th century, taking over the positions previously occupied by the old, essentially landed and noble patriciate.[105] The role played by the Sandherrs, Golls and Vischers is a case-in-point.[106] Among the older

Analibus Linckianis"). Whether Sebastian Wilhelm Linck was expulsed from Sélestat for religious reasons in 1556 is very dubious, and that he was banished in the company of Hans Goll is clearly wrong. The above was claimed by Heinrich Rocholl based on Antoine Dorlan's questionable account: cf. above, n. 93.

[100] Cf. above, p. 88.

[101] On Thomas Schoepf, see Matr. Basel, Vo. II, p. 27 (No. 6).

[102] See Erb's references to Schoepf in his correspondence with Heinrich Bullinger: AMS/AST, No. 139, fol. 134 (June 18, 1558): "Thomas Schepfius, Colmarien[sis] physicus, meus familiaris et Dominus et frater ..."; ibid., fol. 179 (March 16, 1565); and ibid., fol. 213 (May 4, 1570, after a visit from Schoepf, now the city-physician of Bern): "Venit ad me nuper de altera ascensionis meus dulcissimus frater, Doctor Thomas Scoppfius Bernensis physicus ..., admodum abituriebat Colmariam ...".

[103] STA, Zürich, E II, 346a, fol. 413 (Schoepf to Bullinger, March 13, 1559): "Tempus est sane, mi domine Bullingere, ut ad tuas datas ad me peramicas literas ... respondeam. ... Res meae in eodem [Euangelicum negotium] quo ante sunt statu, uidelicet ut cupiam reliquum uitę meae consumere in atrio domini. Faxit Dominus Jesus ut aliquando eam in domu domini, et uideam Hierusalem aedificatam ...". Cf. also ibid., fol. 414 (A letter which Schoepf wrote to Bullinger on August 3, 1559, from Mulhouse where he was visiting the Reformed minister Conrad Finck); and ibid., fol. 526 (July 7, 1564).

[104] Cf. above, n. 76.

[105] This process of the formation of a new patriciate was underlined by *Metzenthin*, „Les Goll et leur origine", 56; and, more recently, by *Erdmann Weyrauch*, "Die politische Führungsgruppe in Colmar in der Zeit der Reformation", paper presented at a symposion on Sozialgeschichte der Reformation, held at the Deutsches Historisches Institut London on May 25–27, 1978 (Publication forthcoming; see above, p. 9. n. 36). Weyrauch terms the final phase of this process, as it occurred in the 1550's and 1560's, „eine schichtinterne Elitenzirkulation", which contributed to the strengthening of the oligarchical rule entered upon by Colmar's guilded aristocracy. In 16th century urban history this phenomenom of a "circulation of elites" was by no means unique. A similar shift has been observed, for instance, in the case of Ravensburg. See *Hans Georg Hofacker*, "Die Reformation in der Reichsstadt Ravensburg", ZWLG, XXIX (1970), 76.

[106] Cf. the source-material cited above, n. 93 and 96; and *Fritz Vischer-Ehinger*, Die Familie Vischer in Colmar und Basel, Basel 1933. Although such immigrants as Thomas Schoepf and Johann Jacob Wecker

families, the Kriegelsteins, Buobs and Heckers actively participated in this change.[107] In general, by virtue of its predominantly trade-related orientation (as the source of income), this new generation of patricians shared a less conservative political outlook than their predecessors. Accordingly, most of the important representatives of the new leadership were ultimately in favor of the introduction of the Reformation. It was not without reason that the Dean Jacob Klein warned Bishop Melchior as early as 1560 about the possible effects of the ascent to power of a new generation of *Colmariens*: "especially because, in these dangerous times, all tend to favor reforms and to embrace the liberty of the flesh, so much so that overnight, after the old generation has died away, the jurisdiction of your Princely Grace and our impoverished foundation will perish, and Catholic religion will suffer great losses".[108]

In a nutshell, the spread of the Reformation movement throughout the 1550's and 1560's, involving an ever greater representative proportion of Colmar's population, may be summarized as follows. From the late 1540's throughout the 1550's, a growing indifference to the upkeep of Catholic traditions, coupled with rising feelings of anticlericalism, gradually spread across the community. Toward the end of the 1550',s this movement also reached the higher and ruling ranks of Colmar's society, where it slowly began to spread as well. In the course of the 1560's, based on this increasing indifference and anticlericalism, a gradually more discernible evangelical movement took shape. Although it undoubtedly exerted some influence on the councillors, the evangelical party within the community at large was not strong enough, or dedicated enough, to dictate its intentions to the magistrate and council. Thus, by the end of the 1560's, the authorities themselves took the lead in the movement.

The influence of the neighboring Protestant ministers, as pointed out above, was essential in shaping this evangelical party. Bartholomäus Westheimer, the minister of

(referred to above) undoubtedly contributed to a strengthening of the city's pro-Reformation party during the 1560's and early 1570's, it is, nonetheless, questionable whether these recent immigrants played a crucial role in bringing about the Reformation of 1575, as was claimed by *Joseph M. Clauss*, ed., Historisch-Topographisches Wörterbuch des Elsass (Saverne 1895), p. 209. An in-depth investigation of this claim is not possible because the Colmar *Bürgerbuch* only regularly mentions the geographical origin of persons acquiring citizenship from 1572/73 onward. See *Lucien Sittler*'s observations in *Wertz*, ed., Le livre des bourgeois, pp. x and xiv–xvi. In any case, the impact of the pro-Reformation attitude shared by an increasing number of descendants of patrician families, which were already well established in Colmar by about 1560, was certainly much more decisive. The formation of an exclusive group of thirteen families whose descendants were to occupy alternately the important position of the *Obristmeister* during the following ninety years, had become effective already by about 1540. Cf. *Weyrauch*, ibid.

[107] Cf. *Edouard Metzenthin*, "Anciennes familles Colmariennes: Les Kriegelstein et leur origine", Annuaire de Colmar (1954), 67–76; *Philippe Mieg*, "Notes complémentaires sur les Kriegelstein de Colmar", Annuaire de Colmar (1978), 153; *Edouard Metzenthin*, "La famille Hecker à Colmar", Annuaire de Colmar (1951/52), 33–44; and *Lucien Sittler*, ed., Les listes d'admission à la bourgeoisie de Colmar: 1361–1494, Publ. Arch. Colmar, Vol. I, Colmar 1958.

[108] AAEB, A 41, 31b (February 12, 1560): "... Wiewol wier am hoffen, gnediger her, Es seyen dannocht in gemeltem Magistratt ettlich recht vnd Catholisch gesint, die vilicht kein enderung in gloubens sachen sůchen oder gestatten wurden, So tragen wier doch die grossen fürsorg, ... besonder diser geferlichen zeytt alles auff neuwerung vnd fleischliche freyheit neigt, es möchte über nacht, so die alten entschlaffen, E[uren] F[ürstlichen] G[naden] an Jrer Jurisdiction, vnser verarmbten Stifft zų endtlicher verderbung, aber gemeiner Catholischer Religion ... zu grossem abbruch gelangen ...".

nearby Horbourg, was clearly the most influential among them.[109] Not long after he took over the Horbourg ministry in 1553, the chapter of St. Martin's began to evaluate his activity as a serious threat. On July 25, 1557, Dean Jacob Klein reported to his Bishop:

> I would like your Princely Grace to know that, recently, in matters of religion, I have suffered a setback at the hands of the common people who, in general, are more inclined to favor uproar rather than the keeping of peace and who [in this instance] have been incited by false instruction received from the nearby Württemberg preachers. In their own tricky ways, the latter have succeeded in doing some occasional hedgerow-preaching to the immature crowd, so that I see myself constrained to ward off their poisonous arrows through vigorous instruction and preaching.[110]

Bartholomäus Westheimer administered the parish of Horbourg until his death on Christmas, 1567.[111] An equally eloquent preacher, his successor Colmannus Poyger had no difficulties in maintaining the steady attendance of his services by a good many evangelically-oriented *Colmariens.*[112]

To be sure, the "vigorous preaching" of Jacob Klein and Johann Rasser must have had some success in countering this outside influence. But, despite their dedication, the two priests were unable to muster enough authority to bring about a successful reform of the canons' worldly lifestyle, which continued to feed the community's anticlericalism. This, and (following Rasser's resignation in January, 1565) the chapter's increasing financial and moral difficulties in trying to assure the continued recruitment of qualified preachers, contributed in turn to the growth in influence of Westheimer and his colleagues. The authorities' reproach, addressed to the secular clergy in 1560, was not unwarranted at all: They claimed that the scandalous lifestyle of a fair number of priests was a direct catalyst for the spread of Lutheranism within the community.[113]

Following the death of Bartholomäus Westheimer, Nicolaus Cancerinus (successor of Matthias Erb as superintendent of the church of Horbourg-Riquewihr) estimated the time was ripe for open influence to be exerted on the course of the evangelical movement in Colmar. In December, 1569, he had his recently published pamphlet, entitled *Der alte Glaub von der Rechtfertigung des Menschen . . .,* sent to all of Colmar's councillors. In this

[109] Cf. above, pp. 72–3 and 90–3; and *Philippe Mieg,* "Barhélemy Westheimer, pasteur à Mulhouse et à Horbourg 1499–1567", Annnuaire de Colmar (1956), 41: "On peut en effet le considérer comme le précurseur de l'introduction de la Réforme, en 1575, dans cette ville [Colmar] en raison de l'influence considérable qu'il exerça, dans le domaine spirituel, sur beaucoup de ses habitants".

[110] AAEB, A 41, 31a. An earlier complaint by the chapter about the harmful effect of Westheimer's preaching dates from August, 1554, and is cited above, p. 92, n. 110.

[111] Cf. *Mieg,* "Barthélemy Westheimer", 49; and BMC, Fonds Chauffour, I.Ch. 100 (Letter from the administrator at Riquewihr to the Duke's councillors at Montbéliard of January 23, 1567). Regarding Westheimer's death, cf. AMS/AST, No. 139, fol. 200–202 (Matthias Erb to Heinrich Bullinger, January 18, 1568).

[112] In "Kirchners Elsaessische Chronik", fol. 220r, the renewal in 1569 of the mandate against attendance of Protestant worship outside of Colmar is explained by the observation that "there was a good preacher outside [i. e. in Horbourg] so that many left town to attend the Lord's Supper there".

[113] Amongst other complaints, the magistrate's representatives, Jörg Vogel, Michael Buob and the city-clerk Beat Henslin, protested (according to Dean Jacob Klein's report): ". . . Sed heu uita nostra scandalosa haereses subinde pullulantes, et tempora pessima omni disciplina Christiana carentia tantarum turbarum causa fuerunt, et usque manent, nisi emendatio futura sit Dei omnipotentis cura et inspiratione".

printed version of a sermon he had held two years earlier at Montbéliard, Cancerinus elaborates in popular language on the very substance of Lutheran doctrine by arguing for justification by faith through God's grace, and by simultaneously condemning all faith in the salvific effect of good works. The thrust of his argument is enhanced by a wealth of quotations from the churchfathers and from the works of ancient and medieval scholars. But Cancerinus' friendly gesture proved to be premature: the Colmar authorities had all the pamphlets collected and sent back to their author at once.[114] In light of the later dogmatic development of Colmar's Protestant church[115], the assumption seems justified that it was not only a certain pusillaminity of Colmar's leadership, predominantly inclined toward Protestantism by 1569, which led the councillors to show Cancerinus the cold shoulder. It is quite as possible that, already in the late years of the pre-Reformation period, the evangelically-minded among them hesitated to submit themselves to Württemberg's influence.[116] It is interesting to note in this connection that Andreas Sandherr, one of the main promoters of Protestantism in Colmar, not only maintained contact with Cancerinus, but also entertained an intimate correspondence with the politically more independent minister of the nearby village of Jebsheim, Johannes Cellarius.[117] The village of Jebsheim was subject to the Wetzel von Marsilien, a family of imperial knights. In any case, the scarce evidence does not allow labelling Nicolaus Cancerinus as the "actual reformer" of Colmar, as stated by Heinrich Rocholl and Gabriel Braeuner.[118] In my opinion, Bartholomäus Westheimer would be a more deserving candidate – if such a title is admissable at all in the case of Colmar, where extraneous political factors manifestly exerted an overwhelming influence on the final decision in favor of the Reformation.

As mentioned above, Colmannus Poyger, minister at Horbourg from 1567 to 1587, succeeded in maintaining the religious influence on Colmar's population established by Bartholomäus Westheimer.[119] The authorities' last renewal in 1569, of their old decree

[114] AMC, GG 151, 38, 14 and 34. The complete title of Cancerinus' pamphlet reads as follows: Der alte Glaub von der Rechtfertigung des Menschen: Ein christliche vnd in Gottes wort gegründte Predig wie sich diser Zeit einfeltige Christen in den strittigen glaubens Articul von vergebung der sünden richten sollen damit sie vor Gott gerecht vnd endtlich selig werden. Zu Mumpelgardt den Sechzehenden Sontag nach Trinitatis, Anno. 67. gehalten, Strasbourg 1569. A copy is kept at AMC, GG 151.

[115] Cf. below, Chapter V.

[116] It is noteworthy, in this connection, that on May 11, 1567, Matthias Erb testified to the keen interest of many *Colmariens* in the writings of Heinrich Bullinger of Zürich: AMS/AST, No. 139, fol. 196 (Letter addressed to Heinrich Bullinger).

[117] Cf. the letter from Cellarius to Sandherr of April 28, 1575, encouraging the latter to continue his efforts for the establishment of a Protestant church in Colmar: "... Dabit autem Consilium dominus Jesus Christus quidem Optimus consiliarius. Et dabit optimum quia eius causa agitur. Tu ignaviter inceptis pergito; esto sedulus monitor multum pa ... (?) efficeres, rem enim intelliges et totum negotium est tibi cognitum: Caeteris ut plurimis hoc latet praesertim quod sit in ordine Senatorie, si vnum hoc tantum sciret quantum sic prosit habere bonum predicattorem?": AMC, GG 151, 16.

[118] *Rocholl*, Die Einführung, p. 182; *Gabriel Braeuner*, La Préréforme à Colmar (1522–1575)". Annuaire de Colmar (1975/76), 66–67.

[119] Regarding Poyger's biography, cf. *Marie-Joseph Bopp*, Die evangelischen Geistlichen und Theologen im Elsass und Lothringen: Von der Reformation bis zur Gegenwart (1540–1958), Parts I–III (One Vol.), Bibliothek Familiengeschichtlicher Quellen, Vol. XIV (Neustadt a. d. Aisch 1959–60), p. 420.

prohibiting the attendance of Protestant worship outside their city was mainly prompted by his preaching.[120] The repeated promulgation of the old decrees of 1554 and 1564 indicates what little effect the mandate must have had in the course of the preceding years. Although the evidence discussed so far allows for the assumption that from about 1565 onward there was a Protestant majority among Colmar's councillors, the reiteration of the old prohibition in 1569, demonstrates that this majority did not yet dare to defend their conviction publicly.[121]

The councillors' determination to prevent open disunity within the community,[122] and their fear of the possible grave political consequences resulting thereof, as well as from a premature attempt to introduce the Reformation, must have kept them on their guard. Thus, it is unlikely that the renewal in 1569 of the decree in question was once again based solely on an attempt to suppress the further spread of Protestantism. According to Heinrich Rocholl, the city-clerk Andreas Sandherr, in 1568, petitioned the authorities in the name of a group of Protestants to install a Protestant preacher in the former church of the Franciscans, now called the *Spitalkirche*.[123] On the occasion of the dissolution of the Franciscan monastery in 1543, this church, as we have seen, was transferred to the Colmar city government. I have found no evidence of the reaction of the magistrate and council to Sandherr's petition, but its result indicates that, once more, the votes in favor of mediation and temporizing prevailed. To the great disappointment of the Protestant party, the authorities proceeded to install the Catholic priest Michael Buchinger (d. 1571) at the hospital church.[124] The prohibition, renewed in 1569, was closely connected to the appointment of Michael Buchinger as a city preacher; according to the testimony of Conrad Scherer, the council justified the measure by decreeing "that henceforth, on every Sunday, a preacher was to preach at the hospital at 8 o'clock. Those who disliked joining the priests at the *Münster* [St. Martin's] would now be able to go to the hospital".[125] Thus, the mandate of 1569 was *also* based on the

[120] Cf. above, n. 112.

[121] This assumption is substantiated by Christian Wurstisen's contemporaneous observation that, at this time, a real suppression of Protestantism in Colmar was out of question because "even among the ruling upper classes there were secret *Nicodemi* who always advised leniency and forbearance in these matters": cf. idem, Basler Chronick, p. dcliii.

[122] Cf. ibid., p. dclii.

[123] I have been unable to come up with archival evidence in this instance. The incident is, however, reported by *Rocholl*, Die Einführung, p. 132.

[124] Cf. Conrad Scherer's report in "Kirchners Elsaessische Chronik", fol. 220r: "Anno 1569 anfangs des jahres haben die herren allhie einen newen prediger ins Spitthal angenommen, der was eines Bürger Sohn und hieß Michel Buchinger . . ., vnd thut die erste predigt auff den 23. tag Januarij, vnd frewden sich die Burgerschafft gar sehr, dann man meinte, er würde predigen dass der Augsburgischen Confession gemäß were, aber es geschahe nicht". For Buchinger's biography and a discussion of his work, see *Nikolaus Paulus*, "Michael Buchinger: ein Colmarer Schriftsteller und Prediger des 16. Jahrhunderts", Arch. EKG, V (1930), 199–223. A later report from January, 1576, claims that the Colmar authorities employed a priest from nearby Heitersheim as a preacher at the hospital church before they appointed Michael Buchinger to this position. Cf. AMC, GG 154, 7 (copy) or AAEB, A 41, 123 (original); and the discussion of this report by *Bücking*, Johann Rasser, pp. 26–7. Bücking's hasty identification of this unknown priest with Johannes Schuler is not warranted by the extant evidence on Schuler's activity. See the discussion of this evidence, below, pp. 121–2; and Bücking, ibid., p. 26. Unfortunately, I could not find any supplementary evidence clarifying whether Buchinger had, in fact, a predecessor as preacher at Colmar's hospital church.

[125] "Kirchners Elsaessische Chronik", ibid.

authorities' intention to assert their autonomy as head of Colmar's church, now that they had installed their own preacher at the hospital church. Considering the Protestants' initial disappointment that the call was extended to Michael Buchinger, it is no surprise that his preaching was not successful in reconciling the two religious factions among the parishioners – the schism between them had become too deep.

While Colmar's authorities maintained their outward commitment to Catholicism, the preaching of Johannes Schuler in turn contributed to the further erosion of this allegiance. Schuler was a vicar at St. Martin's from 1563 onward. Lack of mention of him in the records suggests that there was nothing particularly uncommon about his preaching during the period preceding 1571. However, at the beginning of January, 1571, Johannes Schuler delivered two extremely critical sermons primarily directed against disorders and abuses prevailing among the Catholic clergy. What caused Schuler's rather sudden anguish in his religious conviction we do not know. The prominent elements of his sermons were of a purely anticlerical nature so that most of his preaching, as reported by extant correspondence, cannot really be labelled evangelical.[126] Yet, his attack on the widespread contemporaneous Catholic belief in the salvific effect of good works, as part of his scathing criticism of pilgrimages, was akin to genuinely Protestant belief. It would surely help our understanding of Colmar's religious climate in 1571, if we knew more about Schuler's preaching. Unfortunately, the extant information on his two sermons at the beginning of that year is solely contained in a letter from the Colmar Provost Franz von Apponex to the Suffragan Markus Tettinger at Thann.[127] Johannes Schuler allegedly appealed to the Colmar authorities to demand from the Bishop the establishment of catechetical instruction as a means of bringing the local youth back to order and discipline. Also, Schuler apparently criticized the fact that among Colmar's city councillors, only about three were able to converse in a correct Latin. On Epiphany (January 6) 1571, he is reported to have preached "that the three Magi sought the right person, namely God" and that "anybody could do this at home without feeling obliged to run to Santiago di Compostela, to Rome, or to Jerusalem". Moreover, Schuler allegedly found fault with the theological ignorance of the Catholic bishops, including the Bishop of Basel, and the Pope, and is said to have sneered at the questionable lifestyle of some of Colmar's priests.[128]

Quite to the Bishop's relief, Schuler's unruly activity was shortlived. During the month of January, 1571, plagued with a grave illness, he was only able to deliver the

[126] The Suffragan Markus Tettinger called Schuler "a half-way wavering preacher" who ought to be exhorted to show more regularity in his adherence to Catholicism: AAEB, A 41, 74 (Letter addressed to the Bishop of Basel, February 12, 1571).

[127] ADHR, 4 G, 11 (Undated [February 7, 1571], beginning: "Copey ettlicher puncten ...").

[128] Schuler's criticism of the morality of Colmar's clergy was well justified, for even the Bishop felt obliged to admonish the Colmar canons to improve their conduct "so that your unpriestly life and conduct and your disorderly administration will not bring upon me or others the criticism of outsiders": ADHR, 4 G, 11 (Letter from the Bishop to the chapter of St. Martin, June 25, 1571), also in AAEB, A 41, 81 and 82. Furthermore, Schuler's allegations regarding the Bishop were not unfounded either, considering that in 1568 Melchior of Lichtenfels, Bishop of Basel from 1554 to 1575, was severely admonished by Pope Pius V to submit to his priestly ordination without any further delay: *Bücking*, "Die Weihbischöfe", 125.

two sermons summarized here. His only extant letter dates from the following February. It was addressed to his friend the city-clerk Beat Henslin, and mentioned as one of his supporters the court-clerk Andreas Sandherr. Schuler reported to Henslin that he was still very ill.[129] From a letter dated September 11, 1571, we learn that he died shortly thereafter.[130] Contemporaneous testimonies leave no doubt as to the repercussions within Colmar of the few sermons Schuler was able to deliver in 1571. Primarily, they found the approval of the city- and court-clerks and two councillors, Hans Goll and Sebastian Wilhelm Linck, and doubtlessly reassured these men in their commitment to Protestantism. It is also very likely that Schuler's sermons induced the magistrate and council to voice their simultaneous demand that the canons marry their maids and mistresses.[131] Secondly, although there is no direct proof for this point, concurrent correspondence demonstrates quite unambiguously that Bishop Melchior and the Colmar clergy greatly feared the adverse effect of such sermons on the community at large. Therefore, at the end of June 1571, and shortly before his death, Johannes Schuler was dismissed from his function as common priest.[132]

Following his dismissal, the chapter of St. Martin's once more claimed the services of the "spiritual fireman" (J. Bücking) Johannes Rasser, the well-reputed and highly qualified minister of nearby Ensisheim. Assuming the function of Vice-Dean, he administered the parish of St. Martin's during a period of about half a year, starting in June, 1571. But Rasser did not succeed in reversing the predominant trend: The introduction of the Reformation was, by then, only a matter of time.[133] On the contrary, by March, 1575, the increasingly uncompromising Protestant majority within magistrate and council brought the authorities publicly and ultimatively to demand the dismissal of Rasser's successor Matthias Goldenmann, whose sermons they despised because they were not exlusively based on the Gospel.[134] Already a year before, the authorities allegedly prohibited a Dominican from any further preaching.[135] At this juncture, the Bishop and the chapter attached their desperate hopes for a reversal of the tide to the preaching of the experienced Matthias Theodorici, installed at St. Martin's at the

[129] AMC, GG 152, 4a.

[130] AAEB, A 41, 93 (Letter from the Colmar authorities to the episcopal *Offizial*).

[131] Cf. above, n. 58.

[132] On June 25, 1571, the Bishop of Basel, urged by the chapter's Provost Franz von Apponex and by Johann Rasser, ordered the canons to fire Schuler on the spot: ADHR, 4 G, 11. Cf. also, AAEB, A 41, 80 (Letter from Johann Rasser and Franz von Apponex to the Bishop, June 23, 1571). For a crude, anonymous pamphlet caused by Schuler's preaching and directed against the canons, cf. AMC, GG 152, 5.

[133] Cf. *Bücking*, Johann Rasser, pp. 21–22, and the source material indicated there. In addition, cf. also ADHR, 4 G, 11 (Letter from the chapter's Provost to the Suffragan, February 7, 1571); and AAEB, A 41, 77 (Bishop to Suffragan, May 14, 1571).

[134] AMC, GG 151, 24 (Copy of a letter from the Suffragan to the Bishop, March 14, 1575): "... Jtem, jüngst verschinen haben die heren vom Capitel für sich im Rath erfordert und angezeigt, demnach ein Lobl. Reichstatt Collmar nit nuhr in eüsserlichen Sachen, sunder auch in geistlichen ein einsehen zu haben Fueg und Gwaldt, der jezig Praedicant [Matthias Goldenmann] aber ahnstatt dess h. Evangelij allein dandt [?] mehr verkhündige, item auch etliche personen uff der Cantzel schmähe. So wolle ein Ehrsamber Rath ein Capitel ernstlich vermahnen, jhne M. Mathiam fürderlich abzueschaffen, damit die nit andere Mittel fürzuenemen verursacht werden ...".

[135] AAEB, A 41, 114 (Letter from the Suffragan to the Bishop, January 13, 1575).

beginning of April, 1575.[136] But Theodorici's intervention came much too late and he was utterly unable to prevent the introduction of the Reformation on May 15, 1575.

At the end of April, the Colmar authorities asked the Strasbourg jurist Dr. Johannes Nervius to formulate his written opinion on whether, notwithstanding the fact that the imperial Bailiwick of Haguenau, whose protection Colmar was subject to, was now pledged to Habsburg-Austria, their city was entitled to an unrestricted *ius reformandi* and whether it was thus in a legal position to install a Lutheran preacher.[137] In his written statement of early May[138], Nervius expressly acknowledged Colmar's right to reform, and in his covering letter encouraged the councillors to proceed swiftly with the engagement of an evangelical preacher. In their meeting of Saturday, May 14, 1575, the magistrate and council decided to introduce Lutheran worship at once. They did so without even consulting the council of jurors. Early the following morning, the five members of the magistrate instructed the ten guilds, one by one, about their decision and in the same morning at the hospital church, Johannes Cellarius, the minister of neighboring Jebsheim, delivered the first Lutheran sermon officially preached in Colmar.[139]

[136] Cf. AMC, GG 151, 25 (Copies of correspondence concerning the appointment of Matthias Theodorici, March 20–21, 1575).

[137] AMC, GG 151, 42 (Undated [End of April, 1575]): "Summarische puncten daruber des herren doctoris bedencken zû begeren". The city-clerk's memorandum, (undoubtedly a short-form of the letter sent to Nervius), argues that Colmar's clergy had long been subject to the city's secular control in wordly affairs such as debts, sales, taxes and the like. Only recently, the Suffragan and Vice-Dean Markus Tettinger had attempted to free "himself and his bunch" ("sich und sein hauffen") from secular control and had finally driven the chapter of St. Martin into seeking Archduke Ferdinand's official protection, thus creating a situation considered intolerable by the city government. Nervius is then asked the following two questions: "Obe meine herren nit befugt, die pfaffen dahin zû uermogen, das sie new angenhomenen schurm wider auffkhundeten vnnd meiner herren schurm sich bewegen liessen oder gar von meinen herren hinweg ziehen vnnd auch meiner herren schurm verlassen muessen; item, dieweil die pfafen jnn gemain sich so ergerlich auch gotslesterlich jnn Leer vnnd leben halten, mit was fugen meinen herren ein gelerten Mann, der die Warheit predigte vnnd Augspurgischer Confession gemess bekhennen, anstellen . . . mochten vnnd vermogen Religionsfriden sich dessen gegen der Kaiserlichen Maijestät, wo sie darumb angerathen, zu entschuldigen".

[138] AMC, GG 151, 1; cf. also the covering letter sent by Nervius on the same date, ibid., 30. For the details of Nervius' advice, see the printed version of his statement in *Rocholl,* Die Einführung, pp. 223–234.

[139] AMC, GG 151, 32 (Letter from magistrate and council to Dr. Johannes Nervius, May 16, 1575); and TLA, Ferdinandea, fasc. 139, *sub* "Colmar" (Letter from the Ensisheim Regency to Archduke Ferdinand II, Mai 26, 1575). This second letter contains a detailed account of the Colmar events of May 15, 1575. For its forthcoming publication, cf. above, p. ix, n. 1.

CHAPTER V

THE PROTESTANT COMMUNITY AND CHURCH FROM 1575 TO 1628

A. THE MINISTERIAL RECRUITMENT AND DOCTRINAL DEVELOPMENT OF THE PROTESTANT CHURCH: THE TRANSITION FROM LUTHERANISM TO CALVINISM

The minister of Jebsheim, Johannes Cellarius, who preached the first Protestant sermon in Colmar on May 15, 1575, was only temporarily retained as administrator of the Protestant parish. If we are to believe Nicolaus Cancerinus' unfavorable report, his sermons did not find much acclaim. Therefore, at the end of May, the authorities replaced him with Colmannus Poyger, the pastor of Horbourg, who served the church intermittently before the arrival of Colmar's first minister Christian Serinus.[1] Very little is known about Cellarius' doctrinal position. Endowed with a stipend from Count George of Württemberg, he had studied at Lausanne, Zürich and Tübingen. Later he served the school and church of Riquewihr before he became the minister of Jebsheim in 1564. He subsequently signed the Lutheran Formula of Concord[2], and must have been, at least in outward appearance, a good Lutheran. His administration of the Lord's Supper on May 29, 1575, the first officially celebrated in Colmar, apparently found the sanction of the Lutheran Basel *Antistes* Simon Sulzer.[3]

Why did the Colmar authorities, at least initially, opt for Cellarius' service rather than the help of a Strasbourg preacher or a Württemberg minister from among the pastors of the adjacent principality of Horbourg-Riquewihr? Immediately following the introduction of the Reformation in Colmar, the superintendent of Horbourg-Riquewihr went out of his way (documented by his correspondence with the court-clerk Andreas Sandherr) to bring the doctrinal orientation of Colmar's Protestant church into accord with the Lutheran orthodoxy professed by his church. He forwarded copies of his church's current ordinance, catechism and book of psalms, and suggested that the Colmar authorities make good use of them, trying, at the same time, to dissuade the latter from adopting the Strasbourg catechism. He argued that Johann Brenz's catechism

[1] AMS/AST, No. 155, I, pp. 27–9 (Cancerinus to Pappus, June 13, 1575).

[2] For Cellarius' stay in Lausanne and Zürich, see AMS/AST, No. 139, fol. 68r (Matthias Erb to Heinrich Bullinger, August 1, 1551). For supplementary data on his career: *Marie-Joseph Bopp*, Die evangelischen Geistlichen und Theologen im Elsass und Lothringen: Von der Reformation bis zur Gegenwart (1540–1958), Parts I–III, Bibliothek Familiengeschichtlicher Quellen, Vol. XIV (Neustadt a. d. Aisch 1959–60), p. 100.

[3] This qualification of Cellarius' commitment to Lutheranism is suggested by his correspondence, in 1586 and 1589, with the Calvinist Basel *Antistes* Johann Jacob Grynaeus, and by the fact that he sent his son to study theology in Basel: cf. UB Basel, Hs., G II, 3, pp. 600–602 and 604 (Cellarius to Grynaeus, October 15, 1586 and May 23, 1589).

was also put to use at nearby Munster and at Haguenau, as well as in the adjacent villages under his spiritual control. He reminded his correspondent of the fact that many *Colmariens* had accustomed themselves to Brenz's catechism while attending Protestant worship at Horbourg and warned that the common man would almost certainly feel disconcerted about the use of a different catechism. Furthermore, Cancerinus suggested the establishment of a matrimonial court based on Württemberg's matrimonial ordinance.[4] Despite his insistance, his efforts had no immediate effect. Shortly thereafter, moved by strong feelings of frustration, he informed the Strasbourg theologian, Dr. Johannes Pappus, that the Colmar authorities were not dedicated enough to the cause of reform, or else they would already have tried to recruit a qualified and well-educated preacher and reformer able to give the young church an efficient organization. There could be no doubt, according to Cancerinus, that this lack of commitment was due to the adverse influence Johannes Cellarius had exerted on Colmar's leadership. He complained that Cellarius had not been inclined to *share* the honor of being the reformer of the city's Protestant church. Thus, the superintendent made no secret of his great satisfaction about the recent replacement of Cellarius by Colmannus Poyger. He added that he was continuing his efforts to persuade the *Colmariens* that they ought to assure themselves of the services of a qualified and erudite minister.[5] The man of his choice was his correspondent Johannes Pappus.[6]

At the end of May, 1575, the Strasbourg lawyer Dr. Johannes Nervius proposed the temporary services of the Strasbourg professor.[7] Cancerinus did not hesitate to support this candidature and in turn recommended Pappus to the court-clerk Andreas Sandherr.[8] In fact, the magistrate and council had previously sought the advice of Nervius about the recruitment of a minister.[9] However, also at the end of May, there was the visit of the Basel *Antistes* and superintendent of the church of Baden-Durlach, Simon Sulzer, who suggested the appointment of Christian Serinus, minister at Eichstetten in the Margraviate of Baden-Durlach. In a letter to Nervius dated June 2, the authorities underlined their inclination to go along with Sulzer's recommendation, arguing that they preferred the installation of a permanent rather than a temporary preacher. They made no secret of the semi-official character of Sulzer's mission – a fact substantiated by a contemporary letter to Colmar from the Basel city councillor Lux Gebhardt.[10] It appears that the Basel city council shared the lively interest voiced by the Strasbourgeois and by

[4] See his letters of May, 16, 20 and 24: AMC, GG 151; 42, 39 and 41.

[5] AMS/AST, No. 155, I, pp. 27–9 (Letter of June 13, 1575). Denigrating Cellarius with the city's authorities was perhaps part of Cancerinus' strategy, which was designed to bring to bear his and Württemberg's influence on Colmar's young church. See Cancerinus' letter to Andreas Sandherr dated May 20, 1575: AMC, GG 151, 39; and his letter to Johann Pappus of July 1, 1575: AMS/AST, No. 155, I, pp. 23–6.

[6] On Johann Pappus, cf. n. 71, below.

[7] AMC, GG 151, 53 and 19 (Letters of May 28 and 30, 1575).

[8] Ibid., 40 (Letter of May 29, 1575).

[9] Ibid., 32 (Letter of May 16, 1575).

[10] Ibid., 44 (Letter to Nervius, June 2, 1575); and ibid., 23 (Letter from Lux Gebhardt, June 2, 1575).

[11] For the interest demonstrated by Montbéliard, cf. ibid., 45 and 47 (Letters addressed to the Colmar authorities on May 21 and June 5, 1575).

the authorities of Riquewihr and Montbéliard[11] in the imminent recruitment of a Colmar minister and, therefore, in the politico-religious orientation the young Protestant church was about to choose.

When seen in connection with this multilateral, not entirely disinterested, attention devoted to Colmar's pastoral recruitment, the engagement of Cellarius and later of Serinus, appear in their proper perspective: the magistrate and council were determined to keep themselves fully in charge of their city's new church and of its institutional development and were thus inclined to forestall any large-scale outside interference. It appears that this strategy was suggested to them by Johannes Cellarius, who, through his friendship with the crucial man, the court-clerk Andreas Sandherr, had direct access to Colmar's leadership. According to Cellarius' later testimony, it was upon Cellarius' suggestion that Simon Sulzer recommended the appointment of Christian Serinus to Sandherr. Cellarius left no doubt that his suggestion was designed to thwart the installment of Johannes Pappus.[12] At that time, Simon Sulzer tried to bring about a rapprochement between the church of Basel and the Lutheran orthodoxy, newly established in Strasbourg through his colleague Johann Marbach.[13] Sulzer was the head (*Antistes*) of Basel's church from 1553 until his death in 1585. Under the aegis of his successor Johann Jacob Grynaeus, Basel's Protestantism found its re-orientation toward its Reformed heritage, that is, more precisely, toward Calvinism. However, in 1575, the year of Grynaeus' appointment as professor of theology at the University of Basel, this latter development was just beginning.[14] It is, therefore, difficult to see in the Colmar installation of Christian Serinus (who maintained close ties with the church of Basel), a decision in favor of Reformed rather than Lutheran doctrine. In fact, through their successful attempt not to commit Colmar's new church to the confessionalism of the churches of Württemberg and Strasbourg, Cellarius, Andreas Sandherr and their unknown allies among the city's Protestant leadership laid the groundwork for the open religious policy the Protestant authorities were to maintain during the following quarter of a century. Yet, in an age of growing confessionalization, such a policy of confessional nonalignment, as we shall see, was difficult to maintain and ultimately resulted in the alignment of Colmar's Protestant church with Calvinism. This re-orientation became inevitable after the Protestant leaders had provoked their church's increasing isolation within the Lutheran camp because of their refusal to sign the Lutheran Formula of Concord and as a result of the outcome of Colmar's eucharistic controversy in 1589–90. But, notwithstanding the fact that Reformed doctrine gained an increasingly stronger footing within their ranks, they essentially pursued their open religious policy well into

[12] Cf. Cellarius' letter to Johann Jacob Grynaeus of October 15, 1586: UB Basel, Hs., G II, 3 pp. 600–602.

[13] Cf. *Max Geiger,* Die Basler Kirche und Theologie im Zeitalter der Hochorthodoxie (Zollikon-Zürich 1952), pp. 8–13; for Marbach's doctrinal orientation, cf. *James M. Kittelson,* "Marbach vs. Zanchi: The resolution of controversy in late Reformation Strasbourg", The Sixteenth Century Journal, VIII (No. 3, 1977), 31–44. For a brief survey of the doctrinal re-orientation of Strasbourg's Protestant church in those days, see *Bernard Vogler*, "L'affirmation de l'orthodoxie luthérienne", in "Strasbourg au cœur religieux du XVIe siècle", ed. by Georges Livet and Francis Rapp, Société Savante d'Alsace et des Régions de l'Est, Collection 'Grandes Publications', Vol. XII (Strasbourg 1977), pp. 595–602.

[14] *Geiger*, ibid., pp. 13–15.

the 1590's. The ministerial recruitment policy they practiced during this period is a clear case-in-point.

Who were the city's Protestant ministers and deacons in the years preceding the eucharistic controversy of 1589–90? Following the joint agreement of Sulzer, Sandherr and Cellarius on the recruitment of Christian Serinus, Sulzer and the Colmar authorities did their best to bring about his swift engagement.[15] A few days later, Serinus was examined by Sulzer in Basel and on Sunday, June 12, he held his trial sermon in Colmar, interpreting the Lord's Supper based on Luke 14, and found the leading Protestants favorably disposed toward him.[16] Two weeks later, Margrave Karl of Baden-Durlach informed the Colmar authorities that he had released Serinus from his duties at Eichstetten, and on July 12, 1575, the new minister moved to Colmar, where he relieved Colmannus Poyger of his interim service.[17]

Christian Serinus was born in 1540 as a son of Leonhard Serinus or Soer (1514–1573), a former priest turned Protestant and, at that time, a schoolmaster at Kraiburg in Bavaria. In the same year, Leonhard Serinus became a minister at Justingen, near Ulm, where he stayed for four years. Subsequently, he was a preacher at Znaim in Moravia and later in Ulm, where he was forced to emigrate as a result of the *Interim* promulgated by Charles V. After 1550, he occupied the function of administrator of the hospital in the city of Horn in Lower Austria. From here, in 1557, he sent his son Christian to the University of Vienna and in 1559, to the University of Basel where, in his estimation, the "true religion" was being taught.[18] A steadfast Zwinglian, Leonhard Serinus was apparently unaware of the Lutheran orientation imputed to the church and the University of Basel at that time by Simon Sulzer. However, there can be little doubt that his son Christian's Zwinglian upbringing must have decisively shaped that latter's religious thought which, eventually, led him to embrace the Reformed rather than the Lutheran doctrine.[19] In 1560, while at the University of Basel, Christian Serinus acquired a *baccalaureus* in theology and subsequently administered different village parishes in the Margraviate of Baden-Durlach. He kept his ties with Basel after completion of his studies, reinforcing them through his marriage to Ursula Syfrid, the widow of

[15] For Serinus' biography, cf. *Bopp*, Die evangelischen Geistlichen, p. 509. For supplementary evidence: "Historia des Seerinischen Geschlechts ...": UB Basel, Hs., AA II, 2, No. 5; and *Karl Gauss*, "Die Basler Pfarrerfamilie Serin", Basler Zeitschrift für Geschichte und Altertumskunde, XXXIV (1935), 261–270.

[16] Cf. "Historia ...", ibid.; and AMC, GG 151, 46, 12 and 6 (Letters from Simon Sulzer to Colmar authorities of May 30, June 7 and June 18, 1575).

[17] AMC, GG 151, 54 (Margrave Karl to Colmar authorities, June 28, 1575); and ibid., 7 and 8 (Serinus to Colmar authorities, June 22 and July 3, 1575). For Serinus' Colmar salary, cf. AMC, BB 51 ("Eidbuch 1570"), pp. 377-8.

[18] See Matr. Wien, Vol. III, p. 120, "Natio Rhenensium", l. 9: "Christianus Soermus [!] ex Raiburg"; matriculated Fall, 1558. Cf. also Matr. Basel, Vol. II, p. 119.

[19] For the Zwinglian orientation of Leonhard Serinus (d. 1573), cf. Vadianische Briefsammlung, Vol. VI, ed. by Emil Arbenz and Hermann Wartmann, Mitteilungen zur Vaterländischen Geschichte, Vol. XXX (St. Gall 1908), pp. 297–8 (Letter from Martin Frecht of Ulm to Joachim Vadianus of April 5, 1544); and Leonhard Serinus' correspondence with Heinrich Bullinger from 1545, in Ioannis Calvini Opera quae supersunt omnia, Vol. XII, ed. by Wilhelm Baum, Eduard Cunitz and Eduard Reuss, Corpus Reformatorum, Vol. XL (Brunswick 1874), cols. 140–141 and 168–169. The complete correspondence exchanged between Heinrich Bullinger and Leonard Serinus is kept at STA, Zürich, Series E II; and at UB Basel, Hs. It is discussed by *Gauss* "Die Basler Pfarrerfamilie", 263–7.

a Basel tanner, and, following her death in 1565, to Rahel Klein (d. ca. 1629), also the daughter of a Basel burgher. Although only two of his children survived the plague of 1582, Serinus became the founder of a dynasty of Protestant ministers of extraordinary longevity. As Colmar's first Protestant minister, he played an important and influential role within the city which is mirrored by his admission to the patrician association *Zum Waagkeller* in 1583.[20] He exerted a decisive influence, as we shall see, on the re-orientation of the city's Protestant church toward Calvinism. Serinus died on October 6, 1603.

During the first year of his Colmar ministry, Serinus was assisted by the deacon Israel Ulstetter (ca. 1530–1576), a former student at the University of Tübingen and deacon at Riquewihr. Immediately following the introduction of the Reformation, his superior, Nicolaus Cancerinus, dispatched him as interim preacher to Colmar, where he subsequently found regular employment. He died, still a young man, in 1576.[21] Consecutively, two new deacons were associated with Serinus in 1577 – Kaspar Eber and Emanuel Betulejus. Eber was a former student of the Strasbourg Academy and minister at the Lower Alsatian town of Bischwiller. At that time, the church of Bischwiller, under the control of the Palatine Duke Wolfgang of Zweibrücken, clearly adhered to Calvinism. In spite of this, it is difficult to interpret the Colmar installation of Kaspar Eber as a move toward Calvinism because in 1581 he was appointed as minister of the neighboring *Lutheran* village of Bischwihr.[22] However, the second deacon engaged in September, 1577, Emanuel Betulejus, undoubtedly encouraged Serinus' gradual doctrinal shift toward Calvinism.[23]

Emanuel Betulejus was born in Augsburg between 1530 and 1540, a son of the notable scholar and humanist Xystus Betulejus (Sixt Birck).[24] Considering his father's intimate ties to Basel, where, during the 1520's and 30's (following his studies at Erfurt and Tübingen) Sixt Birck was a student, proof-reader and schoolmaster[25], it was only

[20] BMC, Fonds Chauffour, I. Ch. 83, No. 6.

[21] *Bopp*, Die evangelischen Geistlichen, p. 555; and for the arrangement of his regular employment, cf. AMC, GG 151, 11 and 48 (Letter from Colmar to the Regency of Montbéliard, and response by the Regency, June 10 and August 22, 1575). Ulstetter's marriage – shortly before his death – to Salome Vischer, the daughter of the wealthy and important merchant Leonard Vischer, is another case-in-point for the intensive symbiosis uniting Colmar's patriciate and the city's Protestant church. See *Fritz Vischer-Ehinger*, Die Familie Vischer in Colmar und Basel (Basel 1933), pp. 68–9.

[22] *Bopp*, ibid., p. 126; AMC, GG 151, 18 (Letter from the Strasbourg authorities to Colmar, Juli 22, 1577). For Eber's salary, see AMC, BB 51 („Eidbuch 1570"), p. 699. Cf. also Ludwig Rabus' letter to Kaspar Eber of March 4, 1577, admonishing the latter to abstain from excessive consumption of Alsatian wine: AMS/AST, No. 161, I, pp. 87–8.

[23] Jürgen Bücking's assumption that Betulejus served Colmar's Protestant church from the beginning is erroneous. Cf. idem, Johann Rasser (ca. 1535–1595) und die Gegenreformation im Oberelsass, RST, No. 101 (Münster/Westphalia 1970), pp. 30–1. For Emanuel Betulejus' biography, cf. BMC, Fonds Chauffour, I. Ch. 79, No. 1; *Paul Bolchert*, "A la recherche de l'élite intellectuelle de Colmar aux XVIe et XVIIe siècles: Emanuel Bétulejus, 1535?–1588, et André Beck, 1546–1627", Annuaire de Colmar (1964), 39–48; and *Bopp*, Die evangelischen Geistlichen, p. 55. For Betulejus' Colmar salary: AMC, BB 51 ("Eidbuch 1570"), p. 699.

[24] On Xystus Betulejus, cf. ADB, Vol. II, pp. 656–657; and for his activity as a humanist and schoolmaster in Augsburg: *Friedrich Roth*, Augsburgs Reformationsgeschichte, 1517–1530, 4 vols. (Second ed.; Munich 1901–1911), Vol. II, pp. 192–3; and Vol. III, pp. 150–6.

[25] *Rudolf Wackernagel*, Geschichte der Stadt Basel, Vol. III (Basel 1924), pp. 458–9.

		Works		
		No.	In %	
Editions of Bible and parts thereof		3	0.9	
Pre-Reformation authors		5	1.5	
Catholic		9	2.8	
Lutheran	First generation and orthodox	109	33.8	38.8
	Philippists	16	4.9	
Reformed	Zwinglian	116	36.0	51.2
	Calvinist	49	15.2	
Radical Reformation		2	0.6	
Unidentified		14	4.3	

Table I: Emanuel Betulejus' theological library

natural that the son was to study at the University of Basel (1553 to 1559), where he earned a master's degree in theology in 1559.[26] In Basel, Betulejus may have known Serinus, who registered as a student of theology in 1559. From 1561 to 1577, Emanuel Betulejus served as a minister at Sulzburg in the Margraviate of Baden-Durlach. Following the death of his first wife in 1585, he strengthened his ties with Basel by marrying Justitia Trockenbrot (d. 1594), the daughter of a Basel minister. He died in December 1588.[27]

Betulejus was the proud owner of a stately library containing 334 volumes, all of which he donated to Colmar's Protestant church at his death in 1588.[28] His donation later became a part of the library of the Colmar Protestant consistory. The major part of Betulejus' collection was comprised of theological works (323 out of a total of 334

[26] At the University of Basel, Emanuel Betulejus was not a student of the Calvinist professors Johann Jacob Grynaeus and Amandus Polanus, as was claimed erroneously by *Franz Lerse*, Geschichte der Reformation der ehemaligen Reichsstadt Colmar und ihrer Folgen bis 1632 (Second ed.; Mulhouse 1856) p. 43, and subsequently copied by almost all historians who dealt with this aspect of Colmar's Reformation. Grynaeus and Polanus only became professors at the University of Basel in 1575 and 1596, respectively; cf. *Geiger*, Die Basler Kirche, pp. 40 and 46. In 1559, Betulejus established contact with Heinrich Bullinger through whom he had received letters and his annual stipend from his Augsburg patron Georg von Stetten, Jr. Cf. STA Zürich, E II, 356a, fol. 1037 (Letter dated February 26, 1559).

[27] According to the record kept by Sigismund Billing (1742–1796): BMC, Fonds Chauffour, I. Ch. 79, No. 1.

[28] Betulejus' library was reconstituted and analyzed by *Bolchert*, "A la recherche", 39–44, without special attention, however, to the doctrinal orientation of the theological works it contained.

books). An examination of the doctrinal orientation of these theological works[29] reveals a strong preponderance of Reformed, especially Zwinglian, authors in the broadest sense of the term (that is, works of Zürich and "early" Basel theologians and Bucerian authors). The number of Catholic authors, on the other hand, is small.

Among the Zwinglian authors, the best represented are: Rudolf Gwalther (22 works); Heinrich Bullinger (17 works); the Zürich minister Ludwig Lavater (13 treatises); the Hessian Bucerian theologian Andreas Hyperius (5 works); Luther's adversary and later minister in Basel, Andreas Karlstadt; the Zürich theologians Josias Simler and Johannes Wolf; the Bern minister Wolfgang Musculus; and, finally, Peter Martyr Vermigli. The latter are represented with four works each. By comparison, the first generation of Swiss reformers is under-represented: there are only two works by Johannes Oecolampadius and one single treatise by Ulrich Zwingli. The ensemble of Zwinglian works alone constitutes one-fourth of Betulejus' collection of theological authors and testifies to his lively interest in the doctrine advocated and elaborated by these authors.

The Zwinglian works are supplemented by forty-nine works of Calvinist tendency. Among these, Calvin (13 works), the Calvinist Swiss theologian Benedict Aretius (10 works) and Calvin's collaborator and successor Theodore Beza (3 works) stand in the foreground. Thus, the treatises authored by Reformed theologians constitute more than one-half of Betulejus' theological library, whereas the Lutheran works represent less than two-fifths thereof. Among them, Melanchthon's works surpass Luther's by a narrow margin (17 as opposed to 13 works). Four of the Melanchthon treatises are clearly of a Reformed, that is, "Philippist" slant.[30] The attention Betulejus devoted to the study of Philippist publications is further documented by his acquisition of twelve treatises authored by the Danish Philippist Lutheran Nicolaus Hemmingius.

Although Betulejus' interest in humanism is not evident from the composition of his library (he only owned three treatises by Erasmus and a few other humanist works), he gave some evidence of his humanist erudition in the dedication of his father's edition of Lactantius to the city-clerk Andreas Sandherr, where he showed himself a judicious successor to Xystus Betulejus' scholarship.[31] A dedication in another book shows him in personal contact with the Reformed minister of Bern, Johannes Haller, who donated one of his works to the Colmar deacon.[32] In sum, the examination of Betulejus'

[29] The following analysis is based on ibid.; and on *Paul Bolchert*, ed., Catalogue de la Bibliothèque du Consistoire de l'Eglise de la Confession d'Augsbourg à Colmar; Troisième Partie: Livres du XVIe siècle, Colmar 1960, which lists Betulejus' "Ex Libris". For supplementary information, cf. also *Erich Will*, "Die Reformation in Colmar im Spiegel der dortigen Konsistorialbibliothek", ARH, LV (1964), 74–82. For the identification of less well-known authors I have used: HBL, ReThK, and Zedler's Universal Lexicon.

[30] For a concise synopsis of the theological tenets of Philippism, cf. *Jürgen Moltmann*, Christoph Pezel (1539–1604) und der Calvinismus in Bremen, Hospitium Ecclesiae: Forschungen zur bremischen Kirchengeschichte, Vol. II (Bremen 1958), pp. 66–75 ("Grundzüge der Theologie der Philippisten in Wittenberg").

[31] *Bolchert*, "A la recherche", 44. The work in question is listed in idem, ed., Catalogue, pp. 52–3 (No. 941).

[32] Haller's treatise is entitled: Sententiis ex decretis canonicis collectae, Zürich 1572: cf. *Bolchert*, ed., Catalogue, p. 46 (No. 805). Betulejus' acquaintance with Haller probably dates from Haller's stay in Augsburg in 1545–47. See HBL, Vol. IV, p. 58–9.

theological library indicates his prevalent sympathy for Reformed rather than Lutheran doctrine. Beyond this observation, the composition of his library, as well as that of Andreas Beck's, which will be examined below, mirror what has been called the open religious policy of Colmar's Protestant leadership in an age of increasing confessionalization.[33] There is no doubt that Betulejus influenced, or at least encouraged, his colleague Christian Serinus, his friends Andreas Beck and Andreas Sandherr and other notable *Colmariens*, in the pursuit of theological interests which, apparent soon after Betulejus' death in 1588, revealed a similar doctrinal slant.[34]

Very little is known about Betulejus' colleagues, Colmar's first deacons of the 1580's, who succeeded Kaspar Eber after he left the city in 1581: Martin Böhm, deacon from 1581 to 1583; Johann Conberger, deacon from 1583 to 1585; and Johann (Augustin?) Metz, who served the Protestant church of Colmar from 1585 to his death in September, 1589.[35] The first two were both graduates of Tübingen University[36] and left Colmar after a two years' stay to fulfill ministerial functions at nearby Riquewihr. The third, Johann (Augustin?) Metz, attended the universities of Basel, Heidelberg and Jena between 1567 and 1572. Nothing further is known about his career nor about his impact on the doctrinal development of the Protestant church of Colmar. He died before Betulejus' successor, Johann Georg Magnus (Gross), was about to force the city's "Crypto-Calvinists" into the open.

Regarding the open religious policy of Colmar's authorities, it is significant that following Betulejus' death, despite their earlier refusal to sign the Formula of Concord, they once more petitioned the Duke of Württemberg to furnish them with a new deacon. The churchman dispatched by Duke Ludwig was the minister of the village of Gerlingen, Johann Magnus (Gross).[37] When he arrived in Colmar on April 11, 1589, he brought with him a respectable amount of pastoral experience. After his studies at Tübingen University he had been a deacon in Augsburg from 1568 to 1586, and a minister at Gerlingen during the following two years.

Magnus' letter to Johann Pappus of Strasbourg, written in Colmar on May 29, 1589, reveals his commitment to the cause of Lutheran orthodoxy and informs us about the doctrinal division which had occurred among Colmar's Protestants. Magnus men-

[33] *Will*, "Die Reformation in Colmar", 80.

[34] An anonymous, contemporary report claims that Betulejus was a secret Calvinist who converted several notable citizens, particularly city-councillors and members of the magistrate, to his Reformed faith. This report is cited by *Johannes Schmidt*, Gründliche vnd vnvermeidentliche Widerlegung der gifftigen Lästerschrift, welche ein vngenannter Calvinist Anno 1634 ... feindseliger weise ausgesprenget (Strasbourg 1638), p. 167.

[35] For their biographical data, cf. *Bopp*, Die evangelischen Geistlichen, pp. 69, 105 and 366. For Conberger's appointment, cf. also AMC, GG 155, 5 (Letter from Duke Ludwig of Württemberg to the Colmar authorities, March 19, 1583). An autograph letter written by Conberger to Johann Nysaeus at a later date is in AMS/AST, No. 43, fol. 102–3 (dated: Malterdingen [Baden], February 6, 1592). Johann (Augustin?) Metz's death is recorded in *André Waltz*, ed., Chronik des Colmarer Kaufhauses (Colmar 1897), p. 13.

[36] His master's thesis was contained in Emanuel Betulejus' library, cf. *Bolchert*, ed., Catalogue, p. 47 (No. 836).

[37] AMC, GG 158, 35; and ibid., GG 155, 6 (Letters from Duke Ludwig to the Colmar authorities, January 16 and March 21, 1589); cf. also AMC, GG 158, 34 (List of Magnus' travel expenses). For Magnus' biography, see *Bopp*, Die evangelischen Geistlichen, p. 199.

tions that a good number of wellintentioned listeners attended his sermons but emphasizes that "there are, nevertheless, several [*Colmariens*] who are infected by Calvinism and who persist in stinging me with their thorns, whereas those who feel sympathetic toward me, do not dare to fight the others in alliance with me. I realize, therefore, that I have to be moderate and circumspect so that those who may yet be won over by Christ will not feel alienated." He underlines that the sermon he held on Ascension pleased only a few among the city's leading councillors and that it irritated "the Zwinglian hornets" among his listeners.[38] As a result, he announces his intention to visit Pappus in Strasbourg in order to seek his advice for all those who were concerned about the doctrinal vulnerability of Colmar's Protestant church. Finally, Magnus adds that his colleague, Christian Serinus, was suspected by many good men "of various subtle machinations".[39]

Considering Magnus' determination to group Colmar's Lutherans around himself and, with them, to launch an attack against the intrusion of Reformed doctrine in the community and in the ranks of the foremost councillors, it is no surprise that the doctrinal debate soon had to come to a head.[40] When it did, it took the form of a eucharistic controversy erupting in November, 1589, which ultimately led to Magnus' dismissal. The outcome of this controversy was foreshadowed ten years earlier by Colmar's refusal to sign the Lutheran Formula of Concord.

In an nutshell, this confessional document was an attempt to re-define the basic doctrinal tenets of contemporaneous Lutheranism. Championed above all by Duke Ludwig of Württemberg and the Prince-elector August of Saxony, and formulated by their respective theologians in 1577, after long and often tedious negotiations, the Concord, originally a document of theological compromise, soon became the razor's edge definitively separating Lutheranism from all other denominations and their adherents.[41]

[38] According to *Schmidt*, Gründliche Widerlegung, p. 134, this irritation resulted in a citation of Magnus by the magistrate who admonished him to refrain from preaching "new subtleties".

[39] AMS/AST, No. 159, p. 5.

[40] The eucharistic debate of 1589–90 and the subsequent doctrinal re-orientation of Colmar's Protestant church is discussed in some detail by *Schmidt*, Gründliche Widerlegung, Strasbourg 1638. In the following pages I will on occasion rehearse aspects already covered by Schmidt. Due to the polemical and apologetic nature of Schmidt's account and considering that he does not identify the majority of his sources, such a procedure is largely justified.

[41] Its text is contained in Die Bekenntnisschriften der evangelisch-lutherischen Kirche, herausgegeben im Gedenkjahr der Augsburgischen Confession 1930, ed. by Deutscher Evangelischer Kirchenausschuss (Third. ed.; Göttingen 1956), pp. 735–1100. For the history of the Formula of Concord, cf. ibid., pp. XXXII-XLIV; and *Moriz Ritter*, Deutsche Geschichte im Zeitalter der Gegenreformation und des Dreissigjährigen Krieges (1555–1648), Vol. I (Stuttgart 1889), pp. 519–521. Cf. also *Hans Leube*, Kalvinismus und Luthertum im Zeitalter der Orthodoxie, Vol. I (Leipzig 1928), pp. 1–38 ("Die Vollendung der Trennung der protestantischen Konfessionen in der Konkordienformel"). For an in-depth discussion of the history and theology of the Formula of Concord, see especially the recent joint American-German edition of quadricentennial essays by *Lewis W. Spitz* and *Wenzel Lohff*, eds., Discord, Dialogue and Concord: Studies in the Lutheran Reformation's Formula of Concord, Philadelphia 1977; and, by the same editors, Widerspruch, Dialog und Einigung: Studien zum Konkordienwerk der Lutherischen Reformation, Stuttgart 1977. See also *Robert M. Kingdon*, ed., The Formula of Concord: Quadricentennial essays, in The Sixteenth Century Journal, VIII (No. 4, 1977), containing articles by Wenzel Lohff, Gerhard Müller, Lewis W. Spitz and others.

Upon the Concord's completion, the two princes of Saxony and Württemberg, and Prince-elector Johann Georg of Brandenburg, charged themselves with seeking adherence to it from as many Lutheran territories and imperial cities as possible. However, in August, 1577, when the Colmar authorities were petitioned by the Duke of Württemberg to have their ministers and schoolteachers sign the Formula of Concord, they refused to comply. Instead, they referred to the oath[42] taken by the city's churchmen, which stipulated that the latter were to refrain from any public discussion of controversial standpoints differing from their own. Hence, the authorities added that they could not force their ministers to sign a document which not only contained the main articles of pure doctrine but which also meticulously, and point for point, condemned all other teaching.[43] To be sure, the Duke found this an unacceptable excuse and repeated his summons, warning the magistrate and council that their continued refusal would throw a dubious light on the religious teaching of the city's ministers. Despite this pressure, however, Colmar's Protestant leadership steadfastly adhered to their initial refusal and declared that they would have nothing to do with all the subtle fights between the different theological schools and with the resulting doctrinal disputes. They stated, in short, that they preferred to continue their adherence to the old Augsburg Confession alone.[44]

Who among the city's Protestants was responsible for the refusal of the Formula of Concord? What were their *real* doctrinal reasons for doing so? The extant evidence gives no satisfactory answer to these questions. Yet, it is surely not misleading to assume that the stand taken by the city-clerk Andreas Sandherr and by the two ministers Christian Serinus and Emanuel Betulejus had an important impact in prejudicing the Colmar authorities against the new Lutheran confession – even though Serinus apologetically asserted the independence of the magistrate in these matters.[45] There were many officially Lutheran German imperial cities and princes who, for various reasons, refrained from signing the Formula of Concord. Yet, within Alsace, where the Protestant churches of Strasbourg, Munster, Haguenau, Wissembourg and the principality of Horbourg-Riquewihr, all adhered to the new doctrinal guideline, Colmar's refusal ultimately led to the city's increasing politico-religious isolation. The only way out of this adverse situation was Colmar's eventual open acceptance of Calvinism, which permitted an

[42] Cf. below, p. 134.

[43] AMC, GG 153; 10, 11, 7 and 4 (In chronological order; Letters from the Duke of Württemberg to the Colmar authorities, August 17, November 18 and December 5, 1577); and ibid., 5 (Colmar authorities to the Duke, December 10, 1577).

[44] Ibid., 12 (The Duke to Colmar authorities, April 30, 1578); and ibid., 3 and 13 (Colmar authorities to the Duke, May 10, 1578 and November 12, 1579).

[45] Serinus to Johannes Pappus of Strasbourg, May 18, 1578: "Porro est vt quędam etiam ad literas T. D. ante menses aliquot de Bergicae Concordię subscriptione ad me datas, respondeam. . . . Non in nostro situm fuit arbitrio subscribere aut non subscribere, sicut nec in vestro positum fuit. Sed Magistratus noster, cui oblatus est liber, sua authoritate re deliberata subscriptionem recusavit. Honoris tum causa librum istum nobis tradidit perlegendum non subscribendum . . .". See AMS/AST, No. 157, fol. 455. (Copy of this letter in ZB Zürich, Simmleriana, Msc. S., 136, No. 176). It is interesting to note in this connection that the papal nuncio Count Portia informed the Cardinal of Como as early as July 2, 1575, that the *Colmariens* were about to install a Calvinist minister – presumably he was referring to Serinus. See *Karl Schellhass*, ed., Die Süddeutsche Nuntiatur des Grafen Bartholomäus von Portia, in Nuntiaturberichte aus Deutschland, ed. by Königlich Preussisches Institut in Rom, Abteilung III, Vol. V (Berlin 1909), p. 56.

alignment with Basel and the Palatinate. This was the ultimate outcome of the eucharistic controversy unleashed by the preacher Johann Georg Magnus in 1589.

In his full-scale attack on the intrusion of Calvinist and Zwinglian thought among the ranks of Colmar's Protestants, Magnus was forced into an embittered feud with his colleague Christian Serinus, who, by that time, had come a long way toward openly embracing the Reformed doctrine. As a friend of many influential citizens and member of the city's patrician association, Serinus had no difficulty in mobilizing prestigious support against his opponent. Thus, on November 24, 1589, Magnus was cited by the magistrate[46] and admonished to recognize his colleague Christian Serinus as a brother in Christ and to live in friendly harmony with him. He was also admonished to uphold the preacher's oath he had taken.

In this oath, dating from 1575, the city's Protestant preachers swore to preach nothing but the "Evangile" and the teachings of the churchfathers wherever they conformed to Scripture. They were obliged to preach and to administer the sacraments according to the prescriptions of the Augsburg Confession of 1530. Furthermore, they promised in their oath not to calumniate the Roman Catholics and not to start any dispute with their fellow Protestants nor to condemn them in public, but, rather, if need be to admonish them in private with all due modesty. Finally, through the oath they were obliged to take, the preachers pledged to reserve all political matters for the secular authorities and not to infringe upon the competence and prerogatives of magistrate and council.[47]

On December 22, 1589, when the doctrinal dispute between the two ministers had reached a new climax[48], the magistrate presented Magnus with a confessional document especially drafted for the occasion and intended to serve as a basis for the settlement of the ongoing controversy. Although this is not expressly stated in the document, there can be no doubt that it was the city-clerk Andreas Sandherr who drafted its original version, faithfully integrating into his first draft a number of important corrective suggestions, to all appearances from the hand of Christian Serinus.[49] This important document contains the most crucial evidence on the doctrinal position assumed by Colmar's leading Protestants around 1590. It has never been analyzed in detail and requires, therefore, our attention before we resume discussion of the course of events.

In the preamble of this doctrinal stratement, which was later called the Colmar „*Deklarationsschrift*", the drafting of the document was justified by the fact that the

[46] AMC, GG 158, 13. Cf. also, ibid., 30 (Letter from Magnus to the Colmar authorities, n. d.). This citation came about after Serinus allegedly had uttered doubts as to Christ's bodily presence in the Lord's Supper in a sermon held at the beginning of November, 1589, thus urging Magnus to assert publicly the veractiy of the dogma in question. See *Schmidt*, Gründliche Widerlegung, pp. 136–9.

[47] AMC, BB 51 ("Eidbuch 1570"), pp. 377–8 ("Predicanten Ayde").

[48] Cf. *Schmidt*, Gründliche Widerlegung, pp. 139–140.

[49] The original document is contained in AMC, GG 158, 26, and was printed by Johannes Schmidt in his Gruendliche Widerlegung in 1638 (pp. 140–7). Sandherr's original authorship is ascertained in Andreas Beck's letter to Johann Jacob Grynaeus of ca. December 26, 1589: UB Basel, Hs., G II, 2, fol. 116–7. For Sandherr's and Serinus' joint authorship in the drafting of the final version, cf. *Schmidt*, ibid., pp. 147–8 (referring to a now lost account by Serinus). For some of the original drafts in the hand of Andreas Sandherr, cf. AMC, GG 158, 18 and 28; and for Serinus' subsequent corrections, AMC, GG 158, 17.

preachers were not adhering to their oaths calumniating their adversaries from the pulpit or condemning the teaching of Zwingli and Calvin in connection with the interpretation of the Lord's Supper. Such action was branded as a deplorable source of irritation for the common man, who was rendered uncertain in his faith through such doctrinal dispute. Thus, the purpose of the *Deklarationsschrift* was to inform the city's Protestant preachers of the meaning of the oath taken by them and about how the authorities expected them henceforth to interpret two relevant articles of Lutheran creed contained in the Augsburg Confession of 1530 – those pertaining to Christology and the Lord's Supper.

The central passages of the document are divided into two closely interrelated parts containing a discussion of Articles Ten and Thirteen of the Augsburg Confession. The first paragraph of this discussion begins as follows:

> We, the magistrate and council hold that Article Ten of the Augsburg Confession which, in part, is the object of the present debate, is true and we want it to be preached . . . clearly, in the way it is stated: 'About the Lord's Supper we teach that the true body and blood of Christ are really present in the eucharist, administered and taken in the form of bread and wine.' etc.

The following sentence contained in the Augsburg Confession: "Therefore, we reject contradictory teaching[50]," is omitted in the Colmar document. In light of the frequent exhortation in the *Deklarationsschrift* instructing the city's preachers to refrain from any calumniation of Zwingli and Calvin, this omission is quite significant. In their criticism of the Colmar statement, the Lutheran pastors of Wissembourg did not fail to draw attention to this point.[51]

The Colmar document continues:

> Thus, we confess and understand that the body and blood of Christ . . . truly are administered to the believers and received[52] by them in the Lord's Supper with bread and wine ["*mit* brot vnnd Wein"] as a nourishment for the soul rather than the belly. Therefore, the body and blood of Christ are neither eaten ["genossen"] in the manner of the Capernaites[53], nor figuratively or imaginatively . . . but rather supernaturally and in an inscrutable and inexplicable way. Thus, Christ is really present in those who faithfully take the Sacrament ["denen, so daß Sacrament mit glauben nießen"], and they, in turn, are and live in Christ and have communion with his body and blood and are, therefore,

[50] Die Bekenntnisschriften, ed. by Deutscher Evangelischer Kirchenausschuss, p. 64.

[51] Letter addressed to Johann Georg Magnus in Horbourg of July 25, 1590: AMS/AST, No. 98. See also the letter addressed to Johannes Pappus on July 24, 1590, by the Wissembourg minister Peter Bilfinger summarizing his and his colleagues' disapproval of the Colmar confession, which had been sent to them by Magnus: "Non sine lachrymis experti sumus quam lethale vulnus Satanas per semi Cuinglianos et clancularios Calvinistas ecclesiae Colmariensi inflixerit. . . . Ecclesiae Colmariensi afflictissimae pie atque ex animo condolemus . . .". See AMS/AST, No. 154, fol. 229–232. (Copy of this letter in ZB Zürich, Simmleriana, Msc. S., 147, No. 53).

[52] "Received" ("Empfangen") replaced the term "eaten and drunk" contained in the original version of the document.

[53] See John 6, 23. The reservation against the "Capernaite" rite is contained both in Lutheran and Reformed confessions: see *Wilhelm Niesel*, ed., Bekenntnisschriften und Kirchenordnungen der nach Gottes Wort Reformierten Kirche (Second ed.; Zollikon-Zürich [1938]), p. 264 (Confessio Helvetica Posterior, 1566); and Die Bekenntnisschriften, ed. by Deutscher Evangelischer Kirchenausschuss, p. 994 (Formula of Concord, 1577).

furthered in their eternal life, comforted, nourished, fed and imbued ["getrenckhet"], as is said about the Sacrament in the Apology[54] and substantiated by St. Augustine, who said that faith in the attendance of the Sacrament, but not the sacramental act itself, was grounds for justification.[55]

The statement in the above paragraph regarding the real presence of Christ in the Lord's Supper would have been acceptable both to the Reformed and to the Lutheran theologians of that day. The unmistakable rejection of the exclusively tropological, figurative interpretation of the eucharist it contained, was a rejection of Ulrich Zwingli's, but not of *later* Zwinglian doctrine, as advocated by Heinrich Bullinger. As for John Calvin, he had never shared Zwingli's tropological interpretation of the eucharist. Thus, following the 1540's, the basic issue at stake between Bullinger, Calvin and their successors on the one side, and their Lutheran opponents on the other, was not the real presence of Christ in the Lord's Supper as such, but rather the *way* in which Christ was present, i. e. the *modus praesentiae*.[56]

However, on the whole, the paragraph cited above cannot be considered a purely Lutheran statement. At least two points contained in the *Deklarationsschrift*, in fact, suggest that the document had definite Philippist leanings:

1. The substitution in the original draft of the Colmar confession of 1589 (on a suggestion by Christian Serinus)[57] of the term "receiving" the eucharist for the original "eating and drinking", eliminates the only formulation in this document akin to the term *mündliche Niessung* (oral consumption) of the eucharist, consistently used by the 16th century Lutheran theologians in their attempt to emphasize Christ's real bodily presence in the bread and wine of the Lord's Supper, and so prominent in the Formula of Concord of 1577. The term *mündliche Niessung* is missing throughout the Colmar document – an omission which was bitterly criticized by the Lutheran pastors of the sister city of Wissembourg.[58] In fact, in suggesting the replacement of "eating and drinking" by "receiving", Serinus clearly had in mind the spiritual con-

[54] A reference to Philip Melanchthon's *Apologia Confessionis Augustanae* of 1530; cf. Die Bekenntnisschriften ibid., pp. 139–404.

[55] The reference to St. Augustin is contained in ibid., p. 293. However, the interpretation given the citation from the churchfather is more akin to Heinrich Bullinger's of 1566 than to Melanchthon's of 1530: cf. *Niesel*, ed., Bekenntnisschriften, p. 265.

[56] For a brief, succinct discussion of the differences between the Lutheran and Calvinist view of the *modus praesentiae*, see *Hans Emil Weber*, Reformation, Orthodoxie und Rationalismus, Vol. I, Part II, Beiträge zur Förderung christlicher Theologie, Reihe II, Vol. XVL (Gütersloh 1940), pp. 205–209. For Ulrich Zwingli's position, see *Gottfried W. Locher*, "Grundzüge der Theologie Huldrych Zwinglis im Vergleich mit derjenigen Martin Luthers und Johannes Calvins", in idem, Huldrych Zwingli in neuer Sicht: Zehn Beiträge zur Theologie der Zürcher Reformation (Zürich and Stuttgart 1969), pp. 257–265, especially 261. For Heinrich Bullinger's view, see Justus Heer (and Emil Egli), "Bullinger, Heinrich", in REThK, Vol. III, pp. 543 and 545; and *Joseph C. McLelland*, "Die Sakramentslehre der Confessio Helvetica Posterior", in Glauben und Bekennen, Vierhundert Jahre Confessio Helvetica Posterior: Beiträge zu ihrer Geschichte und Theologie, ed. by Joachim Staedtke (Zürich 1966), pp. 379–391. For the specific affinities between the eucharistic theology of Bullinger and Calvin, cf. *Hans Grass*, Die Abendmahlslehre bei Luther und Calvin, Beiträge zur Förderung christlicher Theologie, Reihe II, Vol. XLVII (Gütersloh 1940), pp. 186–190; and *Ernst Bizer's* observations on the same problem: cf. below, n. 61.

[57] Serinus' suggestions for the correction of the original draft of the Deklarationsschrift are contained in AMC, GG 158, 7.

[58] Cf. n. 51, above.

sumption (*geistliche Niessung*) of the eucharist[59], giving the Colmar interpretation of the respective passages of the Augsburg Confession a distinctly Philippist tendency.

2. The above observation is further substantiated by the use of the formula "*mit brot vnnd Wein*" (*with* bread and wine), which, in the Colmar document, replaces the formula *in-, sub-, et cum pane et vino*. In the second half of the 16th century, this reduction to the *cum*-formula was characteristic of Philippist eucharistic theology and was frequently used by the later Melanchthon and his disciples.[60] The Philippist interpretation of the Lord's Supper was of a clearly Reformed slant.

Notwithstanding these unorthodox elements, tenets basically acceptable to both the Lutheran and later Reformed traditions were voiced again in one of the following paragraphs of the *Deklarationsschrift*: that it was not the believer's faith, but rather Christ himself and his eternal, omnipotent word that incorporated his body and blood in the sacrament. Yet, by strongly emphasizing that the believer could count on divine consolation through attendance at the Lord's Supper, the authors distinguished their creed from Heinrich Bullinger's Reformed assertion that the reception of divine grace took place essentially, if not exclusively, before and outside of the act of communion in the Lord's Supper.[61]

The Colmar authors proceeded from there to a condemnation of the important Lutheran assertion that the impious could also receive the body of Christ – only, however, as a divine judgment.[62] They argued that it would be very hard for any poor Christian to understand that Christ could offer his redeeming body to those who believed in him as a vehicle for their communion with him, and simultaneously offer his body to the impious as a means entailing damnation rather than consolation. The Colmar authors did not explicitly reject the participation of the impious in the sacrament of the eucharist, but they refuted the Lutheran notion that the impious could partake, unto their own damnation, in the oral eating of the *res sacramenti* – the body and blood of Christ. Thus, they decisively placed themselves outside the camp of Lutheran orthodoxy, whereas Calvin and Bullinger would have accepted Sandherr's and Serinus' formulation, although they might have wished to see a *positive* statement on how the *Colmariens* interpreted the participation of the impious in the eucharist, going beyond the mere refutation of the Lutheran notion of the *manducatio impiorum* contained in the *Deklarationsschrift*.[63]

[59] Cf. AMC, GG 158,7. See also the refutation of such an exclusively spiritual understanding in the Formula of Concord: Die Bekenntnisschriften, ed. by Deutscher Evangelischer Kirchenausschuss, pp. 989–990.

[60] Cf. *Moltmann*, Christoph Pezel, pp. 20 and 71; and *Edmund Schlink*, Theology of the Lutheran Confessions, trans. by Paul F. Koeneke and H. J. Bouman (Philadelphia 1961), pp. 169–174.

[61] However, Heinrich Bullinger put considerably more weight on the objectivity of the sacrament of the Lord's Supper than his Zürich predecessor Ulrich Zwingli: cf. *Ernst Bizer*, Studien zur Geschichte des Abendmahlsstreits im 16. Jahrhundert (Third ed.; Darmstadt 1972), pp. 243–270. See also the literature cited above, n. 56. On Martin Luther's view, cf. *Bizer*, ibid., p. 312; and for the position of the "fathers" of the Formula of Concord, cf. *Schlink*, Theology, pp. 163–6.

[62] On the central place of the notion of *manducatio impiorum* in 16th century Lutheran eucharistic theology, cf. *Weber*, Reformation, Orthodoxie, pp. 218 and 227.

[63] For Calvin's conception of the *manducatio impiorum*, see *Grass*, Die Abendmahlslehre, pp. 212–3, 226 and 238. For Bullinger's: *McLelland*, "Die Sakramentslehre", pp. 374 and 378.

It is clear that only a strong slant toward the Reformed pneumatological interpretation of the Lord's Supper could lead the Colmar authors to the above rejection. Presuming logical thinking on the part of the authors, their interpretation must have been based on a predominant emphasis on the believer's faith as communicated by Christ's spirit as a necessary prerequisite for the actual partaking in the Lord's Supper. Although not explicitly transparent in the Colmar document, such an understanding came close to the contemporaneous Reformed formulations as outlined in the *Confessio Helvetica Posterior* of 1566, and the *Heidelberg Catechism* of 1563.[64]

The fountainhead of such a position was the christological understanding of the presence of Christ's human nature in the eucharist, which the authors of the Colmar document explained in their interpretation of Article Thirteen of the Augsburg Confession of 1530:

> And to further a final clarification, we profess, hold true, and believe that the contents of Article Thirteen of the Augsburg Confession[65] are true and genuinely Christian.

This is followed by a criticism of those

> scholars who, out of special pertness and ambition, try to investigate and debate [the qualities of] the person of Christ and, thus, of the real, essential Godhead, and who, therefore, anguish . . . the poor [common] man.

Within the context of the subsequent passages, there can be no doubt that this attack was a well-disguised criticism of the Lutheran view of the *communicatio idiomatum*; that is, of the "reciprocal communication of divine and human nature in the person of Christ" (J. Moltmann). The Philippists replaced the Lutheran understanding of the hypostatic union between the two natures of Christ with an anthropologically-oriented dialectical interpretation of the *communicatio idiomatum*: according to them, communication did not take place between the two natures as such; the two natures, they claimed, were solely unified through reciprocal communication within the person of Christ as *mediator*.[66] Like the contemporary Reformed theologians, they thus insisted on the difference between divine and human natures of Christ the *redeemer* and therefore opposed the Lutheran belief that real communication between the two natures could take place after Christ's ascension to heaven.[67]

Not sharing the deep Lutheran *Glaubensinteresse* involved with this issue, the Colmar confession of 1589 followed the Philippist and Reformed interest in ascertaining

[64] *Niesel*, ed., Bekenntnisschriften, p. 264 (Confessio Helvetica Posterior, 1566), and p. 164 (Heidelberg Catechism, 1563; questions and answers 65 and 66). Cf. also the succinct summary of Calvin's position in *Grass*, ibid., p. 255.

[65] Cf. Die Bekenntnisschriften, ed. by Deutscher Evangelischer Kirchenausschuss, p. 68: "Article XIII (On the use of the sacraments): On the use of the sacraments we teach that they were not only established as outward signs whereby Christians can be recognized. They are also signs and the testimony of the divine will and, thus, awaken and strengthen our faith. Therefore, their use requests faith, and they are rightly used, if they are received in faith, whereby the faith in turn is strengthened".

[66] *Moltmann*, Christoph Pezel, p. 67. For the Lutheran position, see *Schlink*, Theology, pp. 161–2.

[67] On the conception of the *communicatio idiomatum* in 16th century Lutheran theology, see *F. Frank* (and *Reinhold Seeberg*), "Communicatio idiomatum", in REThK, Vol. IV, pp. 256–7; and *Weber*, Reformation, Orthodoxie, pp. 151–152, 183–184. For the Reformed view and the christology of the later Melanchthon, cf. *Weber*, ibid., pp. 131–147 (for Melanchthon, especially pp. 143–145). For the christological debate between Lutheran and Reformed theology, see also the succinct analysis in *Grass*, Die Abendmahlslehre, pp. 239–249.

simultaneously the autonomous majesty of the Godhead as well as Christ's true humanity. Thus, it is underlined in the *Deklarationsschrift* "that the Son of God has not suffered for our sin in his divine nature, but rather in his acquired humanity ("sonder allein nach seiner angenohmenen menschheit"), which is unified with God in a personal way". It followed from the Lutheran assertion of the hypostatic union between the natures of the omnipotent God, and of Christ, the Son of man, that the human nature of Christ could partake in the unlocalizable being of the divine Logos. Thus, in their christology and eucharistic theology, Lutheran theologians, especially the Swabians Johann Brenz and Jacob Andreae, claimed the ubiquity of Christ in his divine and human nature alike[68], asserting that Christ can be bodily present whenever, wherever and in whatsoever way he chooses.

Yet, on the basis of their dialectical conception of the *communicatio idiomatum*, the Philippists and Reformed theologians alike were unable to accept the Lutheran dogma of the ubiquity of Christ's human nature. In Germany during the second half of the 16th century, the dogma was rejected by the Philippist theologians of Hessia, Silesia, Nassau and the city of Bremen, and, of course, by the Calvinist theologians of the Palatinate and other territories and cities converting to Calvinism.[69] Considering their preceding assertion, it was logical that the authors of the Colmar *Deklarationsschrift* joined the ranks of these theologians in refuting this Lutheran dogma. In doing so, they once more emphasized their spiritual understanding of the eucharist. They stated:

> We believe steadfastly that Christ the Lord, although he is in heaven, can act through his strong hand, his spirit and giftedness, wherever and whenever he pleases; and, since he promises to be present in his word, he may also be bodily present. But hereby, we do not want to condone the newly invented ubiquity, or try to limit Christ's action, as though Christ, the true God and man, could not and would not want to act through his spirit and giftedness in his [bodily] absence.

In its insistence on Christ's bodily presence in heaven, and, accordingly, on Christ's spiritual action among the believers, as well as in the weakening insertion to the effect that Christ *may* be bodily present in the eucharist, this last paragraph leaves no doubt as to the Reformed doctrinal tendency of its authors. This impression is further substantiated by Serinus' suggestions for the correction of the respective passages in Sandherr's original draft of the *Deklarationsschrift*.[70]

I have already referred to the unfavorable opinion shared by the Lutheran ministers of Wissembourg regarding the Colmar confession of 1589. In summarizing the above observations, let us first look at another contemporaneous review of the Colmar document. In a letter addressed to the Colmar authorities on January 13, 1590, the Strasbourg Lutheran theologian Johannes Pappus observed that the Colmar confession grieved and angered many pious Christians in Strasbourg. This was so

> because, even though it [the Colmar confession] is comprised of several points which reflect the true doctrine of the Holy Evangile and the right understanding of the

[68] *Weber*, ibid., pp. 150–185, especially 151–152 and 164–165.

[69] *Moltmann*, Christoph Pezel, pp. 68–69.

[70] Regarding the rejection of the Lutheran belief in the ubiquity of Christ's human nature Serinus states: "Ubiquitas is justly attributed to the person of Christ, but not to his human nature. This is why I would put the words: 'The refuted ubiquity of the human nature in the person of Christ'": AMC, GG 158, 7.

Augsburg Confession, the major part of the Concept agrees with Zwingli's and Calvin's opinion. . . . It follows necessarily from this that no teacher, whatever opinion he adheres to, and as long he honestly intends to profess publicly what he . . . believes, can really accept this Concept, for, if he truly adheres to the Augsburg Confession, he will only accept the lesser part of the Concept and reject the remainder as contradictory to what he has accepted. However, if he adheres to Zwingli's and Calvin's opinion, he will approve of the major part of the Concept; as for the remainder, he will either impose upon it an interpretation other than the one intended [by its authors], or else reject it in its entirety.[71]

Many of the formulations contained in the Colmar *Deklarationsschrift* were indeed compatible with the basic stance of concurrent Lutheran eucharistic theology; yet, none was genuinely Lutheran. The rejection of a purely tropological and figurative understanding of the Lord's Supper, as advocated by Ulrich Zwingli, was shared by Lutherans and Calvinists alike, and the same was the case with the concomitant assertion that it is not the faith of the believer but rather Christ's grace and his eternal word that incorporate his body into the eucharist.[72] As for the claim of Christ's real presence in the eucharist, it cannot be regarded as genuinely Lutheran when seen within the context of the document. It was stated rather ambigouously. Any comment on the way Christ was present in the Lord's Supper was avoided, whereas the rest of the statement was given a clearly pneumatological slant.

The remainder of the tenets expounded in the document are of an obvious Philippist stance. To be sure, Philippism, as seen both from a theological and historical perspective, was an intermediary position: the solution of its inherent doctrinal contradictions inevitably led to its eventual fusion with Calvinism. Theologically this is exemplified in the path chosen by Christoph Pecelius (1539–1604), and historically by the politico-religious development of the Protestant church of Bremen.[73] The Colmar *Deklarationsschrift* of 1589 was, generally speaking, a Philippist statement in the sense that the majority of the tenets enunciated in it were neither Lutheran nor genuinely Calvinist. The confession drafted by Andreas Sandherr with the help of Christian Serinus documented an intermediary stage in the doctrinal development of the city's Protestant church, which eventually – now that a return to strict Lutheranism would have appeared as a debasing surrender – led to the open acceptance of Calvinist doctrine.

As early as 1590, Colmar's influential Calvinists, such as Andreas Beck, tried to bring about this change in the eucharistic liturgy in use at the hospital church.[74] In practice, this doctrinal development toward open adherence to Calvinism was reinforced by the politico-religious isolation of the city's Protestant church, resulting from the refusal

[71] The letter is printed in *Wilhelm Horning*, Dr. Johann Pappus von Lindau, 1547–1610: Münsterprediger, Universitätsprofessor und Präsident des Kirchenkonvents zu Strassburg (Strasbourg 1891), pp. 292–294. Regarding Pappus' role in Strasbourg, cf. *Anton Schindling*, Humanistische Hochschule und freie Reichsstadt: Gymnasium und Akademie in Strassburg, 1538–1621, Veröffentlichungen des Instituts für Europäische Geschichte Mainz, Vol. LXXVII (Wiesbaden 1977), especially pp. 364–374; and *Vogler*, "L'affirmation de l'orthodoxie luthérienne".

[72] Cf. *Weber*, Reformation, Orthodoxie, pp. 223-226.

[73] Cf. *Moltmann*, Christoph Pezel; and *A. Walte*, "Mittheilungen aus der bremischen Kirchengeschichte", Zeitschrift für historische Theologie, XXXIV (1864), 3–110; XXXVI (1866), 339–428.

[74] Cf. below. p. 147; and *Weber,* Reformation, Orthodoxie, p. 209.

to sign the Formula of Concord and the outcome of the eucharistic controversy of 1589–90. This isolation facilitated and enhanced the spread of Calvinism among the leading Protestants and, eventually, resulted in their close alignment with the church of Basel.

In surveying the *Deklarationsschrift* in its entirety (including the sections not discussed here), it is above all its irenic tone that catches the reader's attention. This irenicism is apparent especially in the repeated attempts to circumvene what the document brands the subtle sophistry of contemporaneous theology in revitalizing the re-unifying basis of apostolic thought. In fact, this is a theme which is likewise advocated in the preacher's oath of 1575, referred to above. One is tempted to look at this irenicism as a last trace of the humanist climate governing the city's ecclesiastical policy of the 1530's and 1540's. Maybe it was more than just a coincidence that both then, as later (1589–90), the city's crucial ecclesiastical decisions were, above all, taken by educated laymen.[75] To be sure, Serinus' assistance to Sandherr in the drafting of the *Deklarationsschrift* was important; yet politically, the city-clerk's action was encouraged and supported by others. A contemporary source informs us "that the whole past action was carried through solely by several of the foremost jurists rather than by the entire city-council".[76] Considering that the recruitment of Protestant ministers – as is suggested by the installation of Matthias Heinerius in 1604 – was effectively an exclusive privilege of the magistrate, this observation seems all the more plausible. The city-councillors' authority in such matters resided in the right to confirm the candidates previously appointed by the magistrate. Thus, only the members of the magistrate could exert a long-range influence on the church's doctrinal development, which was largely determined through the policy of ministerial recruitment.[77]

In light of Magnus' observation that the majority of the foremost members of city government („Senatores primarii") did not agree with his sermons[78], the assumption that next to Andreas Sandherr, Sebastian Wilhelm Linck[79] and Beat Henslin (both

[75] In this respect, see *H. Trevor-Roper's* thoughtprovoking remarks. He claims that in the Reformation years, „the abuses of the church drove its critics into extremity and the Erasminans wherever they were, found themselves obliged either to surrender at discretion or to admit themselves heretics. If they chose the latter course, they became Calvinists. For Calvin, more than is generally admitted, was the heir of Erasmus: the heir in a more intolerant age, it is true . . . . but still, in essentials the heir": idem, "Religion, the Reformation and social change", in idem, The European Witch-Craze of the Sixteenth and Seventeenth Centuries and Other Essays (New York and Evanston, Ill. 1969), p. 26.

[76] "Dise gantze verloffene handlung [ist] allein durch ettliche der fürnembsten Im recht vnd gar nicht durch einen gemeinen Radt gehandlet worden": AMC, GG 158, 23a (Letter from the Bailiff of Riquewihr to Count Friedrich of Württemberg, December 29, 1589).

[77] See AMC, BB 45 (1598–1604), p. 681: A synopsis of the recruitment procedures in the case of Matthias Heinerius, dated February 11, 1604. See also Johannes Schmidt's observation regarding the outcome of Colmar's eucharistic controversy of 1589–90. He claims that everything "durch die Obrigkeit vnd zwar, eigentlich zu reden, nur durch etliche wenige Personen auß dero Mittel berathschlaget, gehandlet, beschlossen vnd ausgemacht worden; da haben die vbrige Stände, das Ministerium vnd das gemeine Volck nichts zu thun gehabt . . .." See *Schmidt*, Gründliche Widerlegung, pp. 117–8.

[78] AMS/AST, No. 159, I, p. 5.

[79] For his (and Sandherr's) concurrent correspondence with the Calvinist Basel *Antistes* Johann Jacob Grynaeus, cf. AMC, GG 158, 8. For Sandherr's and Linck's role, cf. also Andreas Beck's remark to Johann Jacob Grynaeus: „. . . spero in te nihil desideratum iri. Poteris hac causa uel D. praetori Sebastiano

members of the magistrate) played an instrumental role in the eucharistic controversy of 1589 seems entirely justified. As for the other members of the magistrate, the participation of the *Obristmeister* and influential cloth-merchant Ludwig Kriegelstein is insufficiently evidenced, but nonetheless strongly suggested by the weigth of his Dutch and English trading connections.[80] Furthermore, at least in one case, this group could count upon influential support from outside their ranks: the role played by Andreas Beck is a case-in-point. He was a close friend and relative of Andreas Sandherr and, in all likelihood, an *intimus* of Serinus as well. Although he never became a councillor, his impact on the doctrinal development of Colmar's Protestant church must have been extremely important ever since he acquired citizenship in Colmar in 1579.[81] Therefore, his career and doctrinal stand deserve a closer look.

Andreas Beck was born the son of a well-to-do family in neighboring Catholic Ammerschwihr in 1546. In 1565, he registered as a student at the Catholic University of Freiburg im Breisgau, where he must have experienced a religious conversion, for, in 1568, we find him at the Calvinist University of Heidelberg, where he studied law. He later entered the services of the Upper Alsatian landed nobleman, Claus von Hattstatt, whose lands he continued to administer until 1610, following Hattstatt's heirless demise in 1585. In this function, Beck maintained an intensive correspondence with Basilius Amerbach of Basel regarding various legal problems, while Amerbach furnished him with learned works of jurisprudence.[82] In 1591, Beck was entrusted with the position of Bailiff of Sainte-Croix-en-Plaine (Heiligkreuz). As Colmar's Bailiff, he later fulfilled several important diplomatic missions in the service of the city council and must have continuously exerted a great influence on the city's politics. He died in 1627, and, like his close friend Emanuel Betulejus (d. 1588), he donated his library to Colmar's Protestant church.[83] Although Andreas Beck (unlike Betulejus) was a layman, his library contained almost exclusively theological works. The examination of Beck's 313 theological works makes a strong case for their owner's Reformed conviction.

Wilhelmo Linckio, uel archegrammateo Andreae Sandtero (hi enim soli collent literas, caeteri amusi) rescribere": UB Basel, Hs., G II, 2, fol. 116–117 (Letter of ca. December 26, 1589).

[80] Cf. *Edouard Metzenthin*, "Anciennes familles colmariennes: Les Kriegelstein et leur origine", Annuaire de Colmar (1954), 69. In February or March, 1590, Ludwig Kriegelstein warned the new deacon David Hiemeyer from maintaining any association with Magnus and his followers: BMC, Fonds Chauffour, I. Ch. 23, No. 8, fol. 1v. Cf. also below, p. 146. The reference to the merchant Kriegelstein in this respect, is purely speculative, it is true. However, his case might encourage an eventual examination on how the predominant orientation of Colmar's 16th century trade toward the Netherlands and Switzerland influenced the leading *Colmariens'* doctrinal position. The important role played by merchants in the spread of the Reformation is underlined by *Harold J. Grimm*, "The Reformation and the urban social classes in Germany", in Luther, Erasmus and the Reformation: A Catholic-Protestant reappraisal, ed. by John C. Olin, James D. Smart and Robert E. McNally, S. J. (New York 1969), p. 75.

[81] For his biography, see *Bolchert*, "A la recherche", 46–48. Bolchert, however, was unaware of Beck's active concern for the prosperity of Colmar's Protestant church. For Beck's correspondence with Johann Jacob Grynaeus of Basel, and for his role in the 1600 appointment of the minister Ambrosius Socinus, cf. below, pp. 149–50.

[82] This correspondence from the years 1588–90 is contained in: UB Basel, Hs., G^2 II, 67, fol. 147–169.

[83] For an analysis of his library, see *Bolchert*, "A la recherche", 39–44; and for supplementary observations *Will*, "Die Reformation in Colmar". The "Ex-Libris" of the books owned by Andreas Beck are indicated in *Bolchert*, Catalogue.

		Works		
		No.	In %	
Editions of Bible and parts thereof		11	3.5	
Pre-Reformation authors		11	3.5	
Catholic		31	9.9	
Lutheran	First generation and orthodox	58	18.6	23.1
	Philippists	14	4.5	
Reformed	Zwinglian	79	25.3	53.5
	Calvinist	88	28.2	
Unidentified		19	6.1	

Table II: Andreas Beck's theological library

The list of Andreas Beck's collection of theological authors testifies to his broad interest. Unlike Betulejus', his library included, for instance, treatises written by the French Huguenot nobleman Philippe du Plessis-Mornay (two works), by the Dutch Calvinist nobleman Philippe de Marnix, and even by Englishmen such as William Perkins and William Whitaker (one work each). Generally, however, Beck devoted his interest to the collection of German and Swiss Calvinist and Zwinglian authors, an undertaking which was facilitated by his contact with the Zürich printer Christoph Froschauer and by his friendship with Hans Jacob Fries (1546–1611), a Zürich professor of philosophy and theology.[84] Another important feature of Beck's library is the strong representation of 16th century humanism: the ten Erasmian treatises Beck owned are a case-in-point. The example of the Calvinist jurist Andreas Beck thus re-emphasizes the frequently made observations on the intrinsic affinity between humanism and Calvinism.[85]

The analysis of the Philippist position and Calvinist tendency of the Colmar *Deklarationsschrift* of 1589, and the subsequent discussion of its authorship, in the widest possible sense of the term, allows us to turn our attention back to the course of events at the end of the year 1589. The distinguished Strasbourg church historian and a

[84] Christoph Froschauer presented him with a treatise by Heinrich Bullinger, and Hans Jacob Fries donated one of his own works and a Zürich eucharistic confession of 1545. Cf. *Bolchert*, Catalogue, pp. 29 (No. 463), 42 (No. 726) and 82 (No. 1561). On Hans Jacob Fries, cf. also HBL, Vol. III, p. 338.

[85] Cf. *Bernard Vogler*, Le clergé protestant rhénan au siècle de la Réforme (1555–1619), Association des Publications près les Universités de Strasbourg (Paris 1976), p. 309; and for concise theological observations on the problem: *Roland H. Bainton*, The Reformation of the 16th century (Boston 1952), pp. 69–70. Cf. also above, n. 75.

former minister in Colmar, Henri Strohl, once keenly observed that, after the introduction of the Reformation in 1575, Colmar's Protestants "upheld their commitment to the original tradition of the churches of Strasbourg and Württemberg, namely, to entertain a good *entente* with all Protestants".[86] It is not surprising, then, that the city-clerk finished his harangue, delivered against the controversial preaching of Johann Georg Magnus on November 24, 1589, with a reference to the Wittenberg Concord of 1536: "The Upper German cities and the Wittenberg theologians have agreed to remain true to the plain statements [jointly established], and to refrain from further harmful disputes".[87] Ironically, what could have unified the Protestant church of Colmar with the churches of Strasbourg and Württemberg in 1536, could only contribute to their separation sixty years later.

Since the deacon Johann Georg Magnus refused to adjure the *Deklarationsschrift*, he was dismissed by the authorities at the end of December, 1589.[88] The young and very recently appointed deacon Bartholomäus Haller (the successor of Johann [Augustin?] Metz, and a former student of Johann Pappus in Strasbourg), in turn, refused to sign the doctrinal statement and shared Magnus' plight. Subsequently, the church of Württemberg attempted to hold on to its old influence on Colmar's religious climate by installing Magnus in neighboring Horbourg.[89] Magnus' move to this town sealed the doctrinal split between Colmar and Württemberg: in a letter written in late January, 1590, pertaining to Magnus' dismissal, Duke Ludwig of Württemberg concluded that the Colmar *Deklarationsschrift* was unacceptable to any "pure and trust-worthy" minister because it contained two inherently contradictory lines of argumentation – one Lutheran, and the other Zwinglian or Calvinist. The Duke severely criticized the "spiritualist" and Reformed elements of the document and, thus, amply defended Magnus' refusal to accept it.[90] At this juncture, the Colmar authorities refrained from any further petitioning of the Duke to supply them with new ministers as they had done in the past. But it is significant for the position they assumed, which speaks for their distinct rejection of all confessional intransigence rather than for the clarity of their doctrinal stand, that Württemberg Lutherans continued to be appointed after 1590 as Colmar ministers – such as Johann Ernst Frisch, a son of the minister of the neighboring Württemberg village of Ostheim.[91]

[86] *Henri Strohl*, "Les experiences d'une église au cours de quatre siècles", in Vom Wesen und Wandel der Kirche: Festschrift für Eberhard Vischer, ed. by Theologische Fakultät der Universität Basel (Basel 1935), p. 117.

[87] AMC, GG 158, 13: "Es haben sich die oberlendische Stedt vnd Wittenberg. Theologi mit einander vereinbart, bei diser einfaldt zu uerpleiben vnd vernerer schedlicher disputationes sich zu enthalten ...".

[88] Cf. *Schmidt*, Gründliche Widerlegung, pp. 148–9.

[89] AMS/AST, No. 159, I, pp. 7–8 (Letter from Magnus to Johannes Pappus of Strasbourg, May 10, 1590). For Haller, cf. *Bopp*, Die evangelischen Geistlichen, p. 211.

[90] AMC, GG 158, 25 (Letter addressed to the Colmar authorities on January 21, 1590). The letter is printed in *Schmidt*, Gründliche Widerlegung, pp. 156–160. Cf. also AMC, GG 158, 36 (Letter from Duke Ludwig of April 21, 1590). The Duke's exhortation resembles the one sent to Colmar by Johann Pappus of Strasbourg in January, 1590, discussed above, pp. 139–40.

[91] Cf. *Bopp,* Die evangelischen Geistlichen, p. 168. On Frisch's understanding with the Lutheran opposition in town, cf. below, n. 109.

Colmar's connection to the church of Strasbourg – disrupted by the dismissal of Bartholomäus Haller – disintegrated before long. In May, 1590, Magnus begged Johann Pappus of Strasbourg to publicize the news about the intrusion of Calvinism into the ranks of Colmar's Protestant leadership. He hoped that Pappus' assistance would provide him with the attendance of Colmar's "many goodhearted" Lutherans at his sermons in Horbourg. He thus petitioned Pappus to publish a brief, critical sermon on the state of Lutheranism in Colmar. I am not aware of Pappus ever having done so, but he did, as we have seen, reprimand the Colmar authorities for their unorthodox *Deklarationsschrift.*[92] Meanwhile, as Magnus had wished, the news about the outcome of Colmar's eucharistic controversy became common knowledge among Strasbourg's ministers and theologians. It is significant that in this new situation Colmar's Protestant leadership, in search of qualified successors for Magnus and Haller, now preferred to seek the advice of those Strasbourgeois, who, in the ongoing doctrinal dispute between the orthodox Lutheran theologian Johannes Pappus and Strasbourg's old Reformed schoolmaster Johannes Sturm, took sides with the latter: on May 13, 1590, the Strasbourg city-clerk Paul Hochfelder recommended to his Colmar colleague the services of young Johann Glossius (or, Closius), thus confirming an earlier letter sent to Andreas Sandherr by his fellow citizen Nicolaus Fuchs.[93] Hochfelder added that the atmosphere prevailing among Strasbourg's theologians was such that Glossius could only come to Colmar if he was previously assured of an engagement there, so as to spare him a return to Strasbourg and almost certain painful exposure to general ostracism. This guarantee was arranged upon Hochfelder's assurance that Glossius did not object to adjuring the *Deklarationsschrift* and Colmar's preacher oath.[94] Subsequently, Johann Glossius, a former student of Tübingen University, served Colmar's church during the following three years. Later, after a stay in Austria, he reappears in the records as a minister in the Calvinist Palatinate.[95] His appointment followed the dismissal of the deacon David Hiemeyer, which, more so than the ousting of Bartholomäus Haller, had provoked the general outrage of Strasbourg's churchmen.

David Hiemeyer and Andreas Irsamer were appointed as deacons in January and February, 1590, on the recommendation of Johannes Pappus of Strasbourg.[96] Andreas Irsamer from Ratisbon was a mature and experienced minister who had served the

[92] AMS/AST, No. 159, I, pp. 7–8 (Letter dated May 10, 1590). For Pappus' letter of January 13, 1590, cf. above, pp. 139–40.

[93] For Nicolaus Fuchs' letter: AMC, GG 158, 23 (January 16, 1590). Fuchs was a draper and member of the Strasbourg city council in 1571 and 1572: Cf. *Jacques Hatt*, ed., Listes des Membres du Grand Sénat de Strasbourg du XIIIe siècle à 1789 (Strasbourg 1963), p. 435.

[94] AMC, GG 158, 19 and 20 (Letters of May 13, and May 18, 1590). In the contemporary doctrinal struggle between the Strasbourg professor Johann Pappus and the old, meritorious Rector Johannes Sturm, Paul Hochfelder, a cousin of the latter, openly took sides in favor of Sturm: *Schindling,*: Humanistische Hochschule, p. 140. Cf. also *Edouard Sitzmann*, ed., Dictionnaire de biographie des hommes célèbres de l'Alsace depuis les temps les plus reculés jusqu'à nos jours (Reprint of first ed., n.p., 1909; Paris 1973), Vol. I, p. 783.

[95] Cf. *Bopp*, Die evangelischen Geistlichen, p. 186. For Glossius' salary: AMC, BB 51 ("Eidbuch 1570"), p. 733. Cf. also AMC, BB 45 (1588–98), p. 187.

[96] Cf. *Horning*, Dr. Johann Pappus, p. 292; and, for Hiemeyer's appointment: BMC, Fonds Chauffour, I. Ch. 23, No. 8, fol. 1r.

Lutheran churches of Phalsbourg and, later, Lingolsheim from 1553 to 1590.[97] Soon after his installation in Colmar, he aligned himself with his fellow minister Christian Serinus, which earned him the derogatory label of "hypocrite and drunkard" from the embittered Magnus.[98] Whether Irsamer was amenable because of doctrinal conviction or rather for material reasons is not clear. However, later evidence shows that his association with Serinus was far from harmonious, and that, in his heart, he must have remained a good Lutheran.[99] He remained a Colmar deacon until his death in August 1600.

For David Hiemeyer (b. 1561 in Nördlingen), who had just graduated from the Strasbourg Academy, the Colmar appointment was his first post in the ministry.[100] Like all other Colmar ministers and deacons, he was obliged to swear the preacher's oath, which, due to the authorities' experience with Magnus and Haller, was now interspersed with the central doctrinal statements of the *Deklarationsschrift* of 1589 (however, only in an attenuated form), which committed future preachers to refrain from public discussion of such issues as the *manducatio impiorum* and the local presence of Christ in the Lord's Supper. The new oath also contained the very Erastian stipulation that all preachers should avoid the introduction of new ecclesiastical ceremonies unless authorized to do so by the magistrate and council.[101] Allegedly, in spite of these detailed orders, David Hiemeyer did not adhere to the oath he had sworn: as early as March, 1590, according to Christian Serinus' testimony, Hiemeyer discarded his oath and publicly calumniated all Calvinists and Zwinglians. At the same time, he provoked the authorities' reprobation for his publication of a short sermon celebrating the imminent 15th anniversary of the introduction of the Reformation in Colmar – a flaming attack on contemporaneous Catholicism. Later, Hiemeyer allegedly dared to administer privately the Lord's Supper to a group of citizens whom Serinus defiantly called "rebellious Magnists" – the unruly followers of the dismissed deacon Johann Georg Magnus. Finally, as Serinus observed, Hiemeyer, in a state of acute drunkenness, had even gone as far as to slander the doctrinal position of his colleagues Serinus and Irsamer. Inevitably, the young deacon's rashness brought about his interrogation by the authorities and, subsequently, his dismissal and expulsion from town on May 1, 1590.[102] This action definitively severed Colmar's official ties with the Lutheran church of Strasbourg.

[97] *Bopp*, Die evangelischen Geistlichen, p. 264.

[98] AMC, GG 158, 3 (Letter from Andreas Irsamer to the Colmar authorities, June 9, 1590). See also Irsamer's own report on how he was recruited at Lingolsheim by a Colmar delegate in *Schmidt*, Gründliche Widerlegung, pp. 164–6. For Magnus' judgment, cf. AMS/AST, No. 159, I, pp. 7–8 (Letter addressed to Johannes Pappus, May 10, 1590). For Irsamer's salary, see AMC, BB 51, ("Eidbuch 1570"), p. 732.

[99] See below, p. 150.

[100] *Bopp*, Die evangelischen Geistlichen, p. 241.

[101] AMC, GG 158, 27 ("Predicanten Aidt").

[102] Hiemeyer's sermon was published under the title: Ernewerung der Kirchen bey den Barfüssern im Spital, der Hoch löblichen Reichsstatt Colmar, die noch vor 16. Jahren dem abgesagten Teuffel selbst, durch seine Baalitische Meßpfaffen . . . gedient . . . , Strasbourg 1590. Serinus' testimony (BMC, Fonds Chauffour, I. Chr. 23, No. 8, fol. 1r–2r) contradicts the claim of *C[harles] A. Hanauer*, "Les Historiens de l'établissement du Protestantisme à Colmar", RCA, I (1859), 442–443, that Hiemeyer actually held this sermon in Colmar and subsequently published it with the magistrate's authorization. As early as April 16,

In the course of Hiemeyer's interrogation, he and his two fellow preachers presented their written testimonies to the magistrate. Hiemeyer's and Serinus' statements are still extant.[103] The young deacon's *Apologia* is rather confusing. The little useful information it contains refers to Serinus' liturgical practice and to the doctrinal split within the Protestant community: Hiemeyer claimed that Serinus not only used real bread during the celebration of the Lord's Supper but that he also, at least in the case of the patrician Andreas Beck, allowed laymen to break the bread themselves according to Zwinglian tradition. In his own testimony, Serinus acknowledged the veracity of the deacon's claim. It is thus evident that by 1590 Serinus was well on the way toward the implementation of a Reformed eucharistic liturgy. Furthermore, Hiemeyer claimed and emphasized that a representative number of city councillors remained in doctrinal agreement with the dismissed Johann Georg Magnus – an assertion which remained unchallenged by Serinus.[104]

Hiemeyer's latter allegation substantiates Serinus' reference to a group of "rebellious Magnists" and evidences that the dismissal of Johann Georg Magnus had brought about the formation of a group of loyally Lutheran citizens, possibly also comprising a small number of city councillors, which found itself in doctrinal opposition to the "Cryptocalvinist" ecclesiastical policy implemented by the magistrate and its allies.[105] The doctrinal division among the parishioners, referred to by Hiemeyer, is further evidenced by a letter from Master Martin Stromeyer, a member of the patrician association *Zum Waagkeller*, who claimed to be the speaker of the Lutheran opposition and whom the magistrate had allegedly forbidden further contact with Magnus, then at Horbourg.[106] Unfortunately, I have found no evidence of the size of the oppositional faction represented by Stromeyer. However, since only parishioners of at least a rudimentary education could grasp the meaning of the ongoing controversy, it can reasonably be supposed that this opposition was composed of relatively influential citizens and that the doctrinal split may have run straight through the ranks of the city's patricians. Did Martin Stromeyer and the Bailiff of Sainte-Croix-en-Plaine (Heiligkreuz), Johann

1590, Hiemeyer wrote a long letter to his Strasbourg colleagues seeking their support for his employment in Strasbourg's ministry. Referring to his Colmar experience, he complained: "Etsi igitur, Charissimi Fratres, non ignorem, Cinglij et Caluini errorem de coena Domini late per orbem Christianum diffusum esse, eique non solum imperitam plebem sed etiam gubernatores potentes applaudere ac patrocinio multorum, que doctrina et autoritate clarent in Ecclesia, defendi. Tamen . . . non passus sum me cunctis Dei miserationibus minorem a labore meo sincere et simplicissime explicandi doctrinam publice de praesentia corporis Christi in Eucharistia deterreri cothurno Colmariense. Nec me fugit, Fratres, quid homines profani atque humanae impudenti ore crocitent, quamquam graui inuidiae me multorum magni nominis uirorum exposuerim. Nota enim atque perspecta mihi sunt ipsorum consilia, quibus Ecclesiae uulneribus mederi conantur . . .". See AMS/AST, No. 158, fol. 153. (Copy in ZB Zürich, Simmleriana, Msc. S., 148, No. 10). For Hiemeyer's dismissal, cf. also his own account in AMC, GG 158, 21 (Letter to the Colmar authorities, September 23, 1590).

[103] BMC, Fonds Chauffour, ibid.

[104] Regarding a similar claim, cf. also the quotation from Hiemeyer's letter of April 16, 1590, cited above, n. 102.

[105] A breach between the two opposed factions of parishioners was also acknowledged by the authorities in their letter to Duke Ludwig of Württemberg defending their dismissal of Magnus: AMC, GG 158, 16 (n. d. [May, 1590]).

[106] AMC, GG 158, 6. For Stromeyer's patrician status, cf. BMC, Fonds Chauffour, I. Ch. 83, No. 6.

Heller, represent the interests of other citizens or just their own, when they, according to Andreas Irsamer's testimony, tried to talk the latter into refusing all cooperation with Christian Serinus, even if such action meant Irsamer's dismissal? Allegedly, they informed Irsamer that, after all, the authorities could not continue indefinitely dismissing one minister after another.[107] In the eyes of the magistrate, the incident represented an act of insubordination on the part of Johann Heller, which may have prompted his dismissal in 1591. His successor was the Calvinist Andreas Beck.[108] The case of Johann Heller demonstrates that the Lutheran opposition, however important its resources may have been, did not succeed in influencing effectively the magistrate's politico-religious decisions. I am not aware of any further open action taken by this group or members thereof, although around 1600 there was still a kernel of influential Lutherans among the Protestant parishioners.[109] Later evidence even suggests that from about 1590 to 1627 the majority of Colmar's Protestants upheld their commitment to Lutheranism and never really followed the example of the patricians in power who quasi-unanimously adhered to Calvinism.[110]

After 1590, as the Protestant leadership gradually consolidated its friendly relations with the churches of Basel and the Palatinate, the estrangement separating the Protestant church of Colmar from the Lutheran churches of Strasbourg and Württemberg became insurmountable. However, the survival of a Lutheran opposition within the Protestant community beyond 1590, and the fact that the so-called "sacramentarians" (Zwinglians and Calvinists) were excluded from the legal recognition of Protestantism by the Peace of Augsburg of 1555, forced the magistrate and its allies among Colmar's patricians to implement their political re-orientation with great caution. This may help to explain why, for the time being, nothing resulted from the contact established with the

[107] AMC, GG 158, 3 (Letter from Andreas Irsamer to the Colmar authorities, June 9, 1590): "Donnerstag nach Judica, welcher der 9 Aprilis war, dieses 1590 Jhars, sein nach dem Morgen essen der Vogt [Johann Heller] sambt Stromeier zu mir kommen, vnd sonderlich der Vogt mich angeredt, ob ich noch des Sinnes sey, mit herren Christiano [Serinus] auf Ostern das Nachtmal zu reichen. Darauff ich ihme diese Andtwort geben: Ja, ich sey es gesinnet, denn ich albereit der leng nach mit ihme geredt, befinde aber nichts an ihme, das ich tadeln könte. Drauff sie zur antwort geben, er stelle sich nur also, es sey ihme nicht ernst. 'Das mag sein (sagte ich), denn ich kan keinem sein herz erforschen, welches allein Gott gebüret'. Sie aber hielten steiff an, ich solte allerdings herren Christiani müssig ghen, vnd solte ich schon drüber Vrlaub fordern, denn man werde nicht so können einen nach dem andern fortschicken . . .". Cf. also AMC, BB 45 (1580–99), pp. 65 and 71.

[108] AMC, BB 51 ("Eidbuch 1570"), p. 383 (Oath taken by Johann Heller on October 22, 1588, and by Andreas Beck on February 27, 1591).

[109] See UB Basel, Hs., G I, 33, fol. 99 (Ambrosius Socinus to Johann Jacob Grynaeus, October 8, 1600). In a note from April, 1601, the Calvinist minister Ambrosius Socinus refers to the Protestant deacon Johann Ernst Frisch as to a personal and doctrinal adversary and central figure within this group of Lutherans. As partisans of Frisch he mentions the patricians Johann Barth, Martin Stromeyer, Egenolph Wetzel and the Latin schoolmaster Christoph Kirchner. Excepting the latter, all of these men belonged to influential Colmar families; but none occupied a high office in city-government. See BMC, Fonds Chauffour, I. Ch. 23, No. 1, fol. 10v. The note is cited by *Schmidt*, Gründliche Widerlegung, pp. 170-1. Christoph Kirchner's later adherence to Calvinism is suggested by his emigration to Basel in 1628 and his employment as a teacher there. Cf. below, p. 160.

[110] Cf. *Schmidt*, ibid., pp. 204–5. But see also ibid., p 220: „Vnläugbar ists, daß die einfaltige Evangelische Burgerschafft in Colmar meistentheils hiebevor in der Meynung gewesen, es werde kein andere, dann die reine Lutherisch-Evangelische Religion in jhren Kirchen ab den Cantzeln von den Predigern gelehret".

Basel *Antistes* Johann Jacob Grynaeus in 1589–90. It was Leonhard Serinus, son of the Colmar minister and one of Grynaeus' students, who first directed his professor's attention toward the eucharistic controversy in progress in Colmar. Subsequently, Grynaeus expressed his sympathy to Christian Serinus and offered his advice and help in overcoming the problems caused by Johann Georg Magnus.[111] During the following two weeks, Grynaeus' initiative brought about an intensive correspondence with the *Colmariens* Andreas Sandherr, Sebastian Wilhelm Linck and Andreas Beck: the Basel *Antistes* was charged with the recruitment of a new deacon and entrusted with a copy of the *Deklarationsschrift*, which he praised as a true and orthodox interpretation of the salient passages of the Augsburg Confession.[112] At once, Grynaeus proposed two candidates for Magnus' succession, but, for reasons unknown, their appointments did not materialize.[113] Instead, the Colmar authorities, as we have seen, appointed Andreas Irsamer and David Hiemeyer. The authorities' affiliation with the Calvinist church of Basel was strengthened only gradually during the following ten years, reaching its full extent in the years following the turn of the century. This evidence imposes the tentative conclusion that, by 1590, the Calvinists among the city's leading Protestants could not muster enough authority to give their church a distinctly Reformed appearance. Moreover, relative doctrinal harmony between the ministers and deacons was not achieved before the end of the century, so that the Calvinist laymen could not count upon the preachers' undivided support.[114]

It was up to the energetic Calvinist minister Ambrosius Socinus, a native of Basel, to bring about increased doctrinal harmony within Colmar's Protestant ministry and to strengthen the ties between the Protestant churches of Colmar and Basel. Unlike the case of the Philippist Christian Serinus, there can be no doubt about Socinus' uncompromising Calvinist position.[115] A graduate of the universities of Basel and Heidelberg, he was dismissed after twenty-one years of service in the Margraviate of Baden-Durlach for continuously refusing to sign the Lutheran Formula of Concord.[116]

[111] Ibid., Hs., Fr. Gr. Ms. I, 19, fol. 27 (Letter of December 21, 1589). For Leonhard Serinus, Jr., cf. *Gauss*, "Die Basler Pfarrerfamilie Serin", 270–1.

[112] Letters from the period December 26–29, 1589: ibid., G II, 2, fol. 116–117 (Andreas Beck to Grynaeus); AMC, GG 158, 12 and and 8 (Sandherr to Grynaeus; Grynaeus to Sandherr and Sebastian Wilhelm Linck).

[113] Letters from the period January 1–5, 1590: UB Basel, Hs., G II, 3, fol. 6–9 (Magistrate and council to Grynaeus); AMC, GG 158, 7 (Andreas Beck to Sandherr); UB Basel, Hs., G II, 2, fol. 114 (Andreas Beck to Grynaeus); AMC, GG 158, 5 and 6 (Grynaeus to the magistrate and council and to Andreas Beck).

[114] In 1594, the Lutheran pastor of Horbourg made a mockery of the "three different religions" the three Colmar ministers allegedly adhered to: AMC, GG 158, 38. These three ministers were Christian Serinus, Andreas Irsamer and Samuel Radspinner. For the career of the latter, cf. *Bopp*, Die evangelischen Geistlichen, p. 423. Radspinner's only extant letter, soliciting a Colmar appointment, contains no clue as to his doctrinal position: AMC, GG 158, 22 (Letter to the Colmar authorities. n. d. [ca. 1592]).

[115] Evidence from the last decade of Serinus' life suggests that he increasingly approached an openly Calvinist position. See, for instance, Basilius Lucius' [Lutz] letter to Serinus of April 24, 1598: UB Basel, Hs., G I, 26, fol. 112. The Calvinist Lucius was the head minister at neighboring Mulhouse. I have not been able to locate Serinus' commentary on several Books of the Old Testament referred to and praised by Lucius in this letter.

[116] UB Basel, Hs., Ms.Ki.Ar., 22c, fol. 85 (Letter from Ambrosius Socinus to Johann Jacob Grynaeus, January 29, 1599). For his career, cf. also *Bopp*, Die evangelischen Geistlichen, p. 516; and *Th.*

Following the death of Andreas Irsamer in late August, 1600, Socinus was appointed as his successor. In one of his first reports from Colmar, he described the deplorable state of the city's Protestant church. Above all, he noted that the wounds inflicted on it by Johann Georg Magnus in 1589 had no healed, and that the deacon Andreas Irsamer had not been much better than Magnus, because he had succeeded in keeping many parishioners away from pious old Christian Serinus. Moreover, Socinus observed that orthodox Lutheranism continued to be advocated and spread by many *Colmariens* and sustained by the neighboring Württemberg preachers at Horbourg. Thus, Socinus expressed his fervent hopes for success in the attempt he was about to launch to strengthen this weak church.[117] The relentless activity he unleashed proved to be quite successful. Subsequently appointed the successor of the head minister Christian Serinus (d. 1603), this new position supplied him with the status necessary for the successful promotion of his cause.

Ambrosius Socinus played an active role in the appointment of a Reformed preacher in 1603 and a Calvinist schoolmaster in 1604, thus, according to his own testimony, trying to thwart any involvement in these matters by the omnipresent Strasbourg theologian Johannes Pappus.[118] Furthermore, in 1604 the transformation of the Latin school into a Protestant *Gymnasium* was, above all, based on his suggestion.[119] When the post of a third deacon was created in 1609, Socinus was successful in recommending the employment of his son Nicolaus Socinus, a graduate of the Heidelberg *Collegium Sapientiae*, who subsequently filled this position up to his death in 1624.[120] In trying to align the Colmar church with the Calvinist camp, Socinus kept in check the new city-clerk Anton Schott (1569–1634), appointed as successor of Andreas Sandherr in 1597, whom he did not trust because of his Strasbourg connections.[121] In 1605, Socinus, who could count upon the full and influential support of Andreas Beck and Sebastian Wilhelm Linck, had the majority of the patrician votes on his side when he suggested the appointment of a second *Gymnasium* teacher.[122] Last but not least, Socinus succeeded in introducing a new hymnbook in Colmar's church – the "*Psalms of David*", translated from the French and edited by Ambrosius Lobwasser – a clearly Calvinist psalter which, in 1606, superseded the Strasbourg hymnbook.[123] Ambrosius Socinus died in 1615.

Burckhard-Piguet, "Aus der Socin'schen Familiengeschichte", Beiträge zur vaterländischen Geschichte, [Basel], XII (1888), 304–8. For Colmar's ministerial recruitment during the period following 1602, cf. the summary presented by *Bernard Vogler*, "Le corps pastoral de Colmar et des environs avant la Guerre de Trente Ans", Annuaire de Colmar (1975/76), 125.

[117] "Deus det aliquem succursum laboribus nostris in infirma ecclesia": UB Basel, Hs., G I, 33, fol. 99 (Letter to Johann Jacob Grynaeus, October 8, 1600). Thus, the suggestion of *Bopp*, ibid., that Socinus was only appointed in 1602, is wrong.

[118] UB Basel, Hs., G II, 11, pp. 303–304 (Letter of September 1, 1603); and ibid., pp. 308–309 (Letter of December 23, 1605); cf. also below, 160. [119] Cf. below, ibid.

[120] *Bopp*, Die evangelischen Geistlichen, p. 516; and BMC, Fonds Chauffour, I. Ch. 79, No. 1.

[121] For Schott's biographical data, see Matr. Basel, vol. III, p. 312 (No. 46).

[122] UB Basel, Hs., G II, 11, pp. 308–309 (Letter to Johann Jacob Grynaeus, December 23, 1605); and ibid., pp. 303–304 (Letter to Grynaeus, September 1, 1603); and *Joseph Schmidlin*, Die katholische Restauration im Elsass am Vorabend des dreissigjährigen Krieges (Strasbourg-Neudorf 1934), p. 143.

[123] *Jacques Betz*, L'église protestante Saint-Matthieu de Colmar et sa paroisse (Strasbourg 1971), p. 44. For a description of Lobwasser's psalms, see *Martin Vogeleis*, ed., Quellen und Bausteine zu einer Geschichte der Musik und des Theaters im Elsass, 500–1800 (Strasbourg 1911), p. 353.

His doctrinal influence on Colmar's religious climate is further mirrored by the city's ministerial recruitment during the first quarter of the 17th century.

Matthias Heinerius, a native of Gotha and deacon from 1604 to his death in 1624, was a former student at the University of Heidelberg and, preceding his Colmar appointment, a preacher in the Palatinate.[124] The Thuringian Georg Hopf was endowed with an official Colmar stipend supporting his studies at the universities of Basel and Heidelberg. Thereafter, he served his patron city as a deacon from 1615 to 1628. Extant letters from his hand addressed to his Basel mentor and patron Johann Jacob Grynaeus demonstrate Grynaeus' continued interest in Colmar's ecclesiastical affairs.[125] The Lower Rhenish Calvinist Matthias Koenen, minister from 1617 to 1628, came to Colmar from Cologne, where he had been a minister of the Reformed church under the cross.[126] Jacob Stephani (d. *ca.* 1676), a son of a notable Colmar family and deacon from 1624 to 1628, was a graduate of the universities of Basel and Geneva. During his student years, he entertained an intimate correspondence with the well-known Hebrewist of Basel University, Johannes Buxtorf.[127] Stephani's colleague Elias Pellitarius (d. 1636) was a Calvinist like the remainder of Colmar's Protestant preachers of the first quarter of the 17th century. A former student at Heidelberg University, he had served the Palatine ministry prior to his Colmar appointment in 1625.[128] It is quite telling that – in the middle of the Thirty Years' War (1628), when

[124] *Bopp*, Die evangelischen Geistlichen, p. 222. The procedure taken in the case of Heinerius' employment is described in AMC, BB 45 (1598–1604), p. 681. For this and the following, note that some of Bopp's data for Colmar's ministers are wrong. They are implicitly corrected here. For the correction of erroneous data contained in Bopp's list of Colmar preachers in idem, Die evangelischen Gemeinden und Hohen Schulen im Elsass und Lothringen von der Reformation bis zur Gegenwart, Parts I–III, Bibliothek Familiengeschichtlicher Quellen, Vol. XVI (Neustadt a. d. Aisch 1963), pp. 271–2, see AMC, GG 158, 4 ("Praedicanten Eyd").

[125] *Bopp*, Die evangelischen Geistlichen, p. 254; idem, Die evangelischen Gemeinden, p. 619; and UB Basel, Hs., G II, 6, fol. 294–5 (Three letters addressed to Grynaeus in the years 1614–15). See in this connection the letter addressed to Johann Jacob Grynaeus by the Colmar city-clerk Anton Schott on December 3, 1613: „Lectae sunt Politarchis nostris, Reverende ac Magnifice Domine Grynee, literae M. Hopfij, quibus significavit bona vestra pace se dimitti. Itaque et ipsi facile consensimus. Hopfium autem hortare cupimus, ne hac libertate in licentiam abutatur. Tibi vero gratias quas possumus habemus maximas, quod et Ecclesiam Colmariensem cordi tibi esse non desistas, et alumnum hunc nostrum domesticum tibi et quam comendatissimum hactenus esse volueris. Speramus plane eum usui nobis aliquando, . . . tibi tuisque abunde recompenset . . .". UB Basel, Hs., G II, 11, pp. 125–6. Cf. also Hopf's letter to the Zürich *Antistes* Johann Jacob Breitinger of August 24, 1628. At that time, having been forced to leave Colmar due to the Counterreformation, Hopf sought Breitinger's support in his search for a new position. See STA Zürich, E II, 39, fol. 1114.

[126] *Bopp*, Die evangelischen Geistlichen, p. 302. See also the polemical discussion of Koenen's view of predestination in *Schmidt*, Gründliche Widerlegung, pp. 187–190. This discussion is based on a sermon published anonymously by Koenen. I have been unable to locate it.

[127] *Bopp*, ibid., p. 529; and idem, Die evangelischen Gemeinden, p. 654. For Stephani's correspondence, see UB Basel, Hs., G I, 63, fol. 50–51 (Two letters from 1623). Ibid., fol. 52, in an admirable although not flawless attempt to write in French, he describes an extended journey he has undertaken upon leaving Geneva: "J'ay, par la grace de Dieu, passé la France, veue une bonne partie d'Angleterre et les plus notables provinces du pais bas. De Coblence, ayant pris la main droicte, Je m'en suis allé à Treve, de la à Metz, d'ici par la Loraine retourné au logis . . .". (Letter dated September 11, 1624). Three later letters from Stephani at UB Basel, Hs., date from his period as a Swiss minister in Aarau and Schöftland.

[128] *Bopp*, Die evangelischen Geistlichen, p. 409. For his correspondence with the Zürich *Antistes* Johann Jacob Breitinger from 1628 and later years, cf. STA Zürich, E II.

Emperor Ferdinand II issued an ultimatum forcing the Colmar Protestants to either abolish their church and return to the fold of the Roman Catholic church or else leave the city at once – Colmar's four Protestant churchmen chose to emigrate to Switzerland, where they found new positions in the Reformed churches of Burgdorf, Biel and Aarau. On their exodus toward Switzerland, they were accompanied (or followed shortly thereafter) by the majority of Colmar's Protestant leadership, who sought refuge at Mulhouse and Basel; comparatively few Protestant *Colmariens* emigrated to the neighboring Lutheran principality of Horbourg-Riquewihr or to the Lutheran city of Strasbourg.[129]

The Counterreformation of 1628 put an end to the Calvinist period of Colmar's Protestant church. In 1632, the re-establishment of Protestantism, under the protection of the Swedish General Horn and his troops, took place under the spiritual supervision of the church of Strasbourg and its vigilant *praeses* Johannes Schmidt. The fact that following the year 1632 a kernel of steadfast Colmar Calvinists survived well into the 1650's, under steady and finally unbearable harassment by the now predominantly Lutheran community, testifies to the great impact of the preaching and the cure of souls previously administered by Ambrosius Socinus and his fellow preachers.[130]

As the unusual doctrinal development of Colmar's Protestant church during the five decades following the introduction of the Reformation in 1575 has not, to date, been dealt with in depth, the results of my research have been presented here in detail.[131] Before proceeding with this analysis, it is therefore appropriate to summarize the aforementioned.

Through the introduction of the Reformation in 1575, Colmar's Protestant church officially joined the German churches professing the Lutheran Augsburg Confession of 1530. Beyond doctrinal considerations, this step was of great political importance because Lutheranism was the only Protestant denomination legally recognized by the Augsburg Peace of 1555 – Zwinglian and Calvinist churches were excluded from this settlement. Although, on the level of doctrinal practice, Colmar's Protestant church left the ranks of the German Lutheran churches during the decades following 1575 in order to align itself with the Reformed churches of Basel and the Palatinate, it outwardly continued to profess the Augsburg Confession for primarily political reasons.

The first indication of a doctrinal change in progress within the city's Protestant leadership was its refusal to sign the Lutheran Formula of Concord during the years 1577–79. The ministers Christian Serinus and Emanuel Betulejus and their lay allies

[129] *Heinrich Rocholl*, "Die Vertreibung evangelischer Bürger aus der freien Reichsstadt Colmar und ihre Aufnahme in der Stadt Basel: Ein Geschichtsbild aus der Zeit der katholischen Gegenreformation, 1628–1630", Beiträge zur vaterländischen Geschichte, n.s., XIV ([Basel] 1896), 307–345; *Philippe Mieg*, "Les réfugiés colmariens à Mulhouse au temps de la Contre-Réforme 1628–32", Annuaire de Colmar (1950), 45–56; *Fritz Vischer-Ehinger*, Die Familie Vischer in Colmar und Basel (Basel 1933), pp. 82–106. Cf. also *Heinrich Rocholl*, Aus dem alten Kirchenbuch einer freien Reichsstadt. Warnende Bilder aus der Vergangenheit für die Gegenwart in der Jesuitenfrage, Schriften für das deutsche Volk, Vol. XXXV, Halle 1900.

[130] *Philippe Mieg*, "Les tribulations d'Augustin Guntzer, bourgeois de Colmar, durant la guerre de Trente Ans", Annuaire de Colmr (1958), 48–65, especially 61–65.

[131] This was all the more necessary because the only existing book-length account of the history of Colmar's Protestantism in the years 1575–1628 by Franz Lerse, first published in 1790, is interspersed with misleading information and factual errors. Cf. *Lerse*, Geschichte der Reformation, *passim*.

and supporters must have been instrumental in backing up this refusal. However, the evidence contains no clues which would be helpful in assessing this group's doctrinal reasons for rejecting the Formula of Concord. We only learn of their commitment to an open religious policy and of their concomitant reluctance to accept the Concord's sharp outline of Lutheran doctrine vis-à-vis all other Protestant teaching. Following their rejection of the Formula, the city's Protestant leaders demonstrated their commitment to an open ecclesiastical and confessional policy by continuing their recruitment of ministers from the centers of Lutheran orthodoxy – Strasbourg and Württemberg.

Colmar could not, however, avoid the impact of the increasing "confessionalization" in progress throughout the Empire: since contradictory doctrinal tenets were advocated simultaneously by different members of Colmar's Protestant church, an eventual confrontation of these antagonistic standpoints was inevitable. This confrontation was brought about by the orthodox Lutheran deacon Johann Georg Magnus upon his appointment in 1589. In challenging his colleague Christian Serinus' Reformed leaning, he provoked an open eucharistic controversy within the city. It led to the official drafting of a confessional document meant to serve as a basis for the necessary settlement of the ongoing dispute. This document, the so-called *Deklarationsschrift* of 1589, testifies to the Reformed sympathies of Colmar's leading Lutherans. Considering the Melanchthonian tenets advocated in this statement, and given its intermediary doctrinal position, situated in the confessional no-man's land between Lutheranism and Calvinism, it must be regarded as a Philippist confession.

Between November, 1589 and May, 1590, the phrasing of the *Deklarationsschrift* led in turn to the dismissal of the deacons Johann Georg Magnus, Bartholomäus Haller and David Hiemeyer, who refused to accept the doctrinal statement. As a result, Colmar's Protestant church was gradually forced into isolation by the other Alsatian Lutherans in general and by Württemberg in particular. The way out of this politico-religious isolation could only consist in closer alignment with the Reformed churches of Basel and the Palatinate, unless the Colmar Protestants were ready to return to the fold of the Lutheran church – which they were not. However, following the year 1590, and during Christian Serinus' lifetime, the city's Protestant church continued to implement its open policy of ministerial recruitment. This was done quite possibly, in part, because of the formation of a Lutheran opposition within the city against Serinus and his supporters. Furthermore, Serinus' new colleague, Andreas Irsamer, appointed in 1590, did not really share Serinus' Reformed sympathies.

It was only after Irsamer's and Serinus' deaths, in 1600 and 1603 respectively, that Colmar's Protestant leaders drew clear consequences from their politico-religious isolation within the Lutheran camp. Under the leadership of the new minister Ambrosius Socinus, they now sought close partnership with the churches of Basel, the Palatine Prince-electorate and with the church of the Palatine Duchy of Zweibrücken. Thus, the period from ca. 1600 to 1628 can clearly be termed the Calvinist era of Colmar's Protestant church, even though the city government was careful to uphold the appearance of its adherence to the Augsburg Confession. The Calvinist era was brought to an end in 1628, at the climax of a Counterreformation intervention initiated by the

Bishop of Basel and implemented by Emperor Ferdinand II, which forced Colmar's Protestant ministers and leading families into emigration and exile. Four years later, the re-establishment of Protestantism in Colmar under Swedish protection took place under the auspices of the orthodox Lutheran church of Strasbourg.

B. THE COMMUNAL INSTITUTIONALIZATION OF THE REFORMATION

In turning our attention to the institutional change brought about by the Colmar Reformation, we must first consider the size of the city's Protestant community, however scarce and self-contradictory the evidence may be in this respect.[132] Not much information can be gained from Nicolaus Cancerinus' assertion that about three thousand *Colmariens* (approximately one-half of the city's population) attended Johannes Cellarius' first Protestant sermon on May 15, 1575. For many, attendance at this sermon was nothing more than a matter of satisfying their curiosity.[133] Hence, all subsequent Catholic accounts claimed that there was still a Catholic majority in town.[134] These accounts were not merely based on propagandistic speculation. In 1604, their accuracy was verified by the Protestant city authorities, who, in this instance, could not be suspected of any exaggeration; they referred to the "... best part of the citizenry which still professes the Roman Catholic religion". There can be no question that the "best" part meant the "major" part.[135] Thus, in 1604, there was still a Catholic majority in town, the term "still" implying that in 1575, this majority was even larger than in 1604. This evidence can be further substantiated. In 1603 and 1613, 1,700 and 1,500 Catholic communicants, respectively, attended the celebration of the Holy Sacrament at St. Martin's church. On the Protestant side, however, there were only 880 communicants on Easter, 1610.[136] Yet, between 1575 and the beginning of the 17th century, there was a steady growth in the size of the Protestant community. On St. Trinity (May 29), 1575, only about one hundred Protestants attended the Lord's Supper, whereas by Whitsun, 1610, their number had risen to 882.[137] This manifest growth of the Protestant community was primarily due to three factors:

[132] Furthermore, a satisfactory account of Colmar's 16th century demography does not exist. For a discussion of extant analyses, cf. above, pp. 13–4.

[133] AMS/AST, No. 155, I, fol. 27–29 (Letter to Johannes Pappus, June 3, 1575). Cf. also *Christian Wurstisen*, Basler Chronick, darinn alles was sich in Oberen Teutschen Landen gedenkwurdigs zugetragen (Basel 1580), p. dcliiii.

[134] See, for instance, TLA, Ferdinandea, fasc. 140, *sub* "M" (Letter from the Haguenau Bailiwick councillors to Archduke Ferdinand II, June 18, 1575); and ibid., fasc. 139, *sub* „Colmar" (Letter from the Ensisheim Regency to Archduke Ferdinand II, May 12, 1576); and the letter from the Papal nuncio Count Portia to the Cardinal of Como, January 17, 1576, in *Schellhass*, ed., Die süddeutsche Nuntiatur, Vol. V, p. 305.

[135] AMC, GG 160, 11 (Letter from the magistrate and council to the Bishop of Basel, May 19, 1604).

[136] *Schmidlin*, Die katholische Restauration, p. 126. The figures for the Protestant communicants are taken from Sigismund Billing's (1742–1796) account, which is based on now lost source material; cf. BMC, Fonds Chauffour, I. Ch. 79, No. 4.

[137] For the 1575 figures, cf. BMC, Fonds Chauffour, I. Ch. 82, No. 3 ("Geschichtt Biechlin ..."); the figures for 1610 are listed in ibid., I. Ch. 79, No. 4.

a. The moral and spiritual crisis of the Catholic clergy of St. Martin's, from which the clergy and Catholic community began to recover only gradually by the end of the 16th century[138];
b. The proselytizing of the Protestant ministers, deacons and schoolteachers (following 1575, the city schools were entirely in Protestant hands);
c. The increasing ostracism, as well as political and economic pressure, exerted upon the Catholic population by the Protestant authorities.[139]

In fact, the pre-eminent social and economic role played by the city's Protestants[140] clearly outweighed the disadvantage of being the religious minority in town. Thus, the Catholic part of the population was gradually pushed into a situation of total political dependence: by 1585, the membership within the magistrate and council was completely Protestant.[141]

Although the Protestant councillors were far from being scrupulous in dealing with the Catholic part of the city population, the Augsburg Peace of 1555 nevertheless forced them to leave the Catholic church and its possessions in town intact, and obliged them to assure that the Catholic community remained, on the whole, unencumbered by their Protestant fellow citizens. In general, the magistrate and council respected the stipulations of 1555. If by nothing else, their attitude was dictated by political caution, which clearly limited the authorities' possibilities of institutionalizing the Reformation outside the Protestant church and parish, that is, within the urban community at large.

To be sure, such institutional change had to have a basis in the organizational structure of the church proper. Unfortunately, very little is known to date about this organization. I have been unable to find an extant copy of a Colmar church ordinance or of a catechism officially in use during the period 1575 to 1628.[142] Thus, our knowledge must remain conjectural. Shortly after the introduction of the Reformation, Nicolaus Cancerinus, the superintendent of the church of Horbourg-Riquewihr, sent to Colmar fifty copies of Johannes Brenz's catechism and two copies of the church ordinance drafted in 1559 and in use in the church of Württemberg.[143] It was these two documents that the original inner organization of Colmar's Protestant church was, at least outwardly, based upon. Largely for political reasons, these constitutional

[138] Cf., for instance, AAEB, A 41, 195 and 198 (Letters from the Regency of Ensisheim and from the espiscopal *Offizial* of Juli 29 and September 9, 1585, pertaining to the state of Colmar's Catholic clergy). Cf. also *Joseph Schmidlin*, "Religiös-sittliche Verfassung und Reformbestrebungen im Weltklerus des Elsass am Vorabend des Dreissigjährigen Krieges", Arch. EKG, XVI (1943), 199–202.

[139] See the grievances of the chapter of St. Martin's presented to the imperial commissaries Wilhelm Böcklin von Böcklinsau and the Bishop of Basel in February, 1579, and the subsequent report by the two commissaries: AMC, GG 154, 5 and 28. Cf. also *Bücking*, Johann Rasser, pp. 24–34.

[140] For the social composition of the Protestant party in about 1575, cf. below, pp. 114–7.

[141] Cf. ADHR, 4 G, 11 (n. d. [December, 1585], „Guttgedunckhen vnd Neben Bericht ..."). The Catholics were again represented by two councillors only in 1623: *Schmidlin*, Die katholische Restauration, p. 154.

[142] *August Ernst* and *Johann Adam*, Katechetische Geschichte des Elsasses bis zur Revolution (Strasbourg 1897), p. 238: "Über die religiöse Unterweisung der Colmarer Jugend in diesem Zeitraum [1575–1633] ist sehr wenig bekannt". The first extant Colmar church ordinance dates from 1648. Cf. *Emile Graff*, "Die Colmarer protestantische Kirchenordnung von 1648", Annuaire de Colmar (1937), 123–128.

[143] AMC, GG 151, 42 and 41 (Letters to Andreas Sandherr of May 16 and May 24, 1575).

documents did not fall prey to the eucharistic controversy of 1589–90, even though this dispute unmistakenly revealed the "Crypto-Calvinist" leanings of the head minister and the city's magistrate.[143a] Initially, they were followed quite faithfully. Thus, the Colmar mandate from October, 1575, listing the holidays hitherto to be observed, reflects the Lutheran stance of the Württemberg ordinance.[143b] Yet, following the turn of the century, the growing impact of Calvinism on the Protestant community called for long overdue adjustments in this policy of make-believe. In 1608, or possibly earlier, Brenz's catechism was replaced by a new catechism of a Reformed rather than Lutheran orientation.[144] Similarly, the church ordinance suffered some significant modifications as, for instance, in 1618, when further private baptism administered by midwives was prohibited[145], not to mention the Philippist and Calvinist interpretation given its doctrinal stance by the ministers Serinus and Socinus. Nevertheless, it is interesting to note that during the first two or three decades after 1575 the institutionalization of the Reformation within the community was officially based upon the Württemberg catechism and church ordinance, despite the authorities' concurrent shift toward adherence to Calvinism.

As has been shown by research to date, the three areas of communal life within which the city Reformation most directly influenced and initiated institutional change were the fields of education, social welfare and the strict enforcement of morality and discipline.[146] This program of institutional change, was partially outlined by Nicolaus

[143a] According to *Schmidt*, Gründliche Widerlegung, p. 152, when Christian Serinus informed the parishioners of Johann Georg Magnus' dismissal at the end of December, 1589, he cautioned his flock against assuming that the authorities had hereby rejected the Augsburg Confession and added: "Inmassen dann auch forthin die Würtembergische agend vnd derselbe Catechismus, auch die äusserliche ritus vnd Kirchengebräuch noch, wie biß anhero beschehen, gehalten werden sollen". See also Apologia Civitatis Imperialis Colmariensis (Colmar 1645), p. 42. (The authorship of the Apologia is still up to debate. For a salient contribution to this discussion, cf. *C[harles] A. Hanauer*, "Les historiens de l'établissement du Protestantisme à Colmar", RCA, II (1860), 172, n. 3); and *Timotheus Wilhelm Röhrich*, Mittheilungen aus der Geschichte der evangelischen Kirche des Elsasses, Vol. I (Strasbourg and Paris 1855), pp. 294–5.

[143b] BMC, Fonds Chauffour, I. Ch. 84 ("Rueff der feyrtag undt fastag halb ausgangen", dated October 22, 1575). For comparative reasons, cf. *Niesel, ed.*, Bekenntnisschriften, pp. 268–270 (Confessio Helvetica Posterior: "De feriis, ieiuniis, ciborumque delectu").

[144] A new recently printed Colmar catechism is mentioned in "Ludwig Kunigs vnd Johan Schroeters verantwortung" of April 7, 1608: AMC, GG 190, 2. In all likelihood, this catechism is identical with the one referred to by *Schmidt*, Gründliche Widerlegung, p. 193: "Weiters daß die hiebevorigen Colmarischen Prediger den Calvinismum fovirt, ist auch daher offenbar, weil sie denselben durch sonderbare Büchlein der Jugend vnvermerckt beyzubringen sich bemühet. Davon nur eines, dessen Titul: 'Einfältiger Vnterricht vnd Anweisung vor die, so zum Tisch des Herrn anfangs gehen wollen', zu Handen kommen, in welchem sonderlich die Lehre von beyden Sacramenten newen Testaments, der Tauffe, vnd dem heiligen Abendmal, pag. 9, 11 & 12, gantz Calvinisch gefasset . . .". Cf. also *Ernst* and *Adam*, Katechetische Geschichte, pp. 238–9.

[145] *Hanauer*, Les historiens, I (1859), p. 454. Previously, the problem of private baptism had been a chief bone of contention in the doctrinal struggle between the Lutheran and Reformed ministers of the principality of Montbéliard. At Riquewihr, the problem ultimately played an important role in the dismissal of the Reformed superintendent Matthias Erb. Cf. *John Viénot*, Histoire de la Réforme dans le pays de Montbéliard depuis les origines jusqu'à la mort de P. Toussain, 1524–1573, Vol. I (Montbéliard 1900), pp. 101–116; and *Röhrich*, Mittheilungen, Vol. I, p. 294.

[146] These changes are outlined succinctly by *Bernd Moeller*, "Die Kirche in den evangelischen freien Städten Oberdeutschlands im Zeitalter der Reformation", ZGORh, CXII (1964), 152–7. A useful synop-

Cancerinus in a letter he sent to the court-clerk Andreas Sandherr. Cancerinus recommended a reform of the Colmar schools, in the sense that the children be instructed not only in reading and writing but also in "the right knowledge of Christ" and that they be taught a Christian way of life. To this end, he suggested regular visitations to the schools by the city council. Moreover, considering that Colmar's Protestants would hitherto refuse to be cited by the episcopal *Offizial*, he recommended the immediate establishment of a matrimonial court.[147]

In what respect and to what degree did the Colmar authorities follow Cancerinus' suggestions? Even taking into account the deplorable scarcity of evidence in this area, it cannot be denied that there was, compared to the city Reformation of the first half of the 16th century, a remarkable lack of any real impetus in the field of communal reform. In the area of enforcement of discipline[148], I am not aware of any general disciplinary ordinance ever having been drafted in Colmar that was in any way comparable to the so-called *Zuchtordnungen*, so characteristic for the early Upper German city Reformation, as in the case of Constance and Strasbourg.[149] Only a relatively restrained tendency toward stricter enforcement of discipline can be observed, for instance, in the prohibition of public dances in 1601, which had still been tolerated in 1575.[150]

In 1581, the Colmar authorities did, however, establish a matrimonial court. It was composed of the presiding *Obristmeister*, two *Stettmeister*, two Protestant preachers, two councillors, and two representatives of the community.[151] Through the establishment of its matrimonial court, the city wrested from the Bishop of Basel a substantial part of his local jurisdiction. Yet, unlike the case of the early Upper German city Reformation,

sis is also *Ernst-Wilhelm Kohls*, "Evangelische Bewegung und Kirchenordnung in oberdeutschen Reichsstädten", ZSavRG, Kan. Abt., LIII (1967), 124–134, although Kohls' questionable distinction between an (essentially a-political) "evangelical movement" and the subsequent "political Reformation" is hardly supported by the evidence. For a discussion of these categories and justified criticism thereof, cf. *Thomas A. Brady, Jr.*, Ruling Class, Regime and Reformation at Strasbourg (1520–1555), SMRT, Vol. XXII (Leiden 1978), p. 200, n. 2; and *Hans-Christoph Rublack*, Gescheiterte Reformation: Frühreformatorische und protestantische Bewegungen in süd- und westdeutschen Residenzen, Spätmittelalter und Frühe Neuzeit: Tübinger Beiträge zur Geschichtsforschung, Vol. IV (Stuttgart 1978), p. 3, n. 1.

[147] AMC, GG 151, 41 (Letter of May 24, 1575). It was Cancerinus' natural assumption that the reforms in question be carried out by the secular rather than by the ecclesiastical authorities. Although Cancerinus took them for granted, the strongly Erastian tendencies of Colmar's communal institutionalization of the Reformation are, nevertheless, very striking.

[148] The standard work in this respect is still *Walter Köhler*, Zürcher Ehegericht und Genfer Konsistorium, 2 vols., Quellen und Abhandlungen zur Schweizerischen Reformationsgeschichte, Vols. VII and X, Leipzig 1932 and 1942, dealing not only with the Swiss Reformation but also with the city Reformation of Upper Germany of the first half of the 16th century.

[149] For the Constance "Zuchtordnung" of 1531, cf. ibid., Vol. II, pp. 106–121; and *Hans-Christoph Rublack*, Die Einführung der Reformation in Konstanz von den Anfängen bis zum Abschluss 1531, Quellen und Forschungen zur Reformationsgeschichte, Vol. XL (Gütersloh and Karlsruhe 1971), pp. 87–92; for Strasbourg, cf. *Köhler*, ibid., Vol. II, especially pp. 387–426.

[150] Cf. AMC, FF 600, 8 (Mandate of 1575); and *Vogeleis*, ed., Quellen und Bausteine, p. 400 (Mandate of 1601). For another disciplinary mandate of 1601, prohibiting widowers from re-marrying within a period of four, and widows within a period of six, months after the death of the spouse, cf. *Waltz*, ed., Chronik des Colmarer Kaufhauses, p. 24.

[151] "Kirchners Elsaessische Chronik": "Anno 81 ward das Ehegericht gesetzt". For the composition of the matrimonial court in 1601, cf. BMC, Fonds Chauffor, I. Ch. 79, No. 11. For the oath taken by the members of the matrimonial court, cf. AMC, BB 51 ("Eidbuch 1570"), p. 725.

Colmar's matrimonial jurisdiction did not encompass the whole urban population as a corporate entity, but pertained only to the conduct of the Protestant segment of the community.[152] The great significance of the Zürich matrimonial court established in May, 1525, "the fountainhead of the consistorial development of the Reformation" (according to Walter Köhler), was that it reached far beyond the jurisdiction practiced by its episcopal predecessors, and that it became a powerful instrument for the enforcement of a new discipline and morality.[153] Ambrosius Socinus' record of the proceedings of Colmar's matrimonial court from the years 1600 to 1615 informs us about the mode and extent of its jurisdiction.[154] Assuming that the minister's notes are complete, we can conclude that this court convened on a fairly irregular basis. In the period of 1601 to 1605, the number of meetings varied from three to nine sessions annually. The court's action was limited to sentencing in such cases as divorce procedures, litigation regarding marriage promises and proposals, and the like. Whenever the city council referred a case to the matrimonial court, it did so under reservation of its right to pass judgment on such matters as blasphemy, adultery, incest, unchastity and the like.[155]

The two following examples are cases-in-point. In 1601, two Colmar women petitioned the court to sanction their divorce, claiming that their husbands had left them more than three years ago. According to custom, the court agreed to issue a public citation of the two men in question. Since the latter did not respond or return to the city within a period of two months, the two women were officially accorded their divorce and thus allowed to re-marry under the condition, however, that their second marriage should proceed without any pomp ("ohn alles Gepreng"). In 1604, the court cancelled Anna Bass' promise of marriage given to Veltin Hauser, Jr., under the condition of her parents' consent. This decision was based on the dissent of Anna's parents and on her youthful age. Subsequently, considering Anna's age (she was not yet sixteen years old),

[152] There is at least no indication that the authorities subsequently altered their policy enunciated in 1580, that Roman Catholics should have the choice of appealing either to the ecpiscopal or to the city court in matrimonial matters: AMC, BB 45 (1580–88), p. 22. However, this Catholic prerogative was in effect severely limited, since such matters as adultery, incest, unchastity and the like, solely pertained to the city council's jurisdiction and not to that of the matrimonial court. This is demonstrated, for instance, by the case of the Catholic Michael Rumersheim who was indicted by Ursula Hafner in 1614 for violating his promise of marriage. Rumersheim petitioned the matrimonial court to have his case referred to the episcopal *Offizial*. This was subsequently granted by the city council. Yet, upon recommendations received from the matrimonial court, the councillors nevertheless condemned him to a fine of ten pounds and to banishment for having had sexual intercourse with the plaintiff under the false pretense of intending to marry her. See AMC, BB 45 (1604–14), pp. 901, 928–9, 941; and BMC, Fonds Chauffour, I. Ch. 23, No. 1 ("Ehegericht", June 30, 1614).

[153] *Köhler*, Zürcher Ehegericht, Vol. I, pp. VIII and 28–230; especially 142–175. Cf. also *Robert M. Kingdon's* interesting observations on the respective situation in Geneva, in idem, "The control of morals in Calvin's Geneva", in The social history of the Reformation, ed. by Lawrence P. Buck and Jonathan W. Zophy (Columbus, Ohio 1972), pp. 9-12.

[154] BMC, Fonds Chauffour, I. Ch. 23, No. 1. Socinus' notes are supplemented by selective observations on the proceedings of the matrimonial court in the years 1616 to 1707, probably added by Sigismund Billing (1742–1796).

[155] See, for instance, AMC, BB 45 (1604–14), p. 901 (March 29, 1614): "Ursula Hafnerin contra Michel Rumersheim. Ist die sach als ein ansprüchige ehe betreffend, hiemit für ein ord[ent]lich eheg[ericht] gewisen, wegen bekanter fleischlischer vermischung begangenen fräuels gebüerender straff vorbeheltlich". For the city council's final judgment in this case, cf. above, n. 152.

she and Veltin were sentenced to be punished. We are not told about the kind of punishment that was applied in this case. Such punishment was administered by the city council rather than by the matrimonial court itself or by the church. This can be inferred from Socinus' frequent observations on cases remitted for punishment to the secular authorities. Secular punishment administered by the city council, must have been the only expiation regularly imposed in Colmar on infractions committed against public morality and discipline. The court did not prosecute cases of unusual laxity in the attendance of worship, blasphemy and the like. This, and the conspicuous lack in Socinus' notes of any reference to ecclesiastical punishments, such as excommunication pronounced by the matrimonial court, not only underlines the essentially secular nature of this institution, but also re-emphasizes our previous observations on the Erastian aspects of Colmar's Reformation.

Thus, we are led to conclude that the extent of Colmar's matrimonial jurisdiction in the period from 1600 to 1628 does not compare to the all-encompassing control of morality and discipline exerted by the Swiss and Upper German urban matrimonial courts established in the first half of the 16th century. The relatively restrained importance and impact of Colmar's matrimonial court was in some respects a result of the biconfessionality of the town, which the Protestant authorities were obliged to respect. Only the reform of the schools and social welfare pertained to the city's entire community as a corporate commonalty. In the case of the schools, this was to have important repercussions on the religious climate of Colmar in general.

Immediately upon the introduction of the Reformation, the Latin school teacher Andreas Meyenbrunn was told by the authorities that he and his pupils were hitherto to refrain from further attendance at the worship celebrated at St. Martin's, and that he ought to instruct his class in the Protestant catechism and the singing of German psalms instead, and take his pupils regularly to the worship held at the hospital church. Since Meyenbrunn refused to comply, he was immediately dismissed.[156] Subsequently, the Latin school was entrusted to Christoph Tonsorius of Strasbourg. From 1576 onward, he was assisted by a *provisor*, who probably taught the school's second class.[157] Whereas the city's German school, starting with its separation from the Latin school in 1539, was entirely under the city's control, the Latin school remained at least nominally attached to the chapter of St. Martin's whose *scholasticus* was in charge of its supervision. In May, 1575, the Latin school was decisively wrested from the hands of the canons. To be sure, this act of expropriation soon became a hotly debated issue between the chapter and the city government. Yet the canons did not gain the upper hand before 1628, when imperial commissaries entrusted the school to the Jesuits. Before 1628, the Protestant

[156] Cf. TLA, Ferdinandea, fasc. 139, *sub* "Colmar" (Letter from the Ensisheim Regency to Archduke Ferdinand II, May 26, 1575). For Meyenbrunn's employment in 1571, cf. AMC, GG 190, 3 (Letter from Meyenbrunn to *Obristmeister* Johannes Goll, March 30, 1571). For his further activity at the school of Ensisheim, cf. *Vogeleis*, ed., Quellen und Bausteine, p. 329.

[157] For the appointment of Tonsorius, see AMC, GG 151, 51 (Letter from Johannes Nervius to Colmar authorities, June 6, 1575); and AMC, BB 51 ("Eidbuch 1570"), pp. 387–392. According to Sigismund Billing (1742–1796), he left Colmar in 1587: BMC, Fonds Chauffour, I. Ch. 79, No. 7. His *provisor*, Johannes N., is mentioned in AMC, GG 152, 4.

authorities steadfastly forbade the canons to open their own Catholic school. The Catholic citizens who wanted their boys to have some education were thus forced to send them to the Protestant school.[158] There can be no doubt, therefore, that the schools were used by the Protestant leadership as an important means of assuring the further spread of the Reformation within the city.

A real effort to reform the city's schools under the auspices of the Reformation was, to all appearances, only initiated in 1603, notwithstanding Nicolaus Cancerinus' pertinent recommendations submitted as early as May, 1575. The *Obristmeister* Sebastian Wilhelm Linck and the city-clerk Anton Schott were appointed as secular supervisors (*Schulherren*) of the city's schools. Together with the minister Ambrosius Socinus, they undertook the first official visitation of the city's Latin and German schools in July, 1603. Unfortunately there is no extant record of this visitation. In the same month, based on the suggestion of Ambrosius Socinus, to which the *Schulherren* lent their full support, the authorities charged a stone-mason with the construction of a new school building. In 1604, the Latin school was moved to this new building and simultaneously transformed into a Protestant *Gymnasium* composed of four different classes.[159]

Following the "communalization" of the Latin school in 1575, the foundation of the *Gymnasium* was a second important reform measure initiated by the Reformation in the area of education. It was followed in 1625 by the establishment of the city's first girls' school entrusted to the teacher Christoph Irsamer (b. 1593), a son of the former minister Andreas Irsamer.[160]

Very little is known about the life and career of the different Colmar teachers. No real pattern is visible, therefore, in their recruitment by the authorities.[161] The most influential among them was clearly Master Christoph Kirchner from Smalkald, the son of a Thuringian minister. He was appointed in 1592 as the successor of Adelarius Gravelius from Thuringia (Latin teacher from 1590 to 1592)[162] and later became the Rector of the new *Gymnasium*. Forced to resign his post in 1628, he emigrated to Basel, where he died as a *Conrector* in 1637. His social weight is mirrored by his marriage to a sister of

[158] For the chapter's complaints, see AMC, GG 151, 26; and ibid., GG 154, 5 (Grievances of August 1575, and February 1579). See also *Karl Albrecht*, "Das ehemalige Evangelische Gymnasium zu Colmar im Elsass: 1604–1794", Mittheilungen der Gesellschaft für deutsche Erziehungs- und Schulgeschichte, XI (1901), 295–296.

[159] *Albrecht*, ibid., 289–294. See Ambrosius Socinus' observations on the school reform decisions of 1603 and the concurrent recruitment of new teachers in BMC, Fonds Chauffour, I. Ch. 23, No. 1. For a description of the 17th century curriculum, cf. *Albrecht*, ibid. The contemporaneous oath taken by the city's Latin and German teachers is contained in AMC, BB 51, ("Eidbuch 1570"), pp. 387–395. It stipulated, amongst other obligations, that the schoolmasters were allowed only to punish their pupils, if need be, through whipping with the cane and in no other way.

[160] Cf. AMC, BB 51 ("Eidbuch 1570"), pp. 387–388; and *Eugen Waldner*, Allerlei aus dem alten Colmar (Colmar 1894), p. 51.

[161] The scarce evidence suffices to qualify the lists supplied by Sigismund Billing (1742–1796) in BMC, Fonds Chauffour, I. Ch. 79, No. 7, and by *Bopp*, Die evangelischen Gemeinden, pp. 478–479, as incomplete.

[162] For Gravelius' appointment: AMC, GG 151, 21 (Letter from Johannes Nervius to Colmar authorities, July 4, 1590); and AMC, BB 51 ("Eidbuch 1570"), pp. 387–392; and ibid., GG 158, 10 (Letter from the *provisor* Johannes Schuslerus to the authorities, July 8, 1592).

the patrician Jacob Bueb and by his admittance to the patrician association *Zum Waagkeller.*[163]

In respect to 16th century social welfare specifically in Upper German cities, it has been observed that the Reformation led to a "radical prohibition of all begging". The indigenous poor, the so-called *Hausarme*, were now to be supported by centralized city funds, whereas the care of foreign beggars was reduced to a strict minimum: they were administered small alms in the form of food and money and expulsed from town immediately thereafter. Foreign beggars were now strictly excluded from public begging.[164] Recent research, however, has been reluctant to admit any causal link between the Reformation and the concurrent restrictions imposed upon the traditional welfare policy. At best, the Reformation is seen as a mere catalyst of this development, insofar as it adopted the changing concept of work, and insofar as it re-strengthened the collective consciousness of the urban community. It has been shown that as early as the 15th century a re-evaluation of the concept of work had been in progress, which resulted in a sharper distinction between involuntary poverty and mere unwillingness to work. This had eventually led to a revision of medieval welfare policy. Hence, the resulting restructuring of public welfare in the course of the 16th century is now frequently thought to have had its roots in social and economic problems rather than in the Reformation message alone.[165]

The case of Colmar in many ways supports this revisionist approach. As in Strasbourg, the demand for the revision of traditional welfare policy "was not a result of the religous crisis" (M. U. Chrisman) and, essentially, the change took place before the introduction of the Reformation in 1575. During the 1520's, as was the case with Colmar's monastic policy[166], the changes implemented in the city's welfare policy closely followed the Strasbourg example. At the end of the social unrest of Spring, 1525, the authorities issued a decree prohibiting citizens from privately lodging outside beggars or other foreigners.[167] This measure was followed in February, 1526, by a new mandate adopting most substantial changes advocated by the Strasbourg poor-law ordinance of 1523: it prohibited begging by all able-bodied "who were only too lazy to work" and restricted alms-giving to those indigenous poor who were clearly unable to earn a

[163] AMC, BB 51 ("Eidbuch 1570"), pp. 387–392; and *Roland Wertz*, ed., Le livre des bourgeois de Colmar, 1512–1609, Publ. Arch. Colmar, Vol. II (Colmar 1961), p. 187; *Vischer-Ehinger*, Die Familie Vischer, p. 102; and Matr. Basel, Vol. III, p. 308 (No. 5).

[164] See *Ingomar Bog*, "Über Arme und Armenfürsorge in Oberdeutschland und in der Eidgenossenschaft im 15. und 16. Jahrhundert", Jahrbuch für fränkische Landesforschung, XXXIV-XXXV (1975), 994–996; and *Moeller*, "Die Kirche in den evangelischen freien Städten", 153–154.

[165] Cf. *Bog*, ibid., 983–1001, whose article also includes a succinct analysis of the structural changes occurring in 15th/16th century poverty; cf. also *Erich Maschke*, "Die Unterschichten der mittelalterlichen Städte Deutschlands", in Gesellschaftliche Unterschichten in den südwestdeutschen Städten, ed. by idem and *Jürgen Sydow*, VKBW, Reihe B, Vol. XIL (Stuttgart 1967), p. 73. For Strasbourg, cf. *Miriam U. Chrisman*, Strasbourg and the Reform: A study in the process of change (New Haven and London 1967), pp. 276–279; and for comparative reasons, the excellent analysis of poor relief in Lyon by *Natalie Z. Davis*, "Poor relief, humanism and heresy", in idem, Society and Culture in early modern France: Eight Essays (Stanford, Cal. 1975), pp. 17–64.

[166] Cf. above, p. 55, n. 78.

[167] „Liber ortę seditionis": AMC, EE 7, 1, fol. 55v (Decree of May 5, 1525).

livelihood on their own. Toward this end, the authorized indigenous beggars were hitherto to receive beggar's badges from the city's supervisor of begging, the so-called *Bettelvogt*.[168]

To be sure, this Colmar ordinance fell short of the contemporary Strasbourg decree. For instance, it contained no reference to a centralization under the city's control of all available welfare funds. Such stipulations were first voiced in a new mandate regarding poor relief issued around 1548. At that time, the citizens inclined to donate alms for the poor were requested to put their contribution into a special poor-box to be established at St. Martin's and to be administered by the city's *Bettelvögte*. Once again, the latter officials were advised to allow foreign beggars to stay at the city hospital for only one night and to lead them out of town early the following morning, not to be readmitted for another overnight stay for at least one month. The *Bettelvögte* were also advised to keep a close eye on all indigenous beggars and to issue official badges only to the really deserving, whereas all able-bodied poor inhabitants should be forced to work.[169] The evidence shows that these directives were vigorously enforced.[170] Thus, a centralized poor-box (*Almosenkasten*), recommended by Martin Luther in his preface to the Leisnig poor-box ordinance of 1523, which served as a guideline for contemporary urban poor law ordinances, was established in Colmar at least two decades before the introduction of the Reformation.[171] Substantial change in Colmar's poor relief policy, therefore, took place mainly between 1526 and ca. 1548, that is, during the pre-Reformation period and parallel to the changes implemented in other Protestant Upper German cities. After the introduction of the Reformation, the city government limited its action to a repeated emphasis on the previously issued ordinances.[172]

[168] AMC, FF 621, 2 (Also contained in ibid., BB 44, p. 38): Mandate of February 18, 1526. For comparative reasons, see the Strasbourg ordinance of 1523, printed in *Röhrich*, Mittheilungen, Vol. I, pp. 156–160. An extant list of Colmar's indigenous beggars dates from 1545. It lists a total of 73 persons (30 women, among them 12 widows; 32 children; and 11 men): AMC, FF 621, 4.

[169] AMC, FF 621, 6 (The mandate is also contained in ibid., BB 44, pp. 246–248). See also the similar 16th century mandate in AMC, FF 621, 8 (n. d.).

[170] See, for instance, AMC, FF 346, pp. 201, 229 and 244.

[171] For the Leisnig ordinance, cf. *Harold J. Grimm*, "Luther's contribution to the Sixteenth-Century organization of poor relief", ARH, LXI (1970), 226–229; and for its impact in Upper Germany: *Eberhard Naujoks*, "Ulms Sozialpolitik im 16. Jahrhundert", Ulm und Oberschwaben, XXXIII (1953), 93. The only reference to the Colmar *Almosenkasten* from the post-Reformation period I have found is in AMC, BB 51 ("Eidbuch 1570"), p. 733 (The deacon Johann Glossius' salary of 1590).

[172] See the city-clerk's amendment to the oath of Colmar's supervisors of poor-relief (*Bettelvögte*): AMC, BB 51 ("Eidbuch 1570"), p. 465.

CHAPTER VI

THE LATE CITY REFORMATION IN GERMANY

A. THE CHARACTERISTIC ASPECTS OF THE COLMAR REFORMATION.

The above study has shown that, in the case of Colmar, both the course of the Reformation as well as its implementation within the urban community differ substantially in many aspects from the common pattern of the German city Reformation of the first half of the 16th century. The following summarizing observations on the Colmar Reformation will make these differences more apparent. They are followed by a comparison of the Colmar events with other cases of late city Reformation, such as the Reformations in Haguenau, Aalen, Essen, Dortmund and Aachen.

1. The Colmar Reformation proceeded in two separate movements which differed from each other primarily in the social origin of their chief agents. The first movement was brought about by the community at large, especially by the agrarian section of the population, whereas the magistrate and council ultimately assumed the leading role during the second movement. The first movement was initiated in 1522 and reached its climax in the social and religious uproar lasting from December 1524 through May 1525. It ultimately lost its impetus due to the authorities' interference. The second movement began, however weakly, in the late 1540's and reached its goal – the introduction of the Reformation – as late as 1575. Although it was originally initiated by communal action, the city council ultimately carried it through, especially after changes in the composition of magistrate and council (1556 to 1565) facilitated the infiltration of pro-Reformation citizens into the ranks of political leadership. The two movements were separated from each other by an intermediary phase in the 1530's and 1540's. During this time, the authorities, anxious to maintain their social and political leadership and thus hostile toward a social and religious movement coming "from below", and, furthermore inspired by Erasmian humanism, adhered to a policy of Catholic ecclesiastical reform.
2. The first movement was an unsuccessful attempt at communal Reformation "from below", common in the 1520's and 1530's in Germany and Switzerland alike.[1]

[1] See *Franz Lau,* "Der Bauernkrieg und das angebliche Ende der lutherischen Reformation als spontaner Volksbewegung", Luther-Jahrbuch, XXVI (1959), 109–134. The salient passages of Lau's article are translated into English in *Kyle C. Sessions,* ed., Reformation and Authority: The meaning of the Peasants' Revolt, Problems in European Civilization (Lexington, Mass. 1968), pp. 94–101. Cf. also *Bernd Moeller,* "Imperial Cities and the Reformation," in idem, Imperial Cities and the Reformation: Three Essays, transl. and ed. by H. C. Erik Midelfort and Mark U. Edwards, Jr., (Philadelphia 1972), pp. 41–115; and *Leonhard von Muralt*, "Stadtgemeinde und Reformation in der Schweiz", Zeitschrift für

The chief reason for its failure was the lack of a competent and outspoken reformer who could have mobilized large sections of the community. Thus, a knowledge of the religious and social issues at stake was shared by too few, making it a relatively simple task for the authorities to intercede and put an end to the unrest. Secondly, the apparent absence of serious social tensions within the community as a whole further contributed to the failure of the movement.

The second movement was an ultimately successful attempt at introducing the Reformation "from above". To be sure, this second movement was initiated by communal forces and *not* by the ruling patriciate. However, the evidence is too scarce to show how important this impetus "from below" originally was, or, more important, how strong it remained after the authorities had taken the lead. It must remain unexplained to what extent the authorities had to repress and re-channel such communal pressure before effectively making this move in the late 1560's.[2]

3. The introduction of the Reformation in Colmar in 1575 was, above all, the work of the city's socially and economically leading men. Mostly members of the city's bourgeois patriciate, they were, at the same time, the undisputed political leaders of the community. Their political position was so strong that they could afford to introduce Protestant worship without even consulting the council of jurors; the inner cohesion of their oligarchy was such that it was not threatened by the fact that such leading patricians as Matthias Be(e)r and Hans Henckel remained Catholic beyond 1575.[3] The astounding cohesion of Colmar's oligarchy was primarily accounted for by three factors:
   a. the frequent intermarriage among members of the city's leading families[4];

Schweizergeschichte, X (1930), 349–384. In his recent case-study on Strasbourg's ruling class and the Reformation, Thomas Brady has successfully modified the interpretation of the early city Reformation as presented by the above authors – in particular by Bernd Moeller. Based on the example of Strasbourg, Brady has demonstrated that the existence of popular urban movements in the first half of the 16th century, which turned out in favor of the Reformation, did not preclude "an independent reforming role of the urban regimes, distinct from their succumbing to pressure from the populus." It is important to note in this connection, that this "independent reforming role" expressed itself largely in the regime's anticipation of reforms, which otherwise might have been initiated by the middle and lower urban classes. Hence, it is obvious that the role of Colmar's ruling aristocracy in 1575 differed significantly from that of Strasbourg's regime in 1523–25. See *Thomas A. Brady, Jr.,* Ruling Class, Regime and Reformation in Strasbourg, 1520–1555, SMRT, Vol. XXII (Leiden 1978), p. 5; cf. also the discussion above, pp. 6–8.

[2] *Christian Wurstisen,* Basler Chronick, darin alles was sich in Oberen Teutschen Landen gedenkwürdigs zugetragen (Basel 1580), p. dclii. Likewise, it is not really clear whether the authorities' claim voiced in 1568, that the chapter's continued refusal to contribute its share to the "Turkish tax" could lead to an anticlerical uproar in town, had an actual *fundamentum in re*, or whether this was a merely rhetorical warning designed to force the canons to cooperate. See AMC, GG 26, 20 ("Bericht Maister vnd Raths der Statt Colmar vff herrn Brobst, dechan vnd Capitel S. Matins Stifft daselbst vngegründte Supplication," n.d. [ca. April, 1568]).

[3] This inner cohesion was demonstrated, for instance, by the joint attendance of the first Protestant sermon officially preached in Colmar by the entire council, that is, by Protestants and Catholics alike. See TLA, Ferdinandea, fasc. 139, *sub* "Colmar" (Letter from the Ensisheim Regency to Archduke Ferdinand II of May 26, 1575). For the forthcoming publication of this source, cf. above, p. ix, n. 1.

[4] The genealogical tables in the appendix to *Fritz Vischer-Ebinger,* Die Familie Vischer in Colmar and Basel, Basel 1933, are a good case-in-point.

b. the relative lack of involvement of Colmar's patriciate with the distribution of prebends by the chapter of St. Martin's[5]: the majority of patricians had no direct material interest in the preservation of Catholicism;
c. the absence of a real reformer in town who, through his preaching, might have mobilized the lower classes in favor of a swift introduction of the Reformation, thereby exerting considerable political pressure on the leadership.

In the absence of such a reformer, the majority of the community continued to adhere to Catholicism or, at least, did not support the introduction of the Reformation. Only the city's craftsmen are said to have actively supported the authorities' decision in favor of the Reformation.[6] Yet, considering the *Colmariens'* predominantly agricultural occupations, the craftsmen represented a small section of the city's population and were thus unable to exert real pressure on the authorities.[7] To all appearances, the larger agricultural section of the population, which played a dominant role in the religious and social unrest of 1524–25, remained passive in 1575. There can be little doubt, therefore, that the Colmar Reformation was ultimately a *Ratsreformation* implemented by the city's ruling patricians.[8] Thus, whether consciously intended by its authors or not, the Reformation in Colmar contributed to a significant strengthening of the patrician oligarchy in town.

4. In the absence of a competent municipal reformer, the central (but *not* the only) motive for the introduction of the Reformation was anticlericalism. The authorities' dedication to Catholic ecclesiastical reform finally died out in the 1560's, deferring to the leadership's growing frustration over the state of the city's church, a frustration intensified by the secular clergy's lack of interest in the contemporary debates on ecclesiastical reform as raised, for instance, by the Council of Trent. The canons remained inactive, seeking material advantage and ignoring the need for reform of worship and priestly lifestyle.[9] Tensions began to rise during the quarrel between the canons and the Abbot of Munster over the salary of the Dean of St. Martin's in the late 1550's, and finally erupted following the departure of Dean Johann Rasser in 1565, when the chapter proved unable to recruit qualified and competent

[5] Cf. my observations on the origin of Colmars's canons and chaplains, above, pp. 27–31.

[6] TLA, Ferdinandea, fasc. 140, *sub* „M" (Letter from the councillors of the Bailiwick of Haguenau to Archduke Ferdinand II of June 18, 1575).

[7] In 1554, the craftsmen constituted, at the most, about one-fourth of the city's ca. 1000 guildmembers. See *Henri Fleurent,* "Essai sur la démographie et l'épidémiologie de la ville de Colmar," Bulletin de la Société d'histoire naturelle de Colmar, n.s., XV (1920/21), 63.

[8] The papal nuncio, Count Portia, was clearly misinformed when he referred to the introduction of the Reformation in Colmar (based on information he had received from Colmar's Dominican prior) by stating: "Gl'authori dice essere stato il popolo minuto infetta per la vicinità d'Horburg . . .". See *Karl Schellhass,* ed., Die Süddeutsche Nuntiatur des Grafen Bartholomäus von Portia, in Nuntiaturberichte aus Deutschland, ed. by Königlich Preussisches Historisches Institut in Rom, Section III, Vol. V (Berlin 1909), p. 44 (Letter addressed to the Cardinal of Como on June 18, 1575). The assessment by *Henri Strohl,* "Les expériences d'une église au cours de quatre siècles," in Vom Wesen und Wandel der Kirche: Festschrift für Eberhard Vischer, ed. by Theologische Fakultät der Universität Basel (Basel 1935) p. 116, is equally erroneous.

[9] See *Joseph Schmidlin,* Die katholische Restauration im Elsass am Vorabend des Dreissigjährigen Krieges (Strasbourg-Neudorf 1934), p. 125.

priests for the Colmar deanery. Furthermore, the questionable lifestyle of probably a majority of the canons[10] increased general frustration over the condition of the city's Catholic church. However, it is indicative of the situation prevailing in Colmar in the late 1560's and early 1570's (marked by passivity in these matters by the community at large) that there is no extant evidence pointing to any large-scale popular protest. It was in the church policy which the authorities practiced after 1568, that this frustration ultimately provoked hostile anticlericalism. The relevant question put to the Strasbourg lawyer Johannes Nervius at the end of April, 1575, is a clear case-in-point. Nervius was asked to what extent the Colmar authorities were entitled to install "an erudite man who would preach the truth according to the Augsburg Confession," considering that the clergy's conduct, both in daily life as in teaching, was "so utterly vexatious and blasphemous."[11] The Catholic patrician and councillor Matthias Be(e)r admitted that the stage for the introduction of the Reformation had been set by the chapter of St. Martin's "which, for some time, has not maintained any pastor of stature, that is, an able and qualified preacher." He added that the canons "had conducted themselves in an unpriestly and vexatious way."[12]

5. Yet, it would be misleading to portray the Colmar Reformation uniquely as the result of anticlericalism – that is, solely as a reaction to the abuses prevailing among the city's secular clergy,[13] although this reaction admittedly created the chief impetus for change. Genuinely religious motives played an important role as well.[14] The manifest negligence on the part of the secular clergy in the fulfillment of their spiritual duties brought about a kind of "spiritual vacuum" in Colmar, which did nothing to hinder the influence of the neighboring Protestant preachers on the city's religious climate. The preaching and cure of souls administered to numerous *Colmariens* by the minister of Horbourg, Bartholomäus Westheimer, in the years 1553 to 1567, is a major case-in-point. Ultimately, it was his activity, and the occasional hedgerow-preaching done within the city itself by Westheimer and his colleagues, which offered the growing anticlericalism of many *Colmariens* a concrete goal and objective. During the 1550's and 1560's, many of the city's foremost citizens, as we have seen, attended Protestant worship in the adjacent Württemberg villages. It would surely be wrong to assume that these educated laymen did not grasp the religious meaning of the Reformation message. The influence of the neighboring Protestant preachers on Colmar was further enhanced, however indirectly, by the daily contact of citizens with the population of the adja-

[10] Idem, "Religiös-sittliche Verfassung und Reformbestrebungen im Weltklerus des Elsass am Vorabend des Dreissigjährigen Krieges," Arch. EKG, XVI (1943), 199–203.

[11] AMC, GG 154, 42 ("Summarische puncten daruber des herren doctoris bedencken zů begeren," n.d. [end of April, 1575]). Cf. the citation from this source, above p. 123, n. 137.

[12] TLA, Ferdinandea, fasc. 139, *sub* „Colmar" (Letter from the Ensisheim Regency to Archduke Ferdinand II of May 26, 1575). This letter was based directly on Matthias Be(e)r's account. For its forthcoming publication, see above, p. ix, n. 1.

[13] Such a mono-causal interpretation is presented by *Jürgen Bücking,* Johann Rasser (ca. 1535–1595) und die Gegenreformation im Oberelsass, RST, Vol. CI (Münster/Westphalia 1970), pp. 18–35.

[14] This assertion differs from Erdmann Weyrauch's interpretation. See the discussion below, n. 21.

cent Protestant villages and towns and by the proliferation of evangelical treatises and pamphlets in town. Thus, the Colmar Reformation was not only rooted in an essentially "passive" reaction to clerical abuse, but also in an "active" embracement of the genuinely religious tenets of the Reformation by the majority of Colmar's leadership.

6. An essential cornerstone for the realization of the Colmar Reformation was the Peace of Augsburg of 1555. Its stipulations freed the *Colmariens* from the assumption, previously dominating the politico-religious considerations of their leadership, that allegiance to the Emperor implied adherence to the Roman Catholic faith.
7. If some Colmar councillors, considering Habsburg-Austria's strong presence in Alsace, were pre-occupied with serious doubts about the actual practicability of the Augsburg decree of 1555 in the case of their own city, the successful introduction of the Reformation in Haguenau in 1565, must have greatly enhanced their optimism. For Colmar, the Haguenau Reformation furnished an encouraging test of the Augsburg stipulations regarding the *ius reformandi* of imperial cities.
8. In addition to the religious considerations already shared by the Colmar councillors, the success of the Haguenau Reformation encouraged them in their own struggle for autonomy vis-à-vis the increasing political and religious influence of Habsburg-Austria. For Colmar's leadership, this latter objective had a far more decisive impact on their decision in favor of the Reformation than the likewise intended emancipation of their city from the influence of the weak Bishop of Basel[15], who, in any case, usually sought the support of the Austrian Regency of Ensisheim when he was involved in conflict in Upper Alsace. Moreover, the Colmar councillors knew well that such an emancipation from the Bishop's tutelage could only be partially achieved because their city had neither the power nor the independence to disregard the respective prohibitions of the Augsburg Peace and, thus, to envisage a secularization of Catholic church-property and a simultaneous wholesale abolition of Catholicism within its walls. The emancipation from Habsburg-Austria's influence, however, was a very real possibility and the introduction of the Reformation was its most certain, although risky, guarantee.[16] In the case of Colmar, this process of emancipation was encouraged and facilitated by the presence of the House of Württemberg in Upper Alsace, indirectly creating the necessary political elbow-room for the city's anti-Habsburg action.

[15] Thus, the anxiety and irritation created among Colmar's leadership by the fact that, in 1571, the chapter of St. Martin's assured itself of Archduke Ferdinand II's official protection, are prominent aspects of the list of legal problems presented by the magistrate to the Strasbourg lawyer Johannes Nervius shortly before the introduction of the Reformation. See AMC, GG 154, 42 (n. d. [end of April, 1575]).

[16] This important aspect of the Colmar (and Haguenau) Reformation did not elude the councillors of the Bailiwick of Haguenau. Cf. their letter addressed to Archduke Ferdinand II on June 18, 1575: "... dieweil sich Ettliche der Fürnembsten [Städte] im Regiment alhie vergangner Zeit souil vernemen haben lassen, dieweil man Jnen täglich an Jren Freyheitten, auch alten herkomen Recht vnnd gerechtigkeiten eintrag zuthun vnnderstannden, seyen sy verursacht worden, (damit sie sich desto bas bej Jren Recht vnnd gerechtigkeitten, auch alten Freyheitten erhalten möchten), Ennderung der Religion fürtzenemen, sonnst wurden sy Letstlich gleich Freyburg vnnd anndern Stetten gar Oesterreichisch gemacht worden sein": TLA, Ferdinandea, *sub* "M".

9. Similarly, the gradual shift from Lutheranism to Calvinism in the years 1575 to 1600 was nourished by doctrinal and political considerations alike. Its political aspect lay in the hope (catalyzing this change) that a conversion from Lutheranism to Calvinism would effectively free Colmar's authorities from the politico-religious influence exerted on them by Strasbourg and Württemberg. Like the introduction of the Reformation in 1575, the conversion to Calvinism was, above all, advocated and implemented by the city's most influential ruling patricians. Yet, despite the similarities between these two events, it would be too bold to call the latter process of conversion a "Second Reformation" such as was simultaneously initiated by Melanchthonian Philippists and Calvinists elsewhere in Germany. Although the evidence is scarce in this respect, there is no indication that the change from Lutheranism to Calvinism in Colmar led to a thorough ecclesiastical and communal reform, as it had, for instance, in the city of Wesel.[17] In Colmar, the doctrinal change only created a noticeable stimulus for reform in the area of public education.[18] As in the case of Bremen, tight secular control over the city's Protestant church remained untouched by the conversion to Calvinism[19]; unlike the case of Wesel, the new Reformed orientation of the church failed to lead to a presbyterial re-organization of the Protestant community and parish.
10. The city of Colmar, confronted with Habsburg-Austria's expansionist Counter-reformation policy, first reassured itself of the Emperor's further protection of its right of immediacy (*Reichsunmittelbarkeit*)[20], before it took the ultimate step in 1575. The political objective – emancipation from the Habsburg-Austrian grasp – critically influenced the religious decision. Although the role played in this change by anticlerical and religious motives shared by the city's leadership was important, we must conclude that political motives and objectives were equally prominent and that they tended to supersede the anticlerical and religious impetus so characteristic of the early German city Reformation of the first half of the 16th century. Unlike early cases of urban Reformation, there was no real, broad, communal movement in Colmar strong enough to influence the authorities' religious and ecclesiastical

[17] For Wesel, cf. *Heinz Schilling,* Niederländische Exulanten im 16. Jahrhundert: Ihre Stellung im Sozialgefüge und im religiösen Leben deutscher und englischer Städte, SVRG, No. 187 (Gütersloh 1972), pp. 87–95.

[18] For the notion of the "Second Reformation", cf. *Jürgen Moltmann,* Christoph Pezel (1539–1604) und der Calvinismus in Bremen, Hospitium Ecclesiae: Forschungen zur bremischen Kirchengeschichte, Vol. II (Bremen 1958), p. 13. Moltmann's assessment has been criticized by Gerhard Zschäbitz, who has reduced the phenomenon of the "Second Reformation" to a mere ideological attribute of rising German territorial absolutism, cf. idem, "Zur Problematik der sog. 'Zweiten Reformation' in Deutschland," Wissenschaftliche Zeitschrift der Karl-Marx-Universität Leipzig, Gesellschafts- und Sprachwissenschaftliche Reihe, XIV (1965), 505–509. To date, the notion needs further definition, as is demonstrated by Werner Bellardi's usage of the term; cf. idem, Die Geschichte der "Christlichen Gemeinschaft" in Strassburg (1546–1550): Der Versuch einer "zweiten Reformation", QFRG, Vol. XVIII, Leipzig 1934.

[19] For Bremen, cf. *Schilling,* Niederländische Exulanten, p. 95; and *Bodo Heyne* "Zur Entstehung kirchlicher Eigenart in Bremen," in Hospitium Ecclesiae: Forschungen zur Bremischen Kirchengeschichte, Vol. I, ed. by idem and Kurt Schulz (Bremen 1954), pp. 13–15.

[20] This is a reference to the joint Colmar and Haguenau mission to the imperial court of 1574/75. Cf. above, pp. 108–10.

policy. From the 1530's onward through 1628, the domineering position of Colmar's oligarchy was never at stake. Due to the authorities' undisputed control over their town and to the bi-confessionality of Colmar's community after 1575, a corporate-communal impetus was virtually missing. This fact goes a long way in explaining the relative slowness of the communal institutionalization of the Reformation in Colmar.

The impact of both the Augsburg Peace and the Haguenau Reformation on Colmar's decision in favor of the Reformation, the emancipatory nature of the decisive step taken in 1575, and the subsequent gradual shift toward Calvinism, all underline the political character of the Colmar Reformation.[21] The case of Colmar clearly suggests that there are substantial differences between the late city Reformation of the 1560's and 1570's and the city Reformation of the first half of the 16th century which, to date, has attracted the almost exclusive attention of Reformation historians. Thus, we will now focus our interest on some other cases of the late city Reformation in Germany.

B. THE REFORMATION IN ESSEN, DORTMUND, AACHEN, HAGUENAU AND AALEN.

The promulgation of the Augsburg Peace in 1555 did not immediately contribute to a stabilization of the confessional borderlines within the Empire. During the reign of Emperor Ferdinand I (d. 1564), Protestantism was still on the advance. In Saxony, Brandenburg and Bremen, entire bishoprics became subject to Protestant control. In the Rhineland, many noble vassals of the Duke of Jülich-Cleves officially embraced Protestantism. Numerous monasteries and abbeys were secularized in the Palatine Prince-electorate, in the Duchy of Württemberg and in other German principalities. And in the imperial cities of Strasbourg, Ulm, Memmingen, Esslingen, Heilbronn, Schwäbisch Hall and others, the Protestants reclaimed substantial positions lost between 1548 and 1552.[22]

[21] This aspect has induced Erdmann Weyrauch to argue that there was no Reformation to speak of in Colmar and that what took place in 1575 was merely a temporary symbiosis between the interests of the city and those inherent in the Reformation. He claims, in other words, that apparent religious motives only served as an ideological cloak used by the Colmar authorities in order to conceal their purely political interest in introducing the Reformation. This interpretation is of only partial accuracy. Therefore, I do not share Weyrauch's conclusion in this present form, as much as I have otherwise been able to profit from his thougtful suggestions regarding my interpretation of the Colmar events. He seems to think that the evidence is not substantial enough to justify any reference to an independent influence of religious factors on the Colmar decision of 1575, distinct from that exerted by political considerations. In my opinion, however, there is sufficient source-material to warrant the assertion of a distinct role of religious factors. I will not rehearse this evidence here. It has been discussed in detail on pp. 111–23, above. Although I agree with Weyrauch that the political nature of the Colmar decision in favor of the Reformation undoubtedly stands in the foreground, I do not see any justification for casting the religious factors influencing this action into the role of mere ideological attributes of an otherwise exclusively political event. See *Erdmann Weyrauch,* "Die politische Führungsgruppe in Colmar in der Zeit der Reformation," in Stadtbürgertum und Adel in der Reformation: Studien zur Sozialgeschichte der Reformation, ed. by Wolfgang J. Mommsen and Robert W. Scribner, Stuttgart 1979.

[22] *Moriz Ritter,* Deutsche Geschichte im Zeitalter der Gegenreformation und des Dreissigjährigen Krieges, (1555–1648), Vol. I (Stuttgart 1908), pp. 89–230; and *Franz Petri,* "Im Zeitalter der Glaubenskämpfe (1500–1648)," in Rheinische Geschichte, 3 vols., ed. by idem and Georg Droege, Vol.

The Catholic powers within the Empire began more actively to resist the further spread of Protestantism only during the 1560's, following the conclusion of the council of Trent in 1563. This resistance first proved successful in the south and southwest of Germany, where the powerful Archduke Ferdinand II of Tyrol (1565–95), who ruled over all Habsburg-Austrian possessions in the southwest of Germany, the equally influential Duke Albrecht V of Bavaria (1550–79), and the Cardinal-Bishop of Augsburg, Otto Truchsess von Waldburg (1552–73), made themselves the champions of the Catholic Counterreformation. But, as of yet, the influence exerted by their party was mitigated by the fact that they lacked a competent leader and that they could not rely on the support of the vacillating Emperor Maximilian II.[23] This situation changed in their favor in 1576, when Rudolf II, a stern Catholic, became Maximilian's successor. In fact, as we have seen, the ambiguous religious position assumed by Maximilian encouraged the authorities of Haguenau and Colmar to introduce the Reformation into their cities; and it is telling that four out of the six cases of late city Reformation discussed here took place during Maximilian's reign.

Whereas in the case of Colmar, Haguenau and Aalen, Maximilian's indecision, along with substantial political support from the Duke of Württemberg, ultimately assured the success of the Reformation, additional and different outside factors played instrumental roles in the cases of Essen, Dortmund and Aachen. In the west of the Empire, the ultimately abortive attempt to introduce the Reformation into the Archbishopric of Cologne (launched by Archbishop Hermann von Wied during the 1540's) had long-lasting repercussions on the religious climate of the Rhineland and the adjacent territories.[24]

Only after the War of Cologne (1582–85), during the era of the Coadjutor and (later) Archbishop Ernst of Bavaria, did the Counterreformation gain a strong basis within this Rhenish Archdiocese.[25] Following the resignation of Hermann von Wied in 1547, Protestantism ceased to spread within those Rhenish villages and towns which were subject directly to the spiritual *and* secular control of the Archbishop and his cathedral chapter.[26] Yet, wherever the spiritual and secular control exercised by the Archbishop and the powerful Duke Wilhelm V of Jülich-Cleves (1539–92) overlapped, the spread of the Reformation was further sustained by the Duke's considerable leniency in religious matters.

Duke Wilhelm V ruled over a vast territory comprised of the Duchies of Jülich, Cleves and Berg, and the Counties of Mark and Ravensberg. Although Wilhelm never openly embraced the Protestant faith, his and his councillors' strong commitment to Erasmian humanism led him to assume an essentially intermediary position between the

II (Düsseldorf 1976), p. 69. Even in small imperial cities, such as Wissembourg in Lower Alsace, Protestantism reconquered important positions after 1555. See *O. R. Landsmann,* Wissembourg: Un siècle de son histoire, 1480–1580 (Rixheim 1903), pp. 156–161.

[23] *Ritter,* Deutsche Geschichte, ibid., pp. 191–312.

[24] *Otto R. Redlich,* Staat und Kirche am Niederrhein zur Reformationszeit, SVRG, No. 164 (Leipzig 1938), pp. 61–69.

[25] *Petri,* "Glaubenskämpfe," pp. 63–64.

[26] Yet, the attempt to suppress Protestantism in these territories faced great difficulties, cf. *Redlich,* Staat und Kirche, pp. 97–99.

two confessional parties, to which he adhered until the 1570's, when he increasingly succumbed to the sternly Catholic influence of some of his younger advisors. During the preceding decades, however, he did little to oppose the spread of the Reformation within territories controlled by his vassals or within territorial cities such as Wesel, Soest and Duisburg.

Likewise, he only mildly resisted the spread of Calvinism, brought to the Rhineland by immigrants and refugees from Flanders and the Low Countries.[27] Protestants met with stiff prosecution throughout the 16th century only in the Habsburg-Spanish principalities bordering on the Rhineland in the west. This repression escalated after open revolt against Spanish rule broke out in the Low Countries during the 1560's. The situation prevailing in the west did not directly involve the cities of Essen and Dortmund, but was to have grave consequences for the fate of Protestantism in Aachen. Such was, in brief and general terms, the politico-religious situation in the west of the Empire where, between 1563 and 1581, the Reformation was introduced in Essen, Dortmund and Aachen.

1. The Reformation in Essen.

With about 3,000 inhabitants during the 16th century, Essen was a city of medium to small size. Approximately one-third of its inhabitants gained their livelihood from agriculture.[28] During the Middle Ages Essen was a member of the *Hansa.* Its well-to-do citizens, along with fellow merchants from Dortmund, took an active part in the exchange of goods managed by the *Hansa* in Prussia, the Baltic countries and in Russia. The volume of Essen's *Hansa* trade, however, always remained relatively modest when compared to that of the neighboring city of Dortmund. During the 15th century, when Essen experienced significant commercial losses in its trade, the city authorities sought to compensate by furthering the establishment of craftsmen in town. As a result, during the 16th century the city was better known for its flourishing wool-weaving and gun-production than for its trade.[29]

[27] See *Petri,* "Glaubenskämpfe," p. 69; and *Redlich,* ibid., pp. 55–7, 70–96. The ecclesiastical policy of the Dukes Johann III and Wilhelm V of Jülich-Cleves has recently been re-assessed by Anton Gail and August Franzen. Both historians strongly emphasize the genuinely Erasmian orientation of this policy, thus correcting some of the confessionalist flaws contained in older accounts, such as in the otherwise informative book by *Redlich*, cited above, n. 24. See *Anton Gail*, "Johann von Vlatten und der Einfluss des Erasmus von Rotterdam auf die Kirchenpolitik der vereinigten Herzogtümer," Düsseldorfer Jahrbuch, XVL (1951), 1–109; and *August Franzen,* "Das Schicksal des Erasmianismus am Niederrhein im 16. Jahrhundert: Wende und Ausklang der erasmischen Reformbewegung im Reformationszeitalter," Historisches Jahrbuch, LXXXIII (1964), 84–112. Cf. also the succinct and concise analysis by *Erwin Mühlhaupt,* "Eigenart und Bedeutung der Reformation im Rheinland," MKR, XIII (1964), 33–58.

[28] Rheinisches Städtebuch, in Deutsches Städtebuch: Handbuch städtischer Geschichte, ed. by *Erich Keyser,* Vol. III, Part III (Stuttgart 1956), pp. 157 and 159.

[29] Ibid., p. 159; and *Robert Jahn,* Essener Geschichte: Die geschichtliche Entwicklung im Raum der Großstadt Essen (Second ed.; Essen 1957), pp. 182–185. See also *Konrad Ribbeck,* Geschichte der Stadt Essen, Part I (only extant part), (Essen 1915), pp. 443, 458–464.

At that time, Essen was only *de facto* an imperial city. *De iure* it was obliged to recognize the overlordship of the princely Abbess of Essen's *Damenstift,* an abbey composed of the daughters of Rhenish, Westphalian and other German counts. The Abbess controlled the higher jurisdiction in town and held the patronage over the majority of the city's churches. Yet, ever since Emperor Charles IV, in 1372 and 1377, acknowledged simultaneously the Abbess' overlordship as well as the city's status as an imperial city, the debate over the legitimacy of the Abbess' suzerainty had never really subsided. Thus, the introduction of the Reformation, as we shall see, served as an attempt to free the city once and for all from the Abess' tutelage.[30]

In the 15th and 16th centuries, Essen was ruled by a small and socially very exclusive city council composed of twelve members, headed by two burgomasters and a *Rentmeister,* charged with the administration of city finances. Generally, the councillors were recruited from the city's merchant-patricians and were appointed for life. Thus, the annual elections were, in effect, something of a formality. The only concession made to the city's lower-class guilds, which resulted from revolts of the guilds in the late 14th and early 15th centuries, was the annual control of the city's financial administration accorded to the communal committee of the XXIV. Lower-strata burghers had no access to the city council.[31]

There were three churches in Essen: the Cathedral church attached to the abbey, St. Gertrudis, which was incorporated into the chapter of Essen's canons in 1522, and St. Johann's. There were also a number of monasteries in town. During the late Middle Ages, the city council acquired the patronage over St. Gertrudis and was successful in imposing its control upon the city hospital and its chapel.[32] Humanism and the *Devotio Moderna,* so prominent in the Rhineland during the late 15th and early 16th centuries, was not well received in Essen before the 1530's. An early attempt by John Rotgerus (a member of the Brotherhouse of Münster in Westphalia and a former student at the school of the Brethren of the Common Life at Deventer) to establish himself as a teacher in Essen ended in failure.[33]

The Reformation message was first brought to Essen in 1524 by preachers presumably from Lippstadt. During the 1530's, its diffusion was augmented by a preacher named Johann Tuber, apparently expulsed from the city in 1533[34], and by the clandestine Anabaptist and "Sacramentarian" propaganda of that day.[35] The Reforma-

[30] See *Jahn,* Essener Geschichte, pp. 166, 207–208; and *Konrad Ribbeck,* "Übersicht über die Verfassung der Stadt Essen bis zum Untergange der städtischen Selbständigkeit," Essener Beiträge, XXII (1902), 20–22.

[31] *Ribbeck,* "Übersicht," 17–26; *Jahn,* Essener Geschichte, pp. 175–175; and *Ribbeck,* Geschichte der Stadt Essen, p. 405.

[32] *A. Kuhlendahl,* "Die Einführung der Reformation und die Geschichte der ersten deutsch-reformierten Gemeinde (1563–71)," Essener Beiträge, LIV (1936), 34–35.

[33] *Konrad Ribbeck,* "Geschichte des Essener Gymnasiums: Erster Teil, bis 1564," Essener Beiträge, XVI (1896), 17–19; and *R[egnerus] R. Post,* The Modern Devotion: Confrontation with Reformation and Humanism, SMRT, Vol. III (Leiden 1968), p. 626.

[34] *Jahn,* Essener Geschichte, pp. 210–211.

[35] Ibid. On Anabaptism in Essen, cf. *Karl-Heinz Kirchhoff,* "Die Täufer im Münsterland: Verbreitung und Verfolgung des Täufertums im Stift Münster, 1533–1550," Westfälische Zeitschrift, CXIII (1963), 45, 49–50 and 57. For the particular significance of Anabaptism for the spread of the Reformation in the

tion spread quickly throughout the community, so that the Lutheran sermons preached by the Saxon court chaplain Friedrich Myconius found much acclaim when the latter passed through Essen in 1534 and 1535.[36] Growing anticlericalism, aroused by the abuses prevailing among the canons of the local chapter, rendered the population all the more ready to embrace the new faith.[37]

The leading and ruling families of Essen and Dortmund, on the other hand, whose material interest was frequently intertwined with the interests of the local church, felt nothing but hostility for the early Reformation movement and kept the respective communities under tight control.[38] At least in some respects this may explain why Essen had no part in the social and religious unrest which seized the communities of Cologne, Münster, Osnabrück and Minden in 1525. During the second half of the 1530's, the Anabaptist revolt at nearby Münster, by provoking widespread severe reactions from city governments and princes, facilitated the authorities' task of suppressing the spread of the Reformation movement. At the same time, Essen's city government tried to bring about a reform of the clergy's lifestyle[39], and to increase its own impact on the recruitment of teachers for the city's Latin school, which was controlled by the princely abbey. From 1532 to 1536, the school was entrusted to the well-reputed humanist Johannes Monheim, a member of the humanist *sodalitas* at Münster in Westphalia.[40] Around 1545, the Erasmian reforms of public education in progress within the principalities of Jülich-Cleves and Dortmund, particularly the foundation of the ducal *Gymnasium* at Düsseldorf, greatly stimulated the city government's reform-plans. As a result, the city council (with the Abbess' and the chapter's consent) transformed the *Stiftschule* into a *Gymnasium* of five classes. However, the subsequent, all too frequent coming and going of Rectors and teachers soon harmed the good reputation of this new school.[41]

Meanwhile, the increasing religious commotion prevailing in the Rhineland and Westphalia, and especially the Reformation initiated in his lands by the Archbishop of Cologne, Hermann von Wied, did not leave Essen untouched. Since about 1540, the parishioners had responded to the abuses among the canons with progressive laxity in the attendance of Catholic worship. On October 23, 1543, the bulk of the community,

Rhineland, cf. *J[ohann] F. G. Goeters,* „Die Rolle des Täufertums in der Reformationsgeschichte des Niederrheins," Rh. Vb., XXIV (1959), 217–236; and *Mühlhaupt,* "Eigenart und Bedeutung," 39–42.

[36] *Ribbeck,* "Geschichte des Essener Gymnasiums, Erster Teil," 31.

[37] For these abuses, cf. *Ferdinand Schroeder,* "Sittliche und kirchliche Zustände Essens in der ersten Hälfte des 16. Jahrhunderts," Essener Beiträge, XVIII (1898), 122–130. In 1535, for instance, the city council warned the clergy against further neglect of their duties, lest they lose those prebends which were under the council's control: ibid., 125.

[38] *Jahn,* Essener Geschichte, p. 212; and *Ribbeck,* "Geschichte des Essener Gymnasiums, Erster Teil," 30–31.

[39] Cf. n. 37, above.

[40] Later, from 1536 to 1545, Monheim (d. 1564) was a teacher at the cathedral school of Cologne, and in 1545, Duke Wilhelm V of Jülich-Cleves appointed him Rector of the newly established humanist *Gymnasium* at Düsseldorf. The traditional claim that Monheim taught Protestant doctrine at Düsseldorf, although he outwardly continued his adherence to Catholicism (cf. *Ribbeck,* "Geschichte des Essener Gymnasiums, Erster Teil," 28–31), has recently been disqualified as a myth created by confessionalist historiography. According to August Franzen, Monheim was one of the most fervent adherents of Lower Rhenish Erasmianism. See idem. "Das Schicksal des Erasmianismus," 110.

[41] *Ribbeck,* ibid., 46–51.

undoubtedly influenced by the simultaneous religious unrest in the Archbishop's cities of Kempen and Neuss and in the neighboring ducal cities of Wesel, Duisburg, Mülheim and Düren, rose to demand from the city council the installation of an evangelical preacher chosen by the people. The reluctant councillors were besieged at the city hall and forced to give in. Yet, the new preacher, who failed to live up to his task, only stayed in Essen for a few weeks. At the same time, the Abbess intervened and took the case to the Imperial Supreme Court, where her position was upheld in its decision in December, 1543. The Court ordered the city authorities to re-establish the ecclesiastical *status quo*.[42]

Simultaneously, the changing politico-religious constellation within the Empire and the Rhineland greatly dampened the thrust of Essen's Protestant party and strengthened, in turn, the city council's hostile attitude toward all religious change. Duke Wilhelm V's defeat in his drive for the possession of the Duchy of Gelderland, sealed by the Treaty of Venlo in September, 1543, and Archbishop Hermann's resignation in 1547, destroyed all hopes for an eventual wholesale victory of the Reformation in the west of the Empire, and must have discouraged Essen's and Dortmund's Protestants. The Emperor's victory over the Protestant Smalkaldic League in 1546/47 brought still further discouragement.[43] The victory of Essen's Protestants was delayed by another twenty years.

However, behind the facade of quiet prevailing in the city during the 1550's, the Reformation message continued to spread across the community. The attendance (by Esseners) of Reformed worship celebrated by preachers from Wesel in the neighborhood of Essen, is a case-in-point. The growth of the Reformation movement was further stimulated by the Peace of Augsburg of 1555[44], the renewed relaxation of Duke Wilhelm's transitory commitment to a policy of strict Catholicism following Charles V's defeat in 1552, and by the influence the learned "Crypto-Calvinist" Rector of the city's *Gymnasium,* Heinrich Birckmann or Betulejus, exerted on the community in the years 1557 to 1560.[45] These various influences helped to promote the adherence to Calvinism (rising throughout the Rhineland during those years) of a significant section of Essen's population. In 1559–60, Duke Wilhelm V's church visitation revealed that Protestantism had spread considerably throughout the majority of the territories controlled by his noble vassals. At the same time, Count Hermann von Neuenahr

[42] Ibid., 44–46., *Petri,* "Glaubenskämpfe," pp. 43–44; and *Jahn,* Essener Geschichte, pp. 213–216. Jahn shows, in particular, that at this point Essen's Reformation movement had not yet fully grasped the meaning of the Reformation message. Its temporary suppression was, thus, all the more easy.

[43] *Ribbeck,* "Geschichte des Essener Gymnasiums, Erster Teil," 46–47; *Petri,* "Glaubenskämpfe," pp. 46–47.

[44] See *Kuhlendahl,* "Die Einführung," 31 and 44.

[45] Ibid.; for Birckmann's career, cf. *Ribbeck,* "Geschichte des Essener Gymnasiums, Erster Teil," 69–75. In the case of Essen's school, as elsewhere in the Rhineland, it is interesting to observe how smooth the transition was from a predominantly humanist orientation to a Calvinist outlook. The Arminian Calvinists of the second half of the 16th century, such as Birckmann, were, in many ways, the direct heirs of Erasmian humanism, well-established in Rhenish and Westphalian cities during the preceding decades. See *Mühlhaupt,* "Eigenart und Bedeutung," 45. For the simultaneous changes within the Duchy of Jülich-Cleves, cf. *Redlich,* Staat und Kirche, pp. 87–91.

introduced the Reformation into the County of Moers in Essen's close vicinity.[46] There can be no doubt that this situation had significant repercussions on Essen's religious climate and that it encouraged the city's Protestant community to take further action.

On Christmas Day 1560, when the community gathered at St. Gertrudis church and sang Protestant psalms, it could count on the changed religious attitude of a good number of city councillors and the support of the influential city-clerk Laurenz Bussensmidt. Indeed, the authorities immediately took the lead of the communal Reformation movement and sanctioned the introduction of German Protestant psalms at St. Gertrudis.[47] In responding to further communal demands, the council intended to introduce the Protestant Lord's Supper on Easter 1562. When Heinrich Saldenberg (a Dominican charged by the canons with the administration of the parish church) refused to comply with this intention, widespread unrest broke out among the parishioners.[48] The council decided to recruit a Protestant preacher at once. On April 28, 1563, the Lutheran minister Heinrich Barenbroch[49] preached his first sermon at the hospital chapel and, a few days later, administered the Lord's Supper at St. Gertrudis in the presence of the majority of the community: only fourteen Catholic citizens did not attend.[50]

In introducing the Reformation, the city council based its action on the Peace of Augsburg, thus invoking the disputed privileges of 1377 granting Essen the status of an imperial city. Its initiative therefore constituted a double threat to the secular and ecclesiastical authority of the princely Abbess. The introduction of the Reformation and its consolidation in Essen was undoubtedly simplified by the relatively weak reign of the Abbess Irmgard von Diepholz (1561–1575), who did not lack strong sympathies for the Reformation. Yet, since the council's action implicitly challenged her suzerainty, she was forced to act swiftly and against her religious conviction. Her first plan was to entrust the city-school to the Jesuits; subsequent negotiations with the latter ended in failure. Instead, in 1563, she chose to appoint the zealous and sternly Catholic teacher Matthias Carden. But her counterattack failed to have the intended effect because in October, 1564, the city council founded an independent Protestant city-school.[51]

At the same time, the Abbess appealed to the Emperor and to Duke Wilhelm V of Jülich-Cleves who, as Bailiff, was in charge of the abbey's secular protection. As a result, the Emperor commissioned Duke Wilhelm and the Archbishop of Cologne with the abolition of the Reformation in Essen and the enforcement of the city's obedience to the

[46] *Petri,* "Glaubenkämpfe," p. 69. An equally significant influence was exerted on Essen by Duke Wilhelm's vassal at nearby Broich, the Protestant nobleman Wirich von Dhaun-Falkenstein: see ibid.

[47] *Ribbeck,* "Geschichte des Essener Gymnasiums, Erster Teil," 75–76; and *Jahn,* Essener Geschichte, pp. 218–219.

[48] Saldenberg, a good Catholic, acted upon orders from the arch-episcopal *Offizial* of Cologne: *Ribbeck,* ibid., 80.

[49] For Barenbroch, cf. the short biography by *Albert Rosenkranz,* "Heinrich Barenbroch," MKR, XVI (1967), 213–219.

[50] *Kuhlendahl,* "Die Einführung," 47–48. Yet, as a result of Duke Wilhelm's intervention, discussed below, Barenbroch was forced to leave Essen again within the same month.

[51] *Ribbeck,* "Geschichte des Essener Gymnasiums, Erster Teil," 81–95; and *Jahn,* Essener Geschichte, pp. 219–222.

Abbess. However, due to the Duke's leniency and the steadfastness of the city council, the Emperor's mandate did not have any effect. The Duke, shrewdly recognizing the Essen Reformation as a chance to increase his direct influence on the city, largely condoned the religious change, and advised the Abbess to appeal to the Imperial Supreme Court. The ensuing trial between the Abbess and the city lasted for almost a hundred years and when the verdict was finally spoken, Essen definitively lost its rights of immediacy, but on the other hand, won a legal acknowledgment of its *ius reformandi.*

Following the introduction of the Reformation in 1563, Duke Wilhelm insisted on appointing a preacher of his own choice for Essen's parish church, and, in so doing, helped the council to take full possession of St. Gertrudis in 1564. Caspar Isselburg, the preacher nominated by Duke Wilhelm, was a Calvinist who soon found widespread acclaim among the parishioners. His installation opened a period of trying confessional disputes in town, reinforced by the simultaneous controversies in neighboring Wesel. The Essen city council only regained control in 1571, when, for largely political reasons, it suppressed the Calvinism which had already become established in the community. In the same year, and definitively in 1572, the city council re-appointed the Lutheran preacher Heinrich Barenbroch. The city-council's authority over the young church was thus secured. At the same time, the overwhelming majority of citizens had already embraced the new faith.[52]

2. *The Reformation in Dortmund.*

When the Reformation was officially introduced in Dortmund in 1570, the city was well past the zenith of economic prosperity. It had experienced its great days in the late Middle Ages, around 1400, when the city had a population of approximately 10,000 inhabitants. Due to a steady economic decline from this date onward, Dortmund dwindled to about 6500 inhabitants in 1500, and by 1800, the once flourishing city had become a fairly insignificant agrarian town of about 4000 inhabitants.[53] In the 13th and 14th centuries, Dortmund was the leading city in Westphalia and an important member of the *Hansa.* Its economic significance was based on trade. Dortmund merchants maintained a widespread network of connections including a variety of places in Eastern Europe (Prussia, the Baltic countries and Russia), the important city of Goslar, Flanders and England, enabling the city's leading merchant families to accumulate great wealth. However, the great Dortmund Feud (1388–90) and the city's involvement in the Soest Feud (1446–49), contributed to a rapid decline of trade and

[52] *Jahn,* ibid., pp. 222–225; *Kuhlendahl,* "Die Einführung," 61–95; *Ribbeck,* "Die lutherische Stadtschule, 1564–1611 (Geschichte des Essener Gymnasiums, Zweiter Teil)," Essener Beiträge, XIX (1898), 3–22; and *W[ilhelm] Rotscheidt,* "Das Religionsgespräch in Essen im Jahre 1571," Monatshefte für Rheinische Kirchengeschichte, XX (1926), 35–67. On further communal unrest initiated by the middle and lower class Calvinists in 1592 and 1600, cf. *Jahn,* ibid., pp. 237–240.

[53] *Luise von Winterfeld,* Geschichte der freien Reichs- und Hansestadt Dortmund (Fourth ed.; Dortmund 1963), p. 80; and Westfälisches Städtebuch, in Deutsches Städtebuch, ed. by *Keyser,* Vol. III, Part II (Stuttgart 1954), p. iii.

impoverished the city. In the late 15th and early 16th centuries, due to the economic efforts undertaken by citizens involved in coal-trade, bell-foundry, wool-weaving and by its goldsmiths, the city rose, briefly and for a last time, to relative prosperity; renewed and chronic economic decline set in around 1550.[54]

Dortmund was ruled by an exclusive noble patriciate gathered in the noble association called the *Junkergesellschaft,* which was jointly composed of the city's old landed noble families and the most successful merchant-patricians. This oligarchy monopolized political power in town, despite concessions made to the six guilds as a result of the latter's revolt in 1400. From 1400 onward, the city council was composed of eighteen members. The twelve higher-ranking positions were reserved for members of the so-called *Erbsassen* families (mostly noble patricians)[55]; the remainder of the council seats were occupied by representatives of the six guilds. Among the highest ranking councillors, there were two burgomasters (a position which throughout the 16th century was monopolized by the noble patricians), two *Rittmeister,* in charge of the city's military affairs, and two chamberlains (*Kämmerer*), responsible for Dortmund's financial administration. Since the end of the 15th century, the councillors were appointed for life, which, as it did in Essen, greatly strengthened the oligarchical structure of the regime.[56]

At the beginning of the Reformation era, Dortmund housed four parish churches, three monasteries (Franciscans, Dominicans and Premonstratensian nuns), and eight chapels. Through their control of pious foundations and prebends, the ruling *Erbsassen* families exerted a considerable influence on the administration of these ecclesiastical establishments.[57] Unlike the neighboring city of Essen, humanism gained a relatively early influence on Dortmund's intellectual life. Timan Kemner, the founder of the well-known humanist school of Münster in Westphalia, apparently began his education at St. Reinoldi's parish school. Later, around 1505, Kemner's friend Peter Nehemius furthered the influence of humanism on the city's schools. Although the humanist teaching of Nehemius and his successors was not to have an immediate resonance in town, it later proved to have a lasting impact on Dortmund's religious and intellectual life through such intermediary figures as Jacob Schöpper and Johann Lambach, who both received their first education at St. Reinoldi's school.[58]

The first Dortmunders to embrace the Reformation message were clergymen – such as a vicar at St. Reinholdi's, who resigned his prebend in April, 1523, in order to get married. In 1526, Urban Homberg, the Rector of St. Reinoldi's school, allegedly began to

[54] *von Winterfeld,* ibid., pp. 60–120; and Westfälisches Städtebuch, ibid.

[55] See *Luise von Winterfeld,* Die Dortmunder Wandschneider: Quellen und Untersuchungen zur Geschichte des Tuchhandels in Dortmund, Beiträge zur Geschichte Dortmunds und der Grafschaft Mark, Vol. XXIX/XXX (Dortmund 1922), p. 73 (table), and the following observations.

[56] Ibid., pp. 3–5; *von Winterfeld,* Geschichte ... Dortmund, pp. 43–45; and Westfälisches Städtebuch, ed. by Keyser, p. 112.

[57] *von Winterfeld,* Geschichte ... Dortmund, pp. 33–34; and *Klemens Löffler,* "Reformationsgeschichte der Stadt Dortmund," Dortmunder Beiträge, XXII (1913), 183.

[58] *von Winterfeld,* ibid., pp. 117–119. The author asserts the direct connection of the Münster humanists, such as Timan Kemner and Peter Nehemius, to the Dutch Brethren of the Common Life. Yet, this connection has recently been subject to serious doubt by *Post,* The Modern Devotion, p. 625. For critical comments on Post's revisionist approach, cf. the literature indicated above, p. 13, n. 4.

teach "the true religion" to his pupils.[59] Meanwhile, the lower-strata burghers manifested their animosity toward the privileges of the clergy in violent protests of anticlericalism in 1518, 1523 and 1525. In 1518, they forced the city council to prohibit the clergy's exercise of any craft or trade – a decision which cost the city six months of being placed under the interdict. Similar protest was voiced again in 1523, in an incident provoked by the greediness of a priest named Johannes Berchem; and another uproar took place in 1525, in connection with the simultaneous social and religious unrest in Cologne, Münster and Osnabrück.

In order to thwart the further spread of revolt within the city, the authorities cooperated with the rebels and, on October 17, 1525, forced the clergy to sign a treaty which contained most of the communal demands. Again, the clergy was to refrain from further exercise of bourgeois trades and crafts, and was prohibited from accumulating agricultural lands outside the city walls. Furthermore, the priests and monks had to promise to refrain from further appeals to foreign courts in matters pertaining to rents, leases and the like, and had to submit to the city's property tax.[60] As of that time, the discontented community had not voiced any religious demands. However, this situation changed quickly. As early as 1527, the representatives of the six guilds petitioned the city council to install evangelical preachers. At this point, only four of the twenty-four guild representatives intended to remain Catholic. But the council immediately moved to suppress the movement.

In trying to explain this relatively quick spread of the Reformation in Dortmund, it has justly been assumed that if was based, above all, on the impact of Lutheran pamphlets in town and on the city's merchants who, because of their outside connections in Protestant cities, had converted to the new faith.[61] The result of the religious and social unrest of 1527 was a considerable strengthening of the city council's authority. The majority of councillors were hostile toward any religious change and managed up to the 1560's to keep the course of the city's Reformation movement under control. The councillors' hostility vis-à-vis the Reformation movement was not only based on their religious conviction, but also on their material involvement with the prebendary economy of the local Catholic church. Their hostility was further nourished by their anxiety about the social and political aspects of the city's Reformation movement, which threatened their privileged social status.[62] Thus, during the decades preceding the official introduction of the Reformation in 1570, an essential precondition for the victory of the Reformation movement was created by the gradual infiltration of the bourgeoisie into

[59] *Luise von Winterfeld*, "Der Durchbruch der Reformation in Dortmund," Dortmunder Beiträge, XXXIV (1927), 57.

[60] *Löffler*, "Reformationsgeschichte," 187–189; and *von Winterfeld*, ibid., 56. Cf. also *von Winterfeld*, Geschichte . . . Dortmund, p. 124.

[61] It is interesting to note that one of the precautionary measures taken by the city council was the confiscation of Protestant pamphlets in 1528. See *Löffler*, "Reformationsgeschichte," 190–192; and *von Winterfeld*, Geschichte . . . Dortmund, p. 124.

[62] The gradual retreat of the patrician *Junker* from commerce and their progressive dependence upon their manorial income alone must have increased their conservative outlook and, thus, their tendency to suppress the Reformation movement. Cf. *von Winterfeld*, Die Dortmunder Wandschneider, p. 5. See also *Löffler*, "Reformationsgeschichte," 183 and 185.

positions previously monopolized by noble city-councillors. Around 1500, the city council was still almost exclusively in the hands of the noble patricians, and by the 1540's, only a small number of bourgeois *Erbsassen* had conquered a council seat, although at this time three-fourths of all *Erbsassen* were non-patricians.

The growing intrusion of these non-patrician *Erbsassen* during the following decades has to be seen in connection with the re-organization of the city's old association of cloth merchants (*Wandschneider-Gesellschaft*) in the years 1541–51. This re-organization took place with the implicit intention of furthering the non-patrician (bourgeois) control over the city council. Its result was a gradual change in the composition of the city council, assisted by the extinction of a number of patrician families. Of the twelve council seats reserved to the *Erbsassen,* six were in the hands of non-patricians as early as 1569–74, and from 1588 onward the bourgeois-merchant element clearly dominated within the council. The majority of these new merchant-councillors were favorably disposed toward the Reformation movement.[63]

Although the bourgeois councillors were instrumental in assuring the ultimate success of Dortmund's Reformation movement, the decisive pressure came, nevertheless, "from below". In 1532, continued clerical abuse, coupled with the effect of the simultaneous Reformations at Soest and Lippstadt, re-activated widespread anticlericalism and religious unrest within the community. The city council was forced to accept most of the communal demands. The major result of these events was the dismissal of the unpopular chaplain Johannes Berchem, and the entrustment of Berchem's prebend at St. Reinoldi's to the Lippstadt reformer Hermann Köthe, a former Augustinian monk.

Simultaneously, evangelical preaching was also introduced in the other three parish churches; however, this success of the Reformation movement was shortlived. The reaction against the Anabaptist revolt at Münster (1534/35) greatly strengthened the authority of the city council. It revoked all concessions made to the Reformation movement in 1532. But not long thereafter, the communal Reformation movement re-gained momentum: it found inspiration both in Anabaptism as well as in the citizens' widespread hostility toward the regime of conservative patricians[64] and soon pressured the councillors into initiating a reform of the city schools and social welfare. The council conceded to the reform of St. Mary's parish school and entrusted it to the reputed humanist Peter Scharpenberg.[65] The council also launched a re-organization of the parish poor-boxes (*Armenschüsseln*) without, however, allowing for the establishment of a centralized urban poor-box (*Armenkasten*).[66]

[63] See *von Winterfeld,* ibid., pp. 11–74. Cf. also *August Meininghaus,* "Vom Dortmunder Honoratiorentum und seinen Geschlechtern," Mitteilungen der Westdeutschen Gesellschaft für Familienkunde, V (1928), cols. 411–422.

[64] *von Winterfeld,* "Der Durchbruch," 60–65; idem, Die Dortmunder Wandschneider, pp. 11–12; *Löffler*, "Reformationsgeschichte," 192–4. For the clerical abuses prevailing in Dortmund at the time, cf. also *Albrecht Stenger,* "Die Reformation in Dortmund," Jahrbuch des Vereins für westfälische Kirchengeschichte, XL/XLI (1939/40), 195.

[65] Scharpenberg was an Erasmian Catholic with strong sympathies for the Reformation. See *von Winterfeld,* "Der Durchbruch," 67–68. In 1552, he was appointed as a teacher in Essen where, at the beginning of the 1560's, he definitively spoke out in favor of the Reformation. Cf. *Ribbeck,* "Geschichte des Essener Gymnasiums, Erster Teil," 62–64, and 101–103.

[66] *von Winterfeld,* ibid.

In 1543, the Reformation initiated by Hermann von Wied within his Archbishopric of Cologne, the favorable disposition toward the Reformation of the Bishop of Münster, the relative leniency demonstrated by Duke Wilhelm V of Jülich-Cleves, the simultaneous religious unrest in Essen and the introduction of the Reformation into the adjacent towns of Weitmar and Oberwengern, all combined to secure the temporary success of Dortmund's Reformation movement. The city council was now forced to respond to this new situation by the establishment of a city school independent from the local Catholic clergy – a concession still refused in 1539.

The organization of the *Archigymnasium,* founded in 1543, was entrusted to the humanist Johann Lambach, a champion of Catholic-Erasmian church reform. The school, organized by Lambach along the principles established by Johann Sturm of Strasbourg and Philip Melanchthon, soon gained a widespread reputation for a high standard of excellence.[67] In these years, Johann Lambach and his friend, the preacher Jacob Schöpper (d. 1554), took over the spiritual leadership of the community. Schöpper was an irenic Erasmian with strong evangelical tendencies. Like Lambach, he hoped for an eventual reconciliation of Protestantism and Catholicism. Due to his activity and the generally precarious situation of German Protestantism during those years, religious dispute remained relatively subdued in Dortmund.[68]

One year after the promulgation of the Augsburg Peace in 1555, the course of the Reformation movement entered its decisive phase. In 1556, communal pressure and the votes of some Protestant councillors brought about the appointment of Johann Heitfeld as a preacher at St. Mary's, against the will of the patrician councillors. The city council conceded to this energetic Calvinist preacher the administration of the Lord's Supper in both kinds, refusing, however, to tolerate Heitfeld's subsequent objection to saying Mass. Mobilizing their last resources, the authorities succeeded once more in reasserting their authority vis-à-vis the now almost exclusively Protestant community: Heitfeld was expelled from town in the Spring of 1557.[69] Despite this success, the patrician councillors, who consistently opposed the Reformation, fought a losing battle, and were soon forced to grant highly compromising concessions. Again in 1562, as in the early 1540's, the community (represented within the city council by the deputees of the six guilds) knew how to profit from the precarious situation of city finances. At the same time, its resistance was supported by the outside agitation unleashed by the preachers Johann Heitfeld and Hermann Hamelmann, and, in all likelihood, by the concurrent events in neighboring Essen. Thus, the guild representatives in the council only agreed to condone an increase in taxes in exchange for substantial religious concessions.

The result of the ensuing confrontation within the council was the city government's religious edict of March 19, 1562, in which the authorities granted the ministration of the Lord's Supper in both kinds, but forbid any further attendance of Protestant

[67] *Ibid.,* 70–76; *Löffler,* "Reformationsgeschichte," 190. Cf. also, *von Winterfeld,* Geschichte ... Dortmund, pp. 151–152.

[68] *von Winterfeld,* "Der Durchbruch," 76–85; and *Löffler,* ibid., 197–198, who, however, underestimates the Protestant tendencies of Jacob Schöpper. For justified criticism of Löffler's assessment, cf. *Stenger,* "Die Reformation," 198–203.

[69] *von Winterfeld,* ibid., 87–88; and *Löffler,* ibid., 205–210.

celebrations of the Lord's Supper outside the city.[70] Advances of the Protestant movement were also facilitated by the timely deaths (between 1561 and 1566) of three major opponents of the Reformation among the patrician councillors. The council's position was further weakened by the continuing intrusion of Protestants into its ranks. In 1564, in response to petitions presented by the parishioners, the city government was forced to allow the singing of German Protestant psalms in the four parish churches and had no choice later on but to sanction the celebration of Mass in German rather than Latin. The final introduction of the Reformation was by then only a matter of time.

Very little is known about the establishment of exclusively Protestant service within the majority of Dortmund's parish churches during the late 1560's. By 1570, the number of patrician councillors had dropped to five and the remainder of the councillors were thus in a position to take the decisive step. They summoned the city's preachers to submit statements of their religious confession, and the latter responded by presenting a Lutheran eucharistic confession, the *Confessio Praedicantium Tremonensium.* Subsequently, the council decreed that this document be adjured by all present and future preachers. Only two preachers who remained Catholic refused to comply, but they were allowed to remain in town. As in all other late Reformation cities, Catholicism was not abolished in Dortmund.

The year 1570 marks the official introduction of the Reformation in Dortmund. In 1579, the Catholics lost the last of the four parish churches (St. Nicolai). Thereafter, Catholic worship was only held in the monastery churches. In 1616, one of the monastery churches (the church of the Franciscans) was accorded the status of a parish church – including the right to administer marriages and baptism. The tensions and conflicts between the Catholic patricians and the Protestant community survived the year of the official introduction of the Reformation; although the overwhelming majority of citizens had turned Protestant, the minuscule Catholic party in town continued to exert an important influence on city politics because it was largely composed of patrician burgomasters and councillors.[71]

3. The Reformation in Aachen.

During the Reformation century, next to Cologne, Aachen was the most sizeable imperial city in the west of the Empire. Around 1500, it had a population of about 15–20,000 inhabitants. Since the 12th century, its most important economic resources

[70] The Protestant citizens had become accustomed to attending evangelical worship at the neighboring towns of Brakel and probably also Derne. See *Löffler,* "Reformationsgeschichte," 210. For a detailed discussion of the mandate in question, cf. ibid., 210–214. One of the first burghers to attend the new celebration of the Lord's Supper on Easter, 1562, was the former Erasmian and Rector of the *Archigymnasium,* Johann Lambach who, since 1556, had become a zealous evangelical proselytizer. Cf. also *von Winterfeld,* "Der Durchbruch," 89–93.

[71] In 1600, the Catholic party in Dortmund was composed of only seven families counting a total of about thirty members. See *von Winterfeld,* Geschichte ... Dortmund, p. 131. For details on the events during the years following 1564, cf. idem, "Der Durchbruch," 95–100; and *Löffler*, "Reformationsgeschichte," 220–233.

had been woolweaving and the cloth-trade, and from the beginning of the 15th century onward, Aachen also gained a reputation for its production of tools and objects in brass and copper. By 1500, like Dortmund, Aachen was already past the zenith of economic prosperity.[72] For economic reasons, following the 1540's, the authorities encouraged the immigration of craftsmen and merchants from the Low Countries. The latter, as we shall see, greatly stimulated not only the city economy, but also the Reformation movement in town.

Aachen was predominantly ruled by wealthy patricians, even though, by 1513, as a final result of a series of social and constitutional revolts, the guilds had secured their participation in city government. The government consisted of a small and a great city council which were presided over by two burgomasters. The number of councillors varied greatly from decade to decade. Although, according to the new constitutional agreement of 1513, the small council was supposed to comprise two representatives of each of the fourteen *Gaffeln* (guilds), it only consisted of nineteen members in that year. The situation was similar in the case of the great council. Normally, it was to comprise between 127 and 129 members. As a partner of the small council, it fulfilled advisory functions. All city-councillors were elected for a two-year term.[73]

The city was richly endowed with ecclesiastical establishments. In the 16th century, there were fourteen churches and fifteen chapels within its walls. Four among them were parish churches. In addition, the city housed fifteen monasteries. The ecclesiastical jurisdiction, officially in the hands of the Bishop of Liège, was in fact shared equally by the neighboring Duke of Jülich-Cleves.[74] Humanism found its most dedicated partisans among the secular clergy, but seems to have had little impact on Aachen's intellectual life in the early 16th century. It is indicative of this situation that the first printing press was established relatively late in this city; the first genuine Aachen print dates from 1573.[75] However, it is not unlikely that Aachen's humanist clergymen contributed to a stabilization of the city's religious climate. When Erasmus first passed through the coronation city in 1518, he was greeted by a small circle of enthusiastic admirers – all of them canons of St. Mary's chapter. The connection maintained by the latter to the Erasmians at the court of Jülich-Cleves suggests that their reformist attitude may have played a role

[72] *Gustav Elfert,* "Gewerbe und Handel, ihre wirtschaftliche und rechtliche Verfassung," in Aachener Heimatgeschichte, ed. by Albert Huyskens (Aachen 1924), pp. 150–1.

[73] *Carl Schué,* "Die reichsstädtische Verfassung und ihre Entwicklung," in Aachener Heimatgeschichte, ibid., pp. 176–180. For a differentiated and detailed account of Aachen's constitutional development in the 15th and early 16th centuries, see *Erich Meuthen,* "Der gesellschaftliche Hintergrund der Aachener Verfassungskämpfe an der Wende vom Mittelalter zur Neuzeit," Zs. Aachen, LXXIV/LXXV (1962/63), 299–392. Meuthen revises some of Schué's rather clichéd views of the "democratic" character of guild participation in government. The author demonstrates that, notwithstanding the enhanced guild participation in city government after 1513, the oligarchical nature of the régime prevailed. Cf. also Rheinisches Städtebuch, ed. by *Keyser*, p. 36.

[74] Two among the four parish churches, St. Foillan's and St. Adalbert's, were controlled by influential collegial chapters which were directly subject to the Empire (*Reichsstifte*). See Aachener Heimatgeschichte, ibid., pp. 193–206; and Rheinisches Städtebuch, ibid., pp. 30–32.

[75] *Eduard Arens,* "Vom literarischen Leben in Aachen," in Aachener Heimatgeschichte, ibid., p. 242.

in assuring the community's continued adherence to Catholicism during the 1520's and 1530's.[76]

Like the city of Essen, and unlike neighboring Cologne, Aachen was not involved in the social and religious unrest of 1525.[77] During the first half of the 16th century, there was no real communal Reformation movement in Aachen. During the 1530's, a "Sacramentarian", and later an Anabaptist community succeeded in establishing themselves in town, but by virtue of their rather conspiratorial organization, they could not generate any significant religious movement among the citizens. They did, however, help to prepare the ground for the subsequent spread of the Reformation. Except for the cases of a few monks who were disenchanted with the old church, the role of Aachen's clergy during the first decades of the Reformation century is still largely unknown.[78]

The Reformation movement only gained a stronger basis in town after 1544, when the authorities, for economic reasons, organized the settlement in Aachen of about thirty families of weavers and copper manufacturers from Artois and Flanders. Many of these immigrants were Protestants who stimulated and intensified the spread of the Reformation in town.[79] During the following fifteen years, the relatively tolerant position of the city council, originally based entirely on economic motives (and on partially religious reasons later) permitted the growing influence these immigrants and the subsequent refugees from the Low Countries exerted on Aachen's religious climate.

The differences between Aachen's and Cologne's official religious policy became more and more marked.[80] After 1544, further enhanced by new Walloon immigrants, the Protestant community grew steadily. At the same time, intermarriage between Protestant immigrants and leading Aachen families rendered the authorities more lenient in religious matters. Meanwhile, preachers immigrating from the Low Countries stimulated the spread of the Reformation within the community at large. The predominant creed of the growing group of Protestants was Reformed rather than Lutheran.[81]

[76] See my forthcoming articles on Werner Huyn of Anstenroid, Aegidius Hasenbart, Leonardus Priccardus, Johann Schoenraid and Johann Sudermann, to be included in The Biographical Register in The Collected Works of Erasmus, Toronto 1980.

[77] *Günther Franz*, Der deutsche Bauernkrieg (Tenth ed.; Darmstadt 1975), p. 235.

[78] *Schilling*, Niederländische Exulanten, pp. 22 and 95; *Walther Wolff*, "Beiträge zu einer Reformationsgeschichte der Stadt Aachen," Theol. Arbeiten, n.s., VII (1905), 79–85; and *Redlich*, Staat und Kirche, p. 44, Cf. also *J[ohann] F. G. Goeters*, "Die Rolle des Täufertums," 226–227. Goeters revises Wolff's and Redlich's assertion that there was a genuine Anabaptist community in and around Aachen before the rise of Anabaptism at Münster in Westphalia in 1534–35. He makes a good case for Aachen's early Protestants having been "Sacramentarians" rather than genuine Anabaptists.

[79] See *Schilling*, ibid., pp. 32 and 97. According to Wolff it would be misleading, however, to assume that the Reformation movement in Aachen "was solely created by the immigrants, even if we are not in a position to point out clearly the other influences, aside from Anabaptism:" *Wolff*, ibid., 85–88. Cf. also Goeters' critique of Wolff, n. 78, above.

[80] Unlike Aachen's authorities, those of Cologne, who, during the second half of the 16th century also admitted a substantial number of refugees from the Low Countries, never wavered or compromised in their stern commitment to Catholicism. Compare the respective passages on Aachen and Cologne in *Schilling*, Niederländische Exulanten, pp. 95–121. See also *Rudolf Reuter*, Der Kampf um die Reichsstandschaft der Städte auf dem Augsburger Reichstag 1582, Schwäbische Geschichtsquellen und Forschungen, Book III (Munich and Leipzig 1919), pp. 18–47.

[81] *Schilling*, ibid., 95–98; and *Wolff*, "Beiträge," (1905), 89–95.

By 1559, the adherence of city councillors and common citizens to Protestantism had become so widespread that an outside observer estimated that almost the entire community would embrace the Reformation message if a Protestant preacher were allowed to preach publicly during a period of about eight days.[82] In the same year, the Protestant inhabitants, basing their action on the Augsburg Peace, twice petitioned the authorities to allow evangelical worship to be celebrated publicly in town. The largely sympathetic city council preferred first to gain the support of the imperial estates assembled at the Diet of Augsburg before it took the decisive step. However, the two Aachen delegates charged with the mission of securing this support returned to their city empty-handed. The Calvinist tendency of an Aachen Confession, sent to the Palatine Prince-elector Friedrich III by the preacher Adrian van Haemstede in September, 1559, aroused suspicion among the Duke of Württemberg's theological advisors – who, in turn, thwarted the unanimous support of Aachen's Reformation movement by the Protestant princes.[83]

Thus, the initiative taken by the city's Protestants backfired considerably – stern Catholic reaction set in immediately in 1559. Emperor Ferdinand I forbid the city to undertake any religious change, and King Philip II of Spain, the overlord of the neighboring Low Countries, threatened grave consequences to the city's authorities should they not repress the Reformation movement. At the same time, similar protests and threats were voiced by the Ordinary (the Bishop of Liège), the Archbishop of Cologne and by the Duke of Jülich-Cleves, who, through various prerogatives accorded his ancestors, exerted a considerable influence on the city's affairs.[84] All of these outside protests provoked an instantaneous repression of Protestantism in Aachen, culminating in a council decision in February, 1560, ordering that all Protestants were hitherto to be excluded from election to public office.[85] Although it greatly suffered from this reaction, the Protestant community survived the following difficult years. The upper strata of Aachen's Protestant community steadfastly clung to their religious conviction and in the

[82] See *Wilhelm G. Goeters,* "Adrian van Haemstede's Wirksamkeit in Antwerpen und Aachen," Theol. Arbeiten, n.s., VIII (1906), 76.

[83] Ibid.; Adrian van Haemstede came to Aachen in February, 1559, in the company of Antwerp merchant families fleeing the prosecution of Protestants in their native city. Later, in September 1559, the preacher was in London. The Aachen petition of 1559, which was signed by twenty-nine city councillors and sixty-three heads of old Aachen families, and sent to the Augsburg diet in the same year, is printed in *Wolff,* "Beiträge," (1905), 99–103. Cf. also *Petri,* "Glaubenskämpfe," p. 74.

[84] *Hermann F. Macco,* Zur Reformationsgeschichte Aachens während des 16. Jahrhunderts: Eine kritische Studie (Aachen 1907), p. 26; and *Reuter,* Der Kampf, pp. 19–20. It is interesting to note in this connection, the great differences in Duke Wilhelm's reaction to the religious situation in Aachen in 1559 and Essen in 1563–64. For Essen, cf. above, pp. 175–6. Considering how much attention the case of the strategically located city of Aachen attracted throughout the Empire, the Duke probably had no choice but to support Emperor Ferdinand's policy in this case. Essen's strategic value, on the other hand, was minimal compared to that of Aachen. Accordingly, the Reformation in Essen had no real repercussions to speak of in imperial politics. Secondly, and more important, the Duke was interested in safeguarding the rights he held in Aachen, such as his far-reaching control over the city's jurisdiction and his patronage over some of Aachen's parish churches, as well as his control over the local ecclesiastical court (*Sendgericht*). Cf. *Reuter,* ibid. In short, whereas the Essener Reformation enhanced the Duke's influence on this city, the reverse situation would have resulted from a Reformation in Aachen at that time.

[85] *Reuter,* ibid., p. 21; and *Macco,* ibid., pp. 47–49, who discusses the repressive measures taken at the same time by the episcopal court.

second half of the 1560's their party began to rise to new prosperity. This was partially due to the immigration in 1567 of the entire Calvinist community of Maastricht, accompanied by its preacher Johannes Huckelom. The latter was soon joined by other preachers and schoolmasters fleeing religious persecution in the Low Countries. "Courageous preaching of the Gospel, intensive cure of souls, and diaconic care for the poor, were the spiritual instruments preparing the ground for the spread of Protestantism within the native community." (H. Schilling)

Aachen's unreformed Catholic church failed in its attempt to counter this influence.[86] At the beginning of the 1570's, there were two important Protestant communities in Aachen: the Dutch-Reformed and German-Reformed parishes, administered respectively by Johannes Huckelom and Johannes Christianus Otzenradt. In the middle of this decade, yet another religious community established itself in town: an independent Lutheran parish, founded primarily by refugees from Antwerp. The rise and activity of this community was facilitated by the growing acceptance of Protestantism in Aachen's leading families. As a result, the authorities now dropped all restrictions on further immigration from the Low Countries. In 1574, they abolished the 1560 decree excluding Protestants from public office. The city government gradually came under Protestant control.[87]

Meanwhile, the political chances of a Reformation in Aachen dwindled – first, through the advent to power of Emperor Rudolf II in October, 1576, who was soon to take an uncompromisingly hostile stand against Aachen's Protestants, and, secondly, through the gradual shift of the Duke of Jülich-Cleves toward a sternly Catholic policy.[88] The latter's increasingly absolutist demeanor toward the city of Aachen was difficult to counter because of his substantial rights in town. Considering this shift in Duke Wilhelm's policy, the growing number of Protestant city councillors must have seen the intended introduction of the Reformation as a welcome opportunity to restrengthen the city's autonomy against the Duke's territorial expansionism. Yet, in 1580, the city authorities were faced with the threatening position of their neighbors and did not dare give way to the renewed petitions of Protestant citizens calling for the official introduction of evangelical worship, even though the city council now strongly sympathized with the Reformation. At that time, the approximately 12,000 steadfast adherents of Catholicism in town (Catholic clergy and members of the middle and lower

[86] *Schilling,* Niederländische Exulanten, pp. 98–100; and *Petri,* "Glaubenskämpfe," pp. 74–75. For the career of Johannes Huckelom, cf. *Walther Wolff,* "Beiträge zu einer Reformationsgeschichte der Stadt Aachen," Theol. Arbeiten, n.s., VI (1903), 99.

[87] The 1574 decision was clearly simplified by the transition in 1572 of the governorship of the neighboring Spanish Low countries from the hands of the Duke of Alba into the control of the more lenient Luis de Requesens. Furthermore, the simultaneous failure of an imperial commission to abolish the Protestant church in Haguenau and Emperor Maximilian II's indecision, seem to have had important repercussions in Aachen. See *Macco,* Zur Reformationsgeschichte, pp. 50–51; and *Walter Wolff,* "Beiträge zu einer Reformationsgeschichte der Stadt Aachen," Theol. Arbeiten, n.s., IX (1907), 50–58. According to *Wolff,* ibid., it would be a mistake to attribute too much weight to the impact of the refugees from the Low Countries on the renewed rise of Protestantism in Aachen during the 1570's. The German-Reformed parish, composed mostly of native inhabitants, was more instrumental in this new ascent. For the preacher Otzenradt, cf. *Wolff,* "Beiträge," (1903), 97–98.

[88] See *Ritter,* Deutsche Geschichte, Vol. I, pp. 510–514; and *Macco,* ibid., 51 and 61.

strata of the population) faced a still growing number of about 8,000 Protestants originating primarily from the middle and upper strata of the population.[89] In the Fall of 1580, the Emperor dispatched an imperial commission to Aachen. The Bishop of Liège and the Duke of Jülich-Cleves were in charge of this mission.

A situation very similar to that in Haguenau in 1574 was to repeat itself in Aachen. Based on the ambiguous "city-article", contained in the Augsburg Peace of 1555[90], the commissaries not only denied Aachen's *ius reformandi,* but declared that, considering the Duke of Jülich-Cleves' substantial prerogatives in town, the city could not be granted the status of an "immediate" imperial city. Protestantism, the commissaries argued, was thus to be entirely suppressed in Aachen. Not surprisingly, the city authorities refused to comply with such far-reaching impositions.[91] As a result, the Emperor warned the city council in a severe tone not to disregard its 1560 decison to exclude Protestants from public office in the up-coming city elections of May, 1581. To this the Protestant councillors responded by appealing to the next diet of imperial cities held in Speyer at the end of August, 1581. This measure in turn led to an outburst from the Catholic opposition in town: the Catholic councillors now constituted their own city council.

As a result, Rudolf II appointed a new Catholic imperial commision to intervene on his behalf in Aachen. The commissaries arrived in the city shortly after the tumultuous election of two Protestant burgomasters by the eighty Protestant councillors, and two Catholic "counter-burgomasters" by the forty members of the Catholic council. The commissaries, unable to establish unity in town, called for the abdication of the Protestant councillors. Referring to the rights held in town by the Duke of Jülich-Cleves, they again refused to recognize Aachen as an imperial city. They had not, however, counted on the spontaneous outbreak of Protestant opposition. Thus forced to compromise, they ultimately sanctioned the election of both a Calvinist and a Catholic citizen as the two new burgomasters, and tolerated the Protestant members' retention of their seats.[92] The latter lost no time in officially introducing the Reformation.

By 1581, the case of Aachen had become an arena in which the consolidating confessional parties within the Empire were to test their power. During the early 1580's, the situation looked promising for Aachen's Protestants. The estate of imperial cities, under the leadership of Strasbourg and its energetic city-clerk Paul Hochfelder, made all further payment of subsidies to the Emperor for the war against the Turks contingent on Rudolf II's public recognition of Aachen's *ius reformandi.*[93] However, the Emperor's stubborn and uncompromising position in this matter, underlined by open threats ut-

[89] *Schilling,* Niederländische Exulanten, p. 96; and *Wolff,* "Beiträge," (1907), 55–63. Cf. also the interesting "Supplicatio Catholicarum mulierum Aquensium . . ." of November 27, 1580, printed in *Wolff,* ibid., 63–65.

[90] See above, p. 95.

[91] *Reuter,* Der Kampf, pp. 22–28.

[92] ibid.

[93] For detailed accounts of the different negotiations connected with the case of Aachen, cf. *Johannes Müller,* "Der Konflikt Kaiser Rudolfs II. mit den deutschen Reichsstädten, ca. 1577–85," Westdeutsche Zeitschrift für Geschichte und Kunst, XIV (1895), 257–293; *Heinrich Pennings,* "Die Religionsunruhen in Aachen und die beiden Städtetage zu Speyer und Heilbronn 1581 und 1582," Zs. Aachen, XXVII (1905), 25–108; and especially the succinct analysis by *Reuter,* Der Kampf.

tered against the unruly cities, and the inner dissension among the cities themselves, finally brought about the gradual dissolution of the common urban front. After the Catholic cities of Rottweil, Schwäbisch-Gmünd and Ueberlingen yielded to the Emperor's pressure, it was ultimately the ambiguous position assumed on the issue by such important cities as Cologne, Augsburg, Esslingen, Heilbronn and Frankfurt, which thwarted Strasbourg's attempt to bring about a joint action of the German imperial cities in support of beleaguered Aachen.

Between 1582 and 1585, the cities, one by one, paid their "Turkish taxes" without having obtained the Emperor's concessions which, at the city diets of 1581 and 1582, they had declared to be their common political goal. The confessional differences among them, as well as the continuous decline of urban economy during the second half of the 16th century, enabled a narrow-minded parochialism to invade their positions and increasingly obstruct the pursuit of common political goals. In the 1580's, the cities found themselves a long way away from the proud and united role they had once played during the first decade of the Reformation. The days of great urban prosperity were a thing of the past. After 1582, the cities gave in to the Emperor's policy of threats, although the issue at stake was of a vital political significance, not just for Aachen, but for all of them.

The only concession the cities succeeded in wresting from Rudolf II (with the help of Protestant princes) was a promise to appoint a new, *bi-confessional* commission to bring about the settlement of unresolved issues in Aachen. Such an arrangement was reached in April, 1584, resulting in the further pacification of the religious unrest prevailing in town.[94] Thus, following the year 1581, both Catholic and evangelical worship were officially held in Aachen. The Protestant majority within city government cautious not to violate the rights of the Catholic minority. But this situation was not to last.

After the victory of the Catholic party in the War of Cologne (1582–85)[95], the highly exposed city fell prey to the newly established hegemony of Catholic powers in the west of the Empire. During the following years, the city was increasingly harassed by its neighbors, including the Duke of Jülich-Cleves and Philip II's governor in the Low Countries, the Duke of Parma. In 1593, the Imperial Court Council, influenced by the Emperor, decreed that, based on the "city article" of the Augsburg Peace, imperial cities were not in a position to claim a *ius reformandi* and that Aachen's authorities therefore had to return to their own 1560 decision calling for the exclusion of Protestants from city office.

Aachen's city council refused to comply with this decree. Hence, Rudolf II, strongly urged to do so by Philip II, imposed the imperial ban upon the Aachen city government. The ban was executed in 1598 with military forces under the command of the Spanish Admiral Mendoza and the Archbishop and Prince-elector of Cologne, Ernst of Bavaria, who, as Bishop of Liège, controlled the ecclesiastical jurisdiction in Aachen. The Protestant churches in town were immediately abolished, but survived as secret religious com-

[94] Cf. *Macco,* Zur Reformationsgeschichte, p. 65.
[95] See *Ritter,* Deutsche Geschichte, Vol. I, pp. 587–620.

munities.[96] In 1611, through a revolt against the Catholic city government, the Protestant leaders once more came to power. Their triumph was shortlived, however. Three years later, General Spinola's Spanish troops intervened in Aachen and brought the Catholic council back to power. This military interference, combined with the following Spanish occupation, lasting for several years, forced most leading Protestant families into emigration and exile.[97] By 1614, the Reformation in Aachen had ended in failure.

4. The Reformation in Aalen.

When compared to the other late city Reformations discussed here, the available evidence for 16th century Aalen looks particularly scarce, especially regarding this city's pre-Reformation period.[98] Sixteenth century Aalen was a small imperial city with only 1000 to 2000 inhabitants.[99] The modest prosperity of the town was based on its location at the crossroads between Strasbourg, Nördlingen, Ulm and Crailsheim, as well as on its agriculture. A few of its citizens maintained a small network of trade in wool and wine.[100]

An imperial city since 1360, Aalen controlled its own higher and lower secular jurisdiction and was, thus, relatively autonomous. During the late Middle Ages, its government was in the hands of a small number of patrician city councillors. In 1514, the common people, revolting against the financial policy of the ruling oligarchy, incorporated two communal representatives (*Stättmeister*) into the city council. However, they lost their control of the seats in 1552, when Emperor Charles V re-strengthened the aristocratic make-up of a number of Upper German imperial city governments.[101]

[96] *Ritter,* Deutsche Geschichte, Vol. II (Stuttgart 1895), pp. 154–155; *Petri,* "Glaubenskämpfe," pp. 100–102; and *Macco,* Zur Reformationsgeschichte, pp. 79–83.

[97] *Matthias Classen,* "Die konfessionelle und politische Bewegung in der Reichsstadt Aachen zu Anfang des 17. Jahrhunderts," Zs. Aachen, XXVIII (1906), 286–442; and *Heinz Schilling,* "Bürgerkämpfe in Aachen zu Beginn des 17. Jahrhunderts," Zeitschrift für historische Forschung, I (1974), 175–231.

[98] The basic source of information is *Georg W. Zapf,* ed., Sämmtliche Reformations-Urkunden des Heiligen Römischen Reichs Stadt Aalen, two parts in one vol., Ulm 1770. Tscherning's account is largely based on Zapf; cf. *Julius Tscherning,* Züge aus der Geschichte der Reformation der ehemaligen freien Reichsstadt Aalen auf Grund eines im Jahre der Einführung der Reformation abgefassten, später umgeschriebenen Urkundenbuchs, Aalen 1882. There is no modern account of Aalen's Reformation.

[99] In 1803, there were only 1,932 inhabitants in Aalen. Cf. Württembergisches Städtebuch, in Deutsches Städtebuch, ed. by *Keyser,* Vol. IV, Part II/2 (Stuttgart 1962), p. 31. An early picture of Aalen, from the year 1528, gives a good impression of the small size of this town. The picture is reproduced in *Herbert Plickert,* "Geschichte der freien Reichsstadt Aalen im Wandel der Zeiten," Aquileja: Illustrierte Zeitschrift zur Pflege des Heimatgedankens im Gebiet der Ostalb (1960), 73. For comments on its origin, cf. ibid., 79.

[100] *Plickert,* ibid., 76 and 78; and Württembergisches Städtebuch, ibid.

[101] See *L[udwig] Fürstenwerth,* Die Verfassungsänderungen in den oberdeutschen Reichsstädten zur Zeit Karls V., Göttingen 1892. Although Fürstenwerth only peremptorily touches upon Aalen's situation, he makes clear that the imperial instructions regarding the constitutional changes to be implemented in the cities in question listed Aalen among the loyal towns, such as Überlingen, Buchhorn, and Schwäbisch-Gmünd. The strengthening of aristocratic regime in these cities was primarily designed to re-enforce their commitment to Catholicism. Cf. ibid., pp. 35–6. Cf. also *Moeller*, "Imperial Cities", pp. 108–9.

Following this imperial intervention, Aalen's city council was composed of thirteen members, including three burgomasters and two "secret" councillors who, together with the burgomasters, formed the "Secret Council" in charge of the city's daily administration. The oligarchical nature of this regime was further characterized by the singular lack of council elections during the period 1552 to 1591. To all appearances, the councillors were appointed for life and their successors were nominated through co-optation. This system only changed after the introduction of the Reformation, in 1591, when the community succeeded in regaining control over the composition of city government.[102]

St. Nicolai was Aalen's only parish church in the 16th century. In addition, the city housed three chapels. I have found no mention of any monasteries established in town. After 1532, there seem to have been only three clergymen in Aalen – the parson and two chaplains. The right to appoint these churchmen was held by the powerful Prince-Provost of Ellwangen residing a few miles north of Aalen. By the 16th century, the Provost had brought all of Aalen's ecclesiastical property and the income resulting thereof under his control[103]; as a result, the Provost of Ellwangen had a considerable impact on the city's politics. Beyond the religious motives involved with the Aalen Reformation, the religious change of 1575 was nourished by the city council's intention to free the city from the Provost's increasing influence.[104]

To date, very little is known about the course of the Reformation in Aalen before its official introduction in 1575. During the first half of the 16th century, the city demonstratively upheld its allegiance to Charles V, and thereby its commitment to Catholicism. During the years 1519 to 1534, when the Württemberg territory to the west of town was in the hands of Habsburg-Austria, such a commitment may also have served as a measure of protection against Habsburg's expansionism. We do not know about the repercussions the peasants' revolt of 1525 may have had within the agrarian city of Aalen. It is only known that the city did not become involved in the revolt of the countryside, although some peasants from surrounding villages controlled by the city joined the uprising.[105]

The infiltration of Protestantism into Aalen began after 1529. The increasing laxity of the community in ecclesiastical matters, evidenced by the widespread refusal in 1533 to pay the four offerings[106] to the parson, may have been generated by anticlericalism rather than by genuine religious conviction.[107] At the same time, however, Aalen's

[102] See *Plickert,* "Aalen im Wandel der Zeiten," 73–74; and *Hermann Bauer,* Geschichte und Beschreibung der ehemaligen freien Reichsstadt Aalen, (Second ed.; rev. and ed. by J. G. Röhm; Aalen 1884), p. 32. Cf. also Württembergisches Städtebuch, p. 32.

[103] *Plickert,* ibid., 80; and *Bauer,* ibid., pp. 109–113.

[104] The Counts of Öttingen simultaneously held important rights in Aalen, but an emancipation from their politico-religious influence was unnecessary because the Counts had themselves embraced the Reformation. Cf. *Reinhold Herold,* Geschichte der Reformation in der Grafschaft Öttingen, 1522–1569, SVRG, No. 75, Halle 1902.

[105] *Plickert,* "Aalen im Wandel der Zeiten," 83; and *Bauer,* Geschichte und Beschreibung, p. 55. See also *Wilhelm Zimmermann,* Geschichte des großen Bauernkrieges nach den Urkunden und Augenzeugen, 2 vols., (Second ed.; Naunhof and Leipzig 1939), Vol. II, p. 138.

[106] For the notion of the „four offerings", cf. above, p. 91.

[107] At the same time, Anabaptism was encountered in the Aalen area. See *Plickert,* "Aalen im Wandel der Zeiten," 81.

preacher in the years 1525 to 1535, Conrad Delphinus, seems to have exerted a considerable influence on the city's religious climate. His sympathies for the Reformation were strong enough to earn him a citation from the Bishop of Augsburg in 1531, which was only adjourned upon the city council's public testimony as to Delphinus' orthodoxy. Delphinus revealed his Protestant conviction in 1535 by seeking employment as a preacher within the Protestant Duchy of Württemberg. Unfortunately, we cannot judge the extent of his influence on the religious conviction of his parishioners.

There can be no doubt that in 1534 and beyond, the introduction of the Reformation in the neighboring Duchy by Duke Ulrich of Württemberg must have had an important long-term effect on Aalen's religious life. It undoubtedly helped to sustain the parishioners' growing laxity in ecclesiastical matters which, in 1550, prompted the Abbot of Weingarten to dispatch an alarming report to the Emperor. Meanwhile, the city authorities maintained their commitment to the old church, declaring in 1548 their intention to continue their adherence to Catholicism.[108]

The stipulations of the Augsburg Peace of 1555 filled Aalen's Protestants with new hope for the eventual victory of their cause. This hope was nourished by the increasing influence that the Protestant minister of the neighboring imperial city of Bopfingen, Georg Hummel, exerted on Aalen's parishioners.[109] In 1563, Aalen's parson complained that his flock insisted on singing German psalms before and after his sermons. At the same time, the Reformation message began to seep into the ranks of the councillors.

Thus, a year later the Bishop of Augsburg, Aalen's Ordinary and Provost of Ellwangen, took offense at the city council's advice to the schoolmaster to instruct the local youth and adult parishioners in the reading and recitation of a Protestant catechism – presumably Johannes Brenz's Württemberg Catechism. The Bishop reacted by ordering the chaplain of the chapel of St. John's to begin instruction based on the Tridentine Catechism[110], creating a stalemate which the city council did not dare resolve, although more and more of its members were desirous of introducing the Reformation.

Its opponent was none other than the very powerful Otto Truchsess von Waldburg – Cardinal-Bishop of Augsburg and one of the first great champions of the Counterreformation in Germany. From 1552 to his death in April, 1573, Bishop Otto was also in charge of the Prince-Provostship of Ellwangen.[111] As both Bishop and Provost he held

[108] Ibid., 80; *Bauer,* Geschichte und Beschreibung, pp. 114–115; *[Hermann?] Zeller,* "Die Aalener Reformation 1575," Spion von Aalen: Blätter für Heimatkunde, Beilage zur Kocher-Zeitung und zum Härtsfelder Boten, II and III (February and March, 1926), 10. The existence of a Protestant community within Aalen during the 1540's is referred to in sources dating from the 1620's. See *Zapf,* ed., Sämmtliche Reformations-Urkunden, Part II, pp. 24–26.

[109] The small imperial city of Bopfingen introduced the Reformation in 1546. During the period of the *Interim,* its authorities were forced to re-establish Catholic worship, but shortly thereafter returned to Protestantism (in 1552). Georg Hummel was minister there from 1552 to 1561. See *Gerhard Kumpf,* "Die schwäbische Reichsstadt Bopfingen in den Stürmen der Reformations- und Interimszeit," Blätter für württembergische Kirchengeschichte, LIX (1959), 116–7. For Hummel's career, cf. *Herold,* Geschichte der Reformation, pp. 37–8.

[110] *Bauer,* ibid. and p. 132; and *Zeller,* ibid., 11.

[111] See *Friedrich Zoepfl,* "Kardinal Otto Truchsess von Waldburg, 1514–1573," in Lebensbilder aus dem Bayerischen Schwaben, Vol. IV, ed. by Götz Freiherr von Pölnitz (Munich 1955), pp. 204–248. Cardinal-Bishop Otto's furtherance of the Counterreformation within the territory subject to the

important rights in Aalen. He, above all, must have been the cause of those "other circumstances and obstacles" which, in the words of the city-clerk, had prevented Aalen's authorities from introducing the Reformation at an earlier date.[112] It was only after Bishop Otto's death in 1573 that the city council – now the leader of the Reformation movement in town – could reasonably contemplate an eventual religious change. At this point, the Ellwangen Provostship was assumed by the less powerful Christoph, Baron of Freiberg.[113] Emperor Maximilian II's non-commitment in the dispute over Haguenau's *ius reformandi*[114] may have raised the optimism of the city-clerk Johannes Preu and the burgomaster Andreas Baader, who now appeared as the leaders of Aalen's Protestants.

Sent to Augsburg in February, 1575, to seek Dr. Tradeln's legal counsel about a current litigation between Aalen and the Provost of Ellwangen, these two men simultaneously inquired about the legal possibility of introducing the Reformation. Dr. Tradeln, referring to the Augsburg Peace, dit not hesitate to confirm the city's *ius reformandi*. As a result, the city council dispatched the burgomaster and city-clerk to the diet of imperial cities held at Ulm in February/March, 1575. Their task was to seek the support of Ulm, Esslingen and Nördlingen for the intended religious change. Yet, as happened later in the case of Aachen, these cities hesitated to grant their unconditional assistance and advised the city of Aalen to seek support from its neighbor, Duke Ludwig of Württemberg.[115] The city council, concerned about a possible loss of autonomy resulting from such a course of action, was therefore deeply divided on whether to involve the influential neighbor in its own affairs, even though a number of well-respected citizens and outsiders had urged the councillors to lose no time in introducing Protestant worship. A simultaneous warning from the Bishop of Augsburg mobilized Catholic resistance within the community. The warning showed that further hesitation would only result in possible outside interference. It thus helped to restore the councillors' unity, so that at the beginning of April, 1575, they initiated negotiations with Duke Ludwig.[116]

Initially, the latter hesitated to take the matter entirely into his own hands, although he left no doubt as to Aalen's right to introduce Protestant worship and to force the

Provostship of Ellwangen is recorded in *Julius Schall*, "Reformation und Gegenreformation im Gebiet der Fürstprobstei Ellwangen," Blätter für württembergische Kirchengeschichte, n.s., I (1879), 145–163.

[112] On March 1, 1575, the Aalen delegates present at the diet of imperial cities at Ulm declared that they "sonderlich des publicierten Religion Friedens hoche vnd guetherzige Naiglichait gethragen, Sich durch hilff vnd Segens des Allmechtigen der Roemischen Jrrthumben vnd beschwerden dermahlen Ains zu entladen, vnd zw der Euangelischen Confession zu ercleren, Jedoch durch andern zustennde, vnd vngelegenhaiten, daran vffgehalten vnd verhindert worden ..." See *Zapf*, ed., Sämmtliche Reformations-Urkunden, Part, I, p. 6.

[113] See the paragraph dedicated to the history of the princely chapter of Ellwangen in *Johann N. Vanotti*, "Beiträge zur Geschichte der Orden in der Diözese Rottenburg," Part II, Freiburger Diözesan-Archiv, XVII (1885), 205–217.

[114] Cf. above, pp. 109–10.

[115] *Tscherning*, Züge aus der Geschichte, pp. 3–4; and *Zapf*, ed., Sämmtliche Reformations-Urkunden, Part I, p. 6.

[116] *Tscherning*, ibid., pp. 5–8; for the text of a petition addressed to the city council by fourty-two Protestant citizens on March 8, 1575, see *Zapf*, ibid., pp. 11–17.

Provost of Ellwangen, as the patron of Aalen's city church, to take care of the maintenance of a Lutheran minister and schoolmaster.[117] The Duke finally stepped in when Aalen proved once more unable to mobilize the active support of Ulm and Nördlingen, and when Aalen's councillors began to fear an open clash between the Catholic and Protestant burghers of their city, should there be a further delay in resolving the issue. On June 6, 1575, the city council assembled the entire community and cautioned the citizens against further confessional dispute, forcing those present to state publicly whether they favored the introduction of Protestant worship or preferred to remain Catholic: a majority of about forty citizens revealed their intention to remain loyal to the old church. Among the thirteen city councillors, only two did not state their inclination to embrace the Augsburg Confession. Thus, about a third of Aalen's citizenry, including most of the city's political leadership, turned out in favor of the Reformation. The authorities now petitioned Duke Ludwig to dispatch a qualified preacher.[118]

On June 29, 1575, the Duke's court-chaplain and chancellor of the University of Tübingen, Jacob Andreae, officially introduced the Reformation in Aalen. By the time the latter left town a month later, Adam Salomon had been appointed as Aalen's first Protestant minister. Johann Glaser, a native of Aalen and former student at Jena and Basel, became his assistant and deacon. The authorities took control of the city's Latin school, which they entrusted to a Protestant schoolmaster named Kaspar Tinnelhan.[119] Although in the Spring of the same year the Provost of Ellwangen had voiced warning protests against any religious change in Aalen, once Duke Ludwig involved himself with the city's ecclesiastical affairs, the actual introduction of the Reformation met with surprisingly little resistance from the Provost. Led by the city council and protected by the Duke of Württemberg, Aalen's Lutheran church was to prove prosperous. As in the case of Colmar, the abolition of Protestantism by imperial commissaries in 1628 was to have no lasting effect: the Protestant church was re-established under Swedish protection in 1632.[120]

[117] *Zapf,* ibid., pp. 29–32 (Letter from Duke Ludwig of May 9, 1575); and *Tscherning,* Züge aus der Geschichte, p. 8.

[118] For a report on the communal assembly of June 6, 1575, and for the subsequent petition addressed to Duke Ludwig, see *Zapf,* ed., Sämmtliche Reformations-Urkunden, Part I, pp. 45–51. These documents make clear that there was only a minority of Protestants in Aalen. *Zeller,* "Die Aalener Reformation," 22, must have been unaware of this evidence. See also *Tscherning,* ibid., pp. 8–10. It is possible that there were only eleven instead of thirteen councillors in 1575. In this case, the entire council would have consisted of Protestants.

[119] *Zapf,* ibid., pp. 72–73; *Tscherning,* ibid., pp. 12–15., and *Bauer,* Geschichte und Beschreibung, pp. 116–117 and 132.

[120] After further negotiations the Provost also agreed to provide the salary for the Protestant preachers and the schoolteacher, to which the city council of Aalen, basing its actions on the Peace of Augsburg, was legally entitled. In these, as well as previous, negotiations with the Provost, Aalen was assisted by Duke Ludwig's legal councillors. A final agreement between the city and the Provost of Ellwangen was reached in November 1576. See *Zapf,* ibid., Part I, pp. 88–91 and 199–205. For Aalen's history during the Thirty Years' War, cf. *Bauer,* Geschichte und Beschreibung, pp. 56–7.

5. The Reformation in Haguenau.[121]

Sixteenth century Haguenau was approximately the same size as her sister city Colmar, with 5,000 to 6,000 inhabitants.[122] Haguenau's economy, like that of all other member-cities of the Alsatian *Decapolis,* was primarily based on agriculture. Next to it, the production and trading of cloth represented an important source of income.[123] The hierarchic structure of Haguenau's late medieval and 16th century society was far more pronounced than that of Colmar. Since the 14th century, the city government consisted of a magistrate called the Council of Jurors (*Schöffenrat*), comprising twelve members, and the Council fo the XXIV. During the 16th and early 17th centuries, the Council of Jurors was controlled by the city's new merchant patriciate. The XXIV were elected from the members of the city's guilds. Yet, there was no real communal election of councillors as in Colmar: each guild only had the right annually to nominate three candidates from whom the jurors and the XXIV chose one. The jurors were appointed exclusively by co-optation. Magistrate and council were presided over jointly by a *Stettmeister,* appointed by and among the twelve jurors, and a *Marschalk,* elected by the XXIV from among their own ranks. Hence, it is clear that Haguenau's constitution greatly limited communal influence in the city's administration and that it favored the evolution of strongly oligarchical tendencies within city government.[124] In 1565, it enabled a small, upper-class minority to introduce the Reformation against the will of the majority of citizens.

At the beginning of the 16th century, there were four monasteries in Haguenau. In the Spring of 1535, the Commandery of St. John sold its parish church of St. George to the city authorities; only a few weeks later, a similar transaction took place between the authorities and the Premonstratensians regarding the parish church of St. Nicolaus. Thus, practically overnight, the magistrate and council entered into full possession of the city's two parish churches including their respective *Fabrik.*[125] In addition, in 1546, the authorities were able to buy the practically deserted Franciscan monastery and church, granting the mendicants only the right of an eventual re-occupation of the premises.[126] These combined purchases gave the city government considerable control over the local church and were to facilitate the introduction of the Reformation in 1565.

[121] For further information on 16th century Haguenau, cf. also above, Chapters I and IV.

[122] At the beginning of the 16th century, there were 906 guild members in Haguenau. See *André M. Burg,* "Die unteren Volksschichten in Haguenau," in Gesellschaftliche Unterschichten in den südwestdeutschen Städten, ed. by Erich Maschke and Jürgen Sydow, VKBW, Series B, Vol. XLI (Stuttgart 1967), p. 92. For a comparison with Colmar figures, cf. above, pp. 13–16.

[123] See *Hector Ammann,* „La place de l'Alsace dans l'industrie textile du Moyen-Age," in La bourgeoisie alsacienne, ed. by La Société savante d'Alsace et des régions de l'Est (Strasbourg and Paris 1954), pp. 81–2.

[124] For the annual council election, cf. *Victor Guerber,* Histoire politique et religieuse de Haguenau, 2 vols. (Rixheim 1876), Vol. II, pp. 346–349. Cf. also *[Charles] A. Hanauer,* Le protestantisme à Haguenau (Strasbourg and Colmar 1905), pp. 33–35; and *André M. Burg,* "Patrizier und andere städtische Führungsschichten in Haguenau," in Deutsches Patriziat 1430–1740, ed. by Hellmuth Rössler, Schriften zur Problematik der Deutschen Führungsschichten in der Neuzeit, Vol. III (Limburg/Lahn 1968), pp. 358–360.

[125] *Hanauer,* ibid., pp. 87–89; and *Guerber,* ibid., Vol. II, pp. 93–106.

[126] *Guerber,* ibid., Vol. II, p. 117.

The influence of humanism on the city's upper social strata was increased through the advent of the printing press, first established in Haguenau by Heinrich Gran as early as 1489; but, due to its conservative tendency, Alsatian humanism failed to inspire the leadership's receptivity to the Reformation message. This was brought to Haguenau above all by Heinrich Gran's successors Thomas Anshelm and Johann Setzer.[127] There were a small number of clergymen and city councillors who sympathized with the Reformation, but the bulk of the leadership remained Catholic. In 1525, the Latin schoolmaster Michael Hilsbach, a friend of the Strasbourg reformers Capito and Hedio, was dismissed for having proselytized among his pupils and within the community.[128] An attempt launched by Wolfgang Capito on Palm Sunday and Easter, 1525, to introduce Protestant worship into his native city, was equally unsuccessful.[129] The excesses of the peasants' revolt (although Haguenau did not involve itself in the revolt in the countryside) must have added to the authorities' hostility toward the Reformation movement.[130]

In the late 1520's, only a few "secret" Protestants lived in the lower Alsatian city.[131] During the following years, the authorities were re-confirmed in their religious attitude by the distinguished humanist Hieronymus Gebwiler (d. 1545), who succeeded Michael Hilsbach in 1525. The conservative scholar revealed himself a steadfast opponent of all religious change. Yet, the city government's religious policy during these years was far from intransigent. Despite imperial complaints against the city's printers, the authorities did not prohibit the latter from continuing their publication of Protestant works. The printers were even permitted to publish Michael Servetus' antitrinitarian works whose sale was simultaneously prohibited by the Protestant authorities in nearby Strasbourg.[132]

The Haguenau authorities' attempt to stem the Reformation tide gradually became a losing battle as more and more neighboring cities and principalities (such as Wissembourg and the principality of Hanau-Lichtenberg) introduced the Reformation, thus increasing the Protestant influence which had previously been exerted on Haguenau by Strasbourg and neighboring Bischwiller alone. Ironically, this influence mostly affected Haguenau's leading families who, by virtue of their mobility and frequent visits to

[127] *Hanauer,* Le protestantisme, pp. 49–57. For a detailed account of printing in Haguenau, cf. *François Ritter,* Historie de l'imprimerie alsacienne aux XVe et XVIe siècles, Publications de l'Institut des Hautes-Etudes Alsaciennes, Vol. XIV (Strasbourg 1955), pp. 369–410.

[128] *Luzian Pfleger,* "Michael Hilspach, ein oberrheinischer Schulmeister des 16. Jahrhunderts," ZGORh, n.s., XX (1905), 254–259. See also *Joseph Knepper,* Das Schul- und Unterrichtswesen im Elsass: Von den Anfängen bis gegen das Jahr 1530 (Strasbourg 1905), p. 223.

[129] *Timotheus W. Röhrich,* Mittheilungen aus der Geschichte der evangelischen Kirche des Elsasses, 3 vols. (Strasbourg and Paris 1855), Vol. II, p. 456.

[130] When the revolt spread throughout the surrounding countryside, only little religious protest was voiced by a few burghers inside the city. See *Johann Adam,* Evangelische Kirchengeschichte der elsässischen Territorien bis zur Französischen Revolution (Strasbourg 1928), p. 438; and *André M. Burg,* "La guerre des paysans dans la région de Haguenau," in La guerre des paysans, 1525, ed. by Alphonse Wollbrett, Etudes Alsatiques édités par la Sociéte d'Histoire et d'Archéologie de Saverne et Environs, Supplemental No. 93 (Saverne 1975), pp. 49–53.

[131] *Guerber,* Histoire politique et religieuse, Vol. I, pp. 201–202.

[132] Ibid., Vol. II, p. 257; *Röhrich,* Mittheilungen, Vol. II, p. 458; and *Adam,* Evangelische Kirchengeschichte, p. 439.

neighboring cities (especially Strasbourg), were more exposed to it than Haguenau's lower classes. As the Palatine Bailiff residing at Haguenau from 1545 to 1553, Heinrich von Fleckenstein was also instrumental in furthering the cause of Protestantism in town.[133] By 1555, a good number of city councillors adhered to the new faith.[134] But, at about the same time, control over the Bailiwick of Haguenau was resumed by Emperor Ferdinand I – an act which ultimately dampened the impact of the Reformation movement both in Haguenau and Colmar. The further events leading to the introduction of the Reformation in 1565, and to the diplomatic mission of the Alsatian *Decapolis* to the imperial court in Vienna in 1574, have been discussed above.[135]

The Haguenau Reformation was brought about primarily by a few leading patrician families (the von Botzheims, Wilwesheims, Scheidts, Theus, Capito [Köpfels] and others), with assistance from the Duke of Württemberg and the city of Strasbourg. These families monopolized the city's magistrate (the council of jurors). It seems that these patricians introduced Protestant worship into the Franciscan church against the will of the majority of the XXIV.[136] At the time of the Reformation in 1565, the overwhelming majority of Haguenau's burghers were Catholic. In the same year, Bailiff Nicolaus of Bollwiller claimed that the number of Protestants in town did not exceed fifty persons.[137] Considering its weak roots within the city's population at large, Haguenau's Protestant church never really had a chance of surviving, even though the number of its parishioners clearly increased after 1565. This growth was met with stiffening resistance from the Catholic majority. As a result, the minority of Protestant jurors and councillors faced a steadily increasing number of Catholics among the XXIV. Later, in 1623, when an imperial commission set about abolishing the remnants of Protestantism in Haguenau, a communal petition demanded "that the oligarchy which up to now has become overbearing, be abolished, and that the council [the XXIV] as well as the community be henceforth allowed more participation in the city's administration." Emperor Ferdinand II readily complied with this demand.[138]

Ultimately, the Haguenau Reformation failed because the common people did not follow the example of the Protestant patricians. Beginning in the 1590's, Protestantism began to lose ground. This development was largely due to the spontaneous reaction of the Catholic community against the exclusive rule of a small Protestant oligarchy. It cannot be denied (as has frequently been done) that this reaction received substantial and important support from the Habsburg-Austrian officials of the Bailiwick of Haguenau,

[133] Cf. above, p. 25.

[134] *Guerber,* Histoire politique et religieuse, Vol. I, p. 228.

[135] See above, pp. 95–9 and 108–10.

[136] See *Charles A. Hanauer,* ed., Cartulaire de l'Eglise S. George de Haguenau, Quellenschriften der Elsässischen Kirchengeschichte, Vol. V (Strasbourg 1898), p. 508. See also *Röhrich,* Mittheilungen, Vol. II, p. 475. As in Colmar, the introduction of the Reformation in Haguenau did not, by any means, entail the abolition of Catholic worship, although, in 1579, the Protestant oligarchy introduced evangelical worship into a second, hitherto Catholic church (St. Nicolaus). Cf. ADBR, C 5, 7 (Letter from the councillors of the Bailiwick of Haguenau to Archduke Ferdinand II of November 10, 1565); and *Guerber,* Histoire politique et religieuse, Vol. II, pp. 104–105.

[137] ADBR, C 5, 6 (Letter addressed to Archduke Ferdinand II of July 3, 1565).

[138] *Hanauer,* ed., Cartulaire de S. George, p. 518; idem, Le protestantisme, pp. 275–277; and *Burg,* "Patrizier", p. 362.

who all resided in town.[139] It is true, however, that the establishment of the Jesuits in the years following 1601 expedited, but by no means initiated, the downfall of Protestantism in the city.[140] The Reformation in Haguenau had already lost all *raison d'être* before it was definitively abolished in 1623.

C. PATTERNS OF THE LATE CITY REFORMATION IN GERMANY.

In approaching the phenomenon of the late city Reformation in Germany in general, we must bear in mind that it took place in a period of general urban decline. Especially in the south and southwest of the Empire, the imperial cities never recovered from the great financial losses the Smalkaldic War (1546/47) and the War of the Princes (1552) imposed on them. Their economic recovery was increasingly obstructed by the growing confinement of their activity through rising princely absolutism.[141] Furthermore, their relationship toward the Emperor, who might have been able to counteract some of the princely influence on the cities, was henceforth marred by suspicion on the part of the imperial court concerning their questionable loyalty:

> To be sure, the political rupture between the Protestant cities and the Empire was neutralized when the cities and the Protestant princes came together in a common faith and united in the Smalkaldic League. But beginning in 1540, difficulties piled up. First with the Diet of Speyer in 1542, open conflict broke out again concerning the right of the cities to cast an equal vote at the diet, a matter that touched directly the legal guarantee of their freedom. In addition, the solidarity between princes and cities in the Smalkaldic League began to weaken.[142]

The German imperial cities responded to this new situation by strengthening the oligarchical structure of their governments. This was clearly "no sign of strength, but signaled, rather, the extinction of both urban creativity and a vigorous communal mentality" (M. Ritter). As a result, the communal idea which once, particularly in Upper Germany, had lent an important impetus to the city Reformation "now went into permanent decline" (B. Moeller), and the political solidarity among the cities was increasingly paralyzed by shortsighted urban particularism as demonstrated by the case of Aachen.[143]

In addition, since the middle of the 16th century, the process of confessionalization, along with the inner consolidation of the Catholic and Protestant parties within the Empire, was well on its way when, in 1563, a new series of urban Reformations was initiated by the introduction of Protestant worship in Essen. The process of confessionalization, it has been claimed, was not identical with the Reformation itself, but

[139] *Hanauer,* Le protestantisme, pp. 212–259, especially pp. 237–238; and *Schmidlin,* Die katholische Restauration, p. 104.

[140] *Hanauer,* ibid., pp. 260–294; and *Schmidlin,* ibid., pp. 112–125.

[141] *Ritter,* Deutsche Geschichte, Vol. I, pp. 52–54.

[142] *Moeller,* "Imperial Cities," pp. 105–106. For the struggle of the imperial cities for their political freedom in those years, cf. also *Max Huber,* "Städtearchiv und Reichsstandschaft der Städte im 16. Jahrhundert," Ulm und Oberschwaben, XXXV (1958), 94–112.

[143] *Moeller,* ibid.; and *Ritter,* Deutsche Geschichte, Vol. I, p. 53. See also the discussion regarding the role of the communal ideal in the early city Reformation, above pp. 3–8.

was rather its result.[144] In the case of the late city Reformation this nexus was reversed. This is illustrated by the example of those late Reformation cities where the 1530's and 1540's were marked by the authorities' effort to launch Erasmian reforms of church and school. In Colmar, Essen and Dortmund, where such efforts are discernible, their continuation fell prey to the pressure of rising confessionalism. All this leads to the conclusion that the economic, social, political and religious pre-conditions of the late city Reformation in Germany differed substantially from those of the early city Reformation.

Due to the changing social and constitutional structure of the cities during the second half of the 16th century, the late city Reformation was primarily a "magistrate's Reformation" introduced "from above". With the exception of Dortmund, this was the case in all of the cities discussed here. Even in Essen and Aachen, where the Reformation movement rested on broad communal participation, it was clearly the ruling patricians or upper class who carried the movement to its goal.[145] In the case of Haguenau, Colmar and Aalen, the phenomenon of a "magistrate's Reformation" was even more pronounced. In these cities, only a minority of burghers supported the Reformation movement – the Reformation was introduced by a numerically small but powerful upper-strata minority. The Protestant authorities of these three cities had in many ways already assimilated the authoritarian methods of the Counterreformation when they went about introducing evangelical worship. In all six cities discussed here, with the exception of Dortmund, the introduction of the Reformation by the ruling class resulted in a significant strengthening of the prevailing oligarchical regime and furthered the decline of the corporate-communal ideal.[146] Following the late introduction of the Reformation, this decline continued as a result of the toleration of both Catholics and Protestants stipulated by the Peace of Augsburg. Even though these Augsburg provisions were "entirely alien to the mentality of the city,"[147] none of the urban governments in question could afford a wholesale abolition of Catholicism in their cities.

To be sure, the strengthening of the ruling oligarchy through the Reformation, prominent particularly in Colmar, Haguenau, Aalen and Essen, only went unchallenged in

[144] *Heide Stratenwerth,* Die Reformation in der Stadt Osnabrück, Veröffentlichungen des Instituts für Europäische Geschichte Mainz, Vol. LXI (Wiesbaden 1971), p. 1. For the process of confessionalization, cf. also *Ernst Walter Zeeden,* Die Entstehung der Konfessionen: Grundlagen und Formen der Konfessionsbildung im Zeitalter der Glaubenskämpfe (Munich and Vienna 1965), pp. 32–46 and 113–137.

[145] The example of Essen constitutes a borderline-case in this respect. It is possible that its case has more elements in common with that of Strasbourg, as described by Brady, than extant accounts are able to convey. This is possible insofar as the city council may have intended to anticipate potential popular pressure in favor of the Reformation when it embarked on a decisive pro-Reformation course in about 1560. Yet, extant accounts give the impression that this shift in policy was so vigorous that the authorities' role in the final phase leading to the introduction of Protestant worship appears as uninfluenced and autonomous. The city council's subsequent difficulties in securing its authority against a Calvinist communal opposition were rather a result of outside interference by the Duke of Jülich-Cleves than the outcome of autogenous urban conflict. For the discussion of Brady's interpretation, cf. above, pp. 6–8.

[146] This is a trend that can already be observed in the early city Reformation. Cf. *Brady,* Ruling Class, Regime and the Reformation, p. 169, n. 23. A comparative study of the communal institutionalization of the Reformation in the six cities in question could further substantiate this argument. However, due to the current unbalanced state of evidence in this area, I have excluded this aspect from the present discussion.

[147] *Moeller,* "Imperial Cities," p. 108.

Colmar. In the other three cities, this process later provoked communal unrest, forcing the authorities to grant the community increased participation in city government[148]; yet, only in Haguenau did the impact of this communal opposition, in a unique case of a Counterreformation "from below", ultimately bring about the failure of the Reformation. A similar Catholic movement "from below", but with a less decisive impact, also existed in Aachen. In the case of Colmar and Aachen, the introduction of the Reformation "from above" clearly hinged on previous changes in the personal composition of city government. However, these changes occurred exclusively within the upper-strata of Colmar's and Aachen's society, and did not entail an increase of lower-strata influence on city government.

In being primarily a "magistrate's Reformation", the late city Reformation differs substantially from the urban Reformation of the first half of the 16th century. As for the latter, research to date has generally agreed with Franz Lau's assessment "that the German Lutheran Reformation as a spontaneous folk-movement continued to go on without interruption beyond the Peasants' Revolt. Indeed, it continued as a spontaneous movement of the common people in the cities, not of the patricians, the city nobility, or the municipal authorities." The fact that Lau made no provision regarding later cases of city Reformation, is indicative of the almost exclusive focus of comprehensive accounts to date on the urban Reformation of the first half of the 16th century.[149] Only recently, this unanimous scholarly agreement with Lau was challenged by Thomas Brady, who argues convincingly that "the question as to whether the post-1525 reform was chiefly a popular or chiefly an official reform ("Volksreformation oder Ratsreformation?") has only one answer: it was both!" Notwithstanding this helpful insight, the present discussion will show that there are, nevertheless, substantial differences between the early and the late city Reformation.[150] Even in accounting for the relatively strong communal impact in Essen and Aachen, we can conclude that in the cases of late urban Reformation in question, the *Ratsreformation* was the rule and the Reformation as a "spontaneous folk movement" the exception.

In all five cities (Colmar, Haguenau, Aalen, Essen and Aachen) where the Reformation took the form of a more-or-less pronounced Reformation "from above", the act of its introduction was fused with an attempt to free the city from outside political interference.[151] This is a second important aspect of the late city Reformation in Ger-

[148] For Aalen and Haguenau, cf. above, pp. 189 and 195. For Essen, cf. above, n. 52.

[149] *Lau,* "Der Bauernkrieg," p. 113, quoted here from the English translation in *Sessions*, Reformation and Authority, p. 96. In general agreement with Lau, see *Moeller,* "Imperial Cities," pp. 60–61; *A. G. Dickens,* The German Nation and Martin Luther (London 1974), p. 181; and *Steven E. Ozment,* The Reformation in the Cities (New Haven and London 1975), pp. 121–126. Among these authors, only Bernd Moeller refers to the different situation in the second half of the 16th century. He points to the role played by the city councils of Colmar and Aachen. See *Moeller,* ibid., p. 60, n. 32.

[150] See *Brady,* Ruling Class, Regime and the Reformation, particularly p. 200; and the discussion of Brady's results above, pp. 6–8.

[151] A similar constellation of motives has been observed in the case of the late and unsuccessful attempt to introduce the Reformation in the episcopal city of Trier. When matters came to a head in 1559, the Protestants (in particular the Protestant minority among the city councillors) coupled their attempt to establish a Protestant church with a renewed drive for the recognition by their overlord, the Bishop and Prince-elector, of Trier's alleged status of an autonomous imperial city. The operation failed because the

many: the "magistrate's Reformation" of the second half of the 16th century was an act of political emancipation. In Colmar and Haguenau, the introduction of the Reformation was intended to free the two Alsatian cities from increasing influence exerted on them by Habsburg-Austria. In Aalen, the Reformation implied the town's emancipation from constant interference by the Prince-Provost of Ellwangen. In Essen, the Reformation served as an attempt to rid the city of the over-lordship of the princely Abbess. And even in the case of the more sizeable Aachen, there are strong indications that the Reformation was supposed to entail a deliverance from increasing interference by the Duke of Jülich-Cleves. Only in the case of Dortmund, where the Reformation was not introduced by the ruling oligarchy, does such an emancipatory objective not appear in connection with the Reformation. In Colmar, Haguenau and Essen, the political emancipation implied in the act of Reformation was the major issue at stake – whereas the emancipation from the ecclesiastical tutelage exercised by the Ordinary played a minor role. The latter was a more important issue only in Aalen and Aachen, since both respective *ordinarii* (the Bishops of Augsburg and Liège) were early champions of the Counter-reformation.

In the second half of the 16th century, most imperial cities were in economic and political decline and could not really act independently in the area of religious politics. Especially in the case of smaller cities like Essen, Colmar, Haguenau and Aalen, the above emancipation would have ended in failure had these cities not been able to rely on important outside support. This is best exemplified by the cases of Aalen and Schwäbisch-Gmünd. In Aalen, as we have seen, an upper-strata evangelical minority with substantial outside assistance from the Duke of Württemberg could introduce the Reformation against the will of a Catholic majority in town; whereas in Schwäbisch-Gmünd, the ruling Catholic minority, kept in power by the Bishop of Augsburg, could maintain the city's official adherence to Catholicism against the manifest will of an overwhelming majority of Protestant burghers.[152] Hence, a third significant aspect of the late city Reformation is the importance of outside political assistance and support.

Such suppport was all the more important because the so-called "city-article" of the Peace of Augsburg was formulated ambiguously enough to leave the question unaswered whether imperial cities were entitled to an *ius reformandi.* To be sure, Emperor Maximilian II (1564–76) took a fairly lenient stand on this open issue, as evidenced by the position he assumed in the case of Haguenau. Furthermore, his only superficially concealed sympathy for Protestantism was no secret among his contemporaries. It is surely more than just a coincidence that four of the six late city Reformations discussed here took place during his reign.

At the same time, however, a fair number of Catholic secular and ecclesiastical princes in both the south and west of the Empire did not share Maximilian's lenient position in

blockade imposed on the city by the Bishop entailed the disintegration of the vital solidarity between the Catholic majority and the Protestants. See *Hans-Christoph Rublack,* Gescheiterte Reformation: Frühreformatorische und protestantische Bewegungen in süd- und westdeutschen geistlichen Reidenzen, Spätmittelalter und Frühe Neuzeit: Tübinger Beiträge zur Geschichtsforschung, Vol. IV (Stuttgart 1978), 93–104.

152 For Schwäbisch-Gmünd, cf. *Gerhard Pfeiffer* „Der Augsburger Religionsfrieden und die Reichsstädte," Zeitschrift des historischen Vereins für Schwaben, LXI (1955), 292.

religious matters. Only *Realpolitik* could bring them to concede an urban *ius reformandi.* It was therefore of great importance for the success of the Reformation in Haguenau, Colmar, Aalen and Essen, that these cities could rely on substantial outside support. It speaks for the decline of urban solidarity that in all these four cases this assistance was granted by a prince and not by a group of cities: in the south by the Duke of Württemberg and in the west (Essen) by the Duke of Jülich-Cleves. The inverse case of Aachen further evidences the importance of outside support. Maximilian's successor Rudolf II (1576–1612) never felt inclined to grant imperial cities the substantial prerogative of an *ius reformandi.* When the desperate appeal for outside assistance voiced by Aachen's Protestants ultimately remained unanswered by the Protestant cities and princes, Rudolf had no qualms about suppressing Protestantism through direct interference in this strategically important city. It was ironic that from 1576 onward, his policy vis-à-vis Aachen was to find acclaim from the Duke of Jülich-Cleves, even though the latter had helped to secure the Reformation in Essen in 1563.[153]

Among the late Reformation cities discussed here, the case of Dortmund represents an exception. Only here did the popular Reformation movement grow strong enough to force the hostile authorities, at least temporarily, to appoint the Protestant preacher Johann Heitfeld. Yet, as we have seen, this was only a shortlived episode. It is, in fact, a fourth prominent aspect of the late city Reformation in Germany that it lacked competent urban reformers. With the exception of the short activity of Johann Heitfeld in Dortmund, even the case of this city conforms to this pattern. The significant exception in this respect was Aachen. Although the Protestant preachers in this city were not appointed officially before the Reformation was introduced in 1581, they had continuously played an influential role in spreading the Reformation message throughout the community since 1558, working during the 1560's under strict concealment. Even in Aachen, however, outside religious influence, originating mainly in the neighboring Low Countries, had an important impact on the religious life of the city.

In Colmar, Haguenau, Aalen, Essen and (in part) in Dortmund, given the lack of municipal reformers, the religious motivation of the Reformation movement was primarily based on outside influences. In Colmar, this came from the surrounding Württemberg villages and towns and their preachers, above all from Horbourg. In Haguenau, the outside influence of Strasbourg, the nearby Protestant community of Bischwiller and the surrounding villages belonging to the principality of Hanau-Lichtenberg, all played an important role. In Aalen, the religious influence originating within the Württemberg villages in the west of the city and within the imperial city of Bopfingen, both had a considerable impact on the town. In Essen, religious influence exerted by the nearby Protestant communities and territories of Broich, Moers and, in particular, Wesel played a substantial role; and in Dortmund, this influence came, above all, from the cities of Soest and Lippstadt, as well as from surrounding towns and villages situated within the County of Mark. For the urban Reformation of the first half of the 16th century, extant research has pointed to the activity of urban preachers of some stature as a *conditio sine qua non* of the thrust of the early Reformation movement.[154]

[153] For a brief discussion of this phenomenon, cf. above, n. 84.

Thus, the lack of a competent municipal reformer is another aspect in which the late city Reformation differed considerably from the early urban Reformation. This lack goes a long way toward explaining the absence in Colmar, Haguenau and Aalen of a noticeable popular movement in favor of the Reformation. It also helps to explain the lateness of the introduction of the Reformation in these cities.

In discussing the outside influences exerted on the religious climate of the late Reformation cities, we must add a word about the impact of Protestant pamphlets imported into these cities from the outside. To all appearances, this impact was considerable throughout, even though it is now difficult to trace in its specific forms. Furthermore, the (lay) religious influence exerted on their fellow citizens by merchants who, through their profession, found themselves in frequent contact with outside Protestants, should not be underestimated, although this aspect of urban Reformation movements is in need of thorough prosopographical research. The impact of merchants is clearly evidenced in Dortmund and Aachen, and may also have played an important role in Colmar and Haguenau.

The late introduction of the Reformation was based on a conglomerate of different motives. At the very beginning of the Reformation movement stood a strong movement of anticlericalism which never really subsided. It is well evidenced in Colmar, Essen, Dortmund and Aalen. Even in Aalen, where hardly any clergymen resided in town, the city council introduced the Reformation "not only because of the vexation of many Christian consciences, but also because it had found the considerable disorder in the school and church all too appalling."[155] Anticlericalism in the six cities discussed here gradually fused with a progressively stronger religious movement.

It is interesting to note that only Calvinism, which was prominent in the west of Germany, was capable of molding anticlericalism into a relatively widespread Reformation movement in the same way the early Reformation message had once done throughout Germany, especially in the south and southwest of the Empire. The orthodox Lutheran influence (as in the case of Colmar, Haguenau and Aalen) failed to function as an appeal to the community at large. The fervor of the religious discussions of the early Reformation years, great religious debates and spontaneous outbursts of iconoclasm, were missing after 1555. Nevertheless, the thrust of the religious motives of those who helped to bring about the Reformation in these cities should not be underestimated, even though it may be difficult to trace in individual cases. The late introduction of the Reformation was based on more than simply political motives, although in all of our cities, except

[154] See, for instance, *Gerhard Pfeiffer,* "Das Verhältnis von politischer und kirchlicher Gemeinde in den deutschen Reichsstädten," in Staat und Kirche im Wandel der Jahrhunderte, ed. by W. P. Fuchs (Stuttgart, Berlin, Cologne and Mainz 1966), p. 87: 'The activity of notable preachers – I will only mention Osiander in Nuremberg, Brenz in Schwäbisch Hall, Rhegius and Oecolampadius in Augsburg, Alber in Reutlingen, Blarer and Zwick in Constance, Thomas Gassner in Lindau, Bucer and Capito in Strasbourg – formed the basis for the success of the Reformation.' Cf. also *Winfried Ehbrecht*, "Verlaufsformen innerstädtischer Konflikte in nord- und westdeutschen Städten im Reformationszeitalter," in Stadt und Kirche im 16. Jahrhundert, ed. by Bernd Moeller, SVRG, No. 190 (Gütersloh 1978), pp. 38–46 ("Zur Bedeutung der Prädikanten in den innerstädtischen Auseinandersetzungen").

[155] *Zapf,* ed., Sämmtliche Reformations-Urkunden, Part I, p. 6.

Dortmund, strong political motives had an important impact on the city council's decision in favor of the Reformation.

The above observations lead to the conclusion that it is not possible to subsume the pattern of the Reformation in the six cities in question under geographical distinctions between the conditions prevailing in the south/southwest and in the west of the Empire. It is true that the Reformation message was able to generate much stronger popular support in Essen, Dortmund and Aachen, than in the three cities of the south and southwest. This difference can be primarily accredited to two factors.

By the 1560's and 1570's, the Catholic Counterreformation had established a much stronger basis in Upper Germany than in the west of the Empire and was, thus, a constant check on the rise of widespread popular Reformation movements. The authorities of Colmar, Haguenau and Aalen must have had a vital interest in suppressing any signs of a broader Reformation movement within their cities, even after they *themselves* already adhered to the Reformation. The rise of broad popular movements would have provoked the danger of outside Catholic interference. When seen from this perspective, the introduction of the Reformation "from above" was practically a political necessity in these three cities. In the west of the Empire, however, the Counterreformation party only gained a stronger footing during the 1570's and only reached a certain degree of consolidation from 1585 onward, after the War of Cologne.

Secondly, Dutch Calvinism with its strong communal ideal, moving into the Rhineland in ever stronger waves after the 1550's, must have been a much more appealing Protestant doctrine for the middle and lower strata city burghers than contemporary Lutheranism. Throughout Germany and Switzerland, "Luther's ideal of liberating the state from the church, Zwingli's plan for coordinating both powers, and other teachings of the Reformation were falsified by their second-rate successors into a reinforcement of the state."[156] It is not surprising that in Colmar, Haguenau and Aalen the orthodox Lutheran doctrine could only have a limited appeal to the respective urban communities. In contemporary Calvinism, however, strong communal ideals were still alive and able to generate broad popular movements in the cities of the Rhineland.[157]

Notwithstanding the importance of the different impact the Counterreformation of the 1560's and 1570's had within the two geographical areas in question, it is primarily the Calvinist influence which accounts for the main differences between the late Reformation of the three west German cities and those of Colmar, Haguenau and Aalen. Yet, it cannot explain another interesting difference between the late Reformation movements in these two geographical areas. In the three Upper German cities, we can basically distinguish two different Reformation movements, one reaching its climax in 1525, and the next beginning in the late 1540's and early 1550's, later to be led to its destination by the authorities.[158] In Essen, Dortmund and Aachen, however, the Refor-

[156] *Moeller,* "Imperial Cities," p. 113.

[157] The fact that, in Essen, it was the city council which finally succeeded in the official establishment of Lutheranism in 1571 against a strong communal Calvinist opposition further supports these oberservations. Cf. also *Moeller,* ibid., p. 114.

[158] Only the case of Aalen does not entirely conform to this pattern; but even here, the lack of extant evidence may conceal significant events occuring in the early Reformation years. A similar distinction

mation movement, except for some shortlived setbacks, was one continuous movement, starting in the 1520's in Dortmund, in the 1530's in Essen, and in the 1540's in Aachen. This difference can only be explained by the general dissimilarities between the course of the Reformation in Upper Germany, the Rhineland and Westphalia.[159] Yet, these general incongruities, based on the specific geographical locations of the six cities in question, cannot conceal that there were, at least in social and political respects, substantial similarities between the late Reformations in Colmar, Haguenau, Aalen, Essen and Aachen.

It is above all the case of Dortmund which differs from all other late city Reformations discussed here. The case of Dortmund is an exception in respect to all three predominant social and political aspects of the late city Reformation outlined above:

a. The Reformation in Dortmund was no "magistrate's Reformation". When the authorities accepted the Reformation in 1570, they only sanctioned a *fait accompli.* At this point the Reformation had already been unofficially introduced into most city churches;
b. as a Reformation which was introduced "from below", that is, primarily by middle-strata burghers who had no direct access to city government, the Dortmund Reformation lacked a clear political and emancipatory objective as observed in the case of the other late Reformations discussed here;
c. there is no evidence that the introduction of the Reformation in this city was assisted and furthered by any important outside power.

The steadfast resistance of Dortmund's ruling patricians to the Reformation up to 1570 was based on religious and material motives alike. Their material interests were deeply intertwined with those of the local Catholic church. In a time of economic decline, the patricians were not pre-disposed to let go of this source of secure income.[160] Furthermore, the almost caste-like social order within their town helped maintain (over many decades) their more and more disputed oligarchical régime. Whereas in Essen the ultimate cooperation of the ruling oligarchy with the Reformation movement took a considerable momentum out of the pressure exerted on the city government "from below", the continued resistance of the ruling patricians in Dortmund steadily increased this pressure until the resistance of the last *Junker* in power was swept aside by the opposition. In considering the ensemble of social, religious and political aspects discussed here, the late Reformation in Dortmund (of all the six cases of late city Reformation in question) thus clearly resembles most the Reformation as a folk movement as it frequently occurred in the first half of the 16th century:[161] the Reformation message and com-

between separate early and late Reformation movements has recently been established by Hans-Christoph Rublack with regard to the case of the episcopal, residential cities of south and west Germany. Accounting for the impact of the process of confessionalization on the late Reformation movements in these cities, Rublack distinguishes an early Reformation movement ("Frühreformatorische Bewegung") ending in 1525, from the Protestant movement ("Protestantische Bewegung") in the second half of the 16th century. See *Rublack*, Gescheiterte Reformation, pp. 125–6.

[159] See *Mühlhaupt*, „Eigenart und Bedeutung'." and above, pp. 170–1.

[160] It is interesting to note that the similar situation in Essen only prevailed during the first half of the 16th century.

[161] See the historiographical discussion in the Introduction to this study.

munal-corporate ideology combined to counteract the impact and power of an oligarchical régime. Only here can we speak, in a sense, of a socio-political as well as spiritual continuity between the late medieval and the Reformation city. Such continuity is marginal to non-existent in all other late Reformation cities discussed here. In the other cities, rather than finding an affinity between the Reformation message and strong communal-corporate opposition to the oligarchical city government, we can observe that the religious message exerted an important influence on the ruling oligarchy's drive for emancipation of itself and its city from outside interference. This act of emancipation, wherever it proved successful, usually strengthened the existing regime.

Comparative analysis, by its very nature, tends to concentrate on similarities and to overlook individual complexities. Thus, the present attempt to outline the salient patterns of the late city Reformation in Germany is far from exhaustive. Its foremost intention is to draw attention to a relatively neglected aspect of the German Reformation, on which much research still needs to be done before our knowledge will become more complete.[162]

The historical weight of the late Reformation movement in German cities should not be overrated. While it is true that the early German Reformation was, above all, an urban phenomenon, it is equally undeniable that "after 1550, the spiritual center of Germany shifted rapidly away from the imperial cities and away from southern Germany to the princely courts of northern and central Germany."[163] However, the urban Reformation movement did not end in 1550. It lasted until 1581, when it was successful for the last time in Aachen. And what about the numerous, now often forgotten, late urban attempts at introducing the Reformation which ended in failure? In Alsace, for instance, the example of Haguenau and Colmar proved contagious. Thus, during the 1560's and 1570's, the number of Protestants once more increased so significantly in such cities as Sélestat and Obernai as to provoke Habsburg-Austrian interference.[164] Likewise, attempts at introducing the Reformation in the small imperial city of Turckheim near Colmar preoccupied the Bishop of Basel as late as the turn of the century.[165] Moreover, late "Protestant movements" spread throughout most episcopal, residential cities of south and west Germany. Toward the end of the century they were gradually forced to yield to the conforming pressure of the Counterreformation. Yet, considering their a-political nature, these movements, with the exception of that in Trier, had only little in common with the late Reformation movements of the majority of cities discussed above, other than the interesting fact that in Trier, Würzburg, Bamberg, and Salzburg, the

[162] This is especially the case in respect to the Reformation in Haguenau and Aalen.

[163] *Moeller,* "Imperial Cities," p. 114.

[164] *Paul Adam,* Histoire religieuse de Sélestat, Vol. I (Sélestat 1967), p. 81. For Sélestat, cf. also TLA, Kopialbücher der Regierung, 1577 (Letters from the Upper Austrian government to Archduke Ferdinand II of June 3 and 17, 1577). For Obernai, cf. *Joseph Gyss,* Histoire de la ville d'Obernai, Vol. I (Strasbourg 1866), pp. 477–485.

[165] *Moeller,* "Imperial Cities," p. 41, has listed Turckheim among the "five small imperial cities in Swabia and Alsace that remained untouched by the Reformation." For the late Reformation movement in this city, see *Auguste Scherlen,* Geschichte der Stadt Türckheim (Colmar 1925), pp. 230–4; *Schmidlin,* Die katholische Restauration, pp. 167–171; and *André Billich,* Histoire d'une ancienne ville impériale: Turckheim (Colmar 1975), pp. 37–55.

"Protestant movement found especially strong support among the groups that occupied the economically and politically leading positions within the respective communities."[166]

We can conclude that the late urban Reformation movement went far beyond those cases where a late introduction of the Reformation was ultimately successful. The late city Reformation in Germany was more than just a negligible *epiphenomenon* of the city Reformation in its great days. It is a historical phenomenon in its own right – a *reformatio sui generis.*

[166] Cf. *Rublack*, Gescheiterte Reformation, especially pp. 122 and 127; idem, "Reformatorische Bewegungen in Würzburg und Bamberg," in Stadt und Kirche im 16. Jahrhundert, ed. by Moeller, pp. 109–124. For the case of Trier, cf. also above, n. 151.

BIBLIOGRAPHY

A. MANUSCRIPT SOURCES

Basel, Staatsarchiv (STA Basel)
Klosterarchiv C 1 (Istein).
Basel, Universitätsbibliothek, Handschriften-Abteilung (UB Basel, Hs.)
AA II; 2,5: "Historia des Seerinischen Geschlechtes." Fr. Gr. Ms. I, 19; Fr. Gr. Ms. II, 9; G I, 26, 33 and 63; G II, 1–3, 6, 11 and 15; G^2 II, 1 and 67; Ms Ki. Ar., 22c, 25b and 25c: 16th and early 17th centuries correspondence.
Colmar, Bibliothèque Municipale (BMC)
"Fonds Chauffour":
Ms. I. Ch. 1: "Kirchners Elsässische Chronik".
Ms. I. Ch. 22, 23, 71, 79, 82, 84, 100.
Colmar, Archives Départementales du Haut-Rhin (ADHR)
4 G, 1–5, 10–12: Archives of chapter of St. Martin's. E 412 and 415: "Seigneuries de Horbourg-Riquewihr."
C 109, 8; C 234, 19: "Actes du gouvernement d'Ensisheim."
Colmar, Archives Municipales (AMC)
AA 74, 76, 84 and 86: Imperial diets and diets of the Alsatian Decapolis; Correspondence.
BB 43: "Le vieux livre rouge."
BB 44: "Le nouveau livre rouge."
BB 45 (1522–1628): "Délibérations du conseil municipal."
BB 51: Register of oaths.
BB 52, "Protocollum Missivarum," (1526–1575).
CC 76–78: Tithes.
EE 7, 1–26: Communal unrest, 1524–25.
FF 15, 6–39; 16, 56–58; 34 bis, 33; 95; 96, 1–40; 346; 355; 358; 522; 600; 626: "Justice, Police, Procedure."
GG 24–27; 28a; 29a and d; 39–41; 49; 71–73; 82–83; 98–101; 144–160; 168: "Affaires religieuses."
GG 190; 193: Schools.
Innsbruck, Tirolisches Landesarchiv (TLA)
Ferdinandea, fasc. 139–140
Kopialbücher der Regierung, 1565–1580
Pestarchiv, XVIII
Porrentruy, Archives de l'Ancien Evêché de Bâle (AAEB)
A 41
Strasbourg, Bibliothèque Nationale et Universitaire (BNUS)
Ms. 667–681: "Thesaurus Baumianus epistolarum reformatorum alsaticorum." (Th. B.)
Strasbourg, Archives Départementales du Bas-Rhin (ADBR)
C 5; 11; 16; 25; 28; 71; 73; 85.
G 1361, 4.
Strasbourg, Archives Municipales (AMS)
Archives du Chapitre de Saint-Thomas (AST):
Ms. 41; 43; 139; 153; 155; 157; 159; 161; 202: 16th century correspondence.
Vienna, Haus-, Hof- und Staatsarchiv (H.H.StA)
Kleinere Reichsstände, fasc. 84.
Zürich, Staatarchiv (STA Zürich)
E II, 346a, 356a and 391: 16th and early 17th centuries correspondence.

Zürich, Zentralbibliothek, Handschriften-Abteilung (ZB Zürich)
Simmleriana, Msc. S.: 16th century correspondence.

B. PRINTED SOURCES

Amtliche Sammlung der älteren Eidgenössischen Abschiede. 8 vols. Vol. IV, Part Ia (1521–1528). Edited by Johannes Strickler. Brugg 1873. Vol. IV, Part Ib (1529–1532). Edited by Johannes Strickler. Zürich 1876. Vol. IV, Part Ic (1533–1540). Edited by Karl Deschwanden. Lucerne 1878.

Apologia Civitatis Imperialis Colmariensis. (Author unknown). Colmar 1645.

Arbenz, Emil, and *Wartmann, Hermann,* eds. Vadianische Briefsammlung. 7 vols. Vols. V and VI, Mitteilungen zur vaterländischen Geschichte, Vols. XXIX and XXX. St. Gall 1903 and 1908.

Baum, Wilhelm; Cunitz, Eduard; and *Reuss, Eduard;* eds. Ioannis Calvini Opera quae supersunt omnia. 59 vols.
Vol. XII, Corpus Reformatorum, Vol. XL. Brunswick 1874.

Bolchert, Paul, ed. Catalogue de la Bibliothèque du Consistoire de l'Eglise de la Confession d'Augsbourg à Colmar, Troisième Partie: Livres du XVIe siècle. Colmar 1960.

Braunsberger, Otto, ed. Beati Petri Canisii societatis Iesu Epistulae et acta. 6 vols. Vol. II. Freiburg i. Br. 1898.

Das Buch der Hundert Kapitel und der Vierzig Statuten des sogenannten Oberrheinischen Revolutionärs. Edited by Annelore Franke with an introduction by Gerhard Zschäbitz. Leipziger Uebersetzungen und Abhandlungen zum Mittelalter, Series A, Vol. IV. Berlin (-East) 1967.

Cancerinus, Nicolaus. Der alte Glaub von der Rechtfertigung des Menschen: Ein christliche vnd in Gottes wort gegründte Predig . . . Zue Mumpelgardt den Sechzehenden Sontag nach Trinitatis, Anno. 67. gehalten. Strasbourg 1569.

Chauffour, Ignaz, ed. "Aus der Ensisheimer Chronik, 1471–1527: Nach Sigismund Billing's Abschrift mitgetheilt." Alsatia (1873/74), 281–297.

Cowie, Murray A., and *Cowie, Marian L.,* eds. The works of Peter Schott (1460–1490). 2 vols. Vol. I. University of North Carolina Studies in the Germanic Languages and Literatures, Vol. XLI. Chapel Hill, N.C. 1963.

Deutscher Evangelischer Kirchenausschuss, ed. Die Bekenntnisschriften der evangelisch-lutherischen Kirche herausgegeben im Gedenkjahr der Augsburgischen Confession 1930. 3rd ed. Göttingen 1956.

Dürr, Emil, and *Roth, Paul,* eds. Aktensammlung zur Geschichte der Basler Reformation in den Jahren 1519 bis Anfang 1534. 6 vols. Vols. I and II. Basel 1921 and 1933.

Finsterwalder, Paul Wilhelm, ed. Colmarer Stadtrechte. Vol. I (only extant vol.). Oberrheinische Stadtrechte, Abteilung III, Vol. III. Heidelberg 1938.

Franz, Günther, ed. Der Deutsche Bauernkrieg: Aktenband. Munich and Berlin 1935.

Gabriel, Astricus L., and *Boyce, Gray C.,* eds. Auctarium Chartulari Universitatis Parisiensis. Tomus VI: Liber Receptorum Nationis Alemanniae. Paris 1964.

Geiger, Ludwig, ed. Johann Reuchlins Briefwechsel. Bibliothek des Litterarischen Vereins in Stuttgart, Vol. CXXVI. Tübingen 1875.

Hanauer, C[harles] A[uguste], ed. Cartulaire de l'Eglise S. George de Haguenau. Quellenschriften der elsässischen Kirchengeschichte, Vol. V. Strasbourg 1898.

Hartmann, Alfred, and *Jenny, Beat-Rudolf,* eds. Die Amerbachkorrespondenz. 8 vols. to date. Vols. VI–VIII. Basel 1967–1974.

Hiemeierus, David. Ernewerung der Kirchen bey den Barfüssern im Spital der Hoch löblichen Reichsstatt Colmar, die noch vor 16. Jahren dem abgesagten Teuffel selbst, durch seine Baalitische Meßpfaffen . . . gedienet . . . Strasbourg 1590.

Horawitz, Adalbert, and *Hartfelder, Karl,* eds. Briefwechsel des Beatus Rhenanus. Leipzig 1886.

Keussen, Hermann, ed. Die Matrikel der Universität Köln. 3 vols., (1389–1559). Publikationen der Gesellschaft für Rheinische Geschichtskunde, VIII. Bonn 1892–1931.

Knod, Gustav., ed. Deutsche Studenten in Bologna (1289–1562): Biographischer Index zu den Acta nationis Germanicae Universitatis Bononiensis. Reprint of first edition: Berlin 1899. Aalen 1970.

Kohls, Ernst Wilhelm, ed. Die evangelischen Katechismen von Ravensburg (1546/1733) und Reichenweier (1547/1559): Ein Beitrag zur oberdeutschen Katechismusgeschichte des 16. Jahrhunderts. VKBW, Reihe A, Vol. X. Stuttgart 1963.

Lötscher, Valentin, ed. Felix Platter: Tagebuch (Lebensbeschreibung). 1536–1567. Basler Chroniken, Vol. X. Basel and Stuttgart 1976.

Mayer, Hermann, ed. Die Matrikel der Universität Freiburg im Breisgau von 1460–1656. 2 vols., 3 parts. Freiburg i. Br. 1907–10.

Pollet, J. V., ed. Julius Pflug: Correspondence. Vol. I. Leiden 1969.

Ritter, François, ed. Catalogue des Incunables et Livres du XVIe siècle de la Bibliothèque Municipale de Strasbourg. Strasbourg and Zürich 1948.

Rupprich, Hans, ed. Der Briefwechsel des Konrad Celtis. Veröffentlichungen der Kommission zur Erforschung der Geschichte der Reformation und Gegenreformation: Humanistenbriefe, Vol. III. Munich 1934.

Schellhass, Karl, ed. Die Süddeutsche Nuntiatur des Grafen Bartholomäus von Portia. 3 vols. Nuntiaturberichte aus Deutschland. Edited by the Königlich Preussisches Historisches Institut in Rom. Abteilung III, Vols. II–V. Vol. V. Berlin 1909.

Sittler, Lucien, ed. Les listes d'admission à la bourgeoisie de Colmar: 1361–1494. Publ. Arch. Colmar, Vol. I. Colmar 1958. Mimeographed.

– Membres du Magistrat, Conseillers et Maîtres des Corporations de Colmar: Listes de 1408–1600. Publ. Arch. Colmar, Vol. III. Colmar 1964. Mimeographed.

Strauss, Gerald, ed. Manifestations of discontent in Germany on the eve of the Reformation. Bloomington, Ind. 1971.

Svaivert, Willy, and *Gall, Franz,* eds. Die Matrikel der Universität Wien. 3 vols., (1451–1579). Vienna, Cologne and Graz 1967–71.

Toepke, Gustav, ed. Die Matrikel der Universität Heidelberg. 7 vols. Vols. I–III (1386–1662). Heidelberg 1884–93.

Trouillat, Joseph, and *Vautrey, Louis,* eds. Monuments de l'histoire de l'ancien Evêché de Bâle. 5 vols. Vols. IV and V. Porrentruy 1861–67.

Vogeleis, Martin, ed. Quellen und Bausteine zu einer Geschichte der Musik und des Theaters im Elsass, 500–1800. Strasbourg 1911.

Volz, Hans, ed. Drei Schriften gegen Luthers Schmalkaldische Artikel von Cochläus, Witzel und Hoffmeister. Corpus Catholicorum, Vol. XVIII. Münster/Westphalia 1932.

Wackernagel, Hans Georg, ed. Die Matrikel der Universität Basel. 3 vols. (1460–1665/66). Basel 1951–62.

Waldner, Eugen, ed. "Vier Briefe von Johannes Hoffmeister." ZGORh, XLV (1891), 172–177.

Waltz, Andreas (André), ed. Sigmund Billings Kleine Chronik der Stadt Colmar. Colmar 1891.

– Chronik des Colmarer Kaufhauses. Colmar 1897.

– Chronique de Colmar de Félix-Henri-Joseph Chauffour dit le Syndic. Colmar 1903.

Wertz, Roland, ed. Le livre des bourgeois de Colmar, 1512–1609. Publ. Arch. Colmar, Vol. II. Colmar 1961. Mimeographed.

Wurstisen, Christian, Basler Chronick, darinn alles was sich in Oberen Teutschen Landen gedenckwurdigs zugetragen. Basel 1580.

Zapf, Georg Wilhelm, ed. Sämmtliche Reformations-Urkunden des Heiligen Römischen Reichs Stadt Aalen. 2 parts, one vol. Ulm 1770.

C. LITERATURE

Adam, Johann. Evangelische Kirchengeschichte der elsässischen Territorien bis zur Französischen Revolution. Strasbourg 1928.

Adam, Paul. Histoire des hospices et hopitaux de Sélestat. Sélestat 1960.

– L'humanisme à Sélestat: l'école, les humanistes, la bibliothèque. Sélestat 1962.

– Histoire religieuse de Sélestat. 2 vols. Vol. I: Des origines à 1615. Publications de la Société des amis de la Bibliothèque de Sélestat. Sélestat 1967.

Albrecht, Karl. "Das ehemalige Evangelische Gymnasium zu Colmar im Elsass, 1604–1794." Mittheilungen der Gesellschaft für deutsche Erziehungs- und Schulgeschichte, XI (1901), 287–306.

Allgemeine Deutsche Biographie. 56 vols. Edited by Die Historische Commission bei der Königl. Akademie der Wissenschaften. Leipzig 1875–1912.

Ammann, Hektor. "Elsässisch-schweizerische Wirtschaftsbeziehungen im Mittelalter." Elsass-Lothringisches Jahrbuch, VII (1928), 36–61.

– "La place de l'Alsace dans l'industrie textile du Moyen-Age." La Bourgeoisie Alsacienne, pp. 81–85.
– "Von der Wirtschaftsgeltung des Elsass im Mittelalter." Alemannisches Jahrbuch (1955), 95–202.
Andreas, Willy. Deutschland vor der Reformation: Eine Zeitenwende. Stuttgart and Berlin 1932.
Angermeier, Heinz. Königtum und Landfriede im Deutschen Spätmittelalter. Munich 1966.
Arens, Eduard. "Vom literarischen Leben in Aachen." Aachener Heimatgeschichte. Edited by Albert Huyskens, pp. 241–245.
Baillet, Lina. "Amandus Farckall, le premier imprimeur de Colmar (Fin 1522?-1er semestre 1524)." Gutenberg-Jahrbuch (1968), 170–182.
– "Un complément à la 'Bibliographie de la ville de Colmar' d'André Waltz (1902)." Annuaire de Colmar (1975/76), 73–79.
– "Deux villes de la Moyenne Alsace: Sélestat et Colmar face aux conflits religieux et sociaux des paysans, 1525." La guerre des paysans, 1525. Edited by Alphonse Wollbrett, pp. 93–102.
– "La Guerre des paysans: Un cas de consience dans la famille de Ribeaupierre." BPH, I (1967), 357–437.
Bainton, Roland H. The Reformation of the 16th century. Boston, Mass. 1952.
Barth, Médard. "Die Rosenkranzbruderschaften des Elsass, geschichtlich gewürdigt." Arch. EA, n.s., XVI (1968), 53–108.
– "Die Sakramentsbruderschaften des Elsass." Arch. EA, n.s., XIX (1971), 211–224.
Barthelmé, Annette. La Réforme dominicaine au XVe siècle en Alsace et dans l'ensemble de la province de Teutonie. Collection d'études sur l'histoire du droit et des institutions de l'Alsace, Vol. VII. Strasbourg 1931.
Bátori, Ingrid. "Das Patriziat der deutschen Stadt: Zu den Forschungsergebnissen über das Patriziat besonders der süddeutschen Städte." Zeitschrift für Stadtgeschichte, Stadtsoziologie und Denkmalpflege, II (1975), 1–30.
– ed. Städtische Gesellschaft und Reformation. Spätmittelalter und frühe Neuzeit: Tübinger Beiträge zur Geschichtsforschung, Kleine Schriften, Vol. II. Stuttgart 1979.
Bauer, Hermann. Geschichte und Beschreibung der ehemaligen freien Reichsstadt Aalen. 2nd rev. ed. Edited by J.G. Röhm. Aalen 1884.
Becker, Joseph. Geschichte der Reichslandvogtei im Elsass: Von ihrer Einrichtung bis zu ihrem Uebergang an Frankreich, 1273–1648. Strasbourg 1905.
– "Die Reichsvogtei Kaysersberg: Von ihrem Ursprung bis zur Französischen Revolution." Supplement added to Jahresbericht des Bischöflichen Gymnasiums zu Strassburg. Strasbourg 1906.
Beiträge zur Wirtschafts- und Stadtgeschichte: Festschrift für Hektor Ammann. Edited by Hermann Aubin, Edith Ennen, *et al.* Wiesbaden 1965.
Bellardi, Werner. Die Geschichte der 'Christlichen Gemeinschaft' in Strassburg (1546–1550): Der Versuch einer 'zweiten Reformation'. QFRG, Vol. XVIII. Leipzig 1934.
Betz, Jacques. "Colmar à travers les textes du XVIe, XVIIe et XVIIIe siècles." Annuaire de Colmar (1959), 7–17.
– L'Eglise protestante de Saint-Matthieu de Colmar et sa paroisse. Strasbourg 1971.
– "Jérôme Boner, un humaniste devenu maire, diplomate et traducteur." Annuaire de Colmar (1975/76), 81–90; (1976/77), 57–66.
Beuchot, Isidore. "Die ehemalige Franziskaner-, jetzige Spitalkirche der Stadt Colmar." Colmarer Katholischer Kirchen-Kalender, VI (1912), 45–88.
– "Die ehemalige Johanniterkirche in Colmar." Colmarer Katholischer Kirchen-Kalender, VII (1913), 43–63.
– "Das ehemalige Katharinenkloster zu Colmar." Colmarer Katholischer Kirchen-Kalender, VIII (1914), 43–69.
– "Die ehemalige Augustinerkirche zu Colmar." Colmarer Katholischer Kirchen-Kalender, IX (1915), 43–73.
– "Das frühere Unterlindenkloster zu Colmar in seiner Blütezeit." Colmarer Katholischer Kirchen-Kalender, XI (1917), 41–101.
– "Das frühere Kloster Unterlinden zu Colmar im 15. und 16. Jahrhundert." Colmarer Katholischer Kirchen-Kalender, XII (1918), 41–75.
– "Das frühere Unterlindenkloster: Niedergang und Auflösung." Colmarer Katholischer Kirchen-Kalender, XIII (1919), 43–73.
– "Das frühere Armenspital zum Heiligen Geist in Colmar." Colmarer Katholischer Kirchen-Kalender, XIV (1920), 35–55.

Billich, André. Histoire d'une ancienne ville impériale: Turckheim. Colmar 1975.

Bischoff, Georges. "Colmar et la crise révolutionnaire de 1524–1525." Annuaire de Colmar (1975/76), 43–54.

– "La Haute-Alsace et la Guerre des Paysans." La guerre des paysans, 1525. Edited by Alphonse Wollbrett, pp. 11–120.

Bizer, Ernst. Studien zur Geschichte des Abendmahlsstreits im 16. Jahrhundert. 3rd ed. Darmstadt 1972.

Blickle, Peter. Die Revolution von 1525. Munich and Vienna 1975.

– ed. Revolte und Revolution in Europa: Referate und Protokolle des Internationalen Symposiums zur Erinnerung an den Bauernkrieg 1525. HZ, Beiheft No. 4 (1975).

– "Thesen zum Thema: Der 'Bauernkrieg' als Revolution des 'gemeinen Mannes'." Revolte und Revolution in Europa. Edited by idem, 127–131.

Bog, Ingomar. "Ueber Arme und Armenfürsorge in Oberdeutschland und in der Eidgenossenschaft im 15. und 16. Jahrhundert." Jahrbuch für fränkische Landesforschung, XXXIV/ XXXV (1975), 983–1001.

Bolchert, Paul. "A la recherche de l'élite intellectuelle de Colmar aux XVIe et XVIIe siècles: Emmanuel Bétulejus, 1535?–1588 et André Beck, 1546–1627." Annuaire de Colmar (1964), 39–48.

Boner, Georg. "Das Bistum Basel: Ein Ueberblick von den Anfängen bis zur Neuordnung, 1828." Freiburger Diözesan-Archiv, LXXXVIII (1968), 5–101.

Boockmann, Hartmut. "Zu den geistigen und religiösen Voraussetzungen des Bauernkrieges." Bauernkriegs-Studien. Edited by Bernd Moeller, pp. 9–27.

Bopp, Marie-Joseph. Die evangelischen Geistlichen und Theologen in Elsass und Lothringen: Von der Reformation bis zur Gegenwart, (1540–1958). 3 parts, one vol. Bibliothek Familiengeschichtlicher Quellen, Vol. XIV. Neustadt a.d. Aisch 1959–60.

– Die evangelischen Gemeinden und Hohen Schulen in Elsass und Lothringen von der Reformation bis zur Gegenwart. 3 parts, one vol. Bibliothek Familiengeschichtlicher Quellen, Vol. XVI. Neustadt a. d. Aisch 1963.

La Bourgeoisie Alsacienne. Edited by la Société savante d'Alsace et des régions de l'Est. Strasbourg and Paris 1954.

Brady, Thomas A., Jr. "Aristocratie et régime politique à Strasbourg à l'époque de la Réforme (1525–1555)." Strasbourg au coeur religieux du XVIe siècle, pp. 19–36.

– Ruling Class, Regime and Reformation in Strasbourg, 1520–1555. SMRT, Vol. XXII. Leiden 1978.

Braeuner, Gabriel. "La Préréforme à Colmar (1522–1575)." Annuaire de Colmar (1975/76), 55–72.

Brandi, Karl. Der Augsburger Religionsfriede vom 25. September 1555. 2nd ed. Göttingen 1927.

Brecht, Martin. "Der theologische Hintergrund der 12 Artikel der Bauernschaft in Schwaben von 1525: Christoph Schappelers und Sebastian Lotzers Beitrag zum Bauernkrieg." Deutscher Bauernkrieg. Edited by Heiko A. Oberman, 174–208.

– "Die gemeinsame Politik der Reichsstädte und die Reformation." ZSavRG, Kan. Abt., LXIII (1977), 180–263.

– "Die gemeinsame Politik der Reichsstädte und die Reformation." Stadt und Kirche im 16. Jahrhundert. Edited by Bernd Moeller, pp. 87–90. [=Summary of above article].

Bruckner, Albert, general ed. Helveti Cacra. Abteilung I, Vol. I: Schweizer Kardinäle; Das apostolische Gesandtschaftswesen in der Schweiz; Erzbistümer und Bistümer, Bern 1972.

Brunner, Otto, "Stadt und Bürgertum in der europäischen Geschichte." Idem. Neue Wege der Verfassungs- und Sozialgeschichte, pp. 213–224.

– "Souveränitätsproblem und Sozialstruktur in den deutschen Reichsstädten der früheren Neuzeit." Idem. Neue Wege der Verfassungs- und Sozialgeschichte, pp. 294–331.

– Neue Wege der Verfassungs- und Sozialgeschichte. Göttingen 1968.

Bücking, Jürgen, "Die Weihbischöfe von Basel Marcus Tettinger (1567–1599) und Franz Beer d. J. (1599–1611)." ZSKG, LXII (1968), 121–141.

– Johann Rasser (ca. 1535–1595) und die Gegenreformation im Oberelsass. RST, Vol. CI. Münster-/Westphalia 1970.

– "Der Bauernkrieg in den vorder- und oberösterreichischen Ländern und in der Stadt Würzburg: Ansätze zu einer Theorie des Bauernkriegs." Bauernkriegs-Studien. Edited by Bernd Moeller, pp. 47–68.

Burckhard-Piguet, Theophil. "Aus der Socin'schen Familiengeschichte." Beiträge zur vaterländischen Geschichte, XII ([Basel] 1888), 295–342.

Burg, A[ndré] M[arcel]. "Die unteren Volksschichten in Hagenau." Gesellschaftliche Unterschichten in den südwestdeutschen Städten. Edited by Erich Maschke and Jürgen Sydow, pp. 90–100.

– "Patrizier und andere städtische Führungsschichten in Hagenau." Deutsches Patriziat 1430–1740. Edited by Hellmuth Rössler, pp. 353–375.
– "La Guerre des Paysans dans la région de Haguenau." La guerre des paysans, 1525. Edited by Alphonse Wollbrett, pp. 49–53.
Cantimori, Delio. "Submission and Conformity: 'Nicodemism' and the expectations of a conciliar solution to the religious question." Translated and edited by Eric Cochrane. The Late Italian Renaissance. Edited by Eric Cochrane, pp. 244–265.
Charles-Quint, le Rhin et la France: Droit pénal et droit savant à la époque de Charles-Quint. Edited by Centre de Recherches Rhénanes et Régionales de l'Université des Sciences Humaines de Strasbourg. Publications de la Société savante d'Alsace et des régions de l'Est: Collection 'Recherches et Documents', Vol. XVII. Strasbourg 1973.
[Chauffour, Félix]. "Notice sur la Société du Waagkeller à Colmar." Curiosités d'Alsace, II (1863), 56–78.
Chrisman, Miriam U. Strasbourg and the Reform: A study in the process of change. New Haven and London 1967.
Classen, Mathias. "Die konfessionelle und politische Bewegung in der Reichsstadt Aachen zu Anfang des 17. Jahrhunderts." Zs. Aachen, XXVIII (1906), 286–442.
Clauss, Joseph M., ed. Historisch-topographisches Wörterbuch des Elsass. Saverne 1895.
Cochrane, Eric, ed. The Late Italian Renaissance. New York, Evanston, Ill., and London 1970.
Cole. Richard G. "The Reformation in print: German pamphlets and propaganda." ARH, LXVI (1975), 93–102.
Davis, Natalie Zemon. "Some tasks and themes in the study of popular religion." The Pursuit of Holiness in Late Medieval and Renaissance Religion. Edited by Charles Trinkaus and Heiko A. Oberman, pp. 307–336.
– "Strikes and salvation in Lyon." Idem. Society and Culture in Early Modern France: Eight Essays, pp. 1–16.
– "Poor relief, humanism and heresy." Idem. Society and Culture in Early Modern France: Eight Essays pp. 17–64.
– Society and Culture in Early Modern France: Eight Essays. Stanford, Cal. 1975.
Demandt, Dieter. "Konflikte um die geistlichen Standesprivilegien im spätmittelalterlichen Colmar." Städtische Gesellschaft und Reformation. Edited by Ingrid Bátori.
Dickens, A. G. The German Nation and Martin Luther. London 1974.
Dictionnaire d'histoire et de géographie ecclésiastiques. 17 vols. to date. Edited by Alfred Baudrillart, Albert Vogt, Urbain Rouziés, *et al.* Paris 1912–1971.
Dohna, Lothar Graf zu. Reformatio Sigismundi: Beiträge zum Verständnis einer Reformschrift des 15. Jahrhunderts. Veröffentlichungen des Max-Planck-Instituts für Geschichte, Vol. IV. Göttingen 1968.
Dollinger, Philippe. "Strasbourg et Colmar, foyers de la mystique rhénane." La Mystique rhénane, pp. 3–13.
Dorlan, A[ntoine]. Notices historiques sur l'Alsace et principalement sur la ville de Schlestadt. 2 vols. Vol. I. Colmar 1843.
Druffel, August von. Der Elsässer Augustinermönch Johannes Hoffmeister und seine Korrespondenz mit dem Ordensgeneral Hieronymus Seripando. Abhandlungen der Königl. bayerischen Akademie der Wissenschaften, III. historische Klasse, Vol. XIV, Abteilung I. Munich 1878.
Ehbrecht, Wilfried. "Bürgertum und Obrigkeit in den hansischen Städten des Spätmittelalters." Die Stadt am Ausgang des Mittelalters. Edited by Wilhelm Rausch, pp. 275–294.
– "Zur Ordnung und Selbstverständnis städtischer Gesellschaft im späten Mittelalter." Blätter für deutsche Landesgeschichte, CX (1974), 83–103.
– "Verlaufsformen innerstädtischer Konflikte in nord- und westdeutschen Städten im Reformationszeitalter." Stadt und Kirche im 16. Jahrhundert. Edited by Bernd Moeller, pp. 27–47.
Eisenstein, Elizabeth L. "L'avènement de l'imprimerie et la Réforme." Annales ESC, VI (1971), 1355–1382.
Eitel, Peter. Die oberschwäbischen Reichsstädte im Zeitalter der Zunftherrschaft: Untersuchungen zu ihrer politischen und sozialen Struktur unter besonderer Berücksichtigung der Städte Lindau, Memmingen, Ravensburg und Ueberlingen. Schriften zur südwestdeutschen Landeskunde, Vol. VIII. Stuttgart 1970.
Elfert, Gustav. "Gewerbe und Handel, ihre wirtschaftliche und rechtliche Verfassung." Aachener Heimatgeschichte. Edited by Albert Huyskens, pp. 147–154.

Endriss, Albrecht. Die religiös-kirchlichen Verhältnisse in der Reichsstadt Wimpfen vor der Reformation. VKBW, Vol. XXXIX. Stuttgart 1967.

– "Phasen der Konfessionsbildung: Aufgezeigt am Beispiel der Reichsstadt Wimpfen im Zeitraum von 1523 bis 1635." Festgabe für Ernst Walter Zeeden, pp. 289–326.

Ernst, August, and *Adam, Johann.* Katechetische Geschichte des Elsaßes bis zur Revolution. Strasbourg 1897.

Festgabe für Ernst Walter Zeeden. Edited by Horst Rabe, Hansgeorg Molitor, and Hans-Christoph Rublack. RST, Supplemental Vol. II. Münster/Westphalia 1976.

Festschrift für Hermann Heimpel zum 70. Geburtstag. 2 vols. Edited by Mitarbeiter des Max-Planck-Instituts für Geschichte. Göttingen 1972.

Fleurent, Henri. "Essai sur la démographie et l'épidémiologie de la ville de Colmar." Bulletin de la Société d'histoire naturelle de Colmar, XV (1920/21), 45–111.

Frank, F., (and *Seeberg, Reinhold*). "Communicatio idiomatum." RETbK. Vol. IV, pp. 254–261.

Franz, Günther. "Die Entstehung der 'Zwölf Artikel' der deutschen Bauernschaft." ARH, XXXVI (1939), 195–213.

– Der Deutsche Bauernkrieg. 10th, rev. ed. Darmstadt 1975.

Franzen, August. Das Schicksal des Erasmianismus am Niederrhein im 16. Jahrhundert: Wende und Ausklang der erasmischen Reformbewegung im Reformationszeitalter." Historisches Jahrbuch, LXXXIII (1964), 84–112.

Friedensburg, Walter. "Der Regensburger Konvent von 1524." Historische Aufsätze dem Andenken an Georg Waitz gewidmet, pp. 502–539.

Frölich, Karl. "Kirche und städtisches Verfassungsleben im Mittelalter." ZSavRG, Kan. Abt., XXII (1933), 188–287.

Fürstenwerth, L[udwig]. Die Verfassungsänderungen in den oberdeutschen Reichsstädten zur Zeit Karls V. Göttingen 1893.

Gäbler, Ulrich, and *Herkenrath, Erland,* eds. Heinrich Bullinger, 1504–1575: Gesammelte Aufsätze zum 400. Todestag. 2 vols. Vol. II. ZBRG, Vol. VIII. Zürich 1970.

Gail, Anton. "Johann von Vlatten und der Einfluss des Erasmus von Rotterdam auf die Kirchenpolitik der vereinigten Herzogtümer." Düsseldorfer Jahrbuch, XLV (1951), 1–109.

Gatrio, A[ndré]. Die Abtei Murbach im Elsass. 2 vols. Vol. II. Strasbourg 1895.

Gauss, Karl. "Die Basler Pfarrerfamilie Serin." Basler Zeitschrift für Geschichte und Altertumskunde, XXXIV (1935), 261–287.

Geiger, Gottfried. Die Reichsstadt Ulm vor der Reformation: Städtisches und kirchliches Leben am Ausgang des Mittelalters. Forschungen zur Geschichte der Stadt Ulm, Vol. XI. Ulm 1971.

Geiger, Max. Die Basler Kirche im Zeitalter der Hochorthodoxie. Zollikon-Zürich 1952.

Gény, Joseph. Die Reichsstadt Schlettstadt und ihr Anteil an den socialpolitischen und religiösen Bewegungen der Jahre 1490–1536. Erläuterungen und Ergänzungen zu Janssens Geschichte des deutschen Volkes, Vol. I, Books V and VI. Freiburg i. Br. 1900.

Ginzburg, Carlo. Il nicodemismo: Simulazione e dissimulazione relgiosa nell' Europa del'500. Turin 1970.

Glauben und Bekennen: Vierhundert Jahre Confessio Helvetica; Beiträge zu ihrer Geschichte und Theologie. Edited by Joachim Staedtke. Zürich 1966.

Goehlinger, François-Auguste. Histoire du Chapitre de l'Eglise Saint-Martin de Colmar. Colmar 1951.

Goeters, J[ohann] F. G. "Die Rolle des Täufertums in der Reformationsgeschichte des Niederrheins." Rh.Vb., XXIV (1959), 217–236.

Goeters, W[ilhelm] G. "Adrian von Haemstede's Wirksamkeit in Antwerpen und Aachen." Theol. Arbeiten, n.s., VIII (1906), 50–95.

Graff, E[mile]. "Die Colmarer protestantische Kirchenordnung von 1648." Annuaire de Colmar (1937), 123–128.

Grane, Leif. "Lutherforschung und Geistergeschichte: Auseinandersetzung mit Heiko A. Oberman." ARH, LXVIII (1977), 302–314.

Graß, Hans. Die Abendmahlslehre bei Luther und Calvin. Beiträge zur Förderung christlicher Theologie, Reihe II, Vol. XLVII. Gütersloh 1940.

Greyerz, Hans von. "Studien zur Kulturgeschichte der Stadt Bern am Ende des Mittelalters." Archiv des Historischen Vereins des Kantons Bern, XXXV (No. 2, 1940), 173–491.

Greyerz, Kaspar von. "La Préréforme à Colmar, 1535-1555: Continuité ou rupture?." BHPF, CXXII (1976), 551–566.

Grimm, Harold J. "The Reformation and the urban social classes in Germany." Luther, Erasmus and the Reformation: A Catholic-Protestant Reappraisal, pp. 75–86.

– "Luther's contribution to the sixteenth-century organization of poor relief." ARH, LXI (1970), 222–234.

Grimm, Heinrich. "Die Buchführer des deutschen Kulturbereiches und ihre Niederlassungen in der Zeitspanne 1490–1550." Archiv für Geschichte des Buchwesens, VII (1966), cols. 1153–1772.

Grosses Universal Lexicon aller Wissenschaften und Künste, welche bishero durch menschlichen Verstand und Witz erfunden worden. 54 vols. Edited by Johann Heinrich Zedler. Reprint of first edition: Halle and Leipzig 1732–47. Graz 1961–62.

Guerber, Victor. Histoire politique et religieuse de Haguenau. 2 vols. Rixheim 1876.

Gyss, Joseph. Histoire de la ville d'Obernai et ses rapports avec les autres villes ci-devant impériales d'Alsace et avec les seigneuries voisines. 2 vols. Strasbourg 1866.

Hanauer, C[harles] A[uguste]. "Les historiens de l'établissement du Protestantisme à Colmar." RCA, I (1859), 249–266, 406–415, 440–455; II (1860), 169–181, 297–313.

– Le Protestantisme à Haguenau. Strasbourg and Colmar 1905.

Hartfelder, Karl. Zur Geschichte des Bauernkriegs in Südwestdeutschland. Stuttgart 1884.

Haselier, Günther. Geschichte der Stadt Breisach am Rhein. Vol. I/1: Von den Anfängen bis zum Jahr 1700. Breisach 1969.

Hatt, Jacques, ed. Listes des Membres du Grand Sénat de Strasbourg du XIIIe siècle à 1789. Strasbourg 1963.

Hauptmeyer, Carl-Hans. "Probleme des Patriziats oberdeutscher Städte vom 14. bis zum 16. Jahrhundert." Zeitschrift für Bayerische Landesgeschichte, XL (1977), 39–58.

Hauswirth, René. Landgraf Philipp von Hessen und Zwingli. Schriften zur Kirchen- und Rechtsgeschichte, Vol. XXXV. Tübingen and Basel 1968.

Headley, John M. "The Reformation as Lay Enlightenment." Reviews in European History, III (1977), 291–299.

Heer, Justus, (and *Egli, Emil*). "Bullinger, Heinrich." REThK. Vol. III, pp. 536–549.

Heitz, Fernand J. "Messire Jérôme Boner, humaniste, diplomate et maire de Colmar." Annuaire de Colmar (1938), 111–134.

Herold, Heinrich. Geschichte der Reformation in der Grafschaft Oettingen, 1522–1569. SVRG, No. 75. Halle 1902.

Hertzog, August. "Die letzten Jahre des Colmarer Barfüsserklosters und Jakob Einfalt aus Geberschweier, dessen letzter Guardian." Jb.G-S-L, XVII (1901), 113–149.

– "Inventare des früheren Franziskanerklosters von Colmar." Jb.G-S-L, XXI (1905), 23–44.

– "Die Bruderschaften am Minoritenkloster zu Colmar." Jb.G-S-L, XXV (1909), 39–53.

Heyne, Bodo. "Zur Entstehung kirchlicher Eigenart in Bremen." Hospitium Ecclesiae: Forschungen zur Bremischen Kirchengeschichte, Vol. I. Edited by idem, and Kurt Schulz. Bremen 1954, pp. 7–21.

Hieronimus, Konrad W. Das Hochstift Basel im ausgehenden Mittelalter (Quellen und Forschungen). Basel 1938.

Hillerbrand, Hans J. "The German Reformation and the Peasants' War." The social history of the Reformation, pp. 106–136.

Hirsch, Rudolf. Printing, Selling and Reading, 1450–1550. Wiesbaden 1967.

Historisch-biographisches Lexikon der Schweiz. 7 vols. Edited by Heinrich Türler, Marcel Godet, Victor Attinger, *et al.* Neuchâtel 1921–34.

Historische Aufsätze dem Andenken an Georg Waitz gewidmet. (No editor indicated). Hannover 1886.

Hofacker, Hans Georg. "Die Reformation in der Reichsstadt Ravensburg." ZWLG, XXIX (1970), 71–125.

Holborn, Hajo. "The social basis of the German Reformation." Church History, V (1936), 330–339.

Horning, Wilhelm. Dr. Johann Pappus von Lindau, 1549–1610: Münsterprediger, Universitätsprofessor und Präsident des Kirchenkonvents zu Strassburg. Strasbourg 1891.

Huber Max. "Städtearchiv und Reichsstandschaft der Städte im 16. Jahrhundert." Ulm und Oberschwaben, XXXV (1958), 94–112.

L'Humanisme en Alsace. Edited by Association Guillaume Budé. Paris 1939.

Die Humanisten in ihrer politischen und sozialen Umwelt. Edited by Otto Herding and Robert Stupperich. Deutsche Forschungsgemeinschaft, Kommission für Humanismusforschung, Mitteilung III. Bonn and Bad-Godesberg 1976.

Huot, Paul. La Commanderie de St-Jean à Colmar: Etude historique (1210–1870). Colmar 1870.

Huyskens, Albert, ed. Aachener Heimatgeschichte. Aachen 1924.

Ingold, A[rmand] M. P. Notice sur l'église et le couvent des Dominicains de Colmar. Colmar and Paris 1894.

– Miscellanea Alsatica. 3 vols. Vols. I and III. Colmar and Paris 1894 and 1897.

Jahn, Robert. Essener Geschichte: Die geschichtliche Entwicklung im Raum der Großstadt Essen. 2nd, rev. ed. Essen 1957.

Jahns, Sigrid. Frankfurt, Reformation und Schmalkaldischer Bund: Die Reformations-, Reichs- und Bündnispolitik der Reichsstadt Frankfurt am Main 1525–1536. Studien zur Frankfurter Geschichte, Book IX. Frankfurt a.M. 1976.

Jenny, Beat Rudolf. "Bullingers Briefwechsel mit dem Elsässer Reformator Matthias Erb (1539–1571)." Heinrich Bullinger, 1504–1575: Gesammelte Aufsätze zum 400. Todestag. Edited by Ulrich Gäbler and Erland Herkenrath. Vol. II, pp. 57–86.

Junghans, Helmar. Review-article on R[egnerus] R. Post, The Modern Devotion. Luther-Jahrbuch, XXXVII (1970), 120–124.

Kageneck, Alfred Graf von. "Ueber das Patriziat im Elsaß und in der Schweiz." Genealogisches Jahrbuch, VIII (1968), 25–40.

Keyser, Erich, ed. Deutsches Städtebuch: Handbuch städtischer Geschichte. 5 vols., 9 parts, to date. Vol. III, Part II: Westfälisches Städtebuch. Stuttgart 1954. Vol. III, Part III: Rheinisches Städtebuch. Stuttgart 1956. Vol. IV, Part II/2: Württembergisches Städtebuch. Stuttgart 1962.

Kiessling, Rolf. Bürgerliche Gesellschaft und Kirche in Augsburg im Spätmittelalter: Ein Beitrag zur Strukturanalyse der oberdeutschen Reichsstadt. Abhandlungen zur Geschichte der Stadt Augsburg, Vol. XIX. Augsburg 1971.

Kindler von Knobloch, Julius. Oberbadisches Geschlechterbuch. 3 vols. Heidelberg 1894–1919.

Kingdon, Robert M. "The control of morals in Calvin's Geneva." The social history of the Reformation, pp. 3–16.

– "Was the Reformation a revolution? The case of Geneva." Studies in Church History, XII (1975), 203–222.

– ed. The Formula of Concord: Quadricentennial essays. The Sixteenth Century Journal, VIII (No. 4, 1977).

Kirchhoff, Karl-Heinz. "Die Täufer im Münsterland: Verbreitung und Verfolgung des Täufertums im Stift Münster, 1533–1550." Westfälische Zeitschrift, CXIII (1963), 1–109.

Kittelson, James M. "Marbach vs. Zanchi: The Resolution of Controversey in Late Reformation Strasbourg." The Sixteenth Century Journal, VIII (No. 3, 1977), 31–44.

Knepper, Joseph. Nationaler Gedanke und Kaiseridee bei den elsässischen Humanisten: Ein Beitrag zur Geschichte des Deutschthums und der politischen Geschichte im Reichslande. Erläuterungen und Ergänzungen zu Janssens Geschichte des deutschen Volkes, Vol. I., Books II and III. Freiburg i. Br. 1898.

– Jacob Wimpfeling (1450–1528): Sein Leben und seine Werke. Reprint of first ed.: Freiburg i. Br. 1902. Nieuwkoop 1965.

– Das Schul- und Unterrichtswesen im Elsass: Von den Anfängen bis gegen das Jahr 1530. Strasbourg 1905.

Köhler, Walter. Zürcher Ehegericht und Genfer Konsistorium. 2 vols. Quellen und Abhandlungen zur Schweizerischen Reformationsgeschichte, Vols. VII and X. Leipzig 1932 and 1942.

König, Johann. Lazarus von Schwendi: Röm. Kaiserl. Majestät Rat und Feldoberst, 1522–1583: Beitrag zur Geschichte der Gegenreformation. Schwendi (Württemberg) 1934.

Kohls, Ernst-Wilhelm. Die Schule bei Martin Bucer in ihrem Verhältnis zu Kirche und Obrigkeit. Pädagogische Forschungen: Veröffentlichungen des Comenius-Instituts, Vol. XXII. Heidelberg 1963.

– "Evangelische Bewegung und Kirchenordnung in oberdeutschen Reichsstädten." ZSavRG, Kan.Abt., LIII (1967), 110–134.

– Die theologische Lebensaufgabe des Erasmus und die oberrheinischen Reformatoren: Zur Durchdringung von Humanismus und Reformation. Arbeiten zur Theologie, Reihe I, Heft 39. Stuttgart 1969.

Kontinuität und Umbruch. Edited by Josef Nolte, Hella Tompert, and Christof Windhorst. Spätmittelalter und frühe Neuzeit: Tübinger Beiträge zur Geschichtsforschung, Vol. II. Stuttgart 1978.

Krone, Rudolf. Lazarus von Schwendi, Kaiserlicher General und Geheimer Rat: Seine kirchenpolitische Tätigkeit und seine Stellung zur Reformation. SVRG, Nos. 106/107. Leipzig 1912.

Kubler, Louis. "François Christian Lersé et le patrimoine artistique du Haut-Rhin." Annuaire de Colmar (1953), 116–123.

Kuhlendahl, A. "Die Einführung der Reformation und die Geschichte der ersten deutsch-reformierten Gemeinde (1563–1571)." Essener Beiträge, LIV (1936), 27–119.

Kumpf, Gerhard. "Die schwäbische Reichsstadt Bopfingen in den Stürmen der Reformations- und Interimszeit." Blätter für württembergische Kirchengeschichte, n.s., LIX (1959), 91–119.

Kurze, Barbara. Kurfürst Ott Heinrich: Politik und Religion in der Pfalz, 1556–1559. SVRG, No. 174. Gütersloh 1956.

Landsmann, O. R. Wissembourg: Un siècle de son histoire, 1480–1580. Rixheim 1903.

Laplatte, C[laude]. "Colmar." Dictionnaire d'histoire et de géographie ecclésiastiques. Vol. XIII, cols. 258–272.

Lau, Franz. "Der Bauernkrieg und das angebliche Ende der lutherischen Reformation als spontaner Volksbewegung." Luther-Jahrbuch, XXVI (1959), 109–134.

Lebensbilder aus dem Bayerischen Schwaben. Edited by Götz Freiherr von Pölnitz. 9 vols. Vol. IV. Munich 1955.

Lerse, Franz. Geschichte der Reformation der ehemaligen Reichsstadt Colmar und ihrer Folgen bis 1632. 2nd ed. Mulhouse 1856.

Leube, Hans. Kalvinismus und Luthertum im Zeitalter der Orthodoxie. Vol. I (only extant vol.). Leipzig 1928.

Locher, Gottfried W. "Grundzüge der Theologie Huldrych Zwinglis im Vergleich mit derjenigen Martin Luthers und Johannes Calvins." Idem. Huldrych Zwingli in neuer Sicht, pp. 173–274.

– Huldrych Zwingli in neuer Sicht: Zehn Beiträge zur Theologie der Zürcher Reformation. Zürich and Stuttgart 1969.

Löffler, Klemens. "Reformationsgeschichte der Stadt Dortmund." Dortmunder Beiträge, XXII (1913), 183–243.

Lohff, Wenzel, and *Spitz, Lewis W.*, eds. Widerspruch, Dialog und Einigung: Studien zum Konkordienwerk der Lutherischen Reformation. Stuttgart 1977.

Lorenzen-Schmidt, Klaus-Joachim. "Die Geistlichen der schleswig-holsteinischen Städte vor der Reformation und ihre Stellung in den Stadtgemeinden." Stadt und Kirche im 16. Jahrhundert. Edited by Bernd Moeller, pp. 125–7.

Luther, Erasmus and the Reformation: A Catholic-Protestant Reappraisal. Edited by John C. Olin, James D. Smart, and Robert E. McNally, S.J. New York 1969.

Macco, Hermann Friedrich. Zur Reformationsgeschichte Aachens während des 16. Jahrhunderts: Eine kritische Studie. Aachen 1907.

McLelland, Joseph C. "Die Sakramentslehre der Confessio Helvetica Posterior." Glauben und Bekennen, pp. 368–391.

Maeder, Kurt. Die Via Media in der Schweizerischen Reformation: Studien zum Problem der Kontinuität im Zeitalter der Glaubensspaltung. ZBRG, Vol. II. Zürich 1970.

Maschke, Erich. "Verfassung und soziale Kräfte in der deutschen Stadt des Spätmittelalters vornehmlich in Oberdeutschland." VSWG, XLVI (1959), 289–349, 433–476.

– and *Sydow, Jürgen,* eds. Gesellschaftliche Unterschichten in südwestdeutschen Städten. VKBW, Vol. XLI. Stuttgart 1967.

Meininghaus, August. "Vom Dortmunder Honoratiorentum und seinen Geschlechtern." Mitteilungen der Westdeutschen Gesellschaft für Familienkunde, V (1928), cols. 411–422.

Mercklen, P[aul] A[lfred]. Les boulangers de Colmar, 1495–1513. Colmar and Mulhouse 1871.

Merkel, Friedemann. Geschichte des evangelischen Bekenntnisses in Baden von der Reformation bis zur Union. VVKB, Vol. XX. Karlsruhe 1960.

Metz, Friedrich. "Die Reichsstädte." Beiträge zur Wirtschafts- und Stadtgeschichte, pp. 29–54.

Metzenthin, Edouard. "La famille Hecker à Colmar." Annuaire de Colmar (1951/52), 33–44.

– "Anciennes familles colmariennes: Les Kriegelstein et leur origine." Annuaire de Colmar (1954), 67–76.

– "Anciennes familles colmariennes: Les Goll et leur origine." Annuaire de Colmar (1955), 56–68.

Meuthen, Erich. "Der gesellschaftliche Hintergrund der Aachener Verfassungskämpfe an der Wende vom Mittelalter zur Neuzeit." Zs. Aachen, LXXIV/LXXV (1962/63), 299–392.

Mieg, Philippe. La Réforme à Mulhouse, 1518–1538. Strasbourg 1948.

– "Les réfugiés colmariens à Mulhouse au temps de la Contre-Réforme 1628–32." Annuaire de Colmar (1950), 45–56.

– "Généalogie de la famille Goll de Colmar." Annuaire de Colmar (1955), 68–72.

– "Barthélemy Westheimer, pasteur à Mulhouse et à Horbourg 1499–1567." Annuaire de Colmar (1956), 41–49.
– "Les tribulations d'Augustin Guntzer, bourgeois de Colmar, durant la Guerre de Trente Ans." Annuaire de Colmar (1958), 48–65.
– "Notes biographiques et généalogiques sur les Güntzer de Colmar, de Sélestat et de Riquewihr." Annuaire de Colmar (1974/75), 159–179.
– "Notes complémentaires sur les Kriegelstein de Colmar." Annuaire de Colmar (1978), 153.
Moeller, Bernd. Reichsstadt und Reformation. SVRG, No. 180. Gütersloh 1962. (English translation as "Imperial Cities and the Reformation." See below).
– "Die Kirche in den evangelischen freien Städten Oberdeutschlands im Zeitalter der Reformation." ZGORh, n.s., LXXIII (1964), 147–162.
– "Frömmigkeit in Deutschland um 1500." ARH, LVI (1965), 5–30. English translation:
– "Piety in Germany around 1500." Translated by Joyce Irwin. The Reformation in medieval perspective. Edited by Steven E. Ozment, pp. 50–75.
– "Kleriker als Bürger." Festschrift für Hermann Heimpel zum 70. Geburtstag, Vol. II, pp. 195–224.
– "Problems of Reformation Research." Idem. Imperial Cities and the Reformation: Three Essays, pp. 3–16.
– "Imperial Cities and the Reformation." Idem. Imperial Cities and the Reformation: Three Essays, pp. 41–115.
– Imperial Cities and the Reformation: Three Essays. Translated and edited by H.C. Erik Midelfort and Mark U. Edwards, Jr. Philadelphia 1972.
– ed. Bauernkriegs-Studien. SVRG, No. 189. Gütersloh 1975.
– Deutschland im Zeitalter der Reformation. Deutsche Geschichte. Edited by Joachim Leuschner. Vol. IV. Göttingen 1977.
– ed. Stadt und Kirche im 16. Jahrhundert. SVRG, No. 190. Gütersloh 1978.
Molitor, Hansgeorg. "Frömmigkeit im Spätmittelalter und früher Neuzeit als methodisches Problem." Festgabe für Ernst Walter Zeeden, pp. 1–20.
Moltmann, Jürgen. Christoph Pezel (1539–1604) und der Calvinismus in Bremen. Hospitium Ecclesiae: Forschungen zur Bremischen Kirchengeschichte, Vol. II. Bremen 1958.
Mommsen, Wolfgang J., and *Scribner, Robert W.,* eds. Stadtbürgertum und Adel in der Reformation: Studien zur Sozialgeschichte der Reformation. Stuttgart 1979.
Mone, [Franz Joseph]. "Zunftorganisation." ZGORh, XVIII (1865), 12–33.
Mossmann, Xavier. "La sécularisation du prieuré de Saint-Pierre à Colmar." Bulletin du Musée historique de Mulhouse, XIV (1889), 1–17.
– La Réforme à Colmar. Colmar 1853.
– Les Anabaptistes à Colmar. Colmar 1869.
– Notes et documents tirés des Archives de Colmar. Colmar 1872.
– Recherches sur l'ancienne constitution de la commune à Colmar. 2nd, rev. ed. Colmar 1878.
– Mémoire présenté au grand bailli d'Alsace sur une insurrection survenue à Colmar en 1424. Colmar 1882.
Mühlhaupt, Erwin. "Eigenart und Bedeutung der Reformation im Rheinland." MKR, XIII (1964), 33–58.
Müller, Johannes. "Der Konflikt Kaiser Rudolfs II. mit den deutschen Reichsstädten, ca. 1577–85." Westdeutsche Zeitschrift für Geschichte und Kunst, XIV (1895), 257–293.
Muralt, Leonhard von. "Stadtgemeinde und Reformation in der Schweiz." Zeitschrift für Schweizer Geschichte, X (1930), 349–384.
La Mystique rhénane. Edited by Centre d'études specialisé d'histoire des religions de Strasbourg. Paris 1963.
Naujoks, Eberhard. "Ulms Sozialpolitik im 16. Jahrhundert." Ulm und Oberschwaben, XXXIII (1953), 88–98.
– Obrigkeitsgedanke, Zunftverfassung und Reformation: Studien zur Verfassungsgeschichte von Ulm, Esslingen und Schwaebisch Gmünd. VKBW, Reihe B, Vol. III. Stuttgart 1958.
– "Obrigkeit und Zunftverfassung in den südwestdeutschen Reichsstädten." ZWLG, XXXIII (1974), 53–93.
Neue Deutsche Biographie. 11 vols., to date. Edited by Historische Kommission der Bayerischen Akademie der Wissenschaften. Berlin 1953–1977.

Niesel, Wilhelm, ed. Bekenntnisschriften und Kirchenordnungen der nach Gottes Wort reformierten Kirche. 2nd ed. Zollikon-Zürich 1938.
Oberman, Heiko A. "Tumultus rusticorum: Vom 'Klosterkrieg' zum Fürstensieg: Beobachtungen zum Bauernkrieg mit besonderer Berücksichtigung zeitgenössischer Beurteilungen." Deutscher Bauernkrieg. Edited by idem, 301–316.
– ed. Deutscher Bauernkrieg. ZKG, LXXXV (No. 2, 1974).
– and *Brady, Thomas A., Jr.,* eds. Itinerarium Italicum: The Profile of the Italian Renaissance in the Mirror of its European Transformations. SMRT, Vol. XIV. Leiden 1975.
– Werden und Wertung der Reformation. Tübingen 1977.
– "Reformation: Epoche oder Episode." ARH, LVIII (1977), 56–109.
Ohl, Ludwig. Geschichte der Stadt Münster und ihrer Abtei. Vorbruck-Schirmeck 1897.
Ozment, Steven E., ed. The Reformation in Medieval Perspective. Chicago 1971.
– The Reformation in the Cities. New Haven and London 1975.
Paulus, Nikolaus. Der Augustinermönch Johannes Hoffmeister: Ein Lebensbild aus der Reformationszeit. Freiburg i.Br. 1891.
– Die deutschen Dominikaner im Kampfe gegen Luther, (1518–1563). Erläuterungen und Ergänzungen zu Janssens Geschichte des deutschen Volkes, Vol. IV, Books I and II. Freiburg i.Br. 1903.
– "Michael Buchinger, ein Colmarer Schriftsteller und Prediger des 16. Jahrhunderts." Arch. EKG, V (1930), 199–223.
Pennings, Heinrich. "Die Religionsunruhen in Aachen und die beiden Städtetage zu Speyer und Heilbronn 1581 und 1582." Zs. Aachen, XXVII (1905), 25–108.
Petri, Franz. "Im Zeitalter der Glaubenskämpfe (1500–1648)." Rheinische Geschichte. Edited by idem, and Georg Droege, pp. 1–217.
– and *Droege, Georg,* eds. Rheinische Geschichte. 3 vols. Vol. II. Düsseldorf 1976.
Pfeiffer, Gerhard. "Der Augsburger Religionsfrieden und die Reichsstädte." Zeitschrift des Historischen Vereins für Schwaben, LXI (1955), 213–321.
– "Das Verhältnis von politischer und kirchlicher Gemeinde in den deutschen Reichsstädten." Staat und Kirche im Wandel der Jahrhunderte, pp. 79–99.
Pfleger, Luzian (Lucien). "Michael Hilspach, ein oberrheinischer Schulmeister des 16. Jahrhunderts." ZGORh, n.s., XX (1905), 254–259.
– Die elsässische Pfarrei: Ihre Entstehung und Entwicklung. Forschungen zur Kirchengeschichte des Elsass, Vol. III. Strasbourg 1936.
Plickert, Herbert. "Geschichte der freien Reichsstadt Aalen im Wandel der Zeiten." Aquileja: Illustrierte Zeitschrift zur Pflege des Heimatgedankens im Gebiet der Ostalb (1960), 71–83.
Plongeron, Bernard, ed. La religion populaire dans l'occident chrétien: Approches historiques. Bibliothèque Beauchesne: Religions, Société, Politique, Vol. II. Paris 1976.
Post, R[egnerus] R. The Modern Devotion: Confrontation with Reformation and Humanism. SMRT, Vol. III. Leiden 1968.
Press, Volker. "Der Bauernkrieg in der deutschen Geschichte." Nassauische Annalen, LXXXVI (1975), 158–177.
Rammstedt, Otthein, "Stadtunruhen 1525." Der Deutsche Bauernkrieg, 1524–26. Edited by Hans-Ulrich Wehler, 239–276.
Rapp, Francis. "La guerre des paysans dans la vallée du Rhin supérieur: Quelques problèmes d'intérpretations." Charles-Quint, le Rhin et la France, pp. 135–156.
– Réformes et Réformation à Strasbourg: Eglise et Société dans le diocèse de Strasbourg (1450–1525). Collection de l'Institut des Hautes Etudes Alsaciennes, Vol. XXIII. Paris 1974.
– "Die soziale und wirtschaftliche Vorgeschichte des Bauernkrieges im Unterelsass." Bauernkriegs-Studien. Edited by Bernd Moeller, pp. 29–45.
– "Die elsäßischen Humanisten und die geistliche Gesellschaft." Die Humanisten in ihrer politischen und sozialen Umwelt, pp. 87–108.
– "Refléxions sur la religion populaire au moyen âge." La religion populaire dans l'occident chrétien: Approches historiques. Edited by Bernard Plongeron, pp. 5–98.
Rausch, Wilhelm, ed. Die Stadt am Ausgang des Mittelalters. Linz 1974.
Realencyklopädie für protestantische Theologie und Kirche. 24 vols. Edited by Albert Hauck. Third ed. Leipzig 1896–1913.
Redlich, Otto R. Staat und Kirche am Niederrhein zur Reformationszeit. SVRG, No. 164. Leipzig 1938.

Reinking, Karl Franz. Die Vormundschaften der Herzöge von Bayern in der Markgrafschaft Baden-Baden im 16. Jahrhundert: Eine Studie zur Geschichte der Gegenreformation. Historische Studien, Heft CCLIIIIV. Berlin 1935.

Renaudet, Augustin. Humanisme et Renaissance. Travaux d'Humanisme et Renaissance, Vol. XXX. Geneva 1958.

Reuter, Rudolf. Der Kampf um die Reichsstandschaft der Städte auf dem Augsburger Reichstag 1582. Schwäbische Geschichtsquellen und Forschungen, Book III. Munich and Leipzig 1919.

Ribbeck, Konrad. "Geschichte des Essener Gymnasiums: Erster Teil, bis 1564." Essener Beiträge, XVI (1896), 1–111.

– "Die lutherische Stadtschule, 1564–1611: (Geschichte des Essener Gymnasiums, Teil 2)." Essener Beiträge, XIX (1898), 1–73.

– "Uebersicht über die Verfassung der Stadt Essen bis zum Untergange der städtischen Selbständigkeit." Essener Beiträge, XXII (1902), 15–28.

– Geschichte der Stadt Essen. Part I (only extant part). Essen 1915.

Ritter, François. Histoire de l'imprimerie alsacienne aux XVe et XVIe siècles. Publications de l'Institut des Hautes Etudes Alsaciennes, Vol. XIV. Strasbourg 1955.

Ritter, Gerhard. Erasmus und der deutsche Humanistenkreis am Oberrhein. Freiburger Universitätsreden, No. 23. Freiburg i.Br. 1937.

– Die Neugestaltung Europas im 16. Jahrhundert: Die kirchlichen und staatlichen Wandlungen im Zeitalter der Reformation und der Glaubenskämpfe. Berlin 1950.

Ritter, Moriz. Deutsche Geschichte im Zeitalter der Gegenreformation und des Dreissigjährigen Krieges, (1555–1648). 3 vols. Stuttgart 1889–1908.

Rocholl, Heinrich. Anfänge der Reformationsgeschichte in Kolmar: Ein Beitrag zur Reformationsgeschichte des Elsass. Colmar 1875.

– Die Einführung der Reformation in der ehemaligen freien Reichsstadt Colmar: Ein Beitrag zur Reformationsgeschichte des Elsass. Leipzig 1876.

– "Die Vertreibung evangelischer Bürger aus der freien Reichsstadt Colmar und ihre Aufnahme in Basel: Ein Geschichtsbild aus der Zeit der katholischen Gegenreformation 1628–1630." Beiträge zur vaterländischen Geschichte, n.s., XIV ([Basel] 1896), 307–345.

– Aus dem alten Kirchenbuch einer freien Reichsstadt: Warnende Bilder aus der Vergangenheit für die Gegenwart in der Jesuitenfrage. Schriften für das deutsche Volk, No. 35. Halle 1900.

– "Herzog Georg von Württemberg und die Reformation im Ober-Elsass." Kirchliche Monatsschrift, XIX (1900), 475–482, 512–522, 561–578.

– Matthias Erb, ein elsässischer Glaubenszeuge aus der Reformationszeit. Beiträge zur Landes- und Volkeskunde von Elsass-Lothringen, Heft XXVI. Strasbourg 1900.

Röhrich, Timotheus Wilhelm. Mittheilungen aus der Geschichte der evangelischen Kirche des Elsasses. 3 vols. Strasbourg and Paris 1855.

Rössler, Hellmuth, ed. Deutsches Patriziat 1430–1740. Schriften zur Problematik der deutschen Führungsschichten in der Neuzeit, Vol. III. Limburg/Lahn 1968.

Rosenkranz, Albert. Der Bundschuh: Die Erhebungen des südwestdeutschen Bauernstandes in den Jahren 1493–1517. 2 vols. Schriften des Wissenschaftlichen Institutes der Elsass-Lothringer im Reich. Heidelberg 1927.

– "Heinrich Barenbroch." MKR, XVI (1967), 213–219.

Roth, Friedrich. Augsburgs Reformationsgeschichte, 1517–1530. 4 vols. 2nd ed. Munich 1901–1911.

Rott, Jean. "L'Humanisme et la Réforme pédagogique en Alsace." L'Humanisme en Alsace, pp. 64–83.

Rotscheidt, W[ilhelm]. "Das Religionsgespräch in Essen im Jahre 1571." Monatshefte für Rheinische Kirchengeschichte, XX (1926), 35–67.

Rublack, Hans-Christoph. Die Einführung der Reformation in Konstanz: Von den Anfängen bis zum Abschluss 1531. QFRG, Vol. XL. Gütersloh and Karlsruhe 1971.

– "Die Stadt Würzburg im Bauernkrieg." ARH, LXVI (1976), 76–99.

– "Forschungsbericht Stadt und Reformation." Stadt und Kirche im 16. Jahrhundert. Edited by Bernd Moeller, pp. 9–26.

– "Reformatorische Bewegungen in Würzburg und Bamberg." Stadt und Kirche im 16. Jahrhundert. Edited by Bernd Moeller, pp. 109–124.

– Gescheiterte Reformation: Frühreformatorische und protestantische Bewegungen in süd- und westdeutschen geistlichen Residenzen. Spätmittelalter und frühe Neuzeit: Tübinger Beiträge zur Geschichtsforschung, Vol. IV. Stuttgart 1978.

– "Politische Situation und reformatorische Politik in der Frühphase der Reformation in Konstanz." Kontinuität umd Umbruch, pp. 316–330.

Schall, Julius. "Reformation und Gegenreformation im Gebiet der Fürstprobstei Ellwangen." Blätter für württembergische Kirchengeschichte, n.s, I (1897), 25–43, 146–163.

Schanz, Georg. Zur Geschichte der deutschen Gesellenvereine im Mittelalter. Reprint of first ed.: Leipzig, 1876. Glashütten im Taunus 1973.

Schaub, Friedrich. "Der Basler Domherr Franz von Apponex: Seine Studienstiftung und seine Bücher." Freiburger Diözesan-Archiv, LXIX (1950), 92–110.

Scherlen, August(e). Topographie von Alt-Colmar. Colmar [1922].

– Geschichte der Stadt Türckheim. Colmar 1925.

– Colmar, Village et Ville. Colmar 1931.

Schilling, Heinz. Niederländische Exulanten im 16. Jahrhundert: Ihre Stellung im Sozialgefüge und im religiösen Leben deutscher und englischer Städte. SVRG, No. 187. Gütersloh 1972.

– "Bürgerkämpfe in Aachen zu Beginn des 17. Jahrhunderts." Zeitschrift für historische Forschung, I (1974), 175–231.

– "Aufstandsbewegungen in der stadtbürgerlichen Gesellschaft des Alten Reiches: Die Vorgeschichte des Münsteraner Täuferreichs, 1525 bis 1534." Der deutsche Bauernkrieg, 1524–26. Edited by Hans-Ulrich Wehler, 193–238.

Schindling, Anton, Humanistische Hochschule und freie Reichsstadt: Gymnasium und Akademie in Straßburg, 1538–1621. Veröffentlichungen des Instituts für Europäische Geschichte Mainz, Vol. LXXVII. Wiesbaden 1977.

Schlink, Edmund. Theology of the Lutheran Confessions. Translated by Paul F. Koehneke and H.J. Bouman. Philadelphia 1961.

Schmidlin, Joseph. Die katholische Restauration im Elsass am Vorabend des Dreissigjährigen Krieges. Strasbourg-Neudorf 1934.

– "Religiös-sittliche Verfassung und Reformbestrebungen im Weltklerus des Elsass am Vorabend des Dreissigjährigen Krieges." Arch. EKG, XVI (1943), 135–204.

Schmidt, Charles. Histoire littéraire de l'Alsace à la fin du XVe et au commencement du XVIe siècle. 2 vols. Reprint of first ed.: Paris 1879. Hildesheim 1966.

Schmidt, Johannes. Gründliche vnd vnvermeidentliche Widerlegung der gifftigen Lästerschrifft, welche ein vngenannter Calvinist Anno 1634 wider die Anno 1632 in deß Heil. Reichs Stadt Colmar von Johanne Schmidt, Theologiae Doctore, Professore vnd deß Kirchen Convents Praesidenten in Straßburg, gehaltene Christliche Danckpredigt . . . feindseliger weise außgesprenget . . . Strasbourg 1638.

Schmitt, Jean-Claude. "La Confrérie du Rosaire de Colmar (1485)." Archivum Fratrum Praedicatorum, XL (1970), 97–124.

– "Apostolat mendiant et société: Une confrérie dominicaine à la veille de la Réforme." Annales ESC, XXVI (1971), 83–104.

– "Les dernières années d'un béguinage colmarien d'après ses comptes (1510–1531)." Annuaire de Colmar (1975/76), 31–42.

Schroeder, Ferdinand. "Sittliche und kirchliche Zustände Essens in der ersten Hälfte des 16. Jahrhunderts." Essener Beiträge, XVIII (1898), 98–130.

Schué, Carl. "Die reichsstädtische Verfassung und ihre Entwicklung." Aachener Heimatgeschichte. Edited by Albert Huyskens, pp. 176–182.

Schultze, Alfred. Stadtgemeinde und Reformation. Recht und Staat in Geschichte und Gegenwart, No. 11. Tübingen 1918.

Scribner, Robert W. (Bob). "Why was there no Reformation at Cologne?" Bulletin of the Royal Institute for Historical Research, XLIX (1976), 217–241.

– "Is there a social history of the Reformation?" Social History, IV (January 1977), 483–505.

– "Sozialkontrolle und die Möglichkeit einer städtischen Reformation." Stadt und Kirche im 16. Jahrhundert. Edited by Bernd Moeller, pp. 57–65.

Sessions, Kyle C., ed. Reformation and Authority: The meaning of the Peasants' Revolt. Problems in European Civilization. Lexington, Mass. 1968.

Sittler, Luzian (Lucien). "Landwirtschaft und Gartenbau im alten Colmar." Elsass-Lothringisches Jahrbuch, XX (1942), 71–94.

– "Das Elsass im 16. Jahrhundert." Idem, ed. Geschichte des Elsass, Vol. II, pp. 5–32.

– ed. Geschichte des Elsass. 2 vols. 3rd ed. Colmar 1942.

– "Le commerce du vin de Colmar jusqu'en 1789." RdA, LXXXIX (1949), 37–56.

– "Notice sur la famille Sandherr." Annuaire de Colmar (1950), 57–66.
– "Colmar et la Décapole: Une crise au sein de la ligue au XVI siècle." Annuaire de Colmar (1954), 47–54.
– "Les bourgeois de Colmar: Essai d'une vue d'ensemble." La Bourgeoisie Alsacienne, pp. 21–34.
– La Décapole alsacienne des origines à la fin du moyen-âge. Publications de l'Institut des Hautes-Etudes alsaciennes, Vol. XII. Strasbourg 1955.
– La viticulture el le vin de Colmar à travers les siècles. Colmar 1956.
– "Les mouvements sociaux à Colmar du XIVe au XVIe siècle." RdA, XCV (1956), 129–145.
– "Le Ladhof et la navigation colmarienne." Annuaire de Colmar (1957), 13–23.
– "Il y a six siècles: A Colmar en 1358." Annuaire de Colmar (1958), 18–27.
– "Der elsässische Zehnstädtebund, seine geschichtliche Einheit und seine Organisation." Esslinger Studien, X (1964), 59–77.
– "Commerce et commmerçants dans le vieux Colmar." Annuaire de Colmar (1966), 14–48.
– "L'élevage à Colmar au Moyen Age et au début des temps modernes." BHP, I (1967), 49–59.
– "La vie économique de Colmar (jusqu'à 1800)." Annuaire de Colmar (Numéro spécial, 1970), 25–40.
– "Colmar au XVIe siècle." Annuaire de Colmar (1975/76), 13–30; (1976/77), 39–48.
Sitzmann, Edouard, ed. Dictionnaire de biographie des hommes célèbres de l'Alsace depuis les temps les plus reculés jusqu' à nos jours. 2 vols. Reprint of first ed.: n.p. (1909). Paris 1973.
Skalweit, Stephan. Reich und Reformation. Propyläen Bibliothek der Geschichte. Berlin 1967.
The social history of the Reformation: Festschrift in honor of Harold J. Grimm. Edited by Lawrence P. Buck and Jonathan W. Zophy. Columbus, Ohio 1972.
Spitz, Lewis W. "Particularism and Peace: Augsburg 1955." Church History, XXV (1956), 110–126.
– The religious Renaissance of the German Humanists. Cambridge, Mass. 1963.
– The Reformation: Basic Interpretations. 2nd ed. Lexington, Mass., Toronto and London 1972.
– "The course of German Humanism." Itinerarium Italicum. Edited by Heiko A. Oberman and Thomas A. Brady, Jr., pp. 371–436.
– and *Lohff, Wenzel,* eds. Discord, Dialogue and Concord: Studies in the Lutheran Reformation's Formula of Concord, Philadelphia 1977.
Staat und Kirche im Wandel der Jahrhunderte. Edited by Walter Peter Fuchs. Stuttgart, Berlin, Cologne and Mainz 1966.
Staehelin, Ernest. "Bâle et l'Alsace." L'Humanisme en Alsace, pp. 30–41.
Stenger, Albrecht. "Die Reformation in Dortmund." Jahrbuch des Vereins für westfälische Kirchengeschichte, XL/XLI (1939/40), 191–208.
Störmann, Anton. Die städtischen Gravamina gegen den Klerus am Ausgange des Mittelalters und in der Reformationszeit. RST, Nos. 24–26. (One vol.). Münster/Westphalia 1916.
Strasbourg au coeur religieux du XVIe siècle. Edited by Georges Livet and Francis Rapp. Sociéte Savante d'Alsace et des Régions de l'Est: Collection 'Grandes Publications', Vol. XII. Strasbourg 1977.
Stratenwerth, Heide. Die Reformation in der Stadt Osnabrück. Veröffentlichungen des Instituts für Europäische Geschichte Mainz, Vol. LXI. Wiesbaden 1971.
Strauss, Gerald. Nuremberg in the Sixteenth Century. New Dimensions in History: Historical Cities. New York, London and Sydney 1966.
Strohl, Henri. "Les expériences d'une église au cours de quatre siècles." Vom Wesen und Wandel der Kirche, pp. 116–161.
– Le Protestantisme en Alsace. Strasbourg 1950.
Stupperich, Robert. Der Humanismus und die Wiedervereinigung der Konfessionen. SVRG, No. 160. Leipzig 1938.
Süss, Louis. Geschichte der Reformation in der Herrschaft Rappoltstein. Part I: Bis 1648 (only extant part). Saverne 1914.
Tardent, Jean Paul. Niklaus Manuel als Staatsmann. Bern 1968.
Thompson, Lawrence S. "German Translations of the Classics between 1450 and 1550." Journal of English and Germanic Philology, XLII (1943), 343–363.
Trevor-Roper, H. R. "Religion, the Reformation and Social Change." Idem. The European Witch-Craze, pp. 1–45.
– The European Witch-Craze of the Sixteenth and Seventeenth Centuries and other Essays. New York and Evanston, Ill. 1969.
Trinkhaus, Charles, and *Oberman, Heiko A.,* eds. The Pursuit of Holiness in Late Medieval and Renaissance Religion, SMRT, Vol. X. Leiden 1974.

Tscherning, Julius. Züge aus der Geschichte der Reformation der ehemaligen freien Reichsstadt Aalen auf Grund eines im Jahre der Einführung der Reformation abgefassten, später umgeschriebenen Urkundenbuchs. Aalen 1882.

Vanotti, Johann Nepomuk. "Beiträge zur Geschichte der Orden in der Diözese Rottenburg." (Part II). Freiburger Diözesan-Archiv, XVII (1885), 197–243.

Vansteenberghe, M. "Influences Rhénanes." L'Humanisme en Alsace, pp. 10–27.

Vautrey, Louis. Histoire des Evêques de Bâle. 2 vols. Vol. I. Einsiedeln 1884.

Vermeulen, Adeodatus. Der Augustiner Konrad Treger: Die Jahre seines Provinzialates (1518–1542). Rome 1962.

Viénot, John. Histoire de la Réforme dans le pays de Montbéliard depuis les origines jusqu'à la mort de P. Toussain, 1524–1573. 2 vols. Montbéliard 1900.

Vierordt, Karl Friedrich. Geschichte der Reformation im Grossherzogthum Baden. Karlsruhe 1847.

Vischer-Ehinger, Fritz. Die Familie Vischer in Colmar und Basel. Basel 1933.

Vogler, Bernard. "Le corps pastoral de Colmar et des environs avant la Guerre de Trente Ans." Annuaire de Colmar (1975/76), 121–127.

– Le Clergé Protestant Rhénan au siècle de la Réforme (1555–1619). Association des Publications près les Universités de Strasbourg. Paris 1976.

– "L'affirmation de l'orthodoxie luthérienne." Strasbourg au coeur religieux du XVIe siècle, pp. 595–602.

Vom Wesen und Wandel der Kirche: Festschrift für Eberhard Vischer. Edited by Theologische Fakultät der Universität Basel. Basel 1935.

Wackernagel, Rudolf. Geschichte der Stadt Basel. 3 vols. Vol. III. Basel 1924.

Wagner, Adalbert. "Peter Falcks Bibliothek und humanistische Bildung." Freiburger Geschichtsblätter ([Freiburg/Switzerland] 1925), xxv–xxxiii; 1–221.

Waldner, Eugène (Eugen). "La distillation et le commerce de l'eau-de-vie à Colmar au seizième et au dixseptième siècle." Bulletin du Musée Historique de Mulhouse (1891), 3–12.

– "Ein Konflikt zwischen dem Rate und der Bäckerzunft zu Colmar." ZGORh, XLVII (1893), 616–625.

– Allerlei aus dem alten Colmar. Colmar 1894.

– Kurzer Ueberblick über die Geschichte der Stadt Colmar. Colmar 1914.

Walte, A. "Mitteilungen aus der bremischen Kirchengeschichte." Zeitschrift für die historische Theologie, XXXIV (1864), 3–110; XXXVI (1866), 339–428; XLII (1872), 50–159, 448–468, 546–646; XLIII (1873), 163–202.

Weber, Hans Emil. Reformation, Orthodoxie und Rationalismus. 2 parts, 3 vols. Vol. I/2. Beiträge zur Förderung christlicher Theologie, Reihe II, Vol. XLV. Gütersloh 1940.

Wehler, Hans-Ulrich, ed. Der deutsche Bauernkrieg, 1524–26. Geschichte und Gesellschaft: Zeitschrift für Historische Sozialwissenschaft, special No. I (1975).

Werminghoff, Albert. Verfassungsgeschichte der deutschen Kirche im Mittelalter. 2nd ed. Leipzig and Berlin 1913.

Wethly, Gustaf. Hieronymus Boner, Leben, Werke und Sprache: Ein Beitrag zur elsässischen Literaturgeschichte. Strasbourg 1892.

Weyrauch, Erdmann. "Zur Auswertung von Steuerbüchern mit quantifizierenden Methoden." Festgabe für Ernst Walter Zeeden, pp. 97–127.

– "Strasbourg et la Réforme en Allemagne du Sud." Strasbourg au coeur religieux du XVIe siècle, pp. 347–368.

– "Die politische Führungsgruppe in Colmar in der Zeit der Reformation." Stadtbürgertum und Adel in der Reformation: Studien zur Sozialgeschichte der Reformation. Edited by Wolfgang J. Mommsen and Robert W. Scribner.

Wickersheimer, Ernest. "Fries, Lorenz: Arzt, Astrolog und Geograph." NDB. Vol. V, pp. 609–610.

Will, Erich. "Die Reformation in Colmar im Spiegel der dortigen Konsistorialbibliothek." ARH, LV (1964), 74–82.

Winterberg, Hans. Die Schüler von Ulrich Zasius. VKBW, Vol. XVIII. Stuttgart 1961.

Winterfeld, Luise von. "Die Dortmunder Wandschneider: Quellen und Untersuchungen zur Geschichte des Tuchhandels in Dortmund." Dortmunder Beiträge, XXIX/XXX (1922).

– "Der Durchbruch der Reformation in Dortmund." Dortmunder Beiträge, XXXIV (1927), 53–146.

– Geschichte der freien Reichs- und Hansestadt Dortmund. 4th ed. Dortmund 1963.

Wohlfeil, Rainer, ed. Der Bauernkrieg 1524–26: Bauernkrieg und Reformation, Neun Beiträge. Nymphenburger Texte zur Wissenschaft, No. 21. Munich 1975.

Wolff, Christian. "André Sandherr, greffier-syndic de Colmar (1533–1600)." Annuaire de Colmar (1963), 68–79.

Wolff, G. "Sebastian Murrhos Geburts- und Todestag." Anzeiger für Deutsches Alterthum und Deutsche Litteratur, XIV (September 4, 1888), 293–301.

Wolff, Walther. "Beiträge zu einer Reformationsgeschichte der Stadt Aachen." Theol. Arbeiten, n.s., VI (1903), 95–109; VII (1905), 69–103; IX (1907), 50–103.

Wollbrett, Alphonse, ed. La Guerre des Paysans, 1525. Etudes Alsatiques édités par la Société d'histoire et d'archéologie de Saverne et environs, Supplemental No. 93. Saverne 1975.

Yost, John K. "Protestant Reformers and the Humanist via media in the early English Reformation." Journal of Medieval and Renaissance Studies, V (1975), 187–202.

Zeeden, Ernst Walter. Die Entstehung der Konfessionen: Grundlagen und Formen der Konfessionsbildung im Zeitalter der Glaubenskämpfe. Munich and Vienna 1965.

Zeller, [Hermann?]. "Die Aalener Reformation 1575." Spion von Aalen: Blätter für Heimatkunde, Beilage der Kocher-Zeitung und zum Härtsfelder Boten, II and III (February and March, 1926), 9–27.

Zimmermann, Wilhelm. Geschichte des großen Bauernkrieges nach den Urkunden und Augenzeugen. 2 vols. 2nd ed. Vol. II. Naunhof and Leipzig 1939.

Zoepfl, Friedrich. "Kardinal Otto Truchsess von Waldburg, 1514–1573." Lebensbilder aus dem Bayerischen Schwaben. Vol. IV, pp. 204–248.

Zschäbitz, Gerhard. "Zur Problematik der sog. 'Zweiten Reformation' in Deutschland." Wissenschaftliche Zeitschrift der Karl-Marx-Universität Leipzig, Gesellschafts- und sprachwissenschaftliche Reihe, XIV (1965), 505–509.

INDICES

I. INDEX OF PLACE NAMES

This index includes all places referred to in the text and footnotes, except for names of countries ("Germany", "France," etc.), regions ("Lower Alsace", "Sundgau," etc.), and territories ("Jülich-Cleves", "Württemberg," etc.). The cities of Aachen, Aalen, Colmar, Dortmund, Essen, and Haguenau are included in the Subject-Index. The orthography regarding Alsatian places follows the rules described above, p. ix. The single exception is "Heiligkreuz" near Colmar rather than "Sainte-Croix-en-Plaine." Well-known cities are generally rendered in English ("Cologne" rather than "Köln", "Vienna" rather than "Wien"). The Upper Rhenish places listed here have been further identified as lying in Lower Alsace (BR= Bas Rhin), Upper Alsace (HR= Haut Rhin), or the modern state of Baden (B). Swiss places are marked with (S) for "Switzerland."

Aarau (S) 151n, 152
Algolsheim (HR) 72
Altkirch (HR) 100–01
Altwihr (HR) 72
Ammerschwihr (HR) 18
Antwerp 184–5
Appenwihr (HR) 72
Apponex (Savoy) 28
Augsburg 4, 14, 41–2, 128, 129n, 130n, 131, 187, 191, 201n

Baden (S) 84n
Bamberg 204
Basel (Latin: Basilea) (S) 13, 28, 33, 46n, 55n, 64–5, 68, 69n, 70, 78n, 83, 84n, 87, 101, 116, 124–30, 135, 141n, 142, 148–9, 151–3, 160
Bebelnheim (HR) 72
Bern (S) 32, 116n
Biberach 3, 17n
Biel (S) 152
Bischwihr (HR) 72, 128
Bischwiller (BR) 128, 194, 200
Blienschwyler (HR) 14
Bopfingen 190, 200
Brakel (near Dortmund) 181
Breisach (B) 86n, 91n, 103n, 111n
Bregenz 30
Bremen 140, 168–9
Broich 200
Buchhorn 188n
Burgdorf (S) 152
Burgos 45

Châtenois (BR) 29
Cologne 25, 34, 38, 67, 151, 173, 178, 181, 183, 187
Constance 4–5, 28, 30, 157, 201n
Crailsheim 188

Derne (near Dortmund) 181
Deventer 172
Dingsheim (HR) 14
Duisburg 171, 174
Durrenentzen (HR) 72
Düren 174
Düsseldorf 173

Eichstetten (B) 125, 127
Ellwangen 189–92
Ensisheim (HR) 29, 66, 70, 89, 98, 102, 104–6, 122, 159n
Esslingen 4, 169, 187, 191

Frankfurt a.M. 40, 45, 187
Fortschwihr (HR) 72
Freiburg i.Br. (B) 28, 40, 60, 81, 92n, 104n, 111n, 167n
Freiburg (Fribourg) (S) 36, 83

Geislingen (Württemberg) 29
Gengenbach (B) 72
Geneva (S) 1n, 151n
Gerlingen (Württemberg) 131
Giengen (near Ulm) 27
Goslar 4, 176
Gotha 151

Guebwiller (HR) 33
Guémar (HR) 14

Hamburg 4
Heilbronn 169, 187
Heiligkreuz (Sainte-Croix-en-Plaine) (HR) 14, 27, 95n, 142, 147
Heitersheim (HR) 120
Hirtzfelden (HR) 66
Hohenems (near Bregenz) 30
Horbourg (HR) 71–4, 87, 90, 92, 111n, 112, 118–9, 124–5, 144, 147, 149n, 150, 165n, 166, 200
Horn (Lower Austria) 127
Hunawihr (HR) 72–3

Innsbruck 97–8
Isny 3
Istein (B) 28

Jebsheim (HR) 119, 123–4
Jerusalem 121
Justingen (near Ulm) 127

Kaaden (Kadan/Bohemia) 72
Kappel (S) 1n
Kaufbeuren 17
Kaysersberg 23–4, 99, 110
Kempen 174
Kempten 17, 28
Kientzheim (HR) 58, 110
Kirchheim (near Stuttgart) 28
Koblenz 81n, 151n
Kraiburg (Bavaria) 127

Landau 23
Lauffen (Württemberg) 96
Lausanne (S) 124n
Lautenbach (HR) 88
Lehen (near Freiburg i. Br.) (B) 60
Leisnig 162
Leutkirch 3
Lindau 17n, 201n
Lingolsheim (BR) 146
Lippstadt 172, 179, 200
Logelheim (HR) 14
London 184n
Lübeck 4

Maastricht 185
Malterdingen (B) 131n
Memmingen 17, 67, 169
Metternich (near Koblenz) 81n
Metz 14, 151n
Mittelwihr (HR) 72
Moers 175, 200
Minden 173
Molsheim (BR) 29
Montbéliard 72, 86n, 118n, 119, 125n, 126, 128n, 156n
Mulhouse (HR) 3, 23, 116n, 152
Mülheim on the Ruhr 174
Münster (Westphalia) 70, 172–3, 177–8, 183n
Munster (HR) 23–4, 28, 97, 107–110, 125, 133
Muntzenheim (HR) 72
Murbach (HR) 82n

Nambsheim (HR) 14
Naples 27
Neuss 174
Niedermorschwihr (HR) 30n
Nördlingen 188, 191–2
Nordhausen 5
Nuremberg 4–5, 14, 74, 109, 201n

Obernai (BR) 2n, 15, 23–4, 67, 108n, 204
Oberwengern (near Dortmund) 180
Osnabrück 173, 178
Ostheim (HR) 72, 144

Pairis (HR) 14
Passau 94
Payerne (Peterlingen) (S) 31–2
Phalsbourg (BR) 146

Radolfzell 29
Ratisbon 46–8, 84n, 145
Ravensburg 17n, 116n
Reutlingen 4n, 201n
Ribeauvillé (HR) 50, 51n, 60, 78n
Riquewihr (HR) 14, 30n, 50, 71–4, 88, 118n, 124, 126, 128, 131, 156n
Rome 27, 77n, 121
Rosheim (BR) 23
Rottenburg on the Neckar 81
Rottweil 187
Rotwilen (? /diocese of Constance) 30
Rouffach (HR) 29, 30n, 34, 88n, 111n

Salzburg 204
Santiago di Compostela 121
Saverne (BR) 44–5, 78
Scherwiller (BR) 45, 56
Schöftland (S) 151n
Schwäbisch Gmünd 187, 188n, 199
Schwäbisch Hall 5, 169, 201n

Sélestat 2n, 13, 15, 23–4, 34, 36, 40, 45n, 46n, 49, 51n, 53, 55n, 60, 67, 77n, 78, 87, 99, 108n, 111n, 114, 116, 204, 160
Smalkald 160
Soest 171, 179, 200
Soultz (HR) 32
Speyer 60
St. Gall (S) 77n, 88n
St.-Hyppolite (St. Pilt) (HR) 28
Steinach (near Haslach) (B) 36n
Strasbourg (Latin: Argentinum) (HR) 3–5, 13–5, 23–4, 27, 34, 40, 55, 56n, 61n, 69, 78n, 79n, 80n, 84, 86–7, 109, 112, 123–5, 128, 131–3, 139, 140n, 143–6, 147n, 148, 150, 152–4, 157, 159, 161, 164n, 166, 167n, 169, 180, 186–8, 194–5, 200, 201n
Stuttgart 28
Sulzburg (B) 129
Sundhoffen (HR) 72

Thann (HR) 88, 106n, 121
Trier (Treves) 151n, 198n, 204, 205n
Turckheim (HR) 2n, 14, 23–4, 99, 110, 204

Ueberlingen 17n, 187, 188n
Ulm 18, 27, 127, 169, 188, 191–2

Venlo 174
Vienna 96, 109, 115, 195
Volgelsheim (HR) 72

Wangen (Allgäu) 3
Weingarten 190
Weitmar (near Dortmund) 180
Wesel 168, 171, 174, 176, 200
Wettolsheim (HR) 27
Wimpfen 3, 27, 77
Wissembourg (HR) 23–4, 40–1, 133, 135–6, 139, 170, 194
Woffenheim (HR) 14
Wolfgantzen 72
Worms 25, 47
Würzburg 33, 51n, 76n, 204

Znaim (Moravia) 127
Zürich 58, 68n, 116, 119n, 124n, 130, 137n, 143, 151n, 158

II. INDEX OF PERSONAL NAMES

This index includes all names of persons referred to in this book, except for modern authors. The listing follows – with a few exceptions – the orthographie rules described above, p. ix. The main exception is "Nicolaus of Bollwiller" rather than "Niklaus von Bollweiler." The title of "Freiherr" is rendered as "baron." The reader should note that in early modern German orthography the distinction between the following consonants was, at best, accidental: "b" and "p", "c" and "k", "d" and "t", "f" and "v", and "i" and "y." In addition, he should be aware of the interchangeability of short or popularized and regular forms of Christian names, such as Claus (Niklaus or Nicolaus), Diepold (Theobald), Hans (Johann or Johannes), and Jörg (Georg). Birth and death years are supplied wherever possible.

Alba, Duke of. *See* Alvarez de Toledo, Ferdinand
Alber, Matthäus (1495–1570) 201n
Albrecht V (1528–79), Duke of Bavaria (1550–79), 170
Algewer, Michael 29
Alvarez de Toledo, Ferdinand (1508–82), Duke of Alba 185n
Amerbach, Basilius (1534–91) 142
–, Bonifacius (1495–1562) 86
–, Bruno (1485–1519) 35n
–, Johannes (d. 1513) 35n
Andreae, Jacob (1528–90) 96, 139, 192
Angeli, Gregorius 27
Anshelm, Thomas (d. c. 1523) 194
Anstenroid, Werner Huyn of (d. 1534) 183n
Anthony "the Good" (1489–1544), Duke of Lorraine 45
Apponex, Franz von (d. 1591) 28, 121, 122n
–, Petermann von, Abbot of Munster (1540–c. 1544) 28
Aretius (Marti), Benedict (1505–74) 130
August I (1526–86), Prince-elector of Saxony (1553–86) 132–3
St. Augustine 136
Austrius, (Oesterricher), Sebastian, Dr. med. 82, 88, 116

Baader, Andreas, of Aalen 191
Babe, Jacob (d. 1551) 78n
Bader, Jacob, Jr. 57n
–, Jacob, Sr. 50n, 51–4, 57, 66
Barenbroch, Heinrich (d. 1587) 175–6

Bartenstein, Jörg 76n
Barth (fam.) 15, 18
–, Johann 148n
Bass, Anna 158–9
Beck, Andreas (d. 1627) 131, 134n, 140, 142–3, 147–50
Be(e)r (Bär), Franz, Jr. (1543–80) 115n
–, Franz, Sr. (1497–1543) 115n
–, Matthias (1524–c. 1575) 114–5, 164, 166
Belmer, Hans 66
–, Michael 66n
Berchem, Johannes 178–9
Berger, Gregor (d. c. 1587) 114
Berner, Balthasar 115
Betulejus, *see also* Birckmann, Heinrich
–, Emanuel (d. 1588) 128–31, 133, 142–3, 152
–, (Birck), Xystus (1500–54) 128–30
Beza, Theodore (1519–1605) 130
Bilfinger, Johann Peter (d. 1621) 135n
Billing, Sigismund (1742–96) 129n, 154n, 158n, 159n, 160n
Birck, *see* Betulejus, Xystus
Birckmann (Betulejus), Heinrich 174
Birr (fam.) 15
Blarer (Blaurer), Ambrosius (1492–1564) 201n
Blarer von Wartensee, Jacob Christoph (1542–1608),
Bishop of Basel (1575–1608) 26–7
Blunder, Philipp 99
Böcklin von Böcklinsau, Wilhelm (d. 1585) 155n
Böhm, Martin (d. c. 1637) 131
Böschlin, Ambrosius 29, 30n
Bollwiller, Nicolaus, baron of (d. 1588) 25, 96n, 97, 107–8, 195
Boner, Andreas, of Sélestat 87n
–, Hieronymus (d.c. 1555/56) 68, 69n, 81n, 82n, 83,
Botzheim (fam.), of Haguenau 12, 195
–, Rochius von 96, 109
Breitinger, Johann Jacob (1575–1645) 151n
Brenz, Johannes (1499–1570) 124–5, 139, 155–6, 190, 201n
Bucer, Martin (1491–51) 4, 73, 87, 201n
Buchinger, Michael (d. 1571) 120–1
Bullinger, Heinrich (1504–1575) 72n, 73, 108n, 116, 118n, 119n, 124n, 127n, 129n, 130, 136–7, 143
Buob (Bueb), (fam.) 15, 117
–, Jacob (d. 1620) 161
–, Michael (d. 1588) 114, 118n
Busche, Hermann von dem (1468–1534) 58
Bussensmidt, Laurenz, of Essen 175
Buxtorf, Johannes, Jr. (1599–1664) 151

Calvin, John (1509–64) 130, 135, 136–7, 138n, 140
Cancerinus (Krebs), Nicolaus (d. 1579) 73, 118–9, 124–5, 128, 154–7, 160
Canisius, Peter (1521–97) 111n
Capito (Köpfel), (fam.), of Haguenau 195
–, Wolfgang Fabritius (1472–1541) 194, 201n
Capua, Raymond of (c. 1330–99) 32
Carden, Matthias 175
Carpentarii (Zimmermann), Jacob (d. 1541/42) 28, 31, 46–7, 65, 82–4
Cellarius (Keller), Johannes (1533–94) 119, 123–7, 154
Celtis, Conrad (1459–1508) 35n
Charles III (d. 1553), Duke of Savoy (1504–35) 84n
Charles IV (1316–78), Emperor (1346–78) 17n, 23–4
Charles V (1500–58), Emperor (1519–58) 89, 94, 127, 188–9
Cheurodi (Tscheurodi), Jean (d. 1570) 32
Christoph (1515–68), Duke of Württemberg (1550–68) 73
Closius, *see* Glossius, Johann
Conberger, Johann (d. 1594) 131
Cuntz, Hans 69n, 70

Delphinus, Conrad 190
Diepholz, Irmgard von, Abbess at Essen (1561–75) 175
Diesbach, Nicolaus von (1478–1550),
coadjutor of Basel, bishopric (1519–27) 64
Drübein, Stephan 57
Dürninger (fam.) 15
–, Bartholomäus 21

Eber, Kaspar 128, 131
Ehinger (fam.), of Constance 12
Einfalt, Jacob (d. c. 1543/44) 33, 76n
Embs, Hans von (d. 1584) 115
Erasmus, Desiderius, of Rotterdamm (c. 1466–1536) 5, 58, 84, 86, 130, 182
Erb, Matthias (1494–1571) 72–3, 79n, 108n, 114, 116, 118, 119n, 124n, 156n
Ernst (1554–1612), Duke of Bavaria,
Archbishop of Cologne (1583–1612),
Bishop of Liège (1581–1612) 170, 187
Eugly, *see* Oiglin

Fabri, Johannes, of Wimpfen 32n, 77–8, 82, 90
Fabritius (Schmid), Erasmus (c. 1492–1546) 72
Falck, Peter (c. 1468–1519), of Freiburg (Switzerland) 36n
Farckall, Amandus 48n, 49, 57–9
Farnese, Alexander, Duke of Parma (1545–92) 187
Ferdinand I (1503–64), Archduke of Austria (1521/22–31), King (1531–58), Emperor (1558–64) 47–8, 68, 72, 74, 95–6, 107, 169, 184, 195
Ferdiand II (1578–1637), Emperor (1619–37) 152, 154, 195
Ferdinand II (1529–95), Archduke of Tyrol (1564–95) 94, 96–8, 104–5, 107, 123n, 154n, 159n, 164n, 165n, 166n, 167n, 170, 195n, 204n
Finck, Conrad (d. 1567) 116n
Fleckenstein, Heinrich von, baron of Dagstuhl 25, 195
Franck, Sebastian (1499–1542/43) 13, 112n
Frecht, Martin (1494–1556) 127n
Freiberg, Christoph, baron of 191
Friedrich III (1415–93), Emperor (1440–93) 17
Friedrich I (1557- 1608), Count of Württemberg (1581–93), Duke of Württemberg (1593–1608) 73, 141n
Friedrich III "the Pious" (1515–76), Palatine Prince-elector (1559–76) 184
Fries, Hans Jacob (1546–1611) of Zürich 143
Fries (Phrysius), Lorenz (c. 1485–1532) 84
Frisch, Johann Ernst (d. 1618) 144, 148n
Fritsch, Hans 75
Froben, Johannes (c. 1460–1527) 35n
Froschauer, Christoph, Jr. (d. 1585) 143
Fuchs, Nicolaus (d. 1598), of Strasbourg 145
Fürstein, Cornelius, Dr. iur., of Haguenau 96
Fugger (fam.), of Augsburg 12

Gallus, Jodocus (c. 1459–1517) 34
Gasser, Michael (d. c. 1563) 30
Gassner, Thomas (d. 1548) 201n
Gebhardt, Lux (Lucas), (1523–93), of Basel 125
Gebwiler, Hieronymus (d. 1545) 194
Geiler von Kaysersberg, Johann (1445–1510) 13n, 77n, 92
George (1498–1558), Count of Württemberg 66, 72, 124
Gerson, Jean (1363–1429) 12n
Gessler, Vitus 78n
Giger, Claus 70
–, Johannes 36n
Glareanus, *see* Loriti, Heinrich
Glaser, Johann, of Aalen 192
Glossius (Closius), Johann (1561/62–1603) 145, 162n
Godel, Arbogast, of Rouffach 30n
Godel, Heinrich 30n
Goldenmann, Matthias 122
Goll (fam.) 15, 116
–, Hans (Johannes), (d. 1587) 159
Graff (fam.) 15
Gran, Heinrich (d. 1527) 194
Gravelius, Adelarius 160
Gregory IX, Pope (1227–41) 26
Gross, *see* Magnus, Johann Georg
Grossis, Conrad de (d. 1426) 32
Grüninger, Bartholomäus 58
–, Johannes (d. 1556) 28, 100
Grynaeus, Johann Jacob (1540–1617) 124n, 126, 129n, 134n, 141n, 142n, 148n, 149
Güntzer, Augustin 29, 82
–, Matthias (1502–64) 29n, 80n, 81–2, 84, 87–8
Gundelsheim, Jacob Philipp von (1487–1553), Bishop of Basel (1527–53) 26, 64
Gwalther, Rudolf (1519–86) 130
Gyerfalck, Thomas (d. 1560) 35, 83

Haemstede, Adrian van (c. 1525–c. 1562) 184
Hafner, Ursula 158n
Haller, Bartholomäus (d. 1643) 144–5, 153
–, Johannes (1523–75) 130
Hamelmann, Hermann (1526–95) 180
Hammer, Wilhelm (d. c. 1564) 83
Hans, vicar at St. Peter's, Colmar 31n, 45–6, 49, 59–60
Hasenbart, Aegidius 183n
Hattstatt (fam.) 103
–, Nicolaus von (1510–85) 100, 103, 142
Hattstein, Johann von (d. 1546) 71n
Hauser, Veltin, Jr. 158–9
Hecker (fam.) 15, 18, 117
Hedio, Caspar (1494–1552) 72n, 79n, 194
Heerbrand, Philipp (d. 1575) 96
Hegenwald, Erhard 58
Heidelberg, Urban 50n
Heinerius, Matthias (1564–1624) 141, 151
Heitfeld, Johann 180, 200
Heller, Johann 147–8
Hemmingius, Nicolaus (1513–1600) 130

Henckel, Hans 115, 164
Henslin, Beat (d. 1595) 22, 95n, 109, 115, 118n, 122, 141
Heresbach, Conrad von (1496–1576) 86
Hermann V (1477–1552), Count of Wied, Archbishop of Cologne (1515–47) 170, 173–4, 180
Hermann, Bartholomäus (d. c. 1545) 33
Herodianus 58, 85
Hiemeyer, David (1561–1632) 142n, 145–7, 149, 153
Hilsbach, Michael (1483–1570) 194
Hochfelder, Paul (1540–1600), of Strasbourg 145, 186
Höchstetter (fam.), of Augsburg 12
Hoffmeister, Johannes (c. 1509–47) 75, 76n, 79, 81n, 82–3, 88n, 89
Homberg, Urban 177
Hopf, Georg (1590–1631) 151
Horace 87n
Horn, Gustav (1592–1657) 152
Hubert, Conrad (1507–77), of Strasbourg 87, 111n, 112n, 115n
Huckelom, Johannes (d. 1579) 185
Hug, Heinrich 66n
Hummel, Georg 190
–, Hieronymus 89
–, Johannes (d. 1546) 46–7, 52n, 57, 81n, 82n, 88–9
Humpis (fam.), of Ravensburg 12
Hutsch, Ludwig 42
Hyperius, Andreas (1511–64) 130

Ingold (fam.), of Strasbourg 12
Irsamer, Andreas (d. 1600) 145–6, 148–50, 153, 160
–, Christoph (b. 1593) 160
Isselburg, Caspar 176

Jestetten, Heinrich von, Abbot of Munster (1569–73) 108
Johannes N., Colmar schoolteacher 159n
Johann III Duke of Jülich-Cleves (1511–39) 86n, 171n
Johann Georg, Prince-elector of Brandenburg (1571–98) 133
Justinus 85

Kalbfleisch, Eusebius (d. 1558) 29–30
Karl II, Margrave of Baden-Durlach (1552–77) 95, 127
Karlstadt, Andreas (c. 1477–1541) 130
Keller, *see* Cellarius, Johannes
Kemner, Timan 177
Kempf von Angreth, Ambrosius (d. c. 1553/54), of Freiburg i. Br. 92n
Kesselring, Georg 115
Kesselring, Martha, wife of Sebastian Wilhelm Linck 115
Kirchner, Christoph (d. 1637) 148n, 160
Klein, Georg (Jörg), (d. 1551) 28, 70
–, Jacob (d. 1563) 28, 78n, 81n, 99n, 100n, 101–2, 111–3, 117–8
–, Rahel (d. c. 1629) wife of Christian Serinus 128
Klett, Gallus 88
–, Lucas (Lux), Dr. iur. 77n, 88
–, Theobald (Diepolt) 29, 82, 88
Klug, Bartholomäus 30n
Koeltz, Andreas 27
Koenen, Matthias 151
Koenig, *see:* – Regius, Niklaus
–, Kunig, Ludwig
Köthe, Hermann 179
Kopp, Ludwig 46
Kotschareuter, Johann (d. c. 1570) 95n
Krebs, *see* Cancerinus, Nicolaus
Kriegelstein (fam.) 12, 15, 117
–, Ludwig (1542–1625) 158
Krus, Adolf 29
–, Oswalt, Jr. 21
Kunig (Koenig), Ludwig 156n

Lactantius 130
Lambach, Johann (d. 1582) 177, 180, 181n
Landeck, Johann Heinrich von 100, 112
Lavater, Ludwig (1527–86) 130
Lefèvre d'Etaples, Jacques (c. 1450–1536) 36
Leontorius, Conrad (c. 1460–1511) 35
Lichtenfels, Melchior von (1517–75), Bishop of Basel (1554–75) 26, 113, 117, 121n, 122
Linck (fam.) 15, 18
–, Sebastian 115
–, Sebastian Wilhelm (d. 1617) 22, 109, 110n, 115, 116n, 122, 141, 142n, 149–50, 160
Linsen, Claus 66n
Loriti (Glareanus), Heinrich (1488–1563) 81, 87
Louis XIV (1638–1715), King of France (1643–1715) 20
Lucius (Lutz), Basilius 149n
Ludwig IV, the Bavarian (c. 1283–1347), Emperor (1314–47) 17
Ludwig "the Pious" (1554–93),

Duke of Württemberg (1568–93) 131–3, 144, 147n, 191–2
Luther, Martin (1483–1546) 47, 57–8, 79, 83, 130, 137n, 162, 202
Lutz, *see* Lucius, Basilius

Magnus (Gross), Johann Georg (c. 1544– c. 1607) 131–2, 134, 135n, 141, 142n, 144–7, 149–50, 153, 156n
Mantuanus, Baptista (1448–1516) 35
Marbach, Johann (1521–81) 126
Marnix, Philippe de (1538–98) 143
Marti, *see* Aretius, Benedict
Maximilian I (1459–1519), Emperor (1493–1519) 27, 44n
Maximilian II (1527–76), Emperor (1564–76) 96, 98, 105, 107, 109–10, 170, 185n, 191, 199
Melanchthon, Philip (1497–1560) 58, 130, 136n, 137, 138n, 180
Mendoza, Spanish Admiral 187
Menzer, Johannes 33
Merian, Matthäus (1593–1650) 13
Meternus, *see* Tengen, Valentin
Metz, Johann (Augustin ?), (d. 1589) 131, 144
Meyenbrunn, Andreas 18n, 159
Monheim, Johannes (1509–64) 173
Morimont (Mörsberg), Johann Jacob (d. before 1538),
baron of Morimont and Belfort 25
Mülin, Martin 90
–, Veltin 90
Müller, Thomas 57, 69–70
Münster, Sebastian (1488–1552) 13
Murrho, Sebastian, Jr. 35
–, Sebastian, Sr. (1452–94)34–6, 48n
Musculus, Wolfgang (1497–1563) 130
Myconius, Friedrich (1490–1556) 173

Nehemius, Peter 177
Nervius, Johannes, Dr. iur., of Strasbourg 123, 125, 159n, 160n, 166, 167n
Neuenahr, Hermann, Count of,
Count of Moers (1553–78) 174
Nunnenmacher, Peter 53
Nuwgart, Peter 57, 59, 88–9
Nysaeus, Johann (c. 1527–99) 131n

Oecolampadius, Johannes (1482–1531) 83n, 130, 201n
Oesterricher, *see* Austrius, Sebastian
Oiglin (Eugly), Theobald 30n
Orosius 85
Ortlieb, Anton 112, 115
Osiander, Andreas (1498–1552) 201n
Ottheinrich (1502–59),
Palatine Prince-elector (1556–59) 25, 74
Otzenradt, Johannes Christianus (d. 1597) 185

Pappus, Johannes (1547–1610) 124n, 125–6, 131–2, 133n, 139, 144–5n 146n 149, 154n
Parma, Duke of, *see* Farnese, Alexander
Paulus, baptized Colmar Jew 35n
Pecelius, Christoph (1539–1604) 140
Pellicanus, Conrad (1478–1556) 35
Pellitarius, Elias (d. 1636) 151
Perkins, William (1558–1602) 143
Pfeiffer, Marx 105–06
Philesius, *see* Ringmann, Matthias
Philip II (1527–98), King of Spain (1556–98) 184, 187
Phrygio (Sidensticker), Paul (1483–1543) 36n
Phrysius, *see* Fries, Lorenz
Pius V, Pope (1566–72) 121n
du Plessis-Mornay, Philippe 143
Pludenz, (?), Dr. iur. 65n
Plutarch 85
Polanus, Amandus (1561–1610) 129n
Portia, Bartholomäus (d. 1578), Count of, papal nuncio 133n, 154n, 165n
Poyger, Colmannus (d. 1589) 118–9, 124–5
Prechter (fam.), of Strasbourg 12
Preu, Johannes, of Aalen 191
Priccardus, Leonardus (d. 1541) 183n
Pruckner, Nicolaus (c. 1490–1557 35

Rabus, Ludwig (d. 1592) 128n
Radspinner, Samuel (d. 1598) 149n
Rappoltstein (Ribeaupierre), (fam.) 95n
–, Egenolph von (d. 1585) 95, 107
–, Ulrich von (1495/96–1531) 63n
–, Wilhelm von 61n
Rasser, Johann (c. 1535–95) 29, 102, 105, 113–4, 118, 122, 165
Reber, Mathis 46
Regius (Koenig), Niklaus (1497–1561) 73
Requesens, Luis de (d. 1576) 185n
Reuchlin, Johannes (1455–1523) 27, 35
Rhegius, Urbanus (1489–1541) 201n
Rhenanus, Beatus (1485–1547) 35n, 84, 86–8
Riefflin, Jacob 115
Ringlin, Georg 42

Ringmann, Matthias (Philesius), (1482–1511) 34, 36
Ros, Hans 66n
Röttlin (fam.) 15, 18
Rotgerus, John 172
Ruch, Hans 51n
Rudolf I (1218–91), King (1273–91) 17
Rudolf II (1552–1612), Emperor (1576–1612) 170, 185–7, 200
Rüst, Hans von 19
Rumersheim, Michael 158n

Sagittarius (Schütz), Jacob 27
Saldenberg, Heinrich 175
Salomon, Adam 192
Salzmann, Leonhard 30
Sandherr (fam.) 15, 18, 116
–, Andreas (1533–1600) 21, 115, 119–20, 122, 124–7, 130–1, 133–4, 137, 139–42, 145, 149–50, 155n, 157
Sapidus, Johannes (1490–1561) 87
Sartorius, Dietrich 45
Scharpenberg, Peter 179
Scheidt (fam.), of Haguenau 195
Schedlin, Hans 46
Scherer, Conrad 120
–, Mathis 46
Schmid, *see* Fabritius, Erasmus
Schmidt, Johannes (1594–1658) 132n, 152
Schoenraid, Johann (d. 1541) 183n
Schoepf (Schepfius), Thomas (1520–77) 108n, 116
Schöpper, Jacob (d. 1554) 177, 180
Schott, Anton (1569–1634) 150, 151n, 160
–, Peter (1460–90) 12n, 34
Schroeter, Johann 156n
Schuelin, Lux 51n, 54n, 66n
Schuslerus, *see* Schüssler
Schürer, Matthias 35n
Schüssler (Schuslerus), Johannes 160n
Schütz, *see* Sagittarius, Jacob
Schuler, Johannes (d. 1571) 106, 120n, 121–2
Schultheiss (fam.) 15
Schur, Wilhelm 66n
Schuster, Michael 115
Schwager, Christian (d. before 1562) 78n
Schwarzenberg, Ottheinrich, Count of (1535–90) 107–08
Schwendi, Lazarus von (1522–84), baron of 110
Serinus, Christian (1540–1603) 124–9, 131–4, 136–7, 139–42, 146–50, 152–3, 156
–, Leonhard, Jr. (1568–1624) 149
–, (Soer), Leonhard, Sr. (1514–73) 127
Servetus, Michael (1511–53) 194
Setzer, Johann (d. 1532) 194
Sidensticker, *see* Phrygio, Paul
Sigismund (1368–1437), King and Emperor (1410–37) 21
Simler, Josias (1530–76) 130
Singer, Conrad 51, 66n
–, Ulrich 51n
Socinus, Ambrosius (1558–1615) 142n, 148n, 149–53, 156, 158–9, 160
–, Nicolaus (d. 1624) 150
Soer, *see* Serinus, Leonhard, Sr.
Spinola, Ambrosio (1571–1630) 188
Sprung, Augustin 36
Stedli, Jacob 70
Stephani, Jacob (d. c. 1676) 151
Stetten, Georg von, Jr., of Augsburg 129n
Stör, Barbara 78n
–, Johannes Rudolf (1499–1570), Abbot of Murbach (1542–70) 82n
Stoeritz, Blasius 28
Streit, Jacob, Dr. iur., of Freiburg i. Br. 104n
Stromeyer, Martin 147–8
Stumpf, Hans 21
Sturm, Johannes (1507–89) 145, 180
Sudermann, Johann (d. c. 1537) 183
Sulzer, Simon (1508–85) 72n, 124–7
Susanne, Colmar Beguine 57
Syfrid, Ursula (d. 1565) wife of Christian Serinus 127

Taverner, Richard (c. 1505–75) 85n
Tengen, Valentin, of Mettern (?) 81
Tettinger, Marcus (1540–1600), Suffragan of Basel Bishopric (1567–99) 29–30, 110n, 121, 122n, 123n
Theodorici, Matthias 29, 31n, 122–3
Theus (fam.), of Haguenau 195
Tinnelhan, Kaspar 192
Tonsorius, Christoph 159
Tossanus (Toussain, Peter (Pierre), (1498–1573) 72n
Tradeln, (?) Dr. iur., of Augsburg 191
Treger, Conrad (d. 1542) 75
Trockenbrot, Justitia (d. 1594), wife of Emanuel Betulejus 129
Truchsess von Waldburg, Otto (1514–73), (Cardinal-) Bishop of Augsburg (1543–73), Provost of Ellwangen (1553–73) 170, 190–1

Tscheurodi, *see* Cheurodi, Jean
Tuber, Johann 172

Ulmer, Georg 105–6
Ulrich (1487–1550), Duke of Württemberg (1503–50) 72, 190
Ulstetter, Israel (c. 1530–76) 128
Utenheim, Christoph von, Bishop of Basel (1502–27) 12n, 26, 48

Vadianus, Joachim (c. 1484–1551) 77n, 86n, 88, 127n
Vermigli, Peter Martyr (1500–62) 130
Verula, Leonhard 70, 83
Villinger of Schoenberg, Jacob 14
Vischer (fam.) 12, 15, 18, 116
–, Leonhard (c. 1514–96) 15, 116, 128n
–, Salome (d. 1577) 128n
Vlatten, Johann von (d. 1562) 86
Vögelin, Diepolt 35
Vogel, Jörg (d. 1564) 114, 118n
–, Theobald (d. c. 1585) 78n, 105
Vogler, Hans (1489–1567) 77n, 78n, 88

Waldburg, *see* Truchsess von Waldburg, Otto
Wecker, Johann Jacob (1528–86) 110n, 116
Weibel, Bartholomäus 66n
–, Nicolaus 61n
Welfflin, of Hirtzfelden 66
Welser (fam.), of Augsburg 12
Werlin, Balthasar (1521–65) 83
Westheimer, Bartholomäus (1499–1567) 73, 87, 92n, 111n, 112, 114, 115n, 117–9, 166
Wetzel (fam.) 12, 15
–, Egenolph (d. 1627) 148n
Wetzel von Marsilien (fam.) 119
Whitaker, William (1548–95) 143
Wickram, Bartholomäus (d. 1532) 29
–, Conrad (d. c. 1545) 42, 88–9
Widichem, Bernhard 70
Wied, *see* Hermann V, Count of Wied
Wilhelm V, Duke of Jülich-Cleves (1539–92) 86n, 170, 171n, 173n, 174–5, 180, 184–5
Wilmann, *see* Wylman
Wilwesheim (fam.), of Haguenau 195
Wimpfeling, Jacob (1450–1528) 12n, 27, 35, 92
Wölflin, Wilhelm 57
Wolf, Johannes (1521–71) 130
–, Thomas (1475–1509) 36
Wolfgang (1526–69), Palatine Duke of Zweibrücken 128
Würmlin, Ulrich 42
Wurstisen, Christian (1544–88) 87, 112n, 120n
Wydmann, Michael 115
Wylman (Wilmann), Nicolaus 30, 92n

Zanenbentz, Christian 29–30, 105
Zimmermann, *see also* Carpentarii, Jacob
–, Heinrich 57
Zwick, Johannes (c. 1496–1542) 201n
Zwinger, Theodor (1533–88) 110n
Zwingli, Ulrich (Huldrych), (1484–1531) 4, 68n, 130, 135–6, 137n, 140, 202

III. INDEX OF MODERN AUTHORS

This index only includes those modern authors whose works are discussed in the text or the footnotes of this book. Bare citations are not listed.

Adam, Johann 10

Baillet, Lina 53n, 58n
Blickle, Peter 60n, 61–2
Bolchert, Paul 142n
Bopp, Marie-Joseph 151n, 160n
Brady, Thomas A., Jr. 3n, 6–8, 16n, 164n, 198
Braeuner, Gabriel 8–9, 119
Brecht, Martin 5
Brunner, Otto 22
Bücking, Jürgen 8, 74n, 120n, 128n, 166n

Clauss, Joseph M. 117n

Demandt, Dieter 9, 41n, 44n
Dickens, A.G. 8, 14, 58n
Druffel, August von 79n

Ehbrecht, Wilfried 16n, 40n

Franz, Günther 61
Franzen, August 86n, 171n

Gail, Anton 171n
Goehlinger, François-Auguste 27n, 31, 41n
Goeters, Johann F.G. 183n

Hanauer, Charles Auguste 146n
Hillerbrand, Hans 56n
Holborn, Hajo 16n

Jenny, Beat-Rudolf 72n
Junghans, Helmar 13n

Kiessling, Rolf 41
Köhler, Walter 157n, 158
Kohls, Ernst-Wilhelm 4–5, 49n, 157n

Laplatte, Claude 26n
Lau, Franz 198
Lerse, Franz 9, 129n, 152n

Maeder, Kurt 85
Meuthen, Erich 182n
Moeller, Bernd 2–8, 40, 164n, 204n
Mossmann, Xavier 9, 69n

Oberman, Heiko A. 13n
Ozment, Steven E. 6

Paulus, Nikolaus 79n, 83
Pfleger, Lucien 43n
Post, Regnerus R. 13n

Rapp, Francis 61–4, 91
Ritter, Gerhard 2
Rocholl, Heinrich 9–10, 83, 94n, 114, 116n, 119–20
Rublack, Hans-Christoph 3n, 49n, 203n

Scherlen, August(e) 13
Schilling, Heinz 5n
Schmidlin, Joseph 9
Schultze, Alfred 57n
Scribner, Robert W. 6–7
Sittler, Lucien 18n
Spitz, Lewis W. 13n
Strohl, Henri 144, 165n

Trouillat, Joseph 26n

Weyrauch, Erdmann 9, 21n, 116n, 166n, 169n

Yost, John K. 85n, 86n

IV. SUBJECT-INDEX

The simple short-form references to institutions used in the footnotes for the identification of cited 16th and 17th centuries correspondence are not indexed here if they occur throughout (e.g., "Chapter to Bishop", "Colmar authorities to Bishop").

Aachen
  Anabaptism and "Sacramentarians" 182
  Aristocracy 182
  Churches and monasteries 182
    influence of Duke of Jülich-Cleves 182, 184
  Counterreformation 187–8
  Economy 181–2
    importance of immigration 182
      official furtherance 183
  Government
    constitution 182
    oligarchical tendencies 182n
    problem of Protestant participation 184–7
  Humanism 182–3
  Population figures 181
  Reformation 183–7
    Confession of 1559 184
    confessional groups, size 185–6
    impact of immigrants 183, 185n
      of outside resistance 184–6
    political aftermath 186–8
Aalen
  Church and chapels 189
    and Prince-Provost of Ellwangen 189
  Counterreformation 192
  Economy 188
  Government and oligarchical tendencies 188–9
  Population figures 188
  Reformation 189–92
    introduction by minority 192n
    outside resistance and support 190–2
  School 192
Alsace
  Bailiwick of Haguenau 48, 73–4, 94, 96, 107, 123, 167n
    Bailiff 50–1, 65–6, 68, 97–8, 104–5, 107–8, 110, 195
      functions 23–5

Cities
Decapolis (Ten Cities League) 22–5, 74, 87, 94, 96–7, 195
religious policy 23, 67–8
late Reformation movements 2, 204
religious policy
and Habsburg's presence 107
Haguenau Reformation 98, 108–9
Habsburg-Austria, in
political presence 23, 25, 48
Bailiff of Upper Alsace 51n
Regency of Ensisheim 23, 68, 73, 74n, 78n, 82, 100, 105, 107, 167
protection of Colmar clergy 104–5, 123n
religious policy 71, 73–4, 97–8, 107, 167, 204
territorial expansionism 94, 107–9, 167n
Horbourg-Riquewihr, Württemberg principality 71–4, 78n, 152
Protestant church, influence on Colmar 71–4, 90–1, 118, 124–5, 133, 155
Anabaptism 69–70, 74–5, 112–3, 172–3, 179, 183, 189n
Anti-Semitism 50, 59, 63n
Augsburg Confession, 1530 110n, 120n, 123n, 133–5, 137–8, 140, 149, 152–3, 156n, 166, 192
Basel, Bishopric of 64
Bishop 69n, 84n
and Colmar Counterreformation 154, 155n
Colmar's Ordinary 26, 55, 64–6, 92, 99n, 100, 101n, 103–4, 106, 113, 117–8, 121–2, 157, 167
and Turckheim 204
Cathedral chapter 28, 29n
Coadjutor 64
Episcopal court of law 47, 59, 101
Offizial 99–100, 106n, 122n, 155n, 157, 158n
Episcopal officials 57
Cities
Diets (*Städtetage*) 187
Speyer (1574) 109
(1581) 186–7
Ulm (1575) 191
ius reformandi of
cases: Colmar, Essen, Haguenau 108–10, 123, 167, 176
crucial case of Aachen 186–7
and emperors
Maximilian II 109–10
Rudolf II 200
according to Peace of Augsburg 95, 199
oligarchical tendencies 196–8
political and economic decline 187, 196
social and constitutional aspects 16n, 17, 40n
and territorial absolutism 94
Colmar, aristocrcay
bourgeois patriciate 18–9, 59, 116–7, 147
association ***Zum Waagkeller*** 17–9, 110n, 128, 147, 161
and the Protestant church 128n, 148, 168
and the Reformation 164
nobility, association ***Zur Krone*** 19
Colmar, Catholic churches and monasteries 25–34, 47, 51–6, 75–7
number of clergy 25
churches
hospital church (*Spitalkirche*, former Franciscan church) 78n, 120
St. John's 42
parish 31–2
St. Martin's 26–32, 38n, 45, 49, 51, 53, 55, 59, 64–6, 74, 77–9, 81, 84, 88, 90–2, 99–106, 120–2, 155, 159, 162
chapter of 26–31, 46, 52, 77–8, 80–2, 91–3, 99–106, 111–3, 118, 122, 123n, 155n, 159, 164n, 165–6, 167n
Fabrik 42–3, 103
organist 103
origin of clergy 27–31
parish 31–2, 122
St. Peter's 14, 42, 45–6
parish 31–2
monasteries
Augustinians 33–5, 41, 70, 76n, 77, 79, 83
Commandery of St. John's 32, 71
Dominicans 32–4, 38, 41–2, 77–8, 83, 103n, 122, 165n
Franciscans 14, 33–4, 42, 53, 57, 76n, 77, 120
Priorate of St. Peter's 14, 31–2
Çonvents 75
Beguines 34, 42, 57
St. Catherine's 41, 55, 90
Unterlinden 32–3, 41, 51, 55–6, 78n
Colmar, craftsmen
and urban unrest 50
and the Reformation 112, 165
Colmar, Counterreformation 151–4

Colmar, Economy
agriculture 15–6
trade 12, 14–5, 142
Colmar, goverment
city-council 20–22, 114–7
and clergy 41–4, 64–6, 75–83, 99–106
Habsburg interference 104–5, 123n
monastic mandates 55–6, 75–7, 85n
Committee of XIII (*Dreizehner*) 20–2, 46, 52, 115
Committee of VIII (*Echtwer*) 22
communal committee (1525) 52–5
and communal unrest (1524/25) 45–56
constitution 16–7, 19–22
Council of jurors (*Schöffenrat*) 22, 52, 54–5, 123, 164
and the *Decapolis* 23–4, 67–8, 108–10
magistrate (*Meisterschaft*), composition 21
nobility, participation of 19–20
oligarchical tendencies 15n, 18–9, 49, 117n, 164–5, 169
and Protestant church 141–2, 155
and the Reformation 74, 83
early evangelical tendencies 49, 57, 59
introduction 123
outside influences (Habsburg, Württemberg) 167
preventive measures 67–70, 90–3, 111, 113
Protestant tendencies 108, 110, 112–7, 120
Schultheiss (judge, provost), function 21
Colmar, guilds 16, 19–20, 54–5, 123
craftsmen, proportion 165n
journeymen, brotherhoods 38
membership figures 16n
strike of journeymen-bakers 19, 40n
Ackerleute (peasants) 16, 41, 46, 49–50, 53, 61
Rebleute (vine-dressers) 16, 41, 46, 49–50, 53, 61
Zum Adler (weavers, etc.) 16n, 50, 57
Zum Haspel (gardeners, etc.) 16n, 46, 49–50, 53
Zum Holderbaum (masons, etc.) 16n, 50
Zum Kränzchen (bakers, millers) 16n, 50
Zum Löwen (butchers, fishermen) 16n, 22n, 50
Zum Riesen (surgeon-barbers, etc.) 16n
Zur Treue (merchants, tailors, etc.) 15, 16n, 114
Zum Wohlleben (shoemakers) 16n, 92
Colmar, hospital 14, 42–3, 115, 162
Colmar, humanism 34–6, 81, 130, 141
Via Media 83–90
Colmar, poor relief 161–2
Colmar, population figures 13–4
Colmar, printers 48n, 49, 57–9
Colmar, Protestant church
Beginnings, outside influences 119, 124–9
Doctrinal development 152–4
adherence to Lutheranism 152
Calvinist tendencies 131–52, 168
alignment with Basel and Palatinate 134, 141, 148–53
eucharistic confession, 1589, 134–46, 149, 153
eucharistic controversy 126, 132–48
Formula of Concord, refusal of 126, 132–3
separation from Strasbourg and Württemberg 144–8, 152–3
doctrinal factions 147–8
Hospital church (*Spitalkirche*) 123, 140
Hymnbook 150
Matrimonial court 157–9
Number of parishioners 154
Church ordinance and catechism 155–6
Preacher's oath 133–5, 141, 145–6
Colmar, Reformation 119, 163–9
Early spread 45, 49, 53–4
Historiography 8–10
Introduction 123
Outside factors 11
Reformation in Horbourg-Riquewihr 73, 78n, 90–3, 112, 118, 166
Peace of Augsburg 95, 167
Haguenau Reformation 98–9, 108, 110, 167
Pamphlets 111, 113, 167
Protestant party, consolidation 114–22
Colmar, religious life
Anticlericalism 39–41, 53–6, 111
Brotherhoods 38–9
Progressive laxness 90–1
Colmar, schools
before 1575 35–6, 80–1
after 1575 155, 157, 159–60
girl's school 160
Gymnasium 150, 160
Colmar, Territory 14
Bailiwick of Heiligkreuz 14, 95n, 142, 147–8
Colmar, urban unrest (1524/25) 44–64
Thirteen Articles 46–9, 61–2
Cologne, Archbishopric of
Archbishop 175
and Aachen Reformation 184, 187
Reformation in the, effects 170, 173–4, 180

Councils
the planned "national council" 65, 67
Trent 165, 170
Tridentine catechism 190
Counterreformation
Low Countries 171
South/southwest and west of Empire: differences 170, 202
Devotio Moderna 13, 172, 177n
Dortmund
Aristocracy 177
and Catholic church 173, 177, 181
Churches and monasteries 177
Economy 171, 176–7
Government 177
oligarchical tendencies 177
Protestant councillors 178–9, 181
Humanism 177, 179–80
Poor relief 179
Population figures 176
and the Reformation 177–81, 197, 200, 203–4
eucharistic confession (1570) 181
Schools 177, 179–80
Ellwangen, Prince-Provost of
and Aalen 189–92
Essen
Aristocracy and Catholic church 173
Churches and monasteries 172
Economy 171
Government 172
and clergy 103n
and disputed status of Essen 175
Humanism 172
Population figures 171
and the Reformation 172–6
role of the Duke of Jülich-Cleves 175–6, 184n
Schools 173, 175, 179n
Formula of Concord 124, 126, 131–3, 135n, 136, 137n, 141, 149, 152–3
Haguenau
Churches and monasteries 193
Economy 15, 193
Government 24, 193
control over parish churches 193
and the *Decapolis* 23–4
introduction of the Reformation 95–7, 167n
oligarchical tendencies 193, 195
Guilds, membership figures 193n
Humanism 194
and the peasants' revolt 55n, 194
Population figures 193
Printers 58, 194
Protestant church
beginnings 98
catechism 125
and Formula of Concord 133
dissolution 195–6
Reformation 11, 95–7, 194–6
and the *Decapolis* 98, 108–9
and Habsburg 97–8, 167n
introduction by upper-class minority 96–7, 193, 195
outside support 194–5
Humanism 27, 33–4, 85–8, 141, 143
Lower Rhenish 170, 171n, 173, 174n, 177
Imperial Diets
Augsburg (1518) 94
(1530) 40, 68
(1555) 94
(1559) 184
(1566) 104
Nuremberg (1523) 48
Speyer (1526) 65
(1542) 196
(1544) 87a
Imperial Supreme Court 65, 71, 174, 176
Interim of Augsburg (1548) 127, 190n
Liège, Bishop of
Aachen's Ordinary 182
and Aachen Reformation 184, 186–7
Munster (Alsace), Abbot of 26, 28, 99–101, 107–8, 110, 165
Nicodemism 85n, 87–8, 89, 107, 120n
Peace of Augsburg (1555) 82, 94–5, 97, 123n, 155, 167, 174–5, 180, 184, 186–7, 190–1, 192n
"city-article" 95, 199
and politico-religious de-stabilization 169–70
and the Reformed church 148, 152
and late Reformation cities 197
Peasants' revolt 44–5, 54, 60–4
Twelve Articles 47, 61–2
Philippism 130, 136–9, 153
Popular religion 37–8
Reformation in the cities
early and late 1–2, 196–205
discipline enforcement 157–9
historiography 1–8
late city Reformation
cases
Colmar, typical case 163–4, 168–9
Dortmund, a-typical case 197, 200, 203–4
unsuccessful 204–5
characteristic aspects 197–204

geographical differences 202–3
motives 201–2
pre-conditions
Maximilian II's postition 170, 199
Peace of Augsburg 197
Strasbourg, Bishop of 17, 27n, 78n, 108
Tithes, refusals of 100–01, 112
Universities and Academies
Protestant universities 115
Basel 83n, 84, 110n, 116, 124n, 126–7, 129, 131, 149, 151, 192
Bologna 27, 115
Cologne 83n
Erfurt 128
Freiburg i.Br. 28, 34, 36n, 88, 142
Geneva 151
Heidelberg 28, 34, 131, 142, 149–51
Jena 131, 192
Lausanne 124
Montpellier 116
Paris 29, 84n
Strasbourg 128, 146
Tübingen 96, 115, 124, 128, 131, 145
Valence 116
Vienna 127
Wittenberg 87, 110n, 116
Zürich 124

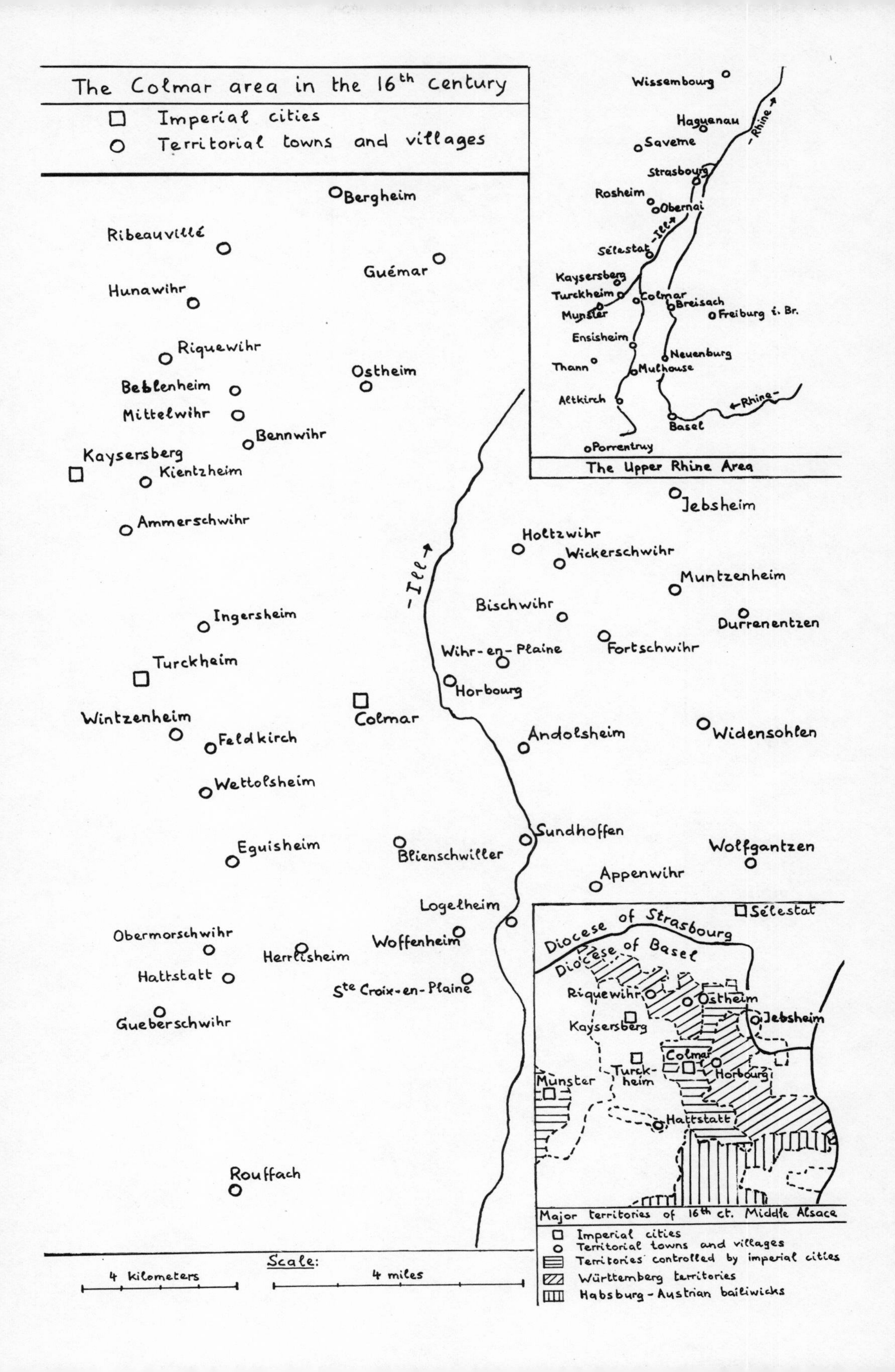
The Colmar area in the 16th century
Imperial cities
Territorial towns and villages
Bergheim
Ribeauvillé
Guémar
Hunawihr
Riquewihr
Ostheim
Beblenheim
Mittelwihr
Bennwihr
Kaysersberg
Kientzheim
Ammerschwihr
- Ill -
Ingersheim
Turckheim
Wintzenheim
Feldkirch
Colmar
Wettolsheim
Eguisheim
Bliensch willer
Logelheim
Obermorschwihr
Herrlisheim
Woffenheim
Hattstatt
Ste Croix-en-Plaine
Gueberschwihr
Rouffach
Jebsheim
Holtzwihr
Wickerschwihr
Muntzenheim
Bischwihr
Durrenentzen
Wihr-en-Plaine
Fortschwihr
Horbourg
Andolsheim
Widensohlen
Sundhoffen
Wolfgantzen
Appenwihr
Scale:
4 kilometers
4 miles
Wissembourg
Haguenau
Saverne
- Rhine
Strasbourg
Rosheim
Obernai
Sélestat
- Ill
Kaysersberg
Turckheim
Colmar
Breisach
Munster
Freiburg i. Br.
Ensisheim
Neuenburg
Thann
Mulhouse
Altkirch
Rhine -
Basel
Porrentruy
The Upper Rhine Area
Sélestat
Diocese of Strasbourg
Diocese of Basel
Riquewihr
Ostheim
Jebsheim
Kaysersberg
Colmar
Turck-heim
Horbourg
Münster
Hattstatt
Major territories of 16th ct. Middle Alsace
Imperial cities
Territorial towns and villages
Territories controlled by imperial cities
Württemberg territories
Habsburg-Austrian bailiwicks

Veröffentlichungen des Instituts für Europäische Geschichte Mainz
Abteilung für Abendl. Religionsgeschichte – Begründet von Joseph Lortz
ab Band 81 herausgegeben von Peter Meinhold

Band 6 **Bernhard von Clairvaux – Mönch und Mystiker.** Internationaler Bernhardkongreß Mainz 1953. Hrsg. u. eingeleitet von *Joseph Lortz. 1955. LVI, 245 S., Ln. DM 20,80*

Band 7 *Hans Wolter S. J.*, **Ordericus Vitalis.** Ein Beitrag zur kluniazensischen Geschichtsschreibung. *1955. VIII, 252 S., 1 Stammtafel, Ln. DM 18,–*

Band 8 *Erwin Iserloh*, **Gnade und Eucharistie in der philosophischen Theologie des Wilhelm von Ockham.** Ihre Bedeutung für die Ursachen der Reformation. Mit einer Einleitung von *Joseph Lortz. 1956. XL, 286 S., Ln. DM 28,–*

Band 18 **Europa und das Christentum.** Drei Vorträge von *Walther von Loewenich, Fedor Stepun, Joseph Lortz.* Hrsg. *J. Lortz. 1959. VIII, 204 S., Ln. DM 18,–*

Band 24 *Gerhard Kaiser*, **Pietismus und Patriotismus im literarischen Deutschland.** Ein Beitrag zum Problem der Säkularisation. *1961. VIII, 302 S., Ln. 32,–*

Band 25 *Hermann Schüssler*, **Georg Calixt – Theologie und Kirchenpolitik.** *1961. XII, 245 S., Ln. DM 28,–*

Band 26 **Paolo Sarpi – Lettere ai Gallicani.** Edizione critica, saggio introduttivo e note a cura di *Boris Ulianich. 1961. CCVII, 308 S., Ln. DM 56,–*

Band 31 bis 34 **Gabrielis Biel Canonis Misse Expositio.** Ediderunt *Heiko A. Oberman* et *William J. Courtenay. Pars Prima (Bd. 31) 1963. XXVI, 363 S., Ln. DM 50,–. Pars Secunda (Bd. 32) 1965. XIII, 462 S., Ln. DM 60,–. Pars Tertia (Bd. 33) 1966. XII, 333 S., Ln. DM 50,–. Pars Quarta (Bd. 34) 1967. XII, 246 S., Ln. DM 50,–* (Siehe auch Bd. 79 = Abschlußbd. der Edition)

Band 40 *Alexandre Ganoczy*, **Le jeune Calvin.** Genèse et Evolution de sa Vocation Réformatrice. Einleitung von *J. Lortz. 1966. XXXII, 382 S., brosch. DM 58,–, Ln. DM 64,–*

Band 42 **Die Texte des Normannischen Anonymus.** Unter Konsultation der Teilausgaben von H. Böhmer, H. Scherrinsky und G. H. Williams neu aus der Handschrift 415 des Corpus Christi College Cambridge herausgegeben von *Karl Pellens. 1966. XLII, 262 S., Ln. DM 60,–* (siehe auch Bd. 69)

Band 46 *Peter Manns*, **Lutherforschung heute.** Krise und Aufbruch. *1967. XVI, 75 S., brosch. DM 14,–*

Band 53 *Robert Stalder*, **Grundlinien der Theologie Schleiermachers.** I. Zur Fundamentaltheologie. *1969. XXIV, 401 S., Ln. DM 48,–*

Band 54 *Georgette Epiney-Burgard*, **Gérard Grote (1340–1384) et les Débuts de la Dévotion moderne.** *1970. XVI, 335 S., Ln. DM 52,–*

Band 57 *Friedhelm Krüger*, **Bucer und Erasmus.** Eine Untersuchung zum Einfluß des Erasmus auf die Theologie Martin Bucers (bis zum Evangelien-Kommentar von 1530). *1970. X, 233 S., Ln. DM 40,–*

Band 58 *Enrique Dussel*, **Les Evêques Hispano-Américains.** Défenseurs et Evangélisateurs de l'Indien 1504–1620. *1970. LXI, 286 S., Ln. DM 56,–*

Band 60 *Vinzenz Pfnür*, **Einig in der Rechtfertigungslehre?** Die Rechtfertigungslehre der Confessio Augustana (1530) und die Stellungnahme der katholischen Kontroverstheologie zwischen 1530 und 1535. *1970. XIII, 432 S., Ln. DM 56,–*

Band 62 *Helmut Feld*, **Martin Luthers und Wendelin Steinbachs Vorlesungen über den Hebräerbrief.** Eine Studie zur Geschichte der neutestamentlichen Exegese und Theologie. *1971. VIII, 277 S., Ln. DM 48,–*

Band 64 *Hans Jörg Urban*, **Bekenntnis, Dogma, kirchliches Lehramt.** Die Lehrautorität der Kirche in heutiger evangelischer Theologie. *1972. X, 401 S., Ln. DM 58,–*

Band 68 *Walther von Loewenich*, **Duplex Iustitia.** Luthers Stellung zu einer Unionsformel des 16. Jhs. Festgabe zum 85. Geburtstag von *Joseph Lortz. 1972. VIII, 84 S., brosch. DM 18,–*

Band 69 *Karl Pellens,* **Das Kirchendenken des Normannischen Anonymus.** *1973. XX, 333 S., Ln. DM 50,–*

Band 71 *Abraham Friesen,* **Reformation and Utopia.** The Marxist Interpretation of the Reformation and its Antecedents. *1974. XVI, 271 S., Ln. DM 52,–*

Band 72 *Gerhard Philipp Wolf,* **Das neuere französische Lutherbild.** *1974. XIV, 370 S., Ln. DM 64,–*

Band 73 *Wolfgang Stein,* **Das kirchliche Amt bei Luther.** *1974. VIII, 225 S., Ln. DM 42,–*

Band 75 *Klaus Bannach,* **Die Lehre von der doppelten Macht Gottes bei Wilhelm von Ockham.** Problemgeschichtliche Voraussetzungen und Bedeutung. *1975. VIII, 424 S., Ln. DM 88,–*

Band 76 *André Sciegienny,* **Homme charnel, homme spirituel.** Etude sur la christologie de Caspar Schwenckfeld (1489–1561). *1975. X, 102 S., brosch. DM 24,–*

Band 78 *Dietrich Kerlen,* **ASSERTIO.** Die Entwicklung von Luthers theologischem Anspruch und der Streit mit Erasmus von Rotterdam. *1976. XII, 377 S., Ln. DM 76,–*

Band 79 **Gabrielis Biel Canonis Misse Expositio.** Dispositio et conspectus materiae cum indice conceptuum et rerum. Curavit *Wilfrid Werbeck.* Abschlußbd. d. Biel-Edition (Bd. 31–34). *1976. XVI, 447 S., DM 64,–*

Band 80 **Bucer und seine Zeit.** Forschungsbeiträge und Bibliographie. Hrsg. von *Marijn de Kroon* und *Friedhelm Krüger. 1976. X, 169 S. u. 1 Taf., Ln. DM 48,–*

Band 81 **Wendelini Steinbach opera exegetica quae supersunt omnia.** Edidit *Helmut Feld.* Vol. I: Commentarius in epistolam S. Pauli ad Galatas. *1976. LXIII, 342 S., Ln. DM 168,–.* Das Werk ist auf 4 Bände vorgesehen.

Band 82 **Der Codex 415 des Corpus Christi College Cambridge.** Facsimile-Ausgabe der Textüberlieferung des Normannischen Anonymus. Herausgegeben und in Verbindung mit *Ruth Nineham* eingeleitet von *Karl Pellens. 1977. XXIV S. u. 320 Taf., Ln. DM 58,–*

Band 83 *Gerd Babelotzky,* **Platonische Bilder und Gedankengänge in Calvins Lehre vom Menschen.** *1977. XII, 276 S., Ln. DM 76,–*

Band 85 **Die Einheit der Kirche.** Dimensionen ihrer Heiligkeit, Katholizität und Apostolizität. Festgabe Peter Meinhold zum 70. Geburtstag. Hrsg. von *Lorenz Hein. 1977. XIV, 513 S. u. 1 Taf., Ln. DM 88,–*

Band 86 *Hermann Schüssler,* **Der Primat der Heiligen Schrift als theologisches und kanonistisches Problem im Spätmittelalter.** *1977. XVI, 312 S., Ln. DM 74,–*

Band 88 *Hans-Jürgen Schönstädt,* **Antichrist, Weltheilsgeschehen und Gottes Werkzeug.** Römische Kirche, Reformation und Luther im Spiegel des Reformationsjubiläums 1617. *1978. XXXVI, 328 S., Ln. DM 80,–*

Band 89 *Stefan Niklaus Bosshard,* **Zwingli – Erasmus – Cajetan.** Die Eucharistie als Zeichen der Einheit. *1978. XVI, 176 S., Ln. DM 48,–*

Band 92 *Ulrich Michael Kremer,* Die Reformation als Problem der amerikanischen **Historiographie.** *1978. X, 265 S., Ln. DM 64,–*

Band 97 *Peter Meinhold,* **Studien zu Ignatius von Antiochien.** *1979. XII, 86 S., Kart. DM 28,–*

Weiterhin auch lieferbar die Bände 12, 20, 39, 43, 44, 48, 56, 61, 66, 67

Kirche und Bekenntnis
Historische und theologische Aspekte zur Frage der gegenseitigen Anerkennung der lutherischen und der katholischen Kirche auf der Grundlage der Confessio Augustana. Hrsg. von *Peter Meinhold.* 1980. 146 S., Kart. DM 19,80

FRANZ STEINER VERLAG GMBH · WIESBADEN